Arms Control
and
Military Preparedness
from
Truman to Bush

American University Studies

Series X
Political Science
Vol. 37

PETER LANG
New York • San Francisco • Bern • Baltimore
Frankfurt am Main • Berlin • Wien • Paris

Martin E. Goldstein

Arms Control and Military Preparedness from Truman to Bush

PETER LANG
New York • San Francisco • Bern • Baltimore
Frankfurt am Main • Berlin • Wien • Paris

Library of Congress Cataloging-in-Publication Data

Goldstein, Martin E.
  Arms control and military preparedness from Truman to Bush / Martin E. Goldstein.
    p. cm. — (American university studies. Series X, Political science ; v. 37)
  Includes bibliographical references.
  1. United States—Defenses. 2. Arms Control—United States—History—20th century. I. Title. II. Series.
UA23.G67   1993   355'.0335'730904—dc20   92-17958
ISBN 0-8204-1955-9   CIP
ISSN 0740-0470

Die Deutsche Bibliothek-CIP-Einheitsaufnahme

Goldstein, Martin E.:
Arms control and military preparedness from Truman to Bush / Martin E. Goldstein. - New York; Bern; Berlin; Frankfurt/M.; Paris; Wien : Lang, 1993
  (American university studies : Ser. 10, Political science ; Vol. 37)
  ISBN 0-8204-1955-9
NE: American university studies/10

Back cover photo by Andrew Einhorn.

This book was designed in Times Roman and Optima and typeset on a Macintosh computer by Janet M. Goldstein.

The paper in this book meets the guidelines for permanence and durability of the Committee on Production Guidelines for Book Longevity of the Council on Library Resources.

© Peter Lang Publishing, Inc., New York 1993

All rights reserved.
Reprint or reproduction, even partially, in all forms such as microfilm, xerography, microfiche, microcard, offset strictly prohibited.

Printed in the United States of America.

This book is dedicated to my wife, Janet, who not only edited and designed the volume, but also provided needed solace and encouragement.

CONTENTS

INTRODUCTION	1
1 TRUMAN	3
The Domestic Setting	3
The International Context	5
Military Doctrine	15
Military Preparedness	17
Arms Control	24
2 EISENHOWER	27
The 1952 Elections	27
The International Context	32
Military Preparedness	40
Arms Control	44
3 KENNEDY	63
The 1960 Elections and the Missile Gap	63
Kennedy's Outlook	64
The International Context	66
Military Preparedness	72
Arms Control	88
4 JOHNSON	97
The Domestic Setting	97
The International Context	99
Vietnam	103
Military Preparedness	108
Arms Control	118

5 NIXON/FORD 125
- The Domestic Setting 125
- The International Context 130
- Vietnam 140
- Military Preparedness 142
- Arms Control 152

6 CARTER 165
- The 1976 Elections 165
- The International Context 168
- Military Preparedness 174
- Arms Control 182

7 REAGAN 195
- The 1980 Elections 195
- The Reagan Administration 196
- The International Context 199
- Military Preparedness 208
- Arms Control 218

8 BUSH 233
- End of the Cold War 233
- Military Preparedness 238
- Arms Control 243

CONCLUSION 257

References 261

Index 264

INTRODUCTION

Throughout the ages, statesmen have pondered the best way to ensure national security. Most fundamentally, national security means freedom from external military attack. A state that has attained a high degree of national security is not, of course, immune from outside influence. Such a state might be subject to economic pressures, subversion, propaganda, international ostracism, and penetration by foreign intelligence agencies. Nevertheless, states have generally placed an extremely high value on minimizing the danger of outside military attack.

Absolute invulnerability from external military attack has grown less attainable with technological improvements in transportation and communication. In biblical times, a state needed to worry about military assault only from its near neighbors. Roman legions vastly extended the distance over which armies of conquest could travel, reaching as far away as Great Britain and North Africa. In the fifteenth century, Europeans began to colonize regions as far away as Asia and North America. In military terms, it seemed that nearly all states dwelled in a single neighborhood by that time.

Yet, bringing large quantities of military power to bear on a distant state was no easy matter. The wars of colonization usually pitted a disciplined, technologically advanced force against loosely organized warriors armed with rudimentary weapons.

For all practical purposes, the United States remained free from the menace of external military attack through World War II. Theoretically, foreign navies could have reached American shores, and invading armies could have poured in from Canada and Mexico. The burning of the White House by British troops in 1812 provides testimony to American vulnerability. The fact of the matter is, however, that neither American neighbor had designs on U.S. territory or the military forces to mount a campaign that held any promise of success. Occasional forays across the border by Mexican bands scarcely qualified as military invasions. At sea, the British navy stood ready to oppose attempts by its European rivals to establish footholds in North America. By the beginning of the twentieth century, none of the maritime powers entertained any plans to land troops on America's shores. Even during the two world wars, American territory was spared from military attack (excepting a couple of random strikes on the West Coast).

The airplane and missile rendered the United States as vulnerable to external military threat as other major powers had been. Once the Soviet Union detonated a nuclear device in 1949, the U.S. became subject to attack by nuclear bombers. Soviet launching of *Sputnik* in 1957 meant that the U.S. would shortly find itself vulnerable to a nuclear missile attack. Ironically, it was the U.S. that perfected both the long-range bomber and inter-continental ballistic missile, the two weapons systems that have left the U.S. most vulnerable to military attack.

These developments, as well as ideological rivalry with communist powers, led the United States to devote unprecedented peacetime attention to enhancing its national security after World War II. Just how to achieve this objective occupied the minds of countless policy-makers and constitutes the principal focus of this volume.

There are, of course, many pathways to national security. Among the tactics available for this purpose are building up one's military forces, reducing an adversary's military forces, strengthening one's allies, acquiring thorough and accurate intelligence, conducting skillful diplomacy, securing strategic bases abroad, acquiring raw materials and processing technology (and denying these to one's foe), and combating subversion at home while conducting it in the homeland of one's potential enemy. The foregoing list could be lengthened. In order to carry out a manageable study of national security, this volume will focus on the first two methods mentioned above. We shall refer to the accumulation of military personnel, equipment and weaponry as military preparedness. Arms control is the term that will be used to signify limits or reductions in arms and military personnel or regulation of their use. Most arms control agreements involve mutual obligations; it is rarely possible to induce one's rival to engage in unilateral arms control. (The most common exception occurs after a war.)

In short, this study will examine the extent to which each president, starting with Truman, relied on military preparedness and arms control to advance U.S. national security. To be sure, every chief executive called on both these tools of diplomacy. However, there are marked differences in emphasis, as the following chapters will reveal.

In order to provide a context for discussing presidential reliance on arms control and military preparedness, it has been necessary to describe the major threats to American security since World War II. Many of these challenges emanated from what used to be known as the Soviet Union. By necessity, therefore, this volume recounts the highlights of U.S.-Soviet relations since the close of the Second World War.

Our narrative begins in those turbulent days.

1
TRUMAN

Harry S Truman assumed the office of President on April 12, 1945, upon the death of Franklin D. Roosevelt. The paramount task facing the American leader was prosecution of World War II to a successful conclusion. Once this goal was achieved in August, 1945, the president and other national leaders turned to the establishment of a new world order both abroad and at home.

THE DOMESTIC SETTING

As the president surveyed the domestic landscape, two promontories stood out that affected questions of arms control and military preparedness. These features were the general desire for a balanced budget and the political attacks of Henry Wallace and his Progressive supporters.

To finance the enormous expenditures of the war, the government had had to borrow mammoth sums of money, generating a gargantuan deficit. Reducing this deficit meant, of course, that the government had to take in more money than it spent. One way to reduce government outlays was to cut military spending. It was hard to think of reasons for not taking draconian measures in this direction. With Germany and Japan lying in smoking ruins and America allied with all the world's major powers, including the Soviet Union, any threat to the peace seemed remote. Apart from occupation forces to prevent the revival of militarism in Tokyo and Berlin and to assure the transition to democracy, there seemed no need for the country to maintain an elaborate armed force.

The American people were ready for change on the home front too. They were tired of rampant inflation fueled by price and wage hikes. An outbreak of strikes and slowdowns darkened the land. People were chafing under shortages of cars, houses and meat, and the citizenry were calling for the government to turn away from foreign matters and rectify the deteriorating domestic situation.

In response to these factors, the United States conducted one of the most precipitous demobilizations in history. By the beginning of 1947, the Army had shrunk from eight million to one million men and the Navy from three and one-half million to less than a million. The Air Force had contracted from over 200 effective combat groups to less than 50 (Ambrose, 1980, p. 122). Other than a very small stockpile of atomic bombs, the United States possessed little with which to confront a potential aggressor. Industrial plants used to produce war goods were rapidly converted back to civilian purposes. These measures greatly pleased the Republican majority returned by the 1946 congressional elections. Senator Robert Taft, the GOP standard-bearer, led the drive for reduced government spending, lower taxes, business as usual (now that the war was over) and demobilization. By early 1947, it appeared that the Republicans were getting all that they craved.

If the Republicans were calling for a return to isolationism in foreign affairs, a different accent was urging the government to recall that "the price of liberty is eternal vigilance." This reminder was voiced by Winston Churchill in his famous "Iron Curtain" speech delivered in Fulton, Missouri, on March 4, 1946. Churchill warned that the Soviet Union had dropped an iron portcullis "from Stettin on the Baltic to Trieste in the Adriatic." Behind that barrier the Soviets were snuffing out freedom and installing communist governments. Churchill urged a policy of toughness on the part of the West. Implementation of such a policy would call for either renewed military preparedness or—less likely—arms control agreements with the Soviets.

Churchill's admonishment was resisted by one of Truman's long-time political allies and then secretary of commerce, Henry A. Wallace. Henry Wallace was appointed secretary of agriculture by President Roosevelt in 1933. Wallace did such a good job in that post that Roosevelt chose him as his running mate in the 1940 election. After retaining Wallace for four years as vice-president, Roosevelt selected Truman for that slot in 1944, moving Wallace over to be secretary of commerce. When Truman became president, he kept Wallace in that post.

An enthusiastic New Dealer, Wallace preserved the idealism of that era in the years following World War II. A strong believer in free trade, Wallace looked with disfavor upon Truman's rising suspicions of the Soviet Union and his dislike of the communists in Eastern Europe and China. Such hostility was bound to restrict commerce in Wallace's view. In September, 1945, Wallace gave a speech in which he cited the need to reach a political understanding with the Soviet Union, even if this meant American recognition of a Soviet security zone in Eastern Europe. Believing that the two systems could compete on a friendly basis, Wallace also called upon the government to share its atomic secrets with Moscow.

This outlook clashed with the point of view that was coalescing at the State Department. In September, 1946, Secretary of State Robert F. Byrnes was in Paris to attend a foreign ministers' meeting. At this time, the United States and Great Britain were beginning to challenge the Soviets concerning the failure to allow democracy in Eastern Europe, as agreed at Yalta. It was at this very moment that Wallace gave a speech in New York City urging the United States and Britain to steer clear of East European affairs, refrain from rearming, and share atomic secrets with the Soviets. Byrnes was furious. Soviet Foreign Minister Molotov had every reason to wonder who was voicing American policy, Byrnes or Wallace. Byrnes sent Truman an ultimatum: either dismiss Wallace, or Byrnes would resign. Truman elected to fire Wallace.

The November, 1946 congressional elections, which resulted in a Republican landslide, indicated widespread disenchantment with Truman and his policies. Sensing that Truman would prove an easy mark in the upcoming 1948 presidential election, Wallace and several other prominent Democrats broke with the party and formed a new party, the Progressive Citizens of America. The Progressive platform called for improved relations with the communist bloc, the cessation of nuclear testing, and an expansion of New Deal programs both at home and abroad. In response to Truman's growing conviction that the Russians would play fair only when confronted with superior force, Wallace said that the two systems were capable of engaging in amicable economic competition, and that the arms Truman was beginning to call for would prove both costly and unnecessarily provocative. If only the United States curbed its belligerency, Wallace said, peace could be preserved.

The Progressives made a determined bid in the 1948 election. However, they received only slightly more than a million votes, half of which came from New York. Thereafter, the Progressive Party faded away, and Wallace never again became a serious candidate.

On the home front, to recapitulate, the desire for a balanced budget, the urge to demobilize, the Republican majority in Congress, and the influence of the Progressives all moved the country away from an activist and interventionist foreign policy. These internal forces, particularly demobilization, stood in the way of military preparedness and inclined the country toward a return to isolationism.

THE INTERNATIONAL CONTEXT

Foreign policy springs from a reaction to external events as well as from the situation at home. The Truman years were a particularly turbulent time, especially in Europe and Asia. If domestic forces disposed the country to discard the weapons of war, occurrences elsewhere suggested the need for military preparedness.

Before exploring these thoughts, it needs to be observed that the Truman administration fell victim to the traditional American distinction between wartime and peacetime. Rather then seeing these two conditions as points along a continuum, Americans tend to view war and peace as opposites. Once at war, Americans tend to hand over policy to the generals and admirals in hope that they will win the war as quickly as possible. The populace rarely concerns itself with the political contours of the world that will emerge after the fighting stops. That is the concern of diplomats and politicians, who take over once peace returns. At that juncture, Americans might wring their hands at the constraints on political choice that the post-war battle-lines impose. Precisely that dilemma arose at the end of World War II. Despite Winston Churchill's admonitions, the Allies agreed that Soviet armies would strike westward across Eastern Europe toward Berlin. The American expeditionary force would move eastward across the continent and meet up with Soviet forces in the German capital. Most Allied generals favored this plan, as it held promise of ending the war as soon as possible with a minimum of Allied casualties. Churchill objected to the arrangement because it would leave Soviet forces in control of Eastern Europe. Given that disposition of forces, the West could do little but plead with Stalin concerning postwar political behavior in Eastern Europe. Churchill put forth a plan whereby Western armies would land in the Balkans and arc up through Eastern Europe in the direction of Berlin. This plan would leave Western armies in control of much of Eastern Europe at the end of the war, and thereby give the West the ability to determine events there. Western military leaders rejected Churchill's plan, arguing that it would prolong the war and result in massive casualties. In traditional fashion, it was decided to win the war as soon as possible and worry about the postwar world afterwards.

Before condemning wartime leaders for short-sightedness, it is worth observing that the breakdown of the alliance between the Soviets and the West was impossible to predict with certainty. Therefore, it was not so clear that leaving Russia in control of Eastern Europe would be detrimental to Western interests.

Nevertheless, when President Truman surveyed the postwar world, he found his political choices constrained by the military strategy followed during the war. Of immediate concern was Eastern Europe, particularly Poland. In February, 1945, Stalin had promised at Yalta to allow free elections throughout Eastern Europe once the war ended. Fulfillment of such a pledge would have vindicated the Western claim that the war was fought to preserve and advance democracy. It would also have yielded, in all probability, East European governments friendly to the West and hostile to the Soviet Union. Such an outcome would have betrayed much of what the Soviets had fought for. For this very reason, Stalin reneged on his pledge. Stalin stated the matter tersely,

> For the Russian people, the question of Poland is not only a question of honor but also a question of security. Throughout history, Poland has been the corridor through which the enemy has passed into Russia. Twice in the last thirty years our enemies, the Germans, have passed through this corridor.... Poland is not only a question of honor but of life and death for the Soviet Union (Ambrose, p. 97).

Stalin aroused Western ire by taking two actions concerning Poland. First, he annexed eastern Poland and said Poland should be compensated with German territory up to the Oder-Neisse line. More infuriating to the West, Stalin refused to permit the democratic elections promised at Yalta. To the contrary, he made sure that communists, not democratic Poles whose leaders were based in London, gained control of the Polish government. Elsewhere in Eastern Europe, as Churchill had predicted, the occupying Soviet troops controlled the press and suppressed freedom of speech, religion and assembly. Nowhere did the promised democratic elections take place.

Chapter 1: Truman

Elsewhere there was also cause for concern. In China, the communists led by Mao Tse-tung resumed their civil war. The situation in Iran was especially irksome. A wartime agreement provided for Soviet occupation of northern Iran until six months after the end of hostilities, the deadline later being set at March 2, 1946. As the deadline approached, the State Department received reports that the Russians, instead of preparing for withdrawal, were actually increasing their presence in Iran. The Russians were also interfering with efforts by the Iranian government to suppress rebellious elements in the northern province of Azerbaijan. Some reports indicated that the Russians were actually helping the rebels, in the hope that they would establish an autonomous entity under Soviet control (Acheson, 1969, p. 197). When the deadline passed without Soviet withdrawal, Washington, backed by London, sent Moscow a strong note of protest. Shortly thereafter the Russians pulled out and the separatist movement collapsed. Despite the successful outcome, the episode left Truman troubled. In the president's words,

> What perturbed me most, however, was Russia's callous disregard of the rights of a small nation and of her own solemn promises. International cooperation was impossible if national obligations could be ignored and the U.N. bypassed as if it did not exist (Truman, 1956, p. 95).

As unsettled as the president and some others were over Soviet behavior, the country was far from contemplating a reversal of demobilization. To the contrary, policy-makers were working on a plan to join with the Russians in preventing the growth and spread of atomic weapons. The pathway to national security appeared to point in the direction of limiting arms, not accumulating more of them.

As early as September 21, 1945, President Truman called a Cabinet meeting to discuss the future of atomic weapons. As Truman (1956) reports, many views surfaced at this meeting. Secretary of War Henry Stimson urged discussions with the Soviet Union on control of the atomic bomb, curbing future work on atomic weapons, and the development of atomic energy for peaceful purposes. The Joint Chiefs, reflecting growing distrust of Moscow, recommended that the United States retain all technological secrets of bomb construction. This division of views foreshadowed the sharp split that was to arise soon after between those who urged cooperation with the Soviet Union and those who counseled against it.

On October 3, President Truman, recognizing that atomic energy and atomic weapons had changed the world in a fundamental way, sent a special message to Congress on atomic energy. "Never in history has society been confronted with a power so full of potential danger and at the same time so full of promise for the future of man and for the peace of the world," the President said (Truman, 1956, p. 530). Truman called for action on two fronts—domestic and international. Domestically, he asked Congress to create an atomic energy commission to manage atomic plants, direct research and establish controls over raw materials. Internationally, he called for global arrangements that would result in renunciation of the use and development of atomic weapons and collaboration in the utilization of atomic energy for peaceful ends.

The following day a bill was introduced in Congress which resulted in creation of the Atomic Energy Commission (AEC). In November, Truman met with British Prime Minister Clement Atlee and Canadian Prime Minister Mckenzie King and urged that control of atomic energy for destructive purposes be lodged with the fledgling United Nations. The Allied leaders agreed, and the three heads of government issued a declaration proposing the establishment of a United Nations atomic energy commission to develop proposals for the international control of the atom. The following month Truman dispatched Secretary of State James F. Byrnes to Moscow to discuss the concept of UN control of atomic energy as well as other postwar matters. Shortly thereafter, the United Nations approved the establishment of its own Atomic Energy Commission (UNAEC), consisting of the representatives of a dozen nations and responsible to the Security Council. Washington appointed elder statesman Bernard Baruch as its representative to the UNAEC. Moscow designated Andrei Gromyko. The new organization had as its mandate to report on methods, by international action, of preventing the use of atomic energy for military purposes.

In support of this arms control effort, Truman appointed Tennessee Valley Authority Chairman David E. Lilienthal head of a group of experts to devise a plan for international control of the atom. Lilienthal worked closely with Under Secretary of State Dean Acheson. In March, 1946, the group produced a document, the Acheson-Lilienthal Report, which became the basis for the first arms control proposal floated in the UNAEC.

The United States formally presented its proposal to the UNAEC on June 14, 1946. In essence, the American proposal, known as the Baruch Plan, said that production of atomic bombs should come to a halt, that existing American bombs (numbering nine at the time) should be dismantled once controls were in place, and that a new international agency should act as the repository of all information concerning production of atomic energy. A control mechanism would be established in successive stages, with the United States to turn over appropriate information and direction of nuclear facilities at each stage. The United States could retain its nine bombs until the final stage, when they would be destroyed.

Washington regarded its proposal as unusually generous, as it involved the eventual surrender of its monopoly over atomic weapons. The Russians, however, were of a different opinion. Moscow objected to three aspects of the Baruch Plan: lack of veto, Western dominance, and inspection. Over Dean Acheson's objection, the Baruch proposal said no country could veto punitive action ordered by the Security Council against violators. The Soviets, taking note of the UN's heavy pro-Western bias at the time, regarded this provision as a way for the West to use the United Nations as a club against the U.S.S.R. Furthermore, Moscow suspected that the new international agency to manage

Chapter 1: Truman

atomic energy, called for by the Baruch Plan, would seek to dominate the development of atomic energy within the U.S.S.R. The Soviets had few illusions concerning Western desires to see the Soviet economy flourish. Inspection represented the third Soviet objection to the Baruch Plan. In Soviet eyes inspection was just another word for espionage. Inspection by a Western-dominated organization would provide the West with strategic data concerning the location and functions of Soviet industrial and military facilities. The Russians were also troubled by the staging contained in the American proposal. Suppose, the Russians said, this previously untried experiment in international control of an essential item collapsed after two or three years. Where would that leave the Russians? They would have neither atomic weapons, nor the know-how to construct them. The United States, however, would not only retain its atomic bombs, but it would possess the knowledge to build additional ones. For all the Soviets knew, Washington would work on increasing the yield of its weapons and so be in a position to build even bigger ones in case the international scheme fell apart. The Baruch Plan included no objective standard of compliance or timetable that would signal the United States to turn over its information to the new international agency. It was left to Washington to make judgments about when, if ever, this transfer would occur.

A few days after Baruch laid the American proposal before the UNAEC, the Russians countered with a proposal of their own. The Soviet plan called for a pledge not to use atomic weapons, the cessation of bomb production, and the destruction of existing stockpiles. After the implementation of these provisions, the Russian overture called for discussions of a control mechanism and arrangements for the exchange of scientific information relating to atomic energy. The United States found the Soviet presentation unacceptable. Moscow's proposal would deprive the United States of all its advantages in the atomic realm in return for nothing more than a promise to agree to control later on. Truman wrote to Baruch on July 10, "We should not under any circumstances throw away our gun until we are sure the rest of the world can't arm against us" (Truman, 1956, p. 11).

After discussion of the two tenders, the UNAEC adopted, over Soviet and Polish objections, the essential elements of the Baruch Plan. When this action reached the Security Council, however, the Soviets vetoed it.

Fundamental to the collapse of this arms control effort was the pervasive mistrust generated by superpower actions extending from Central Europe to Iran. It would be too much to say that in the absence of distrust arms control would surely have succeeded, but it seems fair to say that mistrust made arms control all but impossible to achieve.

It is perhaps worth asking, in light of succeeding events, whether the West would have been pleased had the Soviets agreed to the American plan. Acceptance of the Baruch proposal would have left the West bereft of its nuclear deterrent, while the Soviets could have retained their numerical advantage in conventional forces. This would have left the West with a choice between great expenditures to balance the Soviet forces or the prospect of intimidation at

Soviet hands.

With the demise of efforts to bring the atom under international control, the United States proceeded to organize itself to engage in atomic energy activities. In August, 1946, Truman signed the McMahon Act, which created the Atomic Energy Commission. Truman appointed David E. Lilienthal as chairman. In January of the following year, the AEC took over management of atomic research and production, both civilian and military. By the conclusion of the Truman presidency, the United States had invested $7 billion in nuclear research and development, had constructed a stockpile of atomic bombs and battlefield weapons with atomic warheads, and had successfully tested a hydrogen bomb.

While efforts to preserve security through arms control encountered obstacles at the United Nations, the wider international situation was deteriorating at an alarming rate. On February 9, 1946, Stalin delivered a major address in Moscow. Citing U.S.-Soviet wartime collaboration as nothing more than a temporary phenomenon, the Soviet leader ruled out the prospect of long-term collaboration between the worlds of communism and capitalism. The socialist system had emerged from the war stronger than ever, Stalin said, and it must press its advantage. To buttress this worldwide movement, Stalin announced a 5-year plan to increase heavy industry. To many Americans, Stalin's speech signaled that the Soviets were on the march. The cold war was about to crystallize.

It is not our purpose here to describe in detail the major episodes in the evolution of the cold war. That task has been performed admirably elsewhere. (It should be noted that the author subscribes to the "orthodox" view that the cold war was, in essence, a Western response to Soviet aggression. An alternative, "revisionist" view holds that the West was primarily responsible for the cold war, hoping to capitalize on Russia's postwar weakness to expand Western influence at Moscow's expense. For revisionist accounts, see Kolko, 1969; Fleming, 1961; Williams, 1952; Horowitz, 1971; and Alperovitz, 1965.) To provide a context for the discussion of arms limitation and military preparedness that follows, it is advisable to comment briefly on some of the landmarks in the progress of the U.S.-Soviet confrontation.

In Greece, communist civil war was raging when, in early 1947, Great Britain signaled her intention to withdraw troops from the embattled country and to cease providing Turkey with military and economic assistance. A communist victory in Greece would leave Turkey surrounded by communism. A communist Turkey would provide a corridor for communist penetration of North Africa and the Middle East. Turkey itself was under pressure from the Soviets to agree to joint Soviet-Turkish defense of the strategic Straits of the Dardenelles. Washington feared this amounted to a bid for a Soviet military takeover of Turkey, for if Russian forces entered Turkey to help defend the Straits, Soviet troops could be used to assert hegemony over the entire country. In the eyes of leading officials at the State Department, the British notification of withdrawal from Greece and Turkey "handed the job of world leadership, with all its burdens and all its glory, to the United States" (Jones, 1955, p. 7).

On March 12, 1947, President Truman grasped the role of Western leadership with the enunciation, before a joint session of Congress, of what has become known as the Truman Doctrine. Declaring that "it must be the policy of the United States to support free peoples who are resisting attempted subjugation by armed minorities or by outside pressures," Truman called upon Congress to authorize assistance to Greece and Turkey. In May Congress complied. Soon American personnel and dollars were in Greece and Turkey shoring up their governments with help in such fields as industrialization, agriculture, public finance and public health. These programs helped the two countries survive the communist onslaught.

The Truman Doctrine, coupled with the Greek-Turkish aid program, marked a turning point in American foreign policy. While some may have believed cooperation with the Soviets was still possible, the bulk of opinion held otherwise. Joseph Jones, a participant at the time, asserts that virtually no one in the government, be it the legislature or the executive branch, opposed Truman's announcement, although it was recognized as a major departure in American policy (Jones, 1955, p. 19). Soviet communism was on the march, majority opinion held, and America must halt Moscow's advance. Despite the miscarriage of disarmament talks at the UN, the country was not yet ready to turn to military preparedness. Given the international environment, however, there was little enthusiasm for additional arms limitation efforts.

The label given to the new American policy was containment. As Washington filled out the new doctrine with such efforts as the Marshall Plan, NATO, and military action in Korea—all to be discussed forthwith—containment was to come under attack from three sides (Huntington, 1961, pp. 15–19). Henry Wallace and, to some degree, Secretary of State James F. Byrnes allowed that Moscow's goals were limited and legitimate, and that Soviet expansion was the product of understandable fear, isolation and insecurity. America's hostile and belligerent attitude was largely responsible for U.S.-Soviet tensions. Wallace's defeat in the 1948 election signaled the rejection by the American people of this point of view. A second assault on containment held that America should restrict its strategic concerns to the Western Hemisphere. This variation on the theme of isolationism maintained that events in Europe could have little bearing on America's well-being, and that American involvement in Europe could only weaken the United States. American superiority in air and sea power could seal off the country from any untoward developments in Europe. While never dominant, this point of view gained support once the costs of containment became more apparent with the war in Korea and the expense of maintaining American forces in Europe. The final challenge to containment came from some of those in the Republican Party that called for a showdown with the Soviets. Containment, these critics maintained, was a negative policy that offered no hope of victory. A less extreme version of this point of view was adopted, at least rhetorically, by the Eisenhower administration under the label of liberation. If the United States would not precipitate a final showdown with the Soviet Union, at least America would seek to roll back Soviet advances in such locales as Eastern Europe. When it came time to back such words with action, as at the time of the Hungarian Revolution of 1956, however, Washington failed to follow through.

Following upon the Truman Doctrine, the United States took a wide array of measures to implement containment. Not long after Truman announced the Greek-Turkish aid program, Secretary of State George C. Marshall announced America's intention to provide Western Europe with economic assistance. This effort, to be known as the Marshall Plan, sprang from several motivations. A primary reason was to blunt the threat of communism. Internally, communism threatened to gain control by persuading Europeans that free enterprise coupled with democracy had brought them two world wars and a great depression, and that they should adopt a different system. Externally, the Red Army menaced a European continent that was too weak economically to sustain the military forces needed to thwart a communist attack. Washington hoped that the Marshall Plan would block both communist roads to power. America also had selfish economic reasons to help Europe regain its economic prosperity. A large proportion of America's exports went to Western Europe; only an economically healthy Western Europe could afford to purchase American goods. Finally, both Truman and Marshall hoped that American aid would lead to closer cooperation among European states, which had a bloody tradition of conflict that communists could exploit in the future. Between 1948 and 1952, the United States gave approximately $13 billion to Western Europe. This aid went far toward the accomplishment of the purposes set forth above.

The Marshall Plan received an unexpected boost from a coup in Czechoslovakia in February, 1948. Congress had demonstrated reluctance to appropriate funds for the European recovery program. The communist coup in Czechoslovakia prompted approval of the funding. The events in Czechoslovakia also brought home to the American public the immediacy of the threat Truman had mentioned in his speech the previous year. As a result, Congress passed a selective service bill and appropriated enough money to fund a 70-group air force, a significant expansion of the country's air effort. America was beginning to turn to military strength instead of arms limitation to preserve its security.

Americans were not the only ones moved by the communist seizure in Prague. In March, 1948, England, France and the three Benelux countries signed the Brussels Pact, pledging cooperation in defense matters. Washington applauded the agreement.

In the spring of 1948, one of the most dramatic confrontations of the cold war era occurred in Berlin. The Berlin Blockade can be traced to the failure of the March, 1947, meeting of the foreign ministers of the four occupying powers to agree on the future of Germany. Following this impasse, the Western powers decided to unify their three sectors and bring the new political unit into the anti-Soviet coalition then taking shape. In June, 1948, the Western powers announced their intention to form a West German government. The new-found Western concern for military preparedness was partially responsible for this measure. At the time, West European countries fielded only 12 ill-equipped and poorly trained divisions (Ambrose, 1980, pp. 147–53). The American Joint Chiefs were calling for a huge increase in the number of West European troops to dissuade the Red Army from aggression. A remilitarized West Germany would go a long way toward reaching the goal set by the Joint Chiefs.

Reeling from a succession of foreign policy setbacks—the success of the Marshall Plan, formation of the Brussels Pact and the defection of Tito—the Soviets decided to take strong action against the creation of the West German state. Moscow announced a blockade of all land and water approaches to Berlin, situated in the Russian occupation zone. Fueling this decision was the Soviet perception, which proved well-founded, that the West would use West Germany as an outpost for anti-Soviet espionage and other hostile actions against Soviet interests.

Western leaders viewed the crisis as a test of will. As General Lucius Clay, commander of American forces in Germany, put it, "When Berlin falls, western Germany will be next" (Ambrose, 1980, p. 150). The remainder of Western Europe would soon follow, as these countries came to realize that America could not be counted on to maintain their integrity. To preserve its position in Berlin, the West mounted the largest airlift in history. It was during this episode that Washington made one of its earliest threats to use nuclear weapons. In mid-July, 1948, Truman transferred to England two groups of B-29 bombers, equipped to carry atomic bombs. However, he rejected the Pentagon's request that he transfer authority over use of the weapons to the military (Lafeber, 1967). In March, 1949, the Russians lifted the blockade. Two months later the West German republic came into being.

The West was demonstrating a capacity to work together against potential communist aggression. However, more concrete action was needed to persuade the Soviets that aggression in Europe would not pay, as well as to shore up European confidence so as to stimulate capital investment. In April, 1949, 12 western governments took such a concrete measure by creating the North Atlantic Treaty Organization (NATO). The formation of NATO reflected the lessons learned from 1914 and 1939, namely, that it might be possible to halt aggression by putting the potential aggressor on notice that he would meet strong and determined opposition. But such opposition depended on forces in being, something the West did not possess in great number in the spring of 1949. Accordingly, the Truman administration asked Congress to approve funds for military assistance to Europe. Congress balked, but the Soviet explosion of an atomic bomb in September persuaded Congress to pass the $1½ billion Mutual Defense Assistance Act. Now America would help Europe establish a credible military force against Soviet aggression.

The NATO alliance went beyond a pledge for common defense. The allies agreed to set up a unified defense force, complete with a decision-making structure and a supreme commander. General Dwight D. Eisenhower was the first to assume this post, which he occupied from 1950 until he returned to the United States to campaign for the presidency in 1952.

While Europe was Washington's principal security concern during this period, Washington could not afford to ignore the rest of the world. In his inaugural address of 1949, Truman called for a program of economic assistance to the third world. Truman said that he was not calling for a one-shot injection of emergency aid but a sustained effort to assist the world's poorer countries. This global program, named Point Four, had several objectives. By improving living standards in developing countries, the United States hoped to counter the appeal of communism. Thus, Point Four was part of containment. The program was also designed to aid the American economy. As the poorer countries of the world developed, they could afford to purchase American goods. In 1950, Congress passed legislation that gave life to Point Four.

In Asia, the United States joined other states (but not the Soviet Union) in signing a peace treaty with Japan in September, 1951. The treaty restored Japanese sovereignty over the home islands but not the Bonins or the Ryukus, which housed a large American military base at Okinawa. The treaty allowed for a certain measure of Japanese armaments and provided for the stationing on Japanese soil of American military forces. At the same time, the United States concluded a security pact with Japan. In this agreement, Japan permitted the stationing of American troops and airplanes on its soil but not the forces of any other power. Stalin viewed these developments as clearly hostile, the embryo of an Asian NATO.

In China, meanwhile, communism scored a signal triumph. At the end of 1949 the communists defeated nationalist forces and sent them scurrying to the island of Taiwan.

A half year later, North Korean troops poured across the border into the South. Under the banner of the United Nations, American troops went to battle in large numbers against the communists. Writing later about his thoughts at the time of the North Korean invasion, Truman (1956) said:

> In my generation, this was not the first occasion when the strong had attacked the weak. I recalled some earlier instances: Manchuria, Ethiopia, Austria. I remembered how each time that the democracies failed to act it had encouraged the aggressors to keep going ahead. Communism was acting in Korea just as Hitler, Mussolini, and the Japanese had acted ten, fifteen, and twenty years earlier. I felt certain that if South Korea was allowed to fall Communist leaders would be emboldened to override nations closer to our own shores. If the Communists were permitted to force their way into the Republic of Korea without opposition from the free world, no small nation would have the courage to resist threats and aggression by stronger

Chapter 1: Truman

> Communist neighbors. If this were allowed to go unchallenged it would mean a third world war, just as similar incidents had brought on the second world war. It was also clear to me that the foundations and the principles of the United Nations were at stake unless this unprovoked attack in Korea could be stopped (pp. 332–33).

Such statements convincingly indicate that Truman was not thinking in terms of arms control as an approach to peace. Instead, he looked to military deterrence to discourage communist aggression. As we shall see subsequently, by 1950 Truman and most other top policy-makers had set aside arms limitation in favor of military preparedness as the key to American security.

The last international event that need concern us here was the war in Indochina. Under the leadership of communist Ho Chi Minh, Vietnamese nationalists of various political persuasions were fighting to prevent the French from reasserting their colonial control over Indochina. While Washington had at first sided with the anti-colonial forces, devotion to containment and the pleadings of the French convinced Washington to switch sides. Soon the United States would be funding the French war effort and would later take France's part in fighting the Vietminh.

MILITARY DOCTRINE

In numerous ways, the Second World War represented a watershed for American military policy. As Samuel Huntington (1961) has pointed out, before World War II, it was generally assumed that America would have ample time to prepare for war. By mid-century, this luxury was gone. Before the great global conflagration of 1939–1945, the purpose of military strategy was to win a war. Now it was to deter one. Up to World War II, America placed great reliance on wartime mobilization of personnel and industry. After the war, America had to rely on forces-in-being.

Immediately after World War II, it was assumed that the principal threat to world peace was a vengeful Germany or Japan. This threat was to be contained by the continued cooperation of the wartime alliance of the five great powers, working through the United Nations. It soon became apparent that this vision of the international state system was out of focus. In addition, collective security under the UN Charter foundered on the jagged rocks of U.S.-Soviet enmity. That antagonism itself soon became the fault line along which the advanced countries of the world divided.

America's leaders realized that the country required a new military doctrine to take account of the world that was emerging as the century approached its mid-point. Moscow's explosion of an atomic bomb in 1949, signifying the end of America's nuclear monopoly, and the communist victory in China lent urgency to the task of defining a new military doctrine. In January, 1950, President Truman directed the State and Defense Departments to draw up an overall review and assessment of America's foreign policy. Paul Nitze of State headed the team that in June, 1950, produced a document known as NSC-68. This document set the tone for American foreign policy for many years to come. The paper focused on the nature of the U.S.-Soviet relationship and capabilities of the two powers. After concluding that the Soviets were an expansionist power and likely to remain so for the indefinite future, NSC-68 set forth four alternatives for American policy:

- continuation of the present course without either strengthening American capabilities or reducing American commitments;
- preventive war against the Soviet Union;
- withdrawal to the Western hemisphere;
- development of "free world" capabilities and cooperation.

The paper made a strong case for the last-named alternative. To be specific, the document recommended an immediate and large-scale buildup of the military strength of the United States and its allies, particularly in Western Europe. Only through such military preparedness could the West halt Soviet expansion. NSC-68 thus called for the global application of the Truman Doctrine of preventing Soviet expansion. It also called for an enormous increase in military spending, which Truman had set at $13 billion. Before long, the Korean War would propel this figure toward $50 billion and even beyond.

The government soon began to implement NSC-68's recommendations. In so doing, policy-makers devised a military doctrine for defending Europe and for using atomic air power.

Europe

Given America's limited military capability at the time, Washington decided its first overseas priority must be the defense of Europe. Should there be a war in Europe, most American strategists thought it would resemble World War II in many ways. Atomic weapons suggested a new role for ground forces, namely, that of a tripwire. A Soviet attack would automatically trigger an American nuclear response. In this conception, the number of American troops that needed to be stationed in Europe was very small. Theoretically, that number need not exceed one, so long as that soldier became an early casualty and thereby triggered America's nuclear response.

Not all military planners were enthusiastic about escalating a European war to the nuclear level, especially after the Soviets exploded a nuclear device (1949). NATO doctrine also called for the defense of Europe east of the Elbe River. To achieve this, the West needed sizable conventional forces. While serving as NATO's Supreme Commander, Eisenhower called for 35 to 40 ready divisions and 96 more that could be brought up to strength in a month. He also wanted ten times the existing number of 300 airplanes. At the Lisbon meeting of NATO foreign ministers in 1952, NATO agreed to boost the number of NATO ready divisions to 50. Primarily due to European reluctance, the Alliance has never reached this goal. Still, to increase NATO's capability to contain a Soviet advance east of the Elbe, the United States began in 1952 to equip its infantry forces with battlefield atomic weapons.

Atomic Air Power

Deterring a Soviet attack was also a high priority. In January, 1948, the President's Air Policy Commission, in the "Finletter Report," called for a new strategy to prevent the outbreak of war by the "prospect of a counterattack of the utmost violence," namely, atomic bombs, and to bring victory if war came. The United States still enjoyed a nuclear monopoly. The new doctrine called for an air force capable of destroying Soviet cities and industrial plants with atomic bombs. These instruments of unprecedented destruction underlay the doctrine of atomic air power.

The doctrine had great appeal for those who wanted to limit military spending. Atomic bombs are much cheaper to maintain than infantry divisions. Besides, many thought, the atomic bomb would provide America with influence worldwide without the need to station troops overseas. As we shall see, these expectations were doomed to disappointment.

MILITARY PREPAREDNESS

To support the military stance called for by NSC-68, the United States needed to refurbish its national security capabilities. A beginning had already been made in the form of the National Security Act of 1947. This legislation, since amended, created the Office of Secretary of Defense with authority over the separate armed forces. The law also designated the Joint Chiefs of Staff as the principal source of military advice to the president. To coordinate and give overall direction to foreign policy, the act created the National Security Council. Under it was placed a new organization, the Central Intelligence Agency.

Military Budget

President Truman attached a high priority to a balanced budget. The President normally set aside funds for fixed government expenditures and then allocated one-third of the remaining funds for military purposes. Under this method, military spending was restricted by the revenues the government collected. In the early years of the Truman administration, neither the public nor Congress was enthusiastic about raising taxes or deficit spending. Indeed, Congress wanted to lower taxes.

The military services were not content with their allocations. The Army complained that it lacked the forces needed to carry out the commitments assigned to it and pressed for universal military training. The Air Force said it needed 70 wings to carry out its responsibilities, but funds to sustain these forces were not forthcoming. The military had virtually no capacity to conduct limited warfare. There was a yawning chasm between the country's commitments and its capabilities.

This gap began to narrow following the adoption of NSC-68 and the North Korean attack in June, 1950. NSC-68 provided a comprehensive vision of the future and a plan of action to attain it. Implicit in the document was the need for vastly increased military spending. As already mentioned, the military appropriation for fiscal year 1951 was $13 billion. In early 1951, with the United States fighting Chinese Communist troops in Korea, Truman submitted a defense budget in the amount of $50 billion. He also doubled the number of air groups to 95, boosted the size of the Army by 50% to 3½ million men, and obtained new military bases in Morocco, Libya and Saudi Arabia. In calendar year 1950, national defense consumed 5.2% of GNP. By 1953, the figure had risen to 13.5% of an expanded GNP.

The Korean War, and particularly China's involvement, brought about these increases in defense spending. When the Chinese intervened in October, 1950, many in the West feared that a global war with communism had begun. There were numerous calls among the public and in Congress for a general mobilization. Instead, the administration adopted a partial mobilization, emphasizing the buildup of industrial capacity and manpower in case a full mobilization became necessary. A plan for universal military training was submitted to Congress. In 1952, to the Army's chagrin, Congress voted the program down.

Much of the increase in military spending was allocated for the fighting in Korea as well as the strengthening of the nation's industrial base in preparation for full-scale mobilization. A significant portion of the increase also went to the development of forces to counter-balance the Soviet Union around the globe. These forces were seriously inadequate at the time the buildup began. At mid-1950, the American military included only 10 understrength Army divisions and 11 regimental combat teams, 671 naval vessels, 2 highly understrength Marine divisions, and 48 Air Force wings (including 18 in the Strategic Air Command). Total personnel numbered 1,461,000. If war broke out in Europe, America would be able to do little more than conduct atomic air strikes against the Soviet Union from bases in England, bases that might be vulnerable to Moscow's growing atomic capabilities. Should Soviet nuclear forces neutralize those of the United States, Soviet ground forces in Europe would greatly outnumber those of NATO.

NSC-68 assumed that the Soviet Union would be capable of launching a nuclear attack against the United States by 1954. The document recommended a major increase in nuclear and conventional forces by then. One of the areas

Chapter 1: Truman 19

cited for increased funding was strategic retaliatory forces. It was desirable to fortify these forces so that even if they were hit by the Soviets, there would be enough strength left to deal a devastating blow to the Soviet Union. Another major objective of increased spending was to bolster the West's ground forces in Europe so they could blunt a Soviet land thrust. For both of these objectives, allied assistance was deemed essential. American retaliatory forces, mostly bombers, needed overseas bases where they could be dispersed, rendering their destruction harder to achieve. Assembling ground forces sufficient to halt a Red Army drive required an allied contribution of manpower and equipment.

In December, 1950, the National Security Council set force levels to be attained by July, 1952: for the Army, 18 divisions and 12 regimental combat teams; for the Navy, 1,161 ships plus 2⅓ Marine divisions; for the Air Force, 95 wings. The NSC recommended the total number of men in the armed forces be increased to 3.6 million. To achieve these force levels, Truman proposed a $60 billion defense budget for fiscal year 1953, 20% above his proposal for 1952. The nation did meet these targets. By July 1, 1952, the armed forces included 20 Army divisions and 18 regimental combat teams; the Navy, 3 Marine divisions and 3 Marine air wings; the Air Force, 95 wings. B-36 long-range bombers were improved and production of B-47 medium-range bombers was accelerated. Congress approved construction of some large aircraft carriers. Total military personnel numbered 3,636,000 men. While not all these units were at full strength, there could be no denying that the nation had embarked on a major military buildup.

During the latter half of 1951, the military made another assessment of the strategic balance. The top brass concluded that 1954 represented the time of maximum danger to the West. By then, the buildup of Soviet satellite armies as well as Soviet heavy industry would be complete, and, even more important, the Soviet air force would possess a fleet of strategic bombers equipped with atomic weapons. In consequence, the Joint Chiefs recommended a goal of 143 wings by mid-1954 instead of the then-existing 95. The Truman administration approved this target, but budget restraints moved the target date back to July, 1955.

The expected date of Moscow's acquisition of strategic atomic capability played an important role in America's defense planning. So long as Russia lacked deliverable atomic bombs, the American Air Force could remain relatively small. Invulnerable to a devastating surprise attack, the Air Force's primary task was to punish the Soviet Union in retaliation for an attack upon Western Europe. Once the Soviets gained atomic bombs, however, they might launch a surprise strike against SAC bombers on the ground. To ensure a retaliatory capability, the United States needed a larger air force and one that was more widely dispersed. Thus, as the 1950s progressed, military planners called for increasing the means of delivery (more aircraft as well as missiles), boosting destructive power (hydrogen bombs), and enlarging the atomic stockpile.

European Military Buildup

As we have seen, one of the primary objectives of rearmament and increased military spending was to bolster Western defenses in Europe. The framework for this development was the NATO alliance, concluded in April, 1949. The original signers of the agreement were Canada, the United States, France, Great Britain, Belgium, Luxembourg, the Netherlands, Norway, Italy, Denmark, Iceland and Portugal. NATO committed the United States to Europe's defense, thereby putting Russia on notice that an assault against Western Europe would involve American forces. Along with the Marshall Plan, NATO was designed to give Western Europe the self-confidence to rebuild and stand up to the colossus to the east. The treaty's key clause, Article 5, says:

> The Parties agree that an armed attack against one or more of them in Europe or North America shall be considered an attack against them all and consequently they agree that, if such an armed attack occurs, each of them, in exercise of the right of individual or collective self-defense recognized by Article 51 of the Charter of the United Nations, will assist the Party or Parties so attacked by taking forthwith, individually and in concert with the other Parties, such action as it deems necessary, including the use of armed force, to restore and maintain the security of the North Atlantic area.

No sooner had Washington ratified the NATO treaty than Truman asked Congress to appropriate $1.4 billion in military assistance for the NATO allies and Greece, Turkey and the Philippines. Truman proposed 3 types of military aid:

- transfer of U.S. surplus weapons (mostly World War II stocks);
- dispatch of American military experts to help train and equip friendly forces;
- assistance to friendly nations to help them boost their own production of military items.

Washington hoped that after a quick injection of such assistance, Europe would be able to provide its own military forces. Indeed, once Europe's economic recovery was completed, Washington found it no longer necessary to offer military aid to its NATO allies for purposes of European defense.

In addition to military hardware and funds, Washington sent American troops to Europe. These soldiers were intended to reinforce America's commitment to Europe's defense, help halt a Soviet attack, activate the tripwire that would perhaps trigger an atomic response, and reassure Europeans that America was not losing interest in the area in view of America's growing involvement in Asia (Korea and China). All of these reasons were consistent with NSC-68.

As 1950 opened, America had two divisions in Europe. The primary mission of these troops was the occupation of western Germany. Western Europe did not begin to field the military forces necessary to thwart a Soviet invasion. That role was assigned to America's atomic arsenal. However, once the

Chapter 1: Truman 21

U.S.S.R. acquired a stockpile of deliverable atomic bombs, Washington's threat to use atomic weapons would diminish in credibility. Therefore, during 1950 the United States sent four additional divisions to Western Europe with the main task of blunting a Soviet drive, not occupying Germany. The following year Washington sent two additional divisions to Europe. At about the same time, Great Britain created the Army of the Rhine. The continental powers also commenced a military buildup. NATO established an integrated command, Supreme Headquarters Allied Powers, Europe; General Eisenhower became NATO's first supreme commander. At least a start had been made in shoring up Western defenses in Europe. However, even these forces did not begin to match the gargantuan Red Army. Realizing this, NATO foreign ministers resolved at their 1952 meeting in Lisbon, already mentioned, to set a goal of 90 divisions, half on active duty, by the end of that year. As we have seen, Europe never came close to that goal. During the winter of 1951-1952, many European governments were already stretching out their arms buildups, reducing their military budgets, and cutting the length of service for draftees. To keep military spending low, more and more Europeans called for reliance on American atomic weapons rather than their own forces to deter a Soviet attack.

As military strategists contemplated the problem of defending Europe, it soon became apparent that it would be difficult to do so without a military contribution from Germany. Germany was situated on the fringe of the Iron Curtain. The country possessed the material resources to create a formidable military force. At the same time, few Europeans on either side of the Iron Curtain looked with equanimity upon the prospect of German rearmament. World War II was still a vivid memory. Nonetheless, in the spring of 1950, the Joint Chiefs drew up a plan for German rearmament. For a while the plan lay dormant, but the North Korean attack in June led to its revival. The Korean assault revealed that the communists would not wait until they had achieved atomic parity or superiority before commencing their drive against the West. If they attacked in Asia, they might do so in Europe. The military vacuum in Central Europe had to be filled, and German manpower was the ideal instrument to fill it. During the summer of 1950, officials from State and Defense reviewed the plan drafted by the Joint Chiefs. The final American position suggested the creation of 10 German divisions. To pacify European fears about a rearmed Germany, the United States would place troops of its own in Europe (discussed above), help the Europeans set up their own military forces, and establish an integrated NATO command headed by an American. The last-named provision would serve to prevent the German forces from acting independently from NATO. In September, 1950, Secretary of State Acheson introduced the American proposal to the foreign ministers of Britain and France. The French in particular opposed the scheme. In the face of heavy American insistence, however, France and the other NATO countries accepted Washington's plan. As expected, the Russians vigorously opposed German rearmament.

The Hydrogen Bomb

The Soviet atomic explosion in September, 1949, and the victory of the Chinese communists three months later generated the feeling in Washington that communism was on the warpath around the globe. This concern led officials to consider the development of a weapon even more powerful than the atomic bomb. In November, 1949, Truman formed a special committee of the NSC consisting of Secretary of State Dean Acheson, Atomic Energy Commission Chairman David Lilienthal, and Secretary of Defense Louis Johnson. Truman requested this committee to advise him on whether to construct a hydrogen bomb.

At the very same time two other groups were gathering. Paul Nitze and the Policy Planning Staff at State were drafting the document that came to be known as NSC-68. George Kennan and other members of the Policy Planning Staff were examining international control of the atomic arms race. This concatenation of activity resulted in one of the earliest postwar struggles between the advocates of arms control and those favoring military preparedness.

We have already reviewed the conclusions of NSC-68, which came down clearly on the side of military preparedness. As he was leaving his employ at the State Department, Kennan handed his study to Acheson on January 20, 1950. Kennan (1967) claims that this was the most significant memo he ever wrote for the government. In it he said the government must decide if it truly wanted to abolish atomic weapons, as it maintained in public statements, or if the government wished to retain them for use in case of Soviet aggression, as some military leaders advocated. Kennan favored their elimination, and said in his memo that the United States should forswear first use. He went on to say that the United States should retain its nuclear weapons until the Soviets gave up theirs, but only to prevent their use. Quoting from his memoirs (since the original memo remains classified), Kennan urged the American position to be that

> "we remain prepared to go very far, to show considerable confidence in others, and to accept a certain risk for ourselves, in order to achieve international agreement on their removal from international arsenals; for we can think of nothing more dangerous than a continued international competition in their development" (p. 474).

Kennan argued that atomic weapons are too destructive to be used in a calculated manner; they simply destroy everything in their path. Put differently, atomic weapons do not help nations achieve limited objectives, such as persuading an adversary to desist from aggression against a neighbor. "The results they could produce would mean at best only a deterioration of the conditions of civilization for people everywhere, including ourselves." Kennan believed Washington should rely on non-atomic weapons for deterrence and make another effort (after the Baruch Proposal) to bring about international control of the atom.

Kennan's plea for arms control and atomic restraint was echoed by David

Lilienthal in the deliberations of the special committee of the NSC to study the hydrogen bomb. The AEC chairman advised that the government complete its study (NSC-68) of the overall purposes of American foreign policy before making any decisions regarding the hydrogen bomb. He feared that a decision to build the hydrogen bomb, before a need for it were determined, would prejudice the government in favor of building the bomb and then finding a use for it. Like Kennan, Lilienthal doubted the political utility of such a destructive weapon. Both men favored exploration of international control of atomic weapons. Lilienthal also believed America's first military priority was the acquisition of additional conventional forces; he was shocked when he learned how dependent the country was on the atomic bomb. Further, Lilienthal questioned the morality of a military doctrine that rested on the destruction of large urban targets and their unprotected inhabitants.

Acheson and Johnson, the other two members of the NSC special committee, disagreed with Lilienthal. They both favored an immediate investigation into whether the hydrogen bomb could be built. Lilienthal was outnumbered. The committee voted to recommend an investigation of whether a hydrogen bomb could be constructed. On January 31, 1950, the committee passed its recommendation to the president. At this meeting Lilienthal started to explain his position to Truman, but the president cut him off and approved the committee's recommendation.

As Schilling (1961) explains, numerous American scientists, such as J. Robert Oppenheimer, opposed this decision. They argued that the atomic bomb had already introduced enough evil into the world. In addition, they said that if the United States built a hydrogen bomb, other countries would follow suit, leading to a dangerous arms race. It would be better, they insisted, not to determine whether a hydrogen bomb could be built, for that would put a brake on research directed toward its construction. Some scientists said that if Washington renounced the hydrogen bomb, Moscow might follow that example.

At first the military was not enthusiastic about a hydrogen bomb. The primary impetus for the weapon came not from the top brass but from civilian scientists such as Edward Teller. The military was satisfied that the atomic bomb was an adequate deterrent. After some prodding by civilian scientists, the military came around to support their position, and on October 14, 1949, the Joint Chiefs officially urged development of the hydrogen bomb at a meeting with the Joint Committee on Atomic Energy. Thereafter, the military, especially the Air Force, strongly endorsed the project.

Both the State Department and the Defense Department supported development of the weapon. Both departments assumed that the Soviets would seek to construct a hydrogen bomb regardless of America's course. The diplomats at State worried that the superbomb would give the Russians negotiating leverage, while the Defense Department feared a war in which the Kremlin had the bomb but America did not. Neither department had much faith that Russia was interested in controlling the bomb through arms control negotiations. Efforts to engage the Soviets in such talks, it was widely felt, would only serve to delay American development of the hydrogen bomb and perhaps enable the Russians to gain a head start.

Truman's decision of January 31, 1950, should not be seen as a decision to construct an arsenal of hydrogen weapons. Rather, the President directed that a determination be made whether a hydrogen bomb could be fabricated. In the words of Warner Schilling (1961), the decision bore the aspects of "a conscious search for the course of action that would close off the least number of future alternatives" (p. 38). On February 24, the Joint Chiefs sent Truman a memo urging all-out development of the hydrogen bomb. On March 10 Truman ordered the test of a hydrogen weapon as soon as possible. Twelve months later at Eniwetok the United States conducted the first successful test of a hydrogen bomb.

In retrospect, some observers have wondered whether the United States did not move too hastily to develop the superbomb. Had Washington hesitated and engaged the Soviets in an effort to forebear from building such a weapon, it is possible the two powers would have placed a crucial qualitative cap on the arms race. However, Washington's distrust of Moscow stood in the way of such restraint.

Before Truman left office, he took several other steps to promote the military preparedness of the United States. We have already made mention of the security treaty signed with Japan. Washington also extended aid to France in its war against Ho Chi Minh in Vietnam, initiated the process of adding Greece and Turkey to NATO, and began talks with Franco for the establishment of American military bases in Spain.

As we have seen, the Truman administration placed heavy reliance on military preparedness to preserve American security, especially after the failure of the Soviets to accept the Baruch Plan for international control of the atom. Following the guidelines of NSC-68, the Truman administration embarked on a military buildup both at home and abroad. Nonetheless, American officials continued to make efforts to control the weapons of war, as described in the next section.

ARMS CONTROL

One of the Truman administration's first attempts to guarantee American security involved arms limitation. Following upon the precipitous demobilization of the armed forces, Washington introduced into the United Nations the Baruch Proposal for international control of the atom. The Soviet rejection of this effort occurred at about the time the United States was reassessing its policy toward the Soviet Union. This examination resulted in NSC-68 and containment, both of which called for an emphasis on military preparedness. To this task the nation turned, yet it did not completely turn its back on arms control.

In October, 1950, just a few months after deciding to plumb the feasibility of building a hydrogen bomb, Truman spoke before the General Assembly of the United Nations. Truman told the delegates the United States was prepared to consider a new approach to controlling the implements of war. Until that time, the principal concern of arms control had been to restrain the development of atomic weapons. The Korean War showed, however, that conventional arms remained a threat to peace. America had a highly selfish interest in limiting conventional forces; the large inventory of Soviet troops and conventional weapons would continue to menace American interests even if controls were placed on atomic weapons. Accordingly, Truman told the General Assembly that the United States was ready to consider the control of atomic and conventional weapons together. This new approach led to American support for a General Assembly resolution of January, 1952, to combine the existing UN Atomic Energy Commission and Commission for Conventional Armaments into a single body, the UN Disarmament Commission (UNDC). This resolution passed.

The sixth session of the General Assembly opened in Paris in November, 1951. The United States, United Kingdom and France agreed on an arms control proposal that was announced by Acheson before the General Assembly on November 8 and later elaborated upon in the General Assembly's Political and Security Committee. This proposal called for an international approach to four areas of arms control:

- provision of full, accurate and continuously current data on all armaments of all nations, thus removing the worrisome uncertainty about who had what;
- limitation and reduction of arms;
- abolition of atomic weapons;
- creation of safeguards.

The proposal then called for the UNDC to draw up treaties and agreements that would reduce these four general areas to concrete terms. While the treaties could not go into effect until the fighting in Korea came to a halt, negotiations for formulating the treaties could begin immediately, Acheson said.

The Soviet Union found the Western plan unacceptable and in its place proposed a scheme consisting of the following provisions:

- prohibition of nuclear weapons (without inspection);
- reduction within one year by one-third of the arms and armed forces of the five major powers;
- presentation by all nations of data on arms and armed forces;
- creation of an international control organ under the Security Council (where the Soviets would have a veto).

These provisions reflected previous Soviet positions that the West had found unsatisfactory. To resolve the impasse, the Political and Security Committee set up an ad hoc subcommittee to work out an agreed disarmament plan by December 10. The membership was made up of representatives from the United States, the United Kingdom, France, the Soviet Union, and General Assembly

President Padilla Nervo of Mexico. The subcommittee labored to draw up a mutually acceptable plan but the members were unable to agree, the main stumbling block being verification and inspection. Thus, the Western proposal failed to advance its ostensible purpose, namely the control of arms. In his memoirs, however, Acheson (1969) writes unabashedly about another purpose the Western proposal served rather well. "No doubt existed any longer about who stood where or for what" (p. 583). For the next decade, propaganda was to be a major ingredient in arms control proposals put forth by both sides. Indeed, a curious alliance took shape in the West between the advocates and opponents of disarmament. The advocates favored far-reaching proposals, such as calls for the total elimination of all weapons. The foes of disarmament also relished such proposals, but only because they knew the Soviets found wide-ranging calls unacceptable. By drafting comprehensive proposals that the Soviets would reject but everyone else would applaud, the opponents of disarmament were able to win propaganda battles while at the same time creating a pretext for the construction of additional weapons.

In the spring of 1952 the United States put forth two further arms control proposals, before the country settled down to prepare for the November elections. In April, Washington suggested in the newly established UNDC a verification scheme for disarmament. The plan proposed a team of international inspectors that would operate under a control organ that would have access to the entire national territory of every state. The Soviets objected, raising the by now familiar bugaboo that inspection was nothing more than a cloak for espionage. The following month, France and England joined with the United States in a suggestion to impose manpower ceilings on the armed forces of the world and tie reductions in conventional arms to the elimination of atomic weapons. The Soviets, apparently unwilling to reach an arms control accord so long as they smarted under atomic inferiority, rejected this proposal. It was becoming apparent that the Soviets had little interest in arms limitation as the West conceived it. The Kremlin continued to call for immediate elimination of all atomic weapons with no verification measures.

In looking back at the Truman administration's balancing of disarmament and military preparedness, it is not difficult to discern which element prevailed. After the failure of the Baruch initiative, the United States adjusted its view of the Soviet Union. By the end of the 1940s, Washington perceived Moscow as a dangerous foe with expansionist ambitions. Under the guidelines of NSC-68 and containment, the United States engaged in a major military buildup. While the country put forth some proposals for limiting arms, it seems fair to say that those in high places gave a much higher priority to military preparedness than to arms control. We shall see this pattern continue into the Eisenhower administration.

2

EISENHOWER

THE 1952 ELECTIONS

While foreign policy did not dominate the 1952 election, it certainly played a role. The Korean War was two years old with no end in sight. The Republicans, led by General Eisenhower, criticized the Democrats for waging an inconclusive war without bringing victory. Indeed, the GOP blasted the overall foreign policy of the Roosevelt-Truman period, saying it was self-defeating and, even at its most successful, offered a prospect no better than continued struggle with the Soviet Union at places of the latter's choosing. In seeking to contain Soviet expansion around the world, the Republicans charged the Democrats would eventually spend the country into bankruptcy. Instead, the GOP urged, America should strive to end the U.S.-Soviet struggle once and for all, and with an American victory. Soviet power must be rolled back, not merely contained. The Republican platform branded containment "negative, futile and immoral," inasmuch as it abandoned millions to "a despotism and Godless terrorism."

The GOP vision of pushing back communism and liberating masses of people living under Marxism had undeniable appeal for the American electorate. Such a policy held out the prospect of an end to the U.S.-Soviet confrontation on terms favorable to American democracy.

The GOP never bothered to explain just how it would go about rolling back communism. As we now know, the Republicans had no such plan. Once in power, they failed to push back communism a single inch. Although the rollback described by John Foster Dulles and other Republicans during the 1952 campaign would have meant war with the U.S.S.R., the American people responded positively to the GOP call and swept the Republicans into power. Years later, when GOP foreign policy turned out to resemble very much the containment policy of the Truman years, hardly anyone took notice.

A Balanced Budget

One of the GOP complaints about Truman's foreign policy, particularly its military component, was that it was far too expensive. As Eisenhower (1965) later wrote, "We need an adequate defense, but every arms dollar we spend above adequacy has a long-term weakening effect upon the nation and its security" (p. 622).

Indeed, Eisenhower and the remainder of the Republican leadership were enamored of a balanced budget and a tax decrease. In their view, the best way to achieve these two goals was to reduce military spending. In Eisenhower's view, the country's strength did not rest solely on military might. A strong economy was just as important.

> Excessive spending helps cause deficits, which cause inflation, which in turn cuts the amount of equipment and manpower the defense dollar can buy.... Every addition to defense expenditures does not automatically increase military security. Because security is based upon moral and economic, as well as purely military strength, a point can be reached at which additional funds for arms, far from bolstering security, weakens it (Eisenhower, 1965, p. 217).

Eisenhower feared that a continuation of military spending at the level of the Truman years would lead to runaway inflation, cripple the economy, and thus undermine national security. At the same time, however, he recognized the need for military forces, particularly at a time when the nation was at war (Korea). Besides, the Republicans would need the military wherewithal to roll back communism. How was the country to square diminished military spending with a commitment to fight communism more vigorously than Truman did?

The New Look

The answer was to be found in a restructuring of the American military that has been dubbed the New Look. The Republicans hoped to win the battle against communism by acquiring a different mix of weapons and adopting a new military doctrine.

The New Look was adopted in November, 1953, with the president's approval of a policy paper designated NSC 162/2. In essence, the New Look called for less reliance on conventional military force—the kind used in Korea —and more dependence upon atomic weapons, both strategic and tactical. No longer would atomic weapons be utilized only as a last resort, when the country had its back to the wall. Under the New Look, the nation would deploy nuclear weapons from the outset of combat. The increased firepower provided by nuclear weapons would make up for the reduction in unconventional forces, particularly infantry, foreseen by the new military doctrine. Since atomic weaponry need not be housed, clothed and fed, its maintenance would cost far less than the amount of money required to sustain massive conventional forces. Thus, the country would gain more firepower at less cost, or "more bang for the buck."

While the New Look called for a reduction in military spending, it should not be seen as a move in the direction of arms control or disarmament. Rather, the New Look called for a different mix of military forces designed to accomplish more, not less, militarily. What did this new mix entail? The principal target for cuts in military spending was the Army. Eisenhower opposed the Army's desire to maintain large forces in readiness for fighting limited wars along the lines of Korea. Rather, the president believed wars of the future would be fought with nuclear as well as conventional weapons (Adams, 1961). Henceforth, a smaller army augmented with nuclear weapons would be able to do the job. To fight more effectively, the Army was organized into smaller, more mobile units armed with tactical nuclear weapons—artillery, mines and short-range rockets—as well as conventional weapons. Aircraft designed to support ground troops were equipped with low-yield atomic weapons as well as standard conventional ordnance.

While all branches of the armed services suffered from cuts in military spending, strategic air power suffered least of all. Under the New Look, strategic air power consumed a bigger portion of a smaller military budget, although Eisenhower sheared Truman's goal of 143 Air Force wings by 1956 to 120 wings by 1955 (Huntington, 1961). According to the strategic doctrine of massive retaliation, which accompanied the New Look, strategic air power was to play a central role in stemming communist expansion. When Eisenhower entered office, the United States enjoyed clear strategic superiority over the Soviet Union. The Strategic Air Command (SAC) deployed over 500 B-47 nuclear-capable jet bombers, which could reach Soviet territory from bases in allied countries. Carrier-based aircraft could also deliver nuclear bombs against the Soviet Union. A prototype B-52 intercontinental bomber had already been constructed. By contrast, the Soviets had only a few hundred intermediate-range aircraft, roughly comparable to the B-29 of World War II fame. These airplanes were capable of reaching the United States but could not fly back to base. This balance began to change when Moscow exploded a thermonuclear device in 1953 and displayed a prototype of an intercontinental jet bomber in 1954. The Truman administration had envisioned the use of strategic air power only as a last resort, a threat to be wielded only in response to a Soviet attack against the American homeland or a major strike against Western Europe. Under massive retaliation, Washington threatened to send its strategic bombers into action against Soviet territory as an immediate response to any form of communist expansion. Exactly what communist actions would trigger a strategic nuclear response was left deliberately vague in the hope of dissuading the communists from making any outward thrusts. Supposedly, the communists would desist from aggression, if they knew the price would be the destruction of Soviet cities.

Along with tactical weapons and strategic air power, continental air defense and the Reserves were to become essential elements of national security under the New Look. Eisenhower increased the size of the Reserves and heightened their state of readiness.

The credibility of the New Look and massive retaliation rested in large part upon the military balance between the United States and the Soviet Union. During the first half of the Eisenhower Administration, the United States enjoyed clear nuclear superiority over the Soviet Union and was practically invulnerable to Soviet retaliation against the continental United States. Thus, Washington could threaten atomic strikes against the Soviet Union without having to fear a Soviet response in kind. This situation would not outlast the Eisenhower years. By launching *Sputnik* in 1957, the Soviets demonstrated the capacity to send strategic missiles against American territory.

An additional element of America's new configuration of military force concerned bargaining and diplomacy. By reducing the size of the Army, America sent a signal to Moscow that the United States would have little alternative to nuclear weapons in case of communist aggression. Hopefully, this would deter the communists from adventurousness based on the expectation that Washington was only bluffing in its threats to use atomic power.

The New Look allowed the Eisenhower administration to cut military spending as it had promised. In two years after taking office, Eisenhower reduced Truman's military budget by nearly one-third to approximately $34 billion. Throughout the remainder of the Eisenhower years, defense budgets hovered in the $35–$40 billion range. To provide the needed firepower for massive retaliation, Eisenhower authorized the military to develop the 20-megaton B-41 bomb. From 1953 to 1955, the size of America's nuclear stockpile, tactical as well as strategic, doubled. America also began production of the B-52 long-range jet bomber that would soon replace the B-47. Funds were allocated toward the improved training and competence of flight crews. Finally, America's network of overseas bases, stationed on allied soil, gave the country jumping-off points for attacks against the Soviet Union in case that necessity should arise.

The New Look, together with massive retaliation, was designed to provide the military wherewithal and doctrine to prevent any further expansion of communist influence. The diplomatic strategy for deployment of this military muscle was known as brinkmanship. As explained by Secretary of State John Foster Dulles, brinkmanship entailed threats to go to the brink of war in encounters with communism. With America's tactical and strategic nuclear superiority clearly established, the communists would have no choice but to back down. Two illustrations of brinkmanship will perhaps make the tactic clear. In mid-1953, Korean truce talks were stalled as fighting continued. The major sticking point in the truce negotiations involved the repatriation of POWs. The communists insisted that the United Nations forces return all communist POWs, whether or not they wanted to return. The UN side refused to repatriate North Korean and Chinese soldiers who wished to take up new lives in the non-communist world. Through diplomats in India, Dulles warned China that America might deploy tactical nuclear weapons in Korea if the communists did not give in and agree to a cease-fire. Less than two weeks later, the Chinese agreed to place the question of repatriation before neutral international authorities. In the second case, two years later, Dulles threatened to deploy nuclear weapons against China after the Chinese began to bombard the offshore islands of Quemoy and Matsu. The Chinese soon desisted.

It goes without saying that the United States could not engage in brinkmanship or rely upon massive retaliation unless America enjoyed nuclear superiority over the Soviet Union and its allies. In the early years of the Eisenhower administration, Washington did enjoy such superiority. While America's long-range bombers, based around the periphery of the Soviet Union, could unleash atomic bombs upon Soviet territory, Moscow was unable to retaliate in kind. Similarly, America and its allies were well ahead of the communists in the deployment of tactical atomic weapons. Inasmuch as military superiority provided the foundation upon which Washington constructed its diplomacy, it was most unlikely that the Eisenhower administration would consider bargaining away much military hardware in arms control negotiations. Furthermore, Eisenhower was aware, as was Truman and all presidents who followed them, that the communist nations enjoyed enormous manpower advantages over the Western countries, particularly after China joined the communist fold. In Washington's eyes, atomic weapons provided the only means to offset the communist edge in human resources. America's tactical atomic arsenal served yet another purpose. One element of brinkmanship involved the threat—usually non-spoken—that any military conflict with the West might escalate to a strategic nuclear strike against the Russian or Chinese heartland. But how could Washington make that threat credible? The gulf between conventional weapons and city-busting atomic bombs was as perceivable as it was wide, so much so that the United States might refrain from employing such weapons. But the difference between conventional weapons and tactical atomic weapons, while certainly apparent, was more of a slide than a leap. Once the West started to use atomic artillery, land mines, rockets and bombs fired by close-support aircraft, the shift to larger atomic weapons was much easier to manage. Thus, America's tactical atomic arsenal served the purpose of signaling to the communists that any aggression on their part might culminate in an American atomic attack upon Russia and/or China. Of course, this was not the only purpose that these battlefield atomic weapons served. Eisenhower doubted that limited wars of the future would remain conventional, and so America needed the atomic wherewithal to prevail in the mixed atomic-conventional limited wars of the future. Reducing the size of the Army only confirmed the West's threat to use atomic weapons. With fewer ground troops, what other response could the West make? (By the close of the 1950s, NATO adopted its "tripwire" doctrine. This stated that the Alliance's conventional forces served mainly as a tripwire to activate a nuclear response, in case the Warsaw Pact nations invaded Western Europe.) Although arms control talks continued throughout the Eisenhower era, Washington placed priority on maintaining and extending military superiority, which meant atomic weapons for the most part, over the communists. In this aspect, Eisenhower's approach resembled that of Truman. While both chief executives subscribed to the idea of a disarmed and peaceful world, neither was prepared to take a determined stride in this direction so long as the communists—perceived as aggressive and menacing—shared the planet with the so-called free world. Thus, under both administrations, Washington devoted far more energy to building weapons than to limiting them through mechanisms of arms control.

THE INTERNATIONAL CONTEXT

The eight years of the Eisenhower administration presented an unusually rich tapestry of global events. These occurrences provided the context for the framing of both military policy and arms limitation proposals. We shall examine this international setting before moving on to American military policy and arms control initiatives.

In October, 1952, as the American presidential campaign was moving toward its climax, the Communist Party of the Soviet Union (CPSU) held its nineteenth congress, the first one since 1939. Stalin had been taking a tough line, nearly doubling the size of the Red Army to 4.9 million men and increasing defense spending by 50% in 1951–1952. Stalin's publication of *Economic Problems of Socialism* the month the congress opened set the tone for the gathering. The Soviet leader affirmed an emphasis on heavy industry and predicted the West would soon succumb to economic catastrophe. He also said Western Europe and Japan would rebel against United States domination. Stalin identified two primary tasks facing the Soviet Union: tightening Communist Party control in order to protect the Soviet block against assaults from the capitalist camp, and cooperative efforts with nationalists everywhere, but especially in West Germany, France and Japan, as a means of accelerating the revolt of these nations against American hegemony. Most important, Stalin stressed the inevitability of war between communism and capitalism. Early the next year, Stalin emphasized the theme of capitalist encirclement and said communists must wage "a fierce struggle against the enemy." Thus, as the new administration took office, it was confronted by an angry and hostile Soviet leader, not one seeking accommodation. Stalin's health, however, was failing, and in March, 1953, he died of a stroke.

Events in the third world occupied a significant portion of the Eisenhower administration's attention. The first of these occurred in Iran, which shares its northern border with the Soviet Union. Premier Mohammed Mossadegh had shown his displeasure with the West by nationalizing the British-owned Anglo-Iranian Oil Company. Now he was, in the eyes of John Foster Dulles, cozying up to Iran's communist party, known as the Tudeh Party. Dulles feared that the Russians might use the Tudeh Party as a vehicle for striking a deal with Iran that would extend Soviet influence. The urgency of the situation grew when pro-Mossadegh nationalist mobs rushed into the streets and helped chase pro-Western Shah Mohammed Riza Pahlavi out of the country. CIA Director Allen Dulles reacted by sending Kim Roosevelt—Theodore Roosevelt's grandson—to Teheran with instructions to overthrow Mossadegh and bring back the shah. Roosevelt succeeded in organizing street demonstrations that brought down Mossadegh. The shah returned, severed government ties with the Tudeh Party, and divided oil production among Great Britain (40%), the United States (40%), Holland and France. Covert action had salvaged the situation in Iran.

Truce talks in Korea had been dragging on since the summer of 1951 without any sign of a breakthrough. In the spring of 1953, John Foster Dulles told Indian Prime Minister Jawaharlal Nehru, who was clearly on speaking terms with the Chinese Communists, that Washington might introduce tactical atomic weapons in Korea and bomb Chinese bases and supply sources in North Korea and Manchuria. Whether or not these veiled threats broke the negotiating logjam, a truce was signed in July. Next month Washington signed a security treaty with South Korea aimed at deterring further communist aggression.

Further to the south, fighting was raging in the area now covered by Cambodia, Laos and Vietnam. Communist Ho Chi Minh led a Vietnamese nationalist struggle to win independence from France, which was trying to re-establish its empire. While at first America, under the banner of self-determination and anti-colonialism, had opposed French efforts, by the end of the Truman administration Washington was supporting France under the flag of containment. By 1954, the United States was financing three-fourths of France's war effort in Indochina. Communist China's assistance to Ho Chi Minh's forces persuaded many in Washington that the war had been transformed from a colonial struggle to a cold war battle. The French position continued to deteriorate, as Vietnamese guns pounded a major French redoubt at Dienbienphu. The French, realizing they could not prevail alone, asked Washington in the spring of 1954 to bomb Vietnamese positions on the hills surrounding Dienbienphu. Washington went through an agonizing appraisal of the situation and, in the absence of allied support, ultimately decided not to intervene. France, which was losing stomach for the war, chose to negotiate a settlement. On July 20 an armistice was concluded which divided Vietnam at the 17th Parallel, the North Vietnamese controlling the area above this line and the French controlling the area to the south. A multi-power conference at Geneva worked out a political settlement, which included plans for a country-wide election in two years.

Dulles and Eisenhower shared the general conviction that if the two Vietnams held an election, Ho Chi Minh would emerge the victor. Such an outcome would only further extend the sway of communism. In consequence, Washington backed the refusal of Ngo Dinh Diem, South Vietnam's president, to allow a vote, using the pretext that Ho would not allow genuinely free elections in the region under his control. Washington then began to sustain Diem's government as a bulwark against communism. Eisenhower pledged military and economic aid. In November, 1954, American military advisers arrived to train Diem's army. The United States urged Diem to undertake social and economic reforms in order to win the allegiance of the people. Diem hesitated, but American aid continued to flow. Diem realized that America would continue to support him so long as he maintained his rigid anti-communist stance.

The limited wars in Korea and Indochina presented a dilemma for Washington's New Look military doctrine. The new approach, with its emphasis on atomic air power, pared down the kinds of forces needed for limited engagements. Dulles and Eisenhower sought to fill this military gap by acquiring allies whose armies could be used in limited wars. The security treaty with South Korea was the first display of what some have dubbed "pactomania." Another such effort centered around Southeast Asia and was known as the Southeast Asia Treaty Organization (SEATO). Formed in September, 1954, SEATO included Great Britain, Australia, New Zealand, France, Thailand, Pakistan, the Philippines and the United States. The world's largest democracy, India, was notable for its absence. The parties agreed to consult if any of them felt threatened. A separate protocol extended protection to Laos, Cambodia and South Vietnam.

Before the year was out, the CIA engineered yet another coup, this one in Guatemala. Left-leaning Jacabo Guzman Arbenz came to power denouncing the United States for its past interventions in the Caribbean. When he concluded an arms deal with Czechoslovakia, the CIA decided he was moving too close to communism and installed a more conservative regime.

Next year saw another challenge to America's containment policy, this time in Asia. During the fighting in Korea, the United States gave the green light to Chinese Nationalist forces who wanted to lash back at the mainland. Chinese Nationalist pilots, flying American planes, bombed mainland ports and shipping. Although damage was slight, the mainlanders were furious. In January, 1955, they began bombing the Tachen Islands, 230 miles north of Taiwan and garrisoned by Nationalist troops. These troops elected to withdraw. The mainland Chinese also gathered troops and artillery across from Quemoy and Matsu, where Nationalist troops were placed. A full-scale confrontation over the offshore islands threatened. In an early version of the domino theory, Eisenhower feared that if Quemoy and Matsu fell, Taiwan would shortly follow, and the communists might then be encouraged to seek control in such places as the Philippines, Thailand, Indonesia, Malaya (now Malaysia), Burma, Indochina and perhaps even South Korea and Japan. Eisenhower felt the line had to be held. To achieve this, the president went before Congress on January 14, 1955, for authority to use armed force to protect Taiwan, the Pescadores Islands and "related positions," which included Quemoy and Matsu. By an overwhelming margin, Congress granted him practically a blank check. Despite this clear signal, the Chinese continued to bombard the offshore islands. A war scare ensued. Under the New Look military doctrine, the United States would have to rely upon atomic air power, not ground forces, to subdue the Chinese. Eisenhower and Dulles publicly hinted that they might elect such a course of action. Whether or not such scarcely veiled threats induced the Chinese to desist is not known. However, by May the shelling had stopped, and the crisis passed.

Other events occurred in that highly active month. West Germany joined the NATO alliance. The Soviets formed the Warsaw Pact. In counterpart to these confrontational happenings, the superpowers put their initials on the Austrian State Treaty. This pact gave Austria independence, forbade its union with Germany, and rendered Austria a neutral country permanently. In effect, the superpowers agreed that neither Germany would engineer an *anschluss* with Austria.

These events paved the way for a summit conference. Both sides now had fusion (hydrogen) weapons. Delivery systems were growing more sophisticated. The Taiwan Straits crisis had raised the dread of nuclear war, a war rendered unwinnable on account of nuclear weapons. Common sense suggested an attempt to regulate the great power rivalry and search for common ground within the context of competition. Washington's European allies were especially desirous of an East-West accord. War games had suggested that nearly 200 atomic bombs would probably fall on Europe in the event of a military engagement. Perhaps a summit could avert such a calamity.

The summit meeting opened July 18, 1955. Nikolai Bulganin represented the Soviet Union; Eisenhower, the United States. The most notable proposal tabled at the meeting issued from the American side. This proposal sprang from a common concern about surprise attack. A pre-emptive surprise attack with nuclear weapons would give the perpetrator a military advantage that could prove decisive. Therefore, a strong temptation existed to undertake such a strike. Fear of surprise attack could stimulate a "pre-pre-emptive" strike. This cycle presented a strong danger of unwanted war. It was to prevent such an occurrence that Eisenhower introduced the aerial inspection scheme known as Open Skies. We shall examine the content and fate of this idea in a later section of this chapter.

The major product of the Geneva meeting was a mutual feeling that came to be called "the spirit of Geneva." In essence, this spirit consisted of a joint commitment to dampen the level of great power rivalry and to seek a mutual basis for cooperation. The Austrian State Treaty had capped such an effort. No one believed the cold war had come to an end, but the hope was raised that the two main protagonists would place limits on their efforts to gain advantage over each other. In the nuclear age, such a commitment could make the world much safer.

The emergence of the spirit of Geneva confirmed Secretary Dulles' worst fears about the summit. Dulles worried that photographs of Eisenhower and Bulganin smiling and shaking hands would dash the hopes of anti-communist revolutionaries in Eastern Europe and China who looked to America for support. Accordingly, Dulles advised Eisenhower to look austere and avoid handshakes with his Soviet counterpart in the presence of photographers. However, Eisenhower couldn't resist grinning, and pictures of cordiality appeared in the press.

While the Geneva summit produced no concrete results, it reflected a realization that neither side could win the cold war. For the United States, this realization signified acceptance of communist rule in Eastern Europe and China, a bitter pill for arch anti-communists to swallow. Since communist rule in Eastern Europe and China appeared unshakable, Dulles and other cold warriors turned their efforts increasingly toward the more politically plastic third world.

For the next couple of years, the Middle East moved to the forefront of the policy agenda. In Egypt, King Farouk was overthrown and Colonel Gamal Abdel Nasser emerged as the country's leader. Nasser challenged one of Washington's most cherished values, namely, stability. In Washington's eyes, stability in the third world served as a dike against communist tides. Change offered opportunities for communists to seize power. Yet few inhabitants of the third world shared Washington's enthusiasm for the status quo. The vast bulk of people in the third world desired drastic and immediate change, particularly in the economic sphere. Nasser captured the allegiance of many in Egypt and beyond by blaming the West for the humiliations Moslems, and, by extension, all third worlders, had suffered in the previous century. In huge outdoor rallies, Nasser called upon his considerable oratorical talents to whip up hatred of the West. Nasser also declared himself to be a socialist. The colonel's overall outlook made him a natural ally of the Soviet Union. Soviet policy in the Middle East had been notable for its lack of success. Nasser served as a Trojan horse the Soviets could use to establish a presence in the region. To demonstrate its support for this new anti-Western prophet, Moscow encouraged Czechoslovakia to conclude a large arms deal with Egypt in late 1955. To the West, this arrangement looked like the spearhead of a communist drive to penetrate the Middle East.

Dulles sought to blunt that spearhead by offering Nasser economic aid to build the projected Aswan Dam, designed to harness the power of the lower Nile and generate vast amounts of electric power. Not all Americans, especially high-ranking Republicans, were so enthusiastic about aiding a socialist and a rabid foe of Israel. Dulles himself had numerous second thoughts. In May, 1956, Nasser withdrew diplomatic recognition of the Nationalist regime on Taiwan and extended recognition to the mainland communist government. This so infuriated Dulles that he withdrew the offer of economic assistance.

Dulles' turnabout only confirmed Nasser's suspicions about Western concern, or lack thereof, for the well-being of third world people. In July, the Egyptian leader stunned the West and won resounding plaudits elsewhere by seizing the Suez Canal. A major crisis ensued, culminating in the invasion of Egypt by Israel, England and France, the countries most threatened by Nasser's action. Eisenhower objected to this manifestation of heavy-handed colonialism, and he was angry at the invaders for not informing him beforehand. Washington backed a General Assembly resolution urging a truce. When this did not end the fighting, Washington imposed an oil embargo on England and France and urged them again to call off their attacks. Meanwhile, the Soviets denounced the aggressors in strident terms and threatened to use atomic weapons against them. Faced by opposition from both superpowers, the invading armies declared a cease-fire and withdrew. Under American pressure, Israel returned the captured Sinai to Egypt. But America's bid to win friends and influence Moslems in the Middle East failed. Nasser complained that American reactions were too little and too late. He gave credit to the Soviets for turning back the invasion. As Nasser looked more and more to the Soviet Union for assistance and support, Washington's worst fears about communist penetration of the Middle East seemed about to be realized.

Momentarily, Washington's attentions were diverted back to Europe. Hungarian revolutionaries were attempting to free their country from Soviet control. Fighting broke out in the streets of Budapest. As Soviet tanks began to roll in, the revolutionaries put out a desperate cry for help from the United States. Washington realized that intervention on behalf of the street-fighters would mean war with the Soviet Union. Eisenhower and Dulles were unwilling to assume that risk, and so the calls for assistance went unheeded. As the revolutionaries went down in a hail of machine-gun bullets, Eastern Europeans learned that they had no choice but to strike the best bargains they could with their Soviet masters.

Back in the Middle East, American fears of Soviet penetration increased. Egyptian-Soviet ties warmed markedly. Nasser was evincing ambitions to unite the Arabs under his banner, which would undoubtedly incline at an anti-Western angle. American interests in the Middle East, particularly oil, seemed in jeopardy. To arm himself for future eventualities, Eisenhower went to Congress in January, 1957, to obtain advance permission to intervene in the Middle East whenever a legitimate—meaning non-communist—government asked for assistance on account of a communist threat. Congress assented by passing a joint revolution known as the Eisenhower Doctrine. The Doctrine was designed to give confidence to the governments of the region, which were all non-communist, and warn Moscow of the futility of trying to subvert them. Soon after, Eisenhower greeted Saudi Arabian King Saud in Washington and extended him military aid in return for an American air base at Dhahran.

In April, Washington had another opportunity to manifest its seriousness about checking communist efforts in the Middle East. In Jordan, a clique of pro-Nasser military officers was trying to oust King Hussein. Eisenhower dispatched the Sixth Fleet to the eastern Mediterranean and gave the young monarch $20 million in military aid. Hussein remained on the throne.

In October, 1957, an event occurred that was to have profound effect not only on global politics but also on the superpower military balance and the progress of arms control. On the fourth day of that month, the Soviets fired into orbit the world's first man-made satellite. This epochal scientific achievement caught most American scientists by surprise. It demonstrated that Moscow had perfected rocket boosters large enough to power an ICBM thousands of miles, so that a missile fired from the Soviet Union could strike American territory. Suddenly, America's sea-barrier had become an ocean corridor. In later sections of this chapter, we shall explore *Sputnik*'s effects on military planning and arms control. For the moment, we shall content ourselves in observing that the space shot underlined America's secondary status in space technology and gave rise to a determination to catch up to the Russians. Suddenly, science and engineering programs mushroomed all over America, as the government sought to spur greater scientific achievements to match the Russian accomplishment.

The following year presented Washington with no less than three international crises: Lebanon, the Offshore Islands and Berlin.

Arab radicals with ties to Nasser—and therefore, in Washington's eyes, to Moscow—threatened to topple pro-Western governments in Jordan and Lebanon. To shore up these governments, Britain sent troops to Jordan, and the United States landed Marines in Lebanon (July). These move preserved the regimes in power and thus helped protect Western interests against communism and Arab radicalism.

In August, 1958, the Chinese resumed their shelling of Quemoy and Matsu, both within a dozen miles of the mainland. Under a security treaty signed by the United States and Taiwan in 1954, the United States had committed itself to help protect Taiwan and the Pescadore Islands. A resolution passed by Congress during the 1955 crisis authorized the president to use armed force to protect Taiwan, the Pescadores and "such related positions and territories" as the president deemed necessary. Eisenhower and Dulles decided to use armed force to protect Quemoy and Matsu, both to signal the mainland that aggression does not pay and to maintain morale on Taiwan. The Seventh Fleet escorted Nationalist supply ships to the offshore islands, and the Nationalist air force, using American-supplied air-to-air missiles, prevented the mainland from establishing air supremacy in the skies over the islands. As Chinese bombardments continued, the United States gathered military strength in the area. Troops were landed on Quemoy. Contingency plans were made for nuclear retaliation against the mainland, partly because conventional military resources were at a low level (due to New Look force planning). Nuclear-capable howitzers were deployed on Quemoy. These moves apparently dissuaded the Chinese from any further military action, and the crisis died down.

The last, and potentially most damaging, crisis of 1958 occurred in Germany. In November, Premier Khrushchev announced that the Soviet Union was planning to turn over control of Berlin to East Germany. Thereafter, the West would have to negotiate access rights to the city with the East German government, a regime the West refused to recognize. If the West declined to negotiate with East Germany and tried to force its way into Berlin, Khrushchev stated, Moscow would regard an attack against East Germany as an attack upon the Soviet Union. Under Khrushchev's ultimatum, Berlin would become a free city; Britain, France and the United States would have to withdraw their 10,000 troops from West Berlin.

If Eisenhower gave in, America's allies would question American firmness in the face of future ultimatums. If America capitulated over Berlin, NATO was likely to disintegrate, and the remainder of America's alliances would crumble.

As Khrushchev's six-month deadline neared, a military showdown appeared in the offing. By early 1959, the Soviets had deployed medium-range nuclear rockets targeted on Western Europe. Khrushchev began making speeches in which he hinted at the use of these weapons. To demonstrate firmness of his own, Eisenhower gave a speech in March in which he stressed the dangers of nuclear war and reminded the Soviets that a conventional struggle could escalate to the nuclear level. Apparently in fear of war, Khrushchev withdrew the six-month deadline. The situation remained tense when, in the fall, Khrushchev visited the United States and agreed to a full-fledged summit conference the following spring. Tensions eased and eventually the Soviets accepted the Western presence in Berlin.

At the same time the world's eyes were riveted upon Berlin, many Americans were watching with interest events in neighboring Cuba. There, Fidel Castro and his band of followers were waging a guerrilla war to oust dictator Fulgencia Batista. In January, 1959, Castro prevailed. For a time, Americans hailed the new leader and hoped he would bring a measure of justice and dignity to the Cuban people. It would not take long, however, for Washington to alter its official view of Castro's revolution. As Castro seized more and more American property and closed down opportunities for political dissent, the United States turned against him. Before leaving office in January, 1961, Eisenhower gave the CIA permission to plan an invasion to overthrow the bearded dictator.

The last major international event of the Eisenhower years occurred in May, 1960. This was the time scheduled for the long-awaited summit between Eisenhower and Khrushchev in Geneva. The Soviet leader was sorely in need of a triumph. The Chinese were challenging Soviet leadership of world communism, charging that the Soviets had gone "soft on imperialism." Soviet hawks were unhappy that Khrushchev had not succeeded in prying the West out of Berlin. On May 5, the leaders of the two superpowers were in Geneva in preparation for their meeting. On that day, Khrushchev startled the world by announcing that the Soviets had shot down an American U-2 spy plane flying over Soviet territory. Amidst considerable bluster and posturing, Khrushchev announced that he would not agree to talk with the leader of a country that spied on others. The summit never occurred. Khrushchev came away with a victory of sorts. His tough obstinate stance toward the United States pleased the radicals in

Peking and the hawks in Moscow.

Following the aborted summit conference, the United States, in characteristic fashion, set the rest of the world aside in order to prepare for the upcoming presidential election.

Now that we have reviewed the international context during the Eisenhower years, we can consider American policy in the areas of military preparedness and arms control.

MILITARY PREPAREDNESS

As we have seen, the Eisenhower administration turned to the New Look to contain international communism but at a lower cost than under Truman. Adopted in late 1953, the New Look relied upon atomic weapons, as opposed to conventional forces, to deter communist expansion. As the carrier of atomic bombs, the Air Force enjoyed pre-eminence at the expense of the Army, whose conventional forces were slashed.

Associated with the New Look was the doctrine of massive retaliation. This military doctrine called for atomic attacks against the Soviet heartland in response to communist aggression. No longer would the United States wage battle at the locus of aggression, as in Korea. Another facet of the New Look was brinkmanship. The diplomatic strategy of brinkmanship called for the United States to go to the brink of atomic war in case of communist aggression. Supposedly, America's atomic superiority would compel the Soviets to back away from the brink. By threatening war, therefore, Washington would prevent communist expansion.

During the Eisenhower years, American security rested primarily upon strategic nuclear weapons. Tactical atomic weapons were also important. America enjoyed decisive superiority over the Soviet Union in both categories. Washington's oft-stated intention to use such weapons early on signaled the Soviets that any military conflict with the West was likely to escalate to the nuclear level, perhaps the strategic nuclear level. In that event, the Soviet Union would get bludgeoned, whereas America would receive only a scratch.

From Bombers to Missiles

In the early 1950s, massive retaliation rested upon the long-range bombers of the Strategic Air Command. Soviet deterrence policy, such as it was, also relied upon the long-range bomber. By all accounts, the Soviet bomber fleet was too weak to arouse much concern in the United States.

In the spring of 1957, U-2 flights revealed that the Soviets were building ICBM test sites at Kapustan Yar and Tyuratam. That summer the United States detected test-firings of long-range missiles. The consensus among American planners was that the Soviets were shifting the emphasis of their strategic forces

Chapter 2: Eisenhower 41

from aircraft to missiles.

The United States was in the process of a similar alteration. Throughout the early 1950s, American work on missiles was sporadic; jet bombers remained the principal deterrent. In 1955, however, the NSC assigned a high priority to the development of a liquid-fueled ICBM, to be known as Atlas.

At about the same time, the Killian Commission recommended that the United States concurrently develop intermediate-range ballistic missiles (IRBMs). By the end of the year, the Air Force had started work on a more advanced ICBM, the Titan, as well as the Thor IRBM, planned for deployment in Western Europe. The Army, smarting from its reduced role under the New Look, began work on another IRBM, the Jupiter, which could be launched from ships as well as ground stations. In 1956 the Navy received authorization to develop the Polaris missile. Meanwhile, the Air Force had begun work on a solid-fuel ICBM, the Minuteman. In 1958 the government approved construction of a fleet of Minuteman missiles.

As the various armed services competed with each other to develop missiles, military analysts were touting the virtues of missiles over aircraft. As compared with bombers, missiles offered a higher probability of penetrating Soviet air defenses. Missiles were less vulnerable to a Soviet pre-emptive strike than airplanes on runways. (American planners were growing concerned that Soviet IRBMs could strike American airfields in Western Europe.) Missiles could be protected by concealment, mobility, and hardening, whereas bombers could find safety only while in the air. Protection of these retaliatory forces assumed much greater urgency following the 1957 launching of *Sputnik*, which confirmed Russia's lead over the United States in long-range rocketry. Indeed, as the decade of the 1960s opened, American military planners feared that B-52s based in America might become vulnerable to Soviet ICBMs. In consequence, the United States started developing the Ballistic Missile Early Warning System (BMEWS) across Canada to lower the threat to SAC bombers. Washington also began to think about protecting its just-deployed ICBMs, the Atlas and the Titan, by constructing hardened underground silos for them. Work was accelerated on the Polaris, which planners saw as America's least vulnerable strategic weapons system.

Sufficiency

In 1956 the Eisenhower administration came face to face with a question that has arisen again and again. Should the United States strive for military superiority over the Soviet Union, or should the United States accept strategic parity? The issue presented itself in 1956, when the Air Force and the CIA predicted that, based on current production rates in both countries, the Soviets would enjoy a 2–1 advantage in long-range bombers by the close of the decade. Of course, one way to prevent such an imbalance would have been to conclude an arms control pact limiting the production of strategic bombers. As we shall see, however, no efforts were made in this direction. Instead, the president came under intense pressure from certain military experts and members of the Democratic Party to increase production of long-range bombers. The Air Force in particular insisted national security demanded bomber superiority.

President Eisenhower, reflecting the economic thinking behind the New Look, refused to spend more money to produce more bombers. Instead, he insisted the United States need not match the Soviet Union weapon for weapon. So long as America's deterrent were sufficient to blunt a Soviet attack, he maintained, the security of the country was not in peril. This concept came to be known as the doctrine of sufficiency. To judge the adequacy of America's deterrent, the concept held, one needed to examine all available delivery systems. The nation need not fear a disadvantage in bombers, so long as its overall deterrent could inflict unacceptable damage against the Soviet Union. Eisenhower was convinced this was the case. The Air Force was clearly not pleased with the idea of sufficiency.

By late 1956 and early 1957, the furor over the bomber gap died down, as American intelligence revised downward its estimates of Soviet bomber production. It appeared that the Soviets were using their production facilities to turn out large numbers of medium-range bombers but only a few hundred long-range Bisons and Bears. Indeed, the feared long-range bomber gap never materialized.

Gaither Report

Reports such as those outlined above about Soviet weapons developments stimulated the White House to commission a study of the adequacy of America's deterrent. A panel of scientists from the Office of Defense Mobilization's Science Advisory Committee gathered in April to begin its investigation. The group, named for its chairman H. Rowan Gaither, Jr., released its report in November, one month after *Sputnik*. The report was classified secret, but its gist was leaked to the press.

The Gaither Report painted a gloomy picture of American security. The report's findings included the following:

- Russia's GNP, while smaller than America's, was growing at a faster rate;
- the Soviets were spending as much as the United States on defense and heavy industry;
- Moscow had enough fissionable material for 1,500 nuclear weapons deliverable by 4,500 long-range and medium-range jet bombers and 250–300 long-range submarines;
- the Soviets had an extensive air-defense system;
- by 1959 the Soviets would be able to strike the United States with a

force of 100 ICBMs carrying megaton nuclear warheads;
- if such an attack materialized, the American civilian population would be unprotected, and SAC aircraft would be vulnerable except for a small proportion on airborne alert.

The panel went on to make several recommendations, with a view toward improving America's defenses. The scientists recommended construction of a large network of fallout shelters; upgrading of air-defenses; pooling of technical resources with Western allies; increased forces for limited warfare; increased anti-submarine warfare capabilities; heightened offensive power, especially missiles; and some organizational changes at the Pentagon (a perennial recommendation). At the time, the United States was spending $38 billion annually for defense. The Gaither Commission recommended an increase to $48 billion.

Conceivably, the Gaither Commission could have sought to enhance American security by another route, arms control. The Commission could have recommended that the United States engage the Soviets in intensive arms control negotiations. Since, according to the commission, the Soviets threatened American territory with long-range missiles and submarines, negotiations could have focused on these weapons. As we shall see in the next section, however, prospects for an arms control pact with Moscow were dim. It is understandable that the Gaither Commission did not recommend arms control as the path to greater American security.

The Gaither panel sounded a call for far-reaching action. Failing such action, the scientists said, the nation's security stood in grave peril. Eisenhower disagreed with much of the panel's conclusions. The chief executive had the benefit of reports from U-2s, which had been overflying Soviet territory since 1956. These flights indicated that the Gaither panel's fears of a bomber gap and a missile gap were unfounded. The United States continued to enjoy a lead in strategic weapons.

Nevertheless, Eisenhower faced great public pressure to do something to preserve the nation's integrity. Rather than approving the massive spending program suggested by the Gaither panel, Eisenhower requested $1 billion in supplementary funds in early 1958 to accelerate dispersal of SAC aircraft, place more SAC bombers on 15-minute alert, speed up IRBM and ICBM production, begin construction of the Ballistic Missile Early Warning system across Canada, and place higher priority on the Polaris submarine program. Many of these initiatives represented a response to the Gaither Commission's criticism that American strategic forces, then consisting primarily of SAC bombers, were growing vulnerable to Soviet ICBMs. At the same time, Eisenhower rejected the panel's recommendations for civil defense and an increase in conventional forces.

The president faced a barrage of criticism for doing too little, in light of the Gaither report, to protect the nation's security. But Eisenhower had his own agenda. Believing that too much military spending would damage the country as much as a Soviet strike, the chief executive wanted to keep a lid on such outlays of funds. Besides, Eisenhower disputed the Gaither Commission's conclusion that the American deterrent was in jeopardy. By 1959, two years after the Gaither Report, this deterrent consisted of 600 B-52 and 1,400 B-47 long-range bombers, an array of carrier-based aircraft that could deliver nuclear weapons against targets in the Soviet Union, and Regulus and Snark cruise missiles. Since, according to Eisenhower, the Soviets could not be certain of knocking out all these systems, the American deterrent would still perform its function.

As a further boost to the American deterrent, Washington was working on long-range missiles of its own. On January 31, 1958, the United States launched its first earth-orbiting space satellite. By the end of the year, Thor and Jupiter IRBMs with a capability of hitting targets in the western sector of the Soviet Union were scheduled to be emplaced in Western Europe. In November, 1958, the United States conducted its first full-range test-flight of the Atlas ICBM. Thus, Eisenhower had more confidence than the Gaither Commission in the survivability and effectiveness of America's deterrent.

In confirmation of Eisenhower's perspective, U-2 flights in early 1960 revealed that the Soviet Union was deploying fewer missiles than the Gaither Commission had projected. These reconnaissance flights showed that the Soviets were fielding IRBMs in some quantity; such missiles, of course, could not reach American shores from Europe. The flights also indicated that Moscow was testing ICBMs but was not at the deployment stage. America's deterrent seemed safer than many feared. (U-2 flights ended in May, 1960, when Francis Gary Powers was shot down over Soviet territory.)

By the close of 1960, when Eisenhower was preparing to pack up his office, the Soviet Union had less than 35 operational ICBMs, while Washington had deployed 32 Polaris missiles aboard submarines as well as 9 Atlas ICBMs. The United States was also in the midst of a production run that would shortly reverse the ICBM gap to a position favorable to the United States. Plans in effect when Eisenhower left office called for a total of 250 Atlas and Titan ICBMs to be deployed by 1962 as well as authorization for procurement of 450 Minuteman ICBMs and 19 Polaris submarines. When combined with the existing 600-plus B-52s and nearly 1,400 B-47s, the American deterrent looked healthy indeed.

ARMS CONTROL

The military buildup that began during the Korean War occasioned a clamor by vocal segments of the American public and the world community for controlling the weapons of war. As school children crouched under their desks during air-defense drills—as though this could protect them from an atomic attack—many of their parents insisted that the arms race must be reversed. While the nuclear genie had one leg out of the bottle, it did not seem impossible to

Chapter 2: Eisenhower

stopper him up again if one acted soon. Accordingly, the Eisenhower years, unlike the previous administration, were accompanied by a steady tattoo of arms control negotiations. These efforts yielded but a single accord, the Antarctic Treaty; not one bullet was destroyed as a result of these talks. Yet, not long after the Eisenhower administration had ensconced itself in office, arms control discussions had become an accepted facet of diplomacy. Indeed, it soon became inconceivable that diplomacy should exist without attention being paid to arms control. That tradition has persisted to this day. Despite the diplomatic mood, no administration has renounced arms control negotiations. To do so would appear to display a lack of interest in controlling the most lethal weapons mankind has yet devised. No government could or can afford to take such a stance.

To underline his concern with reducing arms, Eisenhower (1965) created a new governmental position, special assistant to the president for disarmament. In his memoirs, Eisenhower explains that he created the post of special assistant for disarmament in order to help him sort through the multifarious recommendations on disarmament emanating from the bureaucracy. The man Eisenhower chose, Harold E. Stassen, a former governor of Minnesota, was then head of the Foreign Operations Administration, charged with carrying out the mutual security program. Arms control supporters were enthusiastic about the new appointment. Finally, an individual in high places was charged with responsibility for advancing the cause of disarmament. Stassen was to report directly to the president. At the same time, he was to coordinate his activities with State. Here lay the germ of his ruination. How could a disarmer function alongside a secretary of state who was dubious in the extreme about arms control or any agreement with the Russians? In time, Dulles clearly overshadowed Stassen, and Eisenhower abolished the office that Stassen occupied.

Atoms for Peace

The first arms control proposal to emerge from the Eisenhower administration came with a propagandistic title that automatically placed its opponents in bed with the devil. If one were apposed to Atoms for Peace, there was a strong suggestion that one must favor atoms for war. This is not to say that scoring propaganda points was the sole purpose of this initiative, but it does serve to underline the propagandistic content of nearly every arms control proposal floated during the Eisenhower years, not to mention the interval thereafter. It goes without saying that the Soviets have duplicated American behavior in this respect.

President Eisenhower enunciated the Atoms for Peace concept in a speech before the United Nations on December 8, 1953. This was the first plan for international cooperation in atomic research and development since the Baruch Proposal, and it suffered from some of the same flaws. The Atoms for Peace plan called for countries to divert some of their fissile material to a stockpile under United Nations control for the purpose of study and exchange of information on the peaceful uses of atomic energy.

The Soviets rejected the plan for some of the same reasons they turned down the Baruch Proposal. From Moscow's point of view, the United Nations was a hostile, Western-dominated organization, a virtual cog in America's cold war machine. United Nations association with Soviet atomic energy programs would provide the West with reams of valuable information about top-secret Soviet atomic developments. Furthermore, the Soviet Union at the time did not have large stockpiles of fissionable material; to contribute some to the United Nations would severely limit Soviet weapons development, thus perpetuating their inferiority. The prospect of curtailing Russian weapons development reveals that Atoms for Peace was not a wholly disinterested proposal. Rather, the Soviet embrace of the plan would have served American security interests by capping Moscow's atomic arsenal. While the Russians did not accept Eisenhower's offer to create an international atomic R&D center, the United States did gain some propaganda advantage from the proposal. America had proposed Atoms for Peace; the Russians turned it down. Therefore, Moscow must intend its atomic capabilities for something other than peace.

From the standpoint of arms control, Atoms for Peace did spawn a concrete advance. Out of Eisenhower's concept sprang the International Atomic Energy Agency, a United Nations affiliate, one of whose missions is to sponsor international research and development on the peaceful uses of atomic energy.

During the next year and a half, East-West disarmament talks continued in a rather desultory fashion. At the same time, the French were deciding to leave Vietnam, the first Taiwan Straits crisis erupted, West Germany joined NATO, the Warsaw Pact came into being, and the leaders of the two superpowers prepared for the mid-1955 summit.

On the disarmament front, the British and the French in June, 1954, proposed a reduction in conventional forces and the elimination of nuclear weapons once controls were in place. This proposal, which the United States joined with muted enthusiasm, called for weapons reductions in three phases, each to begin once a control organ certified its ability to enforce the measures envisioned. In phase 1, all states would freeze military manpower and spending at the 1953 level. Phase 2 would see implementation of half the agreed cut in conventional arms and manpower and a halt in fabrication of nuclear weapons. In phase 3, countries would carry out the remaining reduction of conventional arms and manpower; atomic weapons would be prohibited; and existing atomic weapons stockpiles would be converted to peaceful purposes.

At first the Soviets rejected this proposal, pushing instead for a one-third reduction in military spending, armaments and manpower. The Soviets continued to hold to their traditional position that unconditional renunciation of the use of nuclear weapons was a necessary first step toward their elimination. Months later, the Soviets relented and indicated an interest in discussing the

Anglo-French proposal. As a means of advancing the discussions, Moscow tabled a proposal of its own in May of 1955.

The Soviet proposal had two discernable purposes. One was to forward the cause of disarmament. The other was to arrest a development that Moscow found highly alarming, namely, the re-arming of West Germany. On May 10, 1955, Moscow set forth a sweeping arms control proposal that was in part a response to the Anglo-French offer of the previous year. The Soviet proposal contained provisions for relaxing international tensions, reducing conventional arms levels, prohibiting nuclear weapons, and establishing international controls to monitor the above. Moscow's use of arms control to advance its own security can readily be seen in the measures it proposed for the relaxation of tensions. The Soviets called for the liquidation of overseas bases (which would result in massive American withdrawals from bases in Europe and Asia), the withdrawal of occupying forces from Germany (which would push back Western forces in Europe, including West Berlin), and the settlement of outstanding questions in Asia. The arms control portion of the Soviet offer went further than any previous Russian position to meet the West's needs. Moscow abandoned its call for a one-third reduction of military spending, conventional arms and manpower and adopted the Anglo-French idea of a ceiling on conventional manpower. Moscow suggested 1 to 1½ million men each for the United States, China and Russia. The control organ in Moscow's proposal had more power than that in any previous Soviet offer, although it contained some ambiguity that left the West uneasy. In contrast to previous Soviet insistence on immediate and comprehensive disarmament—which the West had always interpreted as pure propaganda—the Soviets manifested a willingness to proceed with partial measures on the way to full-scale disarmament. While some distance separated the two sides, the Soviet and Western positions were closer than at any time previously. There were those who thought an agreement was in sight.

What prevented an accord was an ancient bugaboo in arms reduction, namely, distrust. Secretary of States Dulles distrusted arms control in general and the Soviet Union in particular. In Dulles' suspicious eyes, the Soviet proposal was little more than a trick to prevent West German rearmament, which Dulles saw as essential to Western security. Eisenhower aligned himself with Dulles.

But what of the newly-appointed special assistant for disarmament, Harold E. Stassen? Where was his voice on these matters? The fact is that Stassen was not yet totally familiar with his new job and therefore was unable to argue as forcefully as he might have in favor of the Soviet proposal. Dulles had much more bureaucratic clout than Stassen; consequently, the latter's arguments in favor of negotiating on the basis of Moscow's proposal carried little weight. Washington rejected Moscow's offer and instead proposed an idea of its own, which came to be known as Open Skies.

Open Skies

The most controversial and far-reaching disarmament proposal of the Eisenhower administration took form in response to Moscow's May, 1955, counter-proposal to the Anglo-French offer of June, 1954.

President Eisenhower presented his proposal, which he called Open Skies, to Nikita Khrushchev and Nikolai Bulganin at the August 1955 summit meeting in Geneva. Open Skies reflected a relatively new concern in the nuclear age, namely, fear of surprise attack. Weapons designers were conceiving of rockets that could travel long distances and threaten the other side's retaliatory forces. Should one or both sides gain this capability, the incentive to mount a surprise attack might prove irresistible, particularly in a crisis that threatened to generate a nuclear exchange anyway. Open Skies represented a departure from most previous disarmament initiatives. These had called for general and complete disarmament, or at least the abolition of all atomic weapons. These earlier proposals viewed disarmament as an alternative to deterrence. Open Skies accepted deterrence and the armaments that sustained it and sought to enhance deterrence by guaranteeing the survivability of retaliatory forces through the prevention of surprise attack. Parenthetically, we might note that it was much easier to monitor ICBM activity in the 1950s than it is today. Back then, silos were large, clumsy affairs; fueling missiles was a timely and highly visible operation; and mobile missiles were barely on the drawing boards. Furthermore, submarine-launched missiles were in their infancy. If one could monitor the other side's ICBMs, one could reasonably hope to prevent a surprise attack. In later years, as ICBMs went underground in hardened silos and then became mobile, the feasibility of surprise attack schemes like Open Skies declined.

In essence, Open Skies called for the United States and the Soviet Union to exchange blueprints of major military installations and permit each side to inspect the other's facilities from the skies. If aerial inspection revealed activity suggesting imminent surprise attack, the other side could launch its retaliatory planes and missiles and therefore nullify the advantage of a sudden strike. Surprise attack would become a thing of the past.

Was Open Skies a genuine effort to make the world safer, or was it, as Moscow asserted, a scheme to gather intelligence about the Soviet Union? Perhaps both elements were present. While the proposal treated both sides equally, the fact is that the Soviets could learn more about the United States through open sources than the United States could learn about the Soviet Union. Moscow's traditional reluctance to open itself to outsiders prevailed over its desire to prevent surprise attack. The Soviets were also displeased that the proposal covered only the two superpowers but not Western Europe, locus of major American military deployments. (Of course, the West would no doubt have insisted that Eastern Europe also be included.) Skeptics in the disarmament community cited a flaw in Open Skies: information gleaned from blueprints and aerial inspections could allow each superpower to target the other's vulnerable points, thereby *encouraging* a surprise attack. In this viewpoint, Open Skies would have hobbled rather than strengthened deterrence.

In any case, Moscow rejected Eisenhower's offer. The Soviets said aerial surveillance should come only as the final stage of comprehensive disarmament. To prevent surprise attack in the meanwhile, Moscow renewed a proposal first tabled in May. This called for the establishment of fixed control posts at large ports, railway junctions, major highways and airports, but not military bases. Presumably, inspectors at these posts would spot activity in time to provide warning of a surprise attack. The West dismissed this scheme as unreliable. The Soviets also proposed a treaty, to be signed by France and the then nuclear powers (Soviet Union, United Kingdom, United States), barring the first use of nuclear weapons. As a means of preventing full-scale re-armament of West Germany, which had just joined NATO, Moscow also proposed that the armed forces of states other than the Big Five contain no more than 150,000 to 200,000 men. Washington turned down these Soviet proposals.

Open Skies was closed down at the Geneva summit. In retrospect, failure to reach agreement may have cost the Russians more than the Americans. Soon after, American U-2 surveillance aircraft began to overfly Soviet territory. Moscow had no comparable espionage capability. Thus, Washington gained some assurance about surprise attack that the Soviets lacked. Today, of course, surveillance satellites give both sides much of the Open Skies capabilities that Eisenhower envisioned. In the 1990s, negotiations to permit mutual aerial surveillance were reopened.

During the next twelve months, the two powers continued to spar in the disarmament ring. Eisenhower wrote to Bulganin in March, 1956, proposing a mutual cessation in the production of fissionable materials for fabricating nuclear weapons. He also repeated his proposal, advanced in the 1953 Atoms for Peace plan, that the United States and the Soviet Union reduce their atomic stockpiles by transferring agreed amounts of fissionable material from military to peaceful purposes. The Soviets spurned these proposals because they called for on-site inspection, and because the cut-off of material would freeze Soviet inferiority in the amount of fissionable material available for making bombs.

Moscow then offered several proposals, including denuclearized zones in East and West Germany, reducing military budgets by up to 15%, and a halt in nuclear tests. Washington agreed with none of these offers. Of some note, Moscow for the first time agreed to consider aerial photography—a hark back to Open Skies—but only for 800 kilometers (480 miles) on each side of the line dividing NATO and the Warsaw Pact. Washington then reiterated the Open Skies proposals for aerial surveys and the exchange of military blueprints, coupling these with a call for a cut-off in the production of fissionable material for atomic bombs. None of these offers was accepted by the other side. Perhaps the futility of the negotiations can be accounted for as much by the poisonous international atmosphere—Hungary and Suez occurred in 1956—as by the merit or lack thereof in the proposals themselves.

Nuclear Test Ban

For the latter half of the Eisenhower administration, negotiations to bring about a halt to nuclear testing dominated the arms control agenda. As in the case of Open Skies, the American position on a test ban reflected both a desire to fashion a less lethal world and the hope of gaining an advantage over the Soviet Union. There were other reasons why both the United States and the Soviet Union from time to time favored a test ban. A test halt would slow the spread of atomic weapons to other countries. It would conserve the costs of conducting tests. Urging a cessation of tests always gained some favor with the peace-oriented segment of world public opinion.

During the latter half of 1955, the Soviet Union conducted a series of nuclear tests, including a 2–4 megaton blast. The Russians also tested a hydrogen bomb dropped from an airplane as opposed to a testing tower, which was as far as the Americans had gone. The Soviets now had an air-deliverable hydrogen bomb. Upon completion of these tests, the Soviets in late November called for a mutual test halt. This pattern was to become familiar on the part of both the Soviets and the Americans. As soon as one country completed a series of tests—and thus had forged ahead of the other—that country would call for a test suspension, thereby hoping to freeze its advantage. In reaction to Moscow's 1955 call for a testing halt, echoed, it must be noted, by vocal segments of world opinion, the Pentagon raised the prospect that the Soviets were ahead in overall nuclear weapons technology, including nuclear warheads for the ballistic missiles of the not-too-distant future.

The Americans were in a quandary. The Soviet call for a suspension of atomic tests generated plaudits worldwide. Washington did not wish to lose the global propaganda battle to the Russians. Yet the United States feared Moscow was winning the race in nuclear weapons technology and production. Efforts to limit Moscow's missile-building made sense in Washington. The United States was ahead of the Russians in bombers. The Soviets were hoping to redress this balance with missiles. Moscow was ahead of Washington in missile technology and hoped to translate this advantage into actual missiles in the near future. A mutual limitation on missiles would help freeze America's strategic superiority. To prevent the Russians from exploiting the lead Washington feared they had, the American position on a test ban evolved into coupling a test ban with a prohibition on future production of nuclear weapons. Thus, if the Russians were ahead in nuclear technology, a production halt would prevent them from exploiting their advantage. Washington's position was announced by Secretary of State Dulles on January 11, 1956. Dulles rejected Moscow's call for a test ban, adding that America must "keep to the forefront of scientific knowledge in that field" (Divine, 1976, p. 67). Dulles also said a test ban would have to be accompanied by comprehensive disarmament complete with safeguards against cheating. Following this diplomatic exchange, public attention turned away from the test ban issue for a while.

Renewed interest in the topic sprang from the Eisenhower administration's effort to embarrass Moscow by playing to public concern about radioactive fallout. On August 24, 1956, the Soviets resumed testing. With Eisenhower and Strauss acting as point men, the administration vigorously accused the Soviets of hypocrisy in their calls for a test ban.

Democratic presidential candidate Adlai Stevenson decided to capitalize on the public's phobia regarding radioactive fallout. In a major foreign policy speech before the American Legion on September 5, Stevenson called for the United States to halt testing if the Russians did likewise. The next day Vice-President Richard Nixon called Stevenson's proposal "naive" and "dangerous to our national security." Eisenhower echoed the view that a test ban was desirable only if coupled with reliable inspection and a cut-off in the production of fissionable material for military purposes. Thus the issue was joined and became a focus of the 1956 campaign.

Several arguments were advanced on each side. Proponents of a test ban emphasized that it would retard the development of new nuclear weapons. They also pointed out that a ban would prevent additional countries from acquiring nuclear weapons, thereby minimizing the dangers of a proliferated world. Opponents of a test ban generally cited the impossibility of a foolproof inspection system and insisted that Moscow would cheat and forge ahead of the United States. Other opponents argued a test ban would harm deterrence by preventing the development of a "clean" bomb and low-yield nuclear weapons that could realistically be used to deter without also destroying the area one wanted to preserve. Over the next few years, these arguments were to draw the test-ban negotiation along a twisting course. It is advisable to examine these arguments in more detail and trace the course of test ban negotiations.

As we have seen, Eisenhower and his aides opposed a test ban in the 1956 election. Then, in the spring of 1957, the administration began to waver. This mid-course correction sprang not from any new-found thrust for disarmament or desire to patch up differences with the Russians. On the contrary, it was motivated by a fear that Moscow was winning the world opinion battle by its repeated calls for a test ban. American recalcitrance placed Washington in the camp of the incorrigible war-monger. Eisenhower and Dulles began to entertain the idea of a cessation of testing. Those most firmly opposed were Lewis Strauss, Chairman of the Atomic Energy Commission, and the Defense Department, which wanted to develop and test new weapons. Stassen supported a halt in testing.

In the spring of 1957, Washington and Moscow experienced a "near miss" in test ban negotiations. Stassen returned home in May during a break in the five-nation disarmament talks going on in London, convinced that Moscow genuinely desired a test ban. In the negotiations, the Soviets had been calling for a test ban but without inspection. Back in Washington, Stassen suggested that the United States treat a test ban not so much for its own sake but as the first step toward more comprehensive nuclear disarmament. This view began to gain some currency at the top rungs of the administration. Eisenhower, for example, did not rush to support Admiral Arthur Radford, Chairman of the Joint Chiefs of Staff, who said, "We cannot trust the Russians on this or anything. The Communists have broken their word with every country with which they ever had an agreement" (Divine, 1976, p. 144). Rather than backing his top military adviser, Eisenhower remarked at his May 22 press conference that he hoped that the London talks would yield an agreement.

A decision concerning a test ban was finally hammered out at a White House meeting on May 25. In attendance were Eisenhower, Stassen, John Foster Dulles, AEC Chairman Strauss, Radford, Deputy Secretary of Defense Donald Quarles, and National Security Adviser Robert Cutler. The meeting centered on whether to agree to a temporary test ban as the first step toward more comprehensive disarmament. Over the objections of Radford and Strauss, Eisenhower accepted the new concept advocated by Stassen. However, Eisenhower watered down the decision and sent Stassen back to London with a "talking paper" that would offer a brief test halt in return for *future* limits on nuclear weapons production. Eisenhower told Stassen to obtain the approval of the NATO allies before presenting the offer to the Russians. The position detailed in the talking paper marked a departure from the administration's previous stance that a test ban must be linked to an immediate and total halt in weapons production.

Upon returning to London, Stasssen did not handle the matter with the greatest aplomb. He showed the talking paper to the representatives of France and Great Britain, as instructed, but then he revealed it to the Russians before the allies reacted. The British and French protested Stassen's behavior to Eisenhower, who called Stassen back for a reprimand. The British, it turned out, did not care for the American idea, because the cap on weapons production, envisioned for the future, would freeze the British stockpile at a low level. France liked it even less, inasmuch as Paris was working toward a nuclear capability.

Amidst this disarray in the Western camp, the Soviets on June 14 floated a new proposal. Moscow gave up its long-standing call for a permanent and total test ban in favor of a two- to three-year moratorium. Moscow also announced it was prepared to accept some inspection on its soil. Eisenhower termed the Russian offer hopeful. The administration seemed to be leaning in the direction of accepting it.

At this point, domestic opponents of a test ban moved into high gear. The principal opponent was Edward Teller. This Hungarian-born physicist, known as the father of the hydrogen bomb, had a deep distrust of the Soviet Union and possessed unlimited faith in deterrence. At the very time the test ban issue was occupying the Eisenhower administration's attention, Teller and his associates at the Livermore Laboratory were working on new types of bombs and warheads they wanted to see tested and produced. Teller was determined to go ahead with his plans. In a meeting with Eisenhower on June 24, Teller and some of his colleagues told Eisenhower that they had already produced a bomb that was 90% "clean," and that they were on the verge of making a perfectly clean bomb. The scientists went on to argue that clean, low-yield weapons would be ideal for limited wars, such as in the defense of Europe, and for peaceful nuclear explosions (dredging harbors, digging canals, etc.). Teller also insisted any nation could easily cheat on a test ban without detection.

Not every member of the scientific community agreed with Teller. When Eisenhower, at his June 26 press conference, revealed his conversation with Teller, some scientists insisted a perfectly clean bomb was impossible to produce. Some of these scientists claimed the quest for a clean bomb only masked the Pentagon's desire to build and test new weapons.

Division in the scientific community concerning the clean bomb placed Eisenhower in a dilemma and produced a momentary paralysis in policy-making. Into this breach stepped Secretary of State Dulles. Ever sensitive to global accusations that America was spreading deadly radioactivity, yet desirous of maintaining American security through deterrence, Dulles continued to favor tying a test halt to a ban on further production of nuclear weapons. Dulles authorized Stassen to make a new proposal at the London talks. In July, Stassen offered a ten-month test suspension; during this interval the three nuclear powers were to complete the details of an inspection system and finalize an agreement banning the future production of nuclear weapons. At the end of ten months, Washington would decide whether to extend the moratorium, based largely on progress on the other two issues.

Neither London nor Moscow was enthusiastic about Washington's initiative. The British government, eager to augment its meager stocks of atomic bombs, opposed the production halt. Nonetheless, Prime Minister Harold Macmillan sided with Washington, largely in response to widespread domestic furor against testing. Of greater significance, Moscow appeared to be backing away. The Russian delegation met the American offer with a demand for a two-to-three-year test halt under a vague form of international supervision and no curb on the production of more weapons.

The American choice of a ten-month period for suspending tests came as no accident. This was the normal hiatus between series of tests. America had just completed some tests and was not planning to conduct any more before the expiration of ten months. During the interval, American scientists could prepare for the next test series. Should no agreement on a test halt be forthcoming, America would lose nothing.

In late July, 1957, Dulles himself went to London to take personal charge of the negotiations. Agreement proved elusive, however. The Russians appeared to be shilly-shallying, refusing to take a stand. Returning to Washington, Dulles joined with Eisenhower to make one final attempt that would place the Russians in the position of either accepting or rejecting an offer. On August 21, the president announced America's new position. Eisenhower announced that the United States would extend its testing halt for 12 months with an additional 12-month extension, if there were progress in fashioning an adequate inspection system and reaching agreement on ceasing production of nuclear weapons. The Russians grasped at the test halt but rejected the two conditions. The talks had reached an impasse. To put the entirety of the American position on the record, and perhaps to score some propaganda points, the United States joined with Britain and France to offer on August 29 a proposal containing the following elements: a two-year test suspension, open skies, a ban on future production of nuclear weapons, and some other minor points. Moscow turned down the package. The first serious attempt to negotiate a test ban ended in failure.

In October, 1957, the Soviets startled the world—and threw panic into the American scientific community—by launching *Sputnik*. This successful effort to place a satellite into orbit showed that the Russians had perfected a rocket booster large enough to power an intercontinental missile thousands of miles across the Earth's surface. The following month, Moscow sent a dog into orbit. The Russians were clearly ahead in the race to build intercontinental range missiles. Americans knew it would not be long before their invulnerability to a Soviet strategic strike would be a thing of the past.

These Soviet scientific achievements reduced Washington's desire to conclude a test ban treaty. America was now bent on catching up with the Russians in long-range missiles. The country resolved to perfect an ICBM and an antimissile missile, both of which needed testing. In terms of nuclear weapons technology, however, America was ahead. This finding was established by a new scientific advisory panel formed in December, 1957, headed by presidential science adviser James Killian and including some of the nation's top scientists, such as George B. Kistiakowsky, Herbert F. York, Hans Bethe and I. I. Rabi. The new group was called the President's Science Advisory Council (PSAC). In late 1957–early 1958, the PSAC favored a test ban because it believed the United States held "a significant edge" over the Soviets in nuclear weapons technology. The PSAC also "leaned toward a conclusion that a test ban would militarily be advantageous to the United States" (Killian, 1977, p. 153).

On December 10, the Kremlin sent Eisenhower a note calling for a summit conference early the next year and a proposal that the three nuclear powers—the United States, United Kingdom and Soviet Union—halt tests for the next two to three years beginning January 1, 1958. On January 12, Eisenhower replied. The president said he was willing to meet at the summit, but only after substantive issues were resolved at lower levels. Eisenhower also rejected the uninspected test ban called for by Moscow. At the same time, he repeated earlier offers to link a test ban to a cutoff in weapons production.

Moscow scored a propaganda victory in announcing a unilateral test suspension on March 31. The Russians had just completed a series of tests, and they knew the Americans were planning a series of their own.

The Soviet announcement led to a crescendo of calls for the United States to follow suit. In America, scientist Linus Pauling and the Committee for a Sane Nuclear Policy (SANE) led the public campaign for a test halt. An inter-agency panel chaired by physicist Hans Bethe was established in early 1958 to study the feasibility of detecting test ban violations. As reported by Killian (1977), the group unanimously concluded that "the U.S. was ahead [of the U.S.S.R.] in sophisticated weapons, and further testing would permit the Soviets to gain on the U.S.; thus, a test cessation was probably to the military advantage of the U.S." (p. 155). The panel further reported on March 28 the possibility of detecting a Soviet nuclear explosion down to 2 kilotons with an elaborate system of seismic monitors backed by mobile inspection teams that would check the site of a suspected blast. The PSAC then met April 8–10 to consider the findings of Bethe's group. The PSAC concluded that "a cessation in nuclear testing by both sides would leave the United States in a position of technical superiority for at least several years. It would freeze the edge we then had in nuclear weapons technology" (Killian, 1977, p. 156). The PSAC also recommended that the United States reverse its position that a test ban was acceptable only if linked to a halt in bomb production. Killian transmitted these findings to Eisenhower. The president accepted the PSAC's recommendations. In early April, Eisenhower wrote a letter to Khrushchev proposing technical discussions on a test ban inspection system.

Meanwhile, AEC Chairman Strauss sensed a turn in the administration's position and, with the Pentagon's support, argued for a steady course. Strauss advanced three arguments. First, a test ban would prevent the United States from developing important new weapons, including a relatively clean hydrogen bomb, a new generation of thermonuclear warheads, and an anti-missile missile. Secondly, he argued that inasmuch as the Soviets could now strike American soil with atomic weapons, America needed new deterrent weapons that were more sophisticated in design, more accurate, and more numerous than existing ones. Finally, Strauss insisted the gravest danger faced by the United States was nuclear war, and that the United States could prevent this through clear military superiority. If the Russians cheated on a test ban—which Strauss had no doubt they would try to do—they could forge ahead militarily. Therefore, Strauss said, any test ban must be accompanied by a verifiable agreement to cease the production of nuclear weapons.

Meanwhile, the AEC began the most extensive series of tests to date, code-named HARDTACK. On May 9, Khrushchev responded favorably to Eisenhower's letter to open a technical conference to discuss verification. On July 1, 1958, a conference of technical experts opened in Geneva. The following countries were represented: United States, United Kingdom, France, Soviet Union, Poland, Czechoslovakia and Rumania.

The scientists who gathered at Geneva agreed on four methods of detecting nuclear tests: recording acoustical waves, measuring electromagnetic waves, collecting radioactive debris, and examining seismic signals. The most contentious issue concerned the inspection system's extent. The Soviets suggested a network of 110 stations; the United States, 650. Ultimately, the scientists accepted the British suggestion of 170 land stations, 10 shipboard stations and on-site inspection of suspicious events. On August 21, the experts issued a final report, which concluded that it was technically feasible to create an inspection system to detect violations of a test ban.

This timing proved auspicious for the United States, which had just completed the HARDTACK tests. These explosions thrust America's atomic weapons program three to four years ahead of the Soviet program, according to American intelligence. The United States was only too happy to make its lead permanent. Accordingly, on August 22 Eisenhower issued a call for the commencement of negotiations to conclude a test ban. He also offered to suspend tests for one year if Russia reciprocated. The two sides agreed. Atomic tests were suspended.

On October 31, 1958, representatives of the United States, United Kingdom and the Soviet Union gathered at Geneva to negotiate a test ban complete with an inspection system. America's 25 delegates were headed by James Wadsworth, who had succeeded Stassen in the post of disarmament adviser.

Most of the hard bargaining centered around the inspection system. Two issues stood out. The first concerned the power of a 7-person control commission that was to be in charge of the 180-post inspection system agreed to earlier by the technical experts. The Soviets insisted that all members of the control commission must concur, before the commission could rule that an event warranted on-site inspection. In addition, the Soviets insisted no on-site inspection could take place without host-country approval. Washington said this amounted to a veto. The second issue concerned the nationality of the technicians at each of the 180 monitoring posts. Britain and the United States called for mixed teams with equal representation for the Soviets, the West, and neutral countries. The Soviet Union argued for nearly total domination by the host country. Before resolving these issues, the conference adjourned for Christmas.

When the delegates re-convened in January, Wadsworth dropped a bombshell. The American representative said that data from the HARDTACK II tests of 1958 revealed that it was much more difficult than previously thought to detect underground tests by seismic measures. Wadsworth said the tests showed it was possible to distinguish between a test and an earthquake only above the 20-kiloton level. To distinguish down to the 5-kiloton level, he said, it would be necessary to have 500 stations combined with 200–1,000 on-site inspections annually. In his account of the negotiations, Wadsworth (1962) describes the

Chapter 2: Eisenhower 57

effects of his revelation:

> The presentation of the "new data" resulted in the most violent action imaginable. It spread a pall over the negotiations from which they never completely recovered. The Soviets were convinced that the United States was deliberately sabotaging the conference and was simply seeking a pretext to resume testing (p. 24).

In view of the HARDTACK data, the AEC and the Defense Department joined with their hard-line allies in Congress to ask the administration to reconsider its views on testing. John McCone, who had replaced Strauss as AEC chairman on June 30, 1958, led the campaign for renewed testing. McCone urged resumption of underground tests, which did not produce fallout that alarmed the general public. On January 24, 1959, the AEC unanimously recommended a resumption of underground testing both to gather more information about seismic detection and to perfect new weapons. Several members of the congressional Joint Committee on Atomic Energy supported McCone's position. The Senate, meanwhile, in August passed a resolution calling for the negotiation of a comprehensive test ban treaty.

New scientific evidence proved yet more disastrous for those at Geneva trying to work out a treaty. Scientists at the Rand Corporation found it possible to "decouple" a nuclear explosion from the surrounding earth by conducting the blast in a large underground cavern. By this method, the resulting seismic signals could be off by as much as 300 times according to some scientists and 10 times in the opinion of others. Using the more conservative figure, this meant that an actual explosion of 50 kilotons would register only 5 kilotons on seismographs. A country could explode a 10-kiloton warhead with little chance of detection.

Still more disturbing news was to come. In August–September, 1958, the Navy conducted Project Argus, a series of three nuclear explosions in outer space 300 miles above the South Atlantic. The purpose of these blasts was to learn if incoming missiles could by halted by such means (they couldn't). However, these tests went undetected by the world scientific community.

In brief, it appeared that one could reliably detect nuclear explosions in the earth's atmosphere but not underground or in outer space. Given the absence of trust, only a ban on atmospheric tests seemed possible. Accordingly, on April 13, 1959, Eisenhower wrote to Khrushchev proposing an atmospheric test ban as an interim measure, while the experts sought to untangle the detection puzzle in the other environments. Eisenhower suggested that the United States, United Kingdom and Soviet Union halt all tests in the atmosphere up to a height of 50 kilometers. Verification would require only eight posts in Russia with no on-site inspection. Khrushchev replied on April 23, saying a partial test ban would only mislead the public, and that the true goal of a test ban was "preventing the production of new and ever more destructive types of nuclear weapons" (Divine,

1976, p. 257). The Soviet leader urged continuing efforts to conclude a comprehensive test ban. He suggested a limited number of on-site inspections each year but gave no figures.

In Geneva, meanwhile, no progress was evident on the ongoing problems of how much power the control commission should have or the national composition of the control teams. The detection problem proved the most intractable and was the major reason for lack of agreement. The Soviet Union, suspicious of the West to begin with, lost faith in American sincerity when Wadsworth introduced the HARDTACK II data on verification.

Nevertheless, the diplomats labored on. In March, 1960, the parties agreed to ban all atmospheric, underwater and underground tests above 4.75 on the Richter scale (equivalent to 20 kilotons) plus a ban on all smaller underground tests. The latter was to be based on trust, since verification was not achievable. Two issues remained to be resolved before the parties could initial a treaty: the duration of the moratorium on tests below 4.75 and the number of on-site inspections for suspicious events above 4.75. Eisenhower hoped to wrap up these questions and sign a treaty at the upcoming summit meeting in Paris. Back in Washington, the Joint Committee on Atomic Energy, which generally opposed a test ban, held hearings at which eminent scientists expressed strong reservations about detecting blasts below 4.75 and even doubted the possibility of discovering all explosions above 4.75, especially with decoupling. Nonetheless, Eisenhower hoped to tie down an agreement in the French capital.

Hopes ran high as Eisenhower and Khrushchev gathered in Paris. Then the famous U-2 incident destroyed all hope of accord. The Soviets claimed to have shot down a U-2 surveillance aircraft. When Eisenhower denied that the United States was engaged in such high-level espionage, the Russians produced the pilot, Francis Gary Powers (who was supposed to have killed himself). Khrushchev angrily stalked away from the summit, and a test ban agreement fell by the wayside. When John F. Kennedy won the 1960 election, Eisenhower (1965) advised him to resume nuclear testing, as the outgoing chief executive felt the moratorium was hindering America's nuclear weapons program.

Surprise Attack Conferences

While it is true that each side sought, in disarmament negotiations, to improve its strength at the other's expense, it was also the case that both superpowers entertained a genuine fear of surprise attack. With atomic weapons, a surprise attack could be devastating. It was this concern that led Eisenhower to advance his Open Skies proposal in 1955.

Toward the end of 1958, Khrushchev agreed to Eisenhower's proposal that technical experts meet in an attempt to lessen the likelihood of surprise attack. As Kahan (1975) explains, two considerations underlay Soviet willingness to discuss the subject. First of all, the American practice of flying armed SAC bombers in the direction of Soviet territory gave rise to fear of accidental or inadvertent war. Secondly, Khrushchev believed that a cooperative attitude on arms control might slow American strategic programs and avoid a Soviet-American strategic conflict.

The issues discussed at the experts' meeting in Geneva were reminiscent of those brought up during the Open Skies discussions. Washington stressed the need to exchange data and put an inspection plan into place. The latter would serve to reduce suspicions that one side was preparing a surprise attack and provide early warning in case such an attack materialized. Accordingly, the Americans proposed such measures as overflights, sensory devices, and the stationing of observers at airfields, naval bases, transportation centers, and all important military installations. In Washington's eyes, the main objects to be controlled were long-range bombers and conventional forces. The Americans also expressed some interest in putting observation systems at missile sites. The Soviet representatives maintained that preventing surprise attack was less a technical than a political problem, involving intentions more than capabilities. The Russians, always wary about outside inspection, said that the American proposals would actually increase the danger of surprise attack by allowing each side to detect the other's vulnerabilities. The Soviets went on to say that the greatest danger of surprise attack lay along the East-West division in Europe. Here is where emphasis should be placed, the Soviets said, not at military sites on the soil of the superpowers. Conceivably, the reason Moscow opposed inspection of its strategic bases was that Moscow claimed to possess more missiles than it actually had and did not want the Americans to discover the discrepancy. In any case, the meeting ended after six weeks without producing agreement.

In November, 1960, representatives of the United States, United Kingdom, France, Italy and the Soviet Union gathered to devise ways to minimize the possibility of surprise attack. Once again, nothing was achieved.

Antarctic Treaty

This agreement, whose very name suggests the temperature of superpower relations during the Eisenhower years, was the sole arms control agreement concluded during the Eisenhower administration. By the 1950s seven nations claimed sovereignty over areas of Antarctica. Eight others, including the Soviet Union and the United States, had engaged in exploration but had asserted no territorial claims. Future rivalries were possible, perhaps springing from the discovery of economically exploitable resources. Furthermore, the advent of long-range missiles meant that one or more countries might one day seek to station nuclear weapons on Antarctic soil.

The International Geophysical Year of 1956–1957 awakened the desire to preserve Antarctica for scientific research and keep national rivalries away from the region. At Washington's initiative, a conference was held in late 1959 that culminated in a treaty signed by twelve nations on December 1. The Antarctic Treaty provides that Antarctica shall be used for peaceful purposes only. It specifically prohibits "any measures of a military nature, such as the establishment of military bases and fortifications, the carrying out of military maneuvers, as well as the testing of any type of weapons." The treaty provides for inspections by the contracting parties to ensure against violations. Several such inspections have been carried out.

As compared with the Truman administration, Eisenhower engaged the Soviets much more extensively in arms control negotiations. Once American policy under Truman shifted from cooperation with Moscow to containment, Washington's principal strategic interest consisted of putting in place the instruments of the new doctrine. Hence, policy-makers devoted great time, energy and resources to building up America's military might and that of her allies. The scant disarmament activity in the Truman years was more for purposes of propaganda than for genuine arms reduction. In that sense, disarmament never became an integral facet of national security policy under President Truman.

Dwight D. Eisenhower was the first American president to incorporate disarmament into the mainstream of national security policy. The new role accorded disarmament was symbolized by the creation of the office of disarmament advisor, an office that proved less than durable. During the Eisenhower years, scarcely a year passed without an important disarmament initiative. The national security bureaucracy was constantly formulating or debating one aspect or another of arms control. Eisenhower, Stassen, certain scientists and perhaps a few others in the administration had a genuine desire to reach some agreement with the Soviets that would have lessened tensions. But most of the leading policy-makers at the time harbored a deep distrust of the Soviet Union. These officials insisted on such an intrusive degree of on-site inspection and such high levels of verification as to render any agreement with Moscow out of the question. The president, who himself held little affection for the Soviet system, was unwilling to push his own initiatives with sufficient vigor to override the hesitations of Dulles and other arms control skeptics.

America's strategic doctrine did little to advance the cause of disarmament. Under massive retaliation, America had few non-nuclear options. Therefore, Washington could reduce its forces under only the most reassuring of circumstances. Russia's persistent calls for the abolition of all nuclear weapons threatened the very nervous system of America's deterrent. Were the United States to agree, the New Look would have left Washington with precious little military might to offset the gargantuan conventional might of the Soviet Union. Moscow felt threatened by massive retaliation, America's nuclear lead, and Dulles' belligerent remarks about brinkmanship. Washington was hardly reassured by Moscow's bluster concerning world revolution, Russia's preponderance of conventional forces in Europe, and the Kremlin's lead in intercontinental missiles. Thus, the international political environment that prevailed during 1952–1960 was not conducive to arms control.

During the Eisenhower interregnum, the effort to limit military power underwent a vital philosophical shift. The term "disarmament" expresses a time-honored concept inherited by Truman and Eisenhower. This word carries the connotation that the control of weaponry is an alternative to deterrence or any other variant of military strategy. In this conception, successful disarmament would render military strategy obsolete. This view was reflected in the frequent calls by both Moscow and Washington for general and complete disarmament. Advocates assumed security could only be weakened, never enhanced, by the possession of arms. The doctrine of peace through strength was anathema to such people.

So long as American security rested upon deterrence, this conception of disarmament was bound to find few adherents among policy-makers. Proposals that called for complete disarmament were useful for propaganda purposes but contributed little to strategic planning. Knowing the other side— also attached to deterrence—would reject any such proposal placed a premium upon framing extreme positions. One could then claim the other party was obstructing disarmament, while never having to fear that one's own proposal could become reality.

Toward the latter part of the Eisenhower administration, this conception of disarmament underwent an extremely significant alteration. This transition is reflected by the term "arms control," which has come to replace "disarmament" in general usage. "Arms control" suggests not the elimination of arms but rather their limitation. Such limitation may include numbers, areas of deployment (expressed in the term "nuclear-free zone"), types of weapons permitted and disallowed, and conditions under which certain weapons will be used. Seen this way, arms control is not an alternative to deterrence so much as a facilitator of deterrence. An agreement that would authorize the deployment of invulnerable weapons but prohibit deployment of highly vulnerable weapons can be seen as enhancing deterrence. The first type of weapon discourages one party from attacking the other. The second type of weapon encourages commanders to give the "fire" order, based on the notion of "use it or lose it."

"Arms control" thinking appeared in the Eisenhower administration with the Open Skies proposal of 1955. This was not an attempt to abolish great stores of weapons, but had the much more modest objective of preventing surprise attack. Open Skies was perfectly consistent with deterrence. The Surprise Attack Conference of 1958 was another "arms control" effort. At the same time, calls for halting nuclear tests coupled with abolition of atomic weapons reflected "disarmament" thinking.

It has been suggested here that both sides used arms limitation negotiations for national advantage; that is, each side sought to inhibit the other's development of certain weapons while it continued to develop those weapons in which it was dominant. Washington's interest in a test ban exemplifies this approach. Usually ahead of the Soviets in nuclear technology, the United States was only too ready to offer a mutual moratorium at the conclusion of a test series. (Moscow too exhibited this behavior from time to time.) Open Skies and other American calls for on-site inspection also manifested the use of arms limitation talks for unilateral advantage. It has always been easier for the Soviets to collect information about a relatively open society like the United States than vice versa. The presence of international inspectors on Soviet soil might have revealed much that the West wanted to know. However, one must add another motivation for on-site inspection. The West did not trust the Soviet Union. Nor did the Soviet Union trust the West. One might inquire why the Soviets did not accept Eisenhower's call for a test halt coupled with the cessation of constructing nuclear weapons, given Moscow's perception that America enjoyed a nuclear lead. Logic suggests that Moscow erred. If America were ahead in this category of weaponry, Moscow would seem to have every incentive to block the manufacture of America's strongest arms. We may never learn the reasons for Moscow's reluctance to accept a test moratorium under Washington's conditions. Speculation suggests several reasons. Moscow could not bring itself to accept alien inspectors. The Soviets also harbored a deep distrust of the West. Would the United States and the United Kingdom live up to their promises? The international organizations that would oversee inspection were dominated by the West. Moscow felt beleaguered and isolated in a world dominated by Western states that subscribed to two despised concepts, capitalism and democracy. Soviet leaders might well have believed the surest path to national safety lay in the accumulation of weapons that held out the prospect of destruction to their enemies. The Soviets were more interested in acquiring weapons of their own than in signing arms limitation agreements they could not be certain the West would honor.

3
KENNEDY

THE 1960 ELECTIONS AND THE MISSILE GAP

Foreign affairs played a significant role in the 1960 elections. Vice-President Richard Nixon, the GOP candidate, ran on the record of the Eisenhower administration. Democrat John F. Kennedy attacked that record on many fronts, including foreign policy.

Abroad as well as at home, Kennedy criticized Eisenhower for "gazing down the green fairways of indifference," as one party spokesman phrased it. The Democratic front-runner wanted to do more than assure the blessings of democracy and prosperity for the American people. He sought to spread these benefits to the third world. While Eisenhower dutifully confronted problems as they arose, Kennedy eagerly sought out new challenges.

The most salient foreign policy issue of the 1960 election was the "missile gap." Ever since the launch of Sputnik in 1957, Americans had been concerned that the Soviets would vault ahead in missiles. Khrushchev unwittingly exacerbated these apprehensions by bragging about Soviet prowess in rocketry and threatening to outbuild the United States. Secretary of Defense Neil McElroy further aggravated American worries by forecasting in 1959 that the Russians would enjoy a 3–1 advantage in ICBMs over the United States by the early 1960s. At the time of the 1960 elections, America had deployed approximately 30 ICBMs.

During the 1960 campaign, Kennedy roundly criticized the Republicans for allowing the Russians to forge ahead in strategic missiles. The alleged Soviet edge was dubbed the missile gap. Did such a gap exist?

Washington had reliable intelligence on the deployment of Soviet ICBMs from photographs taken by the U-2 spyplane. U-2 flights continued until Francis Gary Powers was shot down in May, 1960. Up until then, U-2 photos showed that Khrushchev had been bluffing. Instead of deploying large quantities of ICBMs targeted on the United States, the Soviets had elected to concentrate on intermediate-range ballistic missiles (IRBMs) targeted on Western Europe. The small number of officials privy to the U-2 intelligence knew the missile gap did not exist. Eisenhower did not wish to reveal this information for fear of informing the Soviets about the capabilities of the U-2.

Following the suspension of U-2 flights after May, 1960, the United States did experience a genuine intelligence gap. It was impossible to verify

Soviet deployments. America was working on a high altitude satellite, Samos, but it would not be ready until the middle of 1961. Some security officials worried that the Soviets were on the verge of forging ahead in ICBM deployment. These officials knew that Moscow had the capacity to produce many more ICBMs than were actually deployed. Might not Moscow be producing these weapons with the intention of a rapid deployment in the near future? If so, the Soviet Union might achieve a first-strike capability. Kennedy and his advisers were troubled by the alleged gap in actual ICBM deployments as well as even more ominous future possibilities.

During the election campaign, Kennedy pilloried the Republicans for permitting a missile gap to develop. The missile gap, Kennedy charged, was only the most egregious example of Republican laxity in matters of defense. It was time for a change, the Democrat argued.

The electorate agreed and put Kennedy in the White House. Shortly thereafter, new intelligence suggested that there was no missile gap. In February, 1961, newly appointed Secretary of Defense Robert McNamara laid the missile gap to rest. By summer, the Samos satellite definitively confirmed the absence of a gap. Kennedy would ensure that no such gap could materialize by authorizing the production of Minuteman ICBMs and Polaris SLBMs.

KENNEDY'S OUTLOOK

The new chief executive's view of both the world and his office differed from that of his predecessor. Whereas Eisenhower tended to see the world's natural condition as being in a steady state, Kennedy viewed it in flux. While Eisenhower cherished stability, Kennedy recognized and welcomed peaceful change. Accepting the reality of the Sino-Soviet rift, Kennedy believed the days of monolithic communism were over. NATO had diminished the military threat to Western Europe; the third world was the new arena of battle between East and West. Kennedy was less sanguine than Eisenhower about military solutions to the world's problems. Economic and political measures were needed to supplement military responses. Even the Soviet Union was open to change, although the young president had no illusions about any immediate alterations. White House Adviser Arthur M. Schlesinger, Jr. (1965), a close associate of the president, characterized Kennedy's policy toward the Soviet Union as "reasoned firmness accompanied by a determination to explore all possibilities of reasonable accommodation" (p. 301).

While Eisenhower sought to prevent untoward modifications of a satisfactory status quo, Kennedy was imbued with a sense of mission to make America and the world a better place. To achieve this goal, he would use both military preparedness and arms control. He noted in his first State of the Union Address, "On the Presidential coat of arms, the American eagle holds in his right talon the olive branch, while in his left he holds a bundle of arrows. We intend to give equal attention to both."

Kennedy rejected Dulles' notion of rolling back communism, believing—as did Dulles if one judges by his actions—that a final confrontation with communism was too dangerous. While no friend of communism, Kennedy was reconciled to living with it. Perhaps, he thought, the West might one day prevail over communism by force of example; other peoples, that is, would grapple democracy to their bosoms because they believed democracy preferable to other systems of government. Such a day was nowhere in sight, however, and Kennedy often warned Americans that the East-West struggle would continue for a very long duration.

At the same time, Kennedy regarded the balance of terror as perilously fragile. He once characterized it as a "sword of Damocles" hanging over humankind by the slenderest of threads. Thus, as we shall see, Kennedy actively engaged the Soviets in efforts to stabilize the superpower rivalry. These efforts took the form of the hotline, decisions to make strategic forces more survivable, and negotiations to curb nuclear testing. Kennedy was also troubled by the prospect of nuclear proliferation, telling Khrushchev's son-in-law Aleksei Adzhubei, "The United States as a matter of national policy...will not give nuclear weapons to any country." (Schlesinger, 1965, pp. 855–56).

But Kennedy did not put undue faith in disarmament. Preparing in August, 1961 for an upcoming address at the United Nations, Kennedy turned down Ambassador Adlai Stevenson's suggestion to make general and complete disarmament a major theme. According to Schlesinger (1965), Kennedy saw little prospect for total disarmament and viewed it primarily as a tool of political warfare. In short, Kennedy understood the propaganda content of calls for total disarmament.

One of the new president's major concerns was the third world. In contrast to Eisenhower, Kennedy felt the third world was the key to the East-West struggle. "The great battleground for the defense and expansion of freedom today is the whole southern half of the globe...the lands of the rising peoples" (Quoted in Ambrose, 1980, p. 248). To prevail on this battleground, Kennedy was prepared to use both the olive branch and the arrow: "Let every nation know, whether it wishes us well or ill, that we shall pay any price, bear any burden, meet any hardship, support any friend, oppose any foes, in order to assure the survival and success of liberty."

To sum up, Kennedy's vision of the world was multi-faceted. While he believed conflict was normal in international relations, he hoped to alleviate it by halting the development and spread of nuclear weapons. While perceiving the Soviet Union as America's cardinal adversary, Kennedy hoped to place the superpower struggle on a more stable footing. Military preparedness was essential to the nation's safety, yet an unchecked arms race threatened the survival of humankind, Kennedy believed. The decisive arena for the East-West contest lay in the third world.

THE INTERNATIONAL CONTEXT

The one thousand days of the Kennedy administration witnessed numerous turbulent events, particularly events that bore on the East-West struggle. These occurrences, in turn, had an important influence on Kennedy's policies regarding arms control and military preparedness.

Soviet Premier Nikita Khrushchev fired the opening salvo with an important speech in Moscow on January 6, 1961, just prior to the inaugural of the new president. Kennedy viewed the speech as an authoritative blueprint of Soviet actions, so much so that he discussed it with his staff and read portions of it aloud at meetings of the National Security Council. Khrushchev declared that communism was riding the crest of history toward inevitable victory over capitalism. The Soviet leaders said that economic and military advances had rendered the Soviet state safe from foreign attack for the first time since 1917. Revolutionary ferment in the third world, he noted, opened new opportunities for communist penetration.

Khrushchev rejected war with the West as suicidal. However, he hailed wars of national liberation, defined as "uprisings of colonial peoples against their oppressors," and vowed Soviet support for the anti-colonialist forces. The Western presence in Berlin must end, he declared, foreshadowing a crisis that was soon to materialize.

A meeting of communist leaders worldwide the previous November had unified communist forces for the coming struggle.

Viewing this speech as a swaggering, bellicose throwing down of the communist gauntlet, Kennedy referred to it in his State of the Union message. Alluding to Russia and China, Kennedy declared,

> We must never be lulled into believing that either power has yielded its ambitions for world domination—ambitions which they forcefully restated only a short time ago. On the contrary, our task is to convince them that aggression and subversion will not be profitable routes to pursue these ends.

This atmosphere of confrontation was to incline the new president to favor military preparedness over arms control at the outset of his tenure.

If Khrushchev's opening barrage was verbal, Kennedy's was behavioral. In his last year in office, Eisenhower had approved a CIA plan to train Cuban exiles in Guatemala for an invasion of Castro's Cuba. Kennedy also gave his assent to the operation.

There was no shortage of reasons for America and Cuba to collide. Americans had offended Cuban sensibilities by intervening three times in the past, maintaining an "alien" presence at Guantanamo Bay, "owning" Cuba through private investment in the island's large enterprises, and supporting hated dictator Fulgencio Batista until the last possible moment before Castro took over. Washington's alarm stemmed from the perception that Castro was rapidly converting the island to communism. The bearded dictator had abolished all political parties other than the communist party. He had received arms and military advisers from Moscow, and he had sent large numbers of Cuban personnel to Eastern Europe and Russia for training. Numerous threads of Cuban-East European trade were weaving Cuba into the communist economic bloc. Lastly, Castro had nationalized American holdings in Cuba. Washington decided to eradicate the communist presence from the Western Hemisphere.

The Bay of Pigs debacle has been amply chronicled elsewhere. By now it is well known that the expected anti-Castro uprising that the invasion was to trigger never materialized. When the invaders, being pounded on the beach, pleaded for American air strikes, Kennedy refused, in a futile attempt to deny America's role in the assault. Khrushchev took note of the president's hesitation and lack of firmness. Castro's forces rounded up the invaders, resulting in one of America's most humiliating setbacks.

Khrushchev's January speech, followed by the American-sponsored invasion of Cuba, did not augur well for the Kennedy-Khrushchev summit held in Vienna June 3–4, 1961. The meeting was not a sterling success. Kennedy urged his Soviet counterpart to accept the prevailing world distribution of power, one which favored the United States. The American president received no such assurances from Khrushchev. To the contrary, Kennedy emerged with the feeling that Khrushchev was determined to support leftist struggles against pro-Western governments. This is precisely what Khrushchev had vowed to do in his speech the previous January. Kennedy warned Khrushchev against such a course of action. Might Khrushchev have questioned the young president's firmness, based on Kennedy's failure to salvage the Bay of Pigs invasion with an American air strike? Khrushchev served notice that the Western presence in Berlin was unacceptable and must be ended within six months. The only point on which the two leaders agreed was to curb the growing conflict in Laos. The meeting gave Kennedy little reason to undertake a major effort in the area of arms control. Indeed, Khrushchev's bellicosity inclined the president to keep his powder dry.

A possible use for that powder occurred during the summer. Khrushchev insisted that the West terminate its presence in Berlin by year's end. The Russians had plenty of reasons for wishing the West out. West Berlin served as a point of exodus for large numbers of young talented people from all over Eastern Europe. The city provided an ideal locus for Western propaganda and espionage targeted on Eastern Europe. West Germany was strengthening its armed forces, and the country was cementing its bond to the remainder of Western Europe. A successful Soviet attempt to pry the West out of Berlin could have substantial consequences. The entire Western alliance would have cause to doubt Washington's commitment; perhaps some members of NATO would drop out of the alliance and seek to reach an accord with the Soviets. NATO might unravel. Countries throughout the world that relied on America's word might panic and seek to make their peace with the Kremlin. The global structure of Western security could crumble.

Kennedy understood the likely consequences of retreat. To bolster the Western position, Kennedy turned to military preparedness. In a major statement on Berlin on July 25, 1961, the president declared that "an attack upon [Berlin] will be regarded as an attack upon us all." Kennedy also hinted at the possibility that nuclear weapons might have to be used to defend the Western position in Berlin, requested additional funds for civil defense, and announced a delay in the planned deactivation of the B-47 bomber fleet. The country also approved an additional $3.2 billion in defense spending, tripled draft calls, extended enlistments, and mobilized 158,000 Reserve and National Guard troops. The president sent an additional 40,000 troops to Europe and designated six Reserve divisions for quick mobilization if that became necessary.

The Berlin crisis was unfolding just after Washington came to realize that the missile gap was a fiction. Khrushchev understood that further efforts to force the West out of Berlin might mean a war that he could have no assurance of winning. Khrushchev's most immediate concern was the steady seepage of people out of Eastern Europe through West Berlin. To block this flow, the Soviets began in August to erect the Berlin Wall. Despite some calls to bulldoze the structure to the ground, Kennedy decided to let it stand. While some critics complained that such inaction signaled lack of resolve, Kennedy figured the American military buildup detailed above would clearly demonstrate Washington's intent to stand firm. By year's end, Khrushchev had ceased insisting that the West evacuate Berlin. The crisis died down.

In the fall of 1962, the world's attention shifted from Europe to the Caribbean, where the most notable event of the Kennedy administration was unfolding. During the summer, the Soviets began secret shipments of intermediate-range missiles and warheads into Cuba. In October, overhead reconnaissance photos provided conclusive proof of this activity. Kennedy knew he faced a major crisis.

A sizeable body of literature has arisen to describe and explain the Cuban missile crisis. (See Allison, 1971, for a classic account.) Several intriguing questions have been posed. Why did the Soviets try to place missiles just 90 miles off America's shore? What made the Kremlin believe it could get away with such an action? What measures other than a blockade might Washington have taken? The extensive literature on the event provides provocative answers to these and other questions surrounding the missile crisis. Here, we are more concerned with the effect of the crisis on U.S.-Soviet relations.

By October, 1962, when Washington conclusively determined that the Soviets had imported missiles into Cuba, Khrushchev and Kennedy were still taking the measure of each other. Cuba, like Berlin and other places, represented various rings where diplomatic sparring between the two leaders took place. Kennedy was especially concerned to demonstrate to Khrushchev that he was not a weak leader. Were the Soviet chairman to conclude otherwise, he might embark on no end of diplomatic adventures that would challenge America's interest, including provocative action in Berlin. Furthermore, Kennedy had to convince America's allies that he would stand firm in the face of a Soviet challenge. The absence of a forceful response to the construction of the Berlin wall, combined with the failure to support fully the invaders at the Bay of Pigs, made Kennedy more concerned than ever to demonstrate toughness in responding to Soviet missiles in Cuba.

Kennedy and his advisers spent several agonizing days deciding what action to take. The measures considered included the entire spectrum from filing a protest at the United Nations to an invasion of Cuba. Eventually, Washington selected a blockade of the island to prevent the shipment of additional missiles, together with an insistence that the Kremlin dismantle and remove missiles presently in Cuba. As Soviet freighters steamed toward the American blockade line, the world approached the closest point to nuclear war in history. At the last minute Khrushchev ordered the ships to turn around. Later, the Soviet leader also agreed to remove the approximately 36 nuclear tipped medium-range ballistic missiles (capable of striking eastern and southern American cities) and nine short-range nuclear missiles from the island (Tolchin, 1992). The crisis subsided.

While the threat of war dissipated, the confrontation over Cuba sparked some deep thinking in both Moscow and Washington. These second thoughts have some relevance for arms control and military preparedness. Leaders in both capitals reminded themselves about the perils of brinkmanship. Actions that could induce escalation must be avoided. Limits must be placed on the superpower rivalry if nuclear war were to be averted. As we shall see later in this chapter, these limits included arms control measures such as the Hot Line and the Limited Test Ban Treaty.

The Cuban missile crisis represented a humiliating defeat for Soviet diplomacy. Kremlin leaders vowed not to let the situation repeat itself. To avert future miscarriages, the Soviets inaugurated a crash program to modernize and strengthen their strategic forces. It was America's strategic preponderance that had forced the Soviet retreat; in strategic warheads, America enjoyed a comfortable 5,000 to 300 lead (McNamara, 1987). Now the Soviets vowed to erase this deficit across the array of strategic weaponry. Unpersuaded that additional Soviet arms were strictly for defensive purposes, the United States elected to match the Soviet buildup. Thus, while stimulating some measures of arms control, the confrontation in Cuba gave rise to a strategic weapons buildup that compounded the task of arms control at a later date.

The confrontations over Berlin and Cuba heightened the awareness in many circles of the need to preserve Western unity. However, an event occurred in late 1962 that helped shatter the unity of NATO.

Two years earlier, President Eisenhower had promised British Prime Minister Harold Macmillan to sell Skybolt missiles to Great Britain. This two-stage ballistic missile, to be launched from bombers, was to constitute the backbone of Britain's nuclear deterrent. Due to technical difficulties, however, Washington cancelled the weapon, leaving the British high and dry. In December, 1962, Kennedy met with Macmillan at Nassau in the Bahamas to discuss the matter.

Europeans watched the talks closely. Would Britain once again render itself dependent upon the United States for its nuclear deterrent, or would London link its survival more closely to Europe? For years Britain had held itself aloof from close involvement with the Continent because of strong ties with the British Commonwealth and Britain's "special relationship" with the United States. Europeans insisted that Great Britain choose between Europe and America. Europe bristled at Britain's refusal to involve itself in the process of European integration. British decisions concerning nuclear weapons would provide a clear barometer of where the country stood as between Europe and America. At Nassau, Macmillan accepted Kennedy's offer to substitute Polaris missiles for Skybolt. Britain had chosen America over Europe. The next month, French President Charles de Gaulle vetoed Great Britain's application to join the European Common Market, asserting that Great Britain valued its ties with America over its connection with Europe. The Nassau meeting, in retrospect, contributed to the fragmentation of Western unity.

One of the more striking differences between Republican and Democratic presidents is their attitude toward the third world. Republican administrations tend to minimize the third world's importance because these states, taken individually, have so little military and economic power. Democratic presidents often stress the significance of developing countries as a collectivity; they also express a moral obligation to assist less fortunate peoples. President Kennedy believed the third world was crucial in the struggle between communism and Western values. Kennedy conveyed an appreciation for the aspirations and travails experienced by the inhabitants of the world's huts and villages. He was the last American president to gain the affections of third world peoples. As opposed to the dualistic world view taken by Eisenhower and Dulles, Kennedy understood why many people in less developed countries preferred a course of nonalignment. He was willing to accept neutralism as well as socialism in the third world. What he would not tolerate was communist conquest, whether by military means or creeping infiltration. His strongest efforts to prevent such conquest occurred in Indochina and Latin America.

When Kennedy came into office, he inherited a small program of economic and military aid to the South Vietnamese government of Ngo Dinh Diem. Kennedy viewed Vietnam as an Asian Berlin. In other words, South Vietnam stood as a symbol of American resistance to communism; were America to allow South Vietnam to fall to communism, America would appear weak, and communists would be encouraged to commit further aggression. During his term in office, Kennedy increased the number of American military advisers in South Vietnam from 500 to 16,000, allowed these advisers to engage in combat if attacked, and authorized U.S. Air Force strikes against communist strongholds in South Vietnam. Kennedy never sent ground combat troops to South Vietnam; that step was left to Lyndon Johnson. However, Kennedy most definitely increased America's commitment to the Saigon regime.

Neighboring Laos was viewed as no less important. This obscure Southeast Asian country bordered on China, both Vietnams, Cambodia, Thailand and Burma. A communist seizure of Laos would put communist cadres on the borders of all these countries. A fragile 1958 agreement among the rightist, centrist and leftist forces in Laos had unraveled, as the right and the center tried to force the left out of the governing coalition. As the country declined into general guerrilla warfare, the communist Pathet Lao turned to the Soviets for military and economic aid. Kennedy sent over 300 military advisers to the country and initiated an economic assistance program. By the time of the Vienna summit in June, 1961, a full-scale proxy war between pro-Soviet and pro-American forces was in the offing; the Pathet Lao already controlled the eastern half of the country. In Vienna, Kennedy and Khrushchev agreed to stop the war. The following year, an international conference neutralized Laos and created a coalition government, removing Laos from the cold war confrontation for a short time.

If Indochina served as a test of American resolve, Latin America acquired its urgency due to its proximity to America's shores. Having failed to oust Castro at the Bay of Pigs and through attempts to assassinate him, Kennedy at the very least wished to prevent the spread of Castro's revolution to the rest of Latin America. Kennedy realized that rampant poverty and oppression made the continent ripe for revolutions of the left. Perhaps he was thinking of Latin America when he remarked that those who make peaceful evolution impossible make violent revolution inevitable. To forestall communist revolutions, Kennedy inaugurated the Alliance for Progress in March, 1961, a ten-year program of economic development assistance for Latin America, totaling $20 billion in American aid. At the conference in Punta del Este in Uruguay that formalized the Alliance, Latin American leaders pledged to invest over $80 billion and undertake land, tax and other socioeconomic reforms. Many of these leaders, however, proved to be among those who made peaceful evolution impossible, as they hesitated to enact reforms that would weaken their privileged status. Washington, for its part, did not insist forcefully enough that Latin governments make needed socioeconomic changes. Instability continued to plague the region; between 1961 and 1966, the military overthrew nine Latin American governments. Castro, meanwhile, was sending cadres to the region to promote revolution. Kennedy responded by training anti-guerrilla forces in the Canal Zone; often these forces acted in support of those very regimes that refused to make the changes called for in the Alliance for Progress. During the Johnson administration, the much-trumpeted Alliance faded away, leaving in place the socioeconomic conditions that sparked the aid program. Latin America was not to know tranquility for many years.

As the foregoing brief survey reveals, international events gave the Kennedy administration an interest in both military preparedness and arms control. Rivalry with the Soviet Union persisted, focusing on such locations as

Berlin, Cuba, Latin America and Indochina. Thus, America had cause to remain well-armed. At the same time, the Cuban missile crisis provoked a genuine fear that an unchecked arms race could lead to the incineration of both nations. Accordingly, leaders in Washington and Moscow showed an interest in placing limits on their rivalry and on capping the arms race. The missile crisis gave rise to a degree of urgency about arms control not felt during previous administrations. To this dual need to both build and control arms we now turn.

MILITARY PREPAREDNESS

Like his predecessor, Kennedy took an essentially bipolar view of world politics. The predominant configuration of power was rivalry between the Soviet Union and its allies, on the one hand, and the United States and its allies, on the other. Not every outcome in international affairs turned on this axis, but the most important events took their coloration from the U.S.-Soviet confrontation. Unlike Eisenhower, Kennedy believed that the third world also merited attention by American policy-makers.

Many tools of diplomacy are useful in global politics. Economics resources, propaganda, foreign assistance, even the quality of diplomacy itself can be used to prevail in the international arena. The most important tool, at the onset of John F. Kennedy's administration, was military power, both for its symbolic value and its potential use in a military confrontation.

In his first annual address as chief executive, on January 30, 1961, Kennedy listed his priorities for waging conflict between "Freedom and Communism." "First," he said, "we must strengthen our military tools." Such a course requires money, and so we turn to defense appropriations.

Military Budget

When Kennedy took office, he was of the opinion that America's military stance was weaker than it should be. He soon learned that the missile gap was a myth. Realizing that the Soviets and Chinese were well aware of this, he feared that the two communist giants would seek to expand their influence by supporting so-called wars of national liberation. To meet this threat, Kennedy called for a 15% increase in defense spending in the first half of 1961. In addition to obtaining more funds, Kennedy revised some of the military spending priorities inherited by Eisenhower. In order to deal with conventional wars of communist expansion, Kennedy doubled the number of combat-ready divisions in the Army's strategic reserve, expanded the Marine Corps, added 70 ships to the fleet, and added two wings to the country's tactical air forces. To enhance America's capacity to respond after a Soviet attack, he called for additional funds to improve command and control systems. He also appointed General Maxwell Taylor as his chief military adviser.

Despite the burial of the missile gap, Kennedy requested more funds for the Polaris and Minuteman strategic missile programs. Two factors underlay this decision. The first of these was bureaucratic, involving primarily the Air Force. Over Air Force objections, Kennedy wanted to eliminate the B-70 strategic bomber, believing it vulnerable to Soviet air defenses. The Air Force insisted that cancellation of the B-70 necessitated more Minuteman missiles, an Air Force program. The Joint Chiefs supported the Air Force and also urged acceleration of the Polaris submarine missile program. Kennedy was not ready for a battle royal with the Defense Department, so he approved increases in Polaris and Minuteman as he scrapped the B-70.

The second consideration concerned relations with the Soviet Union. Some in the Kennedy entourage believed that the defense budget could be used as an instrument of controlling arms. Each budgeting decision conveys a signal about one's intentions. Procurement of coast guard cutters carries a different message than procurement of an aircraft carrier. Kennedy attempted to use the military budget to inform the Kremlin, in a manner more persuasive than words, of his interest in strategic stability. For purposes of stability, Kennedy understood the superiority of weapons that could survive a first strike and could therefore deter it, as opposed to weapons that were useful only for first-strike purposes. This latter category of weapons might in itself provoke a first strike and was therefore destabilizing. But how could the president communicate to the Russians that America was not intent on a first strike and wished only to prevent a first strike by its opponent? By devoting funds to Minuteman and Polaris, as well as more secure command and control systems, Kennedy hoped to achieve this objective. At the same time, he hoped to strengthen his case by eliminating such provocative first-strike weapons as exposed Jupiter missiles in Italy and Turkey (Schlesinger, 1965).

During the Kennedy years, military spending constantly rose. Military spending for fiscal year 1961 totaled $44.7 billion. In fiscal year 1964, by which time Johnson had replaced Kennedy, the figure increased to $52.4 billion.

Flexible Response

The most significant alteration in military doctrine made by the Kennedy administration involved a shift from massive retaliation to flexible response. The nation continues to be influenced by this change.

As formulated during the Eisenhower administration, massive retaliation called for massive atomic strikes against the Soviet homeland in response to communist aggression. Presumably, no expansion of territory would be worth such a price. That being so, communist adventurism would cease. Time after time, however, small increments of communist aggression failed to provoke the promised massive nuclear strike. Massive retaliation had not prevented communist aggression in Korea, Hungary, Quemoy and Matsu, Tibet, Vietnam or

Laos. The Russians had learned that if they grabbed only a thin slice of the salami, America's atomic forces would not respond. Kennedy feared that the Soviets might continue to use such tactics until they were in possession of the entire salami.

Kennedy believed that America's vow to halt communist aggression had become almost meaningless under massive retaliation. The new president said the country needed a range of military options between a nuclear strike and doing nothing. Such a "flexible response" would be a much more credible deterrent to communist aggression than was massive retaliation, the president believed. The country needed the wherewithal to meet communist aggression wherever it occurred and at whatever level of force the invaders employed, be it insurgency, conventional attack, or a nuclear strike. The new doctrine of flexible response called for additional military resources in two areas, counter-insurgency and conventional forces.

Counter-Insurgency

As early as 1954, Kennedy had voiced the need to enlarge the Army so as to preserve non-nuclear options. As a senator he said,

> Our reduction of strength for resistance in so-called brushfire wars, while threatening atomic retaliation, has in effect invited expansion by the communists in areas such as Indochina through those techniques which they deem not sufficiently offensive to induce us to risk the atomic warfare for which we are so ill prepared defensively (Quoted in Schlesinger, 1965, p. 310).

Kennedy also thought that the U.S.-Soviet nuclear standoff had shifted the arena of great-power struggle to the third world. It was here that Khrushchev in his January, 1961 speech vowed to support wars of national liberation. Kennedy saw the need to oppose such wars. Kennedy also realized that counter-insurgency was a method to contain communism with minimal risk of a direct clash with the Soviet Union. As a liberal Democrat, Kennedy hoped that third world leaders would combine counter-insurgency with political and socioeconomic reforms that would earn popular support. In most cases, Kennedy (and his successors) were disappointed in this respect.

Kennedy directed that jungle warfare centers be established at Fort Bragg and the Canal Zone. The Fort Bragg installation started to train troops to confront guerrillas in Southeast Asia. Kennedy reinstated the green beret as the symbol of the new force. At the Canal Zone, a center was established to train soldiers from Central and Latin America in counter-guerrilla tactics. Other counter-insurgency centers were set up in Okinawa, West Germany, and Vietnam.

Conventional Forces

While great-power conflict can theoretically break out anywhere, during the Kennedy years the most probable locus of confrontation was Europe. Thus, most of the debate over conventional forces pertained to this region.

European anxieties were one of the factors underlying the adoption of flexible response. On account of the growing American vulnerability to Soviet strategic weapons, many Europeans voiced doubts that the United States would honor its NATO commitment. During the two world wars, America could come to the defense of Europe without fear of attack. Under massive retaliation, however, an American attack against the Soviet Union would lead to a Soviet counter-strike against American cities. Knowing this, would American leaders order such an attack? Many Europeans said no, and so the very essence of NATO was in jeopardy. On the other hand, if America were in possession of substantial conventional forces, and these forces were thrown into a battle over Europe, the Soviets would have little reason to initiate a nuclear strike against American cities. Thus, a conventional option seemed more credible to a number of European strategists. Not all Europeans accepted this reasoning. Some complained that a conventional option was a convenient way for Americans to spare themselves at Europe's expense. These Europeans, who were in the minority, preferred that Washington continue to rely on its nuclear forces, because an East-West confrontation would then be played out on Soviet and American soil. They also believed that nuclear forces represented a more convincing deterrent than conventional arms. Kennedy and his advisers were of the opinion that a conventional option was more credible than the exclusively nuclear strategy of massive retaliation.

Regional confrontations also called for conventional weapons. During the Cuban missile crisis, all the military options discussed by EXCOMM—naval blockade, surgical air strike, invasion, etc.—relied on conventional forces. The Berlin crisis also highlighted the need for a conventional capacity; Kennedy needed these forces to substantiate his avowal to stand firm, without at the same time catapulting the world into nuclear war.

Once Kennedy made the decision to shift from massive retaliation to flexible response, the question of procurement came to the fore. Conventional forces include a vast array of items, from boots to rifles to airplanes for transporting soldiers to battle. Kennedy believed the Defense Department to be deficient in nearly every category of non-nuclear forces. Consequently, he spent a large sum of money to raise the country's conventional capability across the board. According to a speech by Secretary McNamara at the Economics Club of New York, November 18, 1963—just a few days before Kennedy was assassinated— the administration had increased the number of combat-ready divisions from 11 to 16, had increased the number of tactical air squadrons by 30%, had boosted airlift capabilities by 75%, had doubled warship construction, and had undertaken an extensive program to modernize the fleet. All of these categories of forces had declined during the Eisenhower years, in the expectation they would not be needed. Thus, upon entering office, Kennedy found that 75% of the Air Force's fighter-bomber wings were composed of F-100s, a 1955 aircraft with no all-weather capability. Kennedy also directed the Army to reorganize its divisions to be prepared to fight in conventional combat instead of a nuclear environment, as had been the case under Eisenhower. He also integrated tactical aircraft from the Air Force and Navy into war plans for general purpose forces. The annual procurement rate for conventional weapons and ammunition almost doubled, as did research and development for non-nuclear weapons and ordnance.

While the doctrine of flexible response called for increases in the above categories of forces, the question soon arose: how much is enough? No country can prepare for every conceivable contingency. The Kennedy administration decided on a 2½-war strategy. This meant the country needed to have on hand sufficient forces to handle, simultaneously, a Warsaw Pact attack on Western Europe, a Chinese attack in Asia, and a minor contingency elsewhere. The forces earmarked for these possibilities were known as "general purpose forces." (The following analysis follows Enthoven and Smith, 1971, who occupied policy-making positions in the Kennedy administration.) General purpose forces include forces for all conflicts below the level of general nuclear war. They embrace all Army and Marine Corps land forces, tactical units of the Air Force, and most naval forces other than missile-firing submarines. Increasing these force levels was one of Kennedy's earliest decisions in the military area.

In Europe, we have already noted Eisenhower's rejection, largely on the basis of cost, of NATO's 1952 decision, taken at Lisbon, to raise the number of NATO divisions to 96. Instead, the United States, with NATO's concurrence, elected to defend Europe by rapid resort to nuclear weapons. In late 1954, the North Atlantic Council authorized NATO commanders to base their war plans on the early use of nuclear weapons whether or not the Warsaw Pact used them. In 1957 the Council, chastened by a strong dose of realism, called for 30 combat-ready divisions in Central Europe. It was estimated that the Soviets already had 175 divisions there, of which 140 were said to be active. Western commanders further assumed the Soviets could mobilize a total of 400 divisions within 30 days. Nuclear weapons offered the only hope of withstanding such forces. This was the situation when Kennedy took office.

If nuclear weapons were so crucial in defending Europe, certain questions had to be addressed. What targets should be assigned to these weapons? Should NATO rely on strategic or tactical nuclear forces?

We have already seen that the Kennedy administration rejected its predecessor's reliance on strategic strikes against the Soviet homeland. Massive retaliation was not dissuading the communists from seeking to expand. But what about low-yield, short-range nuclear weapons designed to alter the outcome of particular battles? Such weapons are designated tactical nuclear weapons.

Tactical Nuclear Weapons

Tactical nuclear weapons include artillery shells, land and underwater mines, and low-yield bombs delivered by aircraft, as well as short-range nuclear missiles fired from ships, planes, and land-based launchers. Debate over tactical nuclear weapons was part of the general discussion that arose over flexible response. Like conventional forces, tactical nuclear weapons gave the country an option between total war and defeat. The lower costs of tactical nuclear weapons over conventional forces was another significant advantage. By 1961 the United States had deployed several thousand tactical nuclear weapons in Europe, targeted on tank and infantry units, field headquarters, airfields, logistical installations, and the like. Presumably, the Russians were doing the same thing.

Some strategists from the Eisenhower regime touted these weapons as an affordable alternative to conventional forces for purposes of balancing the Warsaw Pact's manpower advantage. However, numerous Kennedy appointees insisted that reliance on tactical nuclear weapons rested on some doubtful assumptions. In the first place, a war fought with tactical nuclear weapons might require more rather than less manpower. Use of these weapons by both sides would no doubt decimate front-line divisions. Without a sufficient number of troops in reserve, NATO would be unable to force Soviet follow-on divisions to concentrate so as to present a suitable target for destruction by a second round of tactical nuclear weapons. The second questionable assumption concerns limitations on yields, targets and numbers of weapons. Not all targets would be easy to pinpoint and destroy with a single weapon. Each side would probably situate some targets in populated areas. Indeed, in densely populated Europe, many targets already lay in areas surrounded by civilians. Collateral damage would be enormous. Would not the losing side widen its list of enemy targets, thereby extending collateral damage even further? War games showed that a tactical nuclear war in Europe would produce 2–20 million casualties and widespread economic destruction, even if cities were spared. If cities were attacked, casualties would rise to 100 million. Under such circumstances, any victory would be Pyrrhic. Many critics of tactical nuclear war insisted that once the firebreak separating conventional from nuclear warfare were crossed, it would become next to impossible to halt a steady progression to strategic war. Even if the two sides established upper limits on yield, it would be difficult to verify compliance if several weapons were fired at a single target. Precise distinctions are never easy to discern in the fog of war. The above considerations raised serious doubts about reliance on tactical nuclear weapons for the defense of Europe. Nevertheless, the Defense Department defended this option on several grounds. Tactical nuclear weapons stockpiled in Europe reinforced America's commitment to Europe's defense. These weapons helped deter Warsaw Pact use of nuclear weapons; uncertainties about escalation might dissuade the Soviets from taking the first step. Finally, should conventional defense fail, tactical nuclear weapons provided a backup system. Although the Kennedy administration increased the number of tactical nuclear weapons in Europe and Asia by 60%, it stressed their utility for deterring the use of such weapons by others (Kahan, 1975). Kennedy had no enthusiasm for fighting a limited nuclear war in Europe.

All told, conventional defense seemed the best method of preserving Europe. In addition to the factors cited above, conventional defense would avoid the necessity for the several countries of NATO to agree on when to move to nuclear weapons, a potentially divisive step. Conventional forces could support diplomacy in peacetime and buttress firm resistance in a crisis, such as Berlin. Should war erupt, collateral damage and civilian casualties would be lower than those produced by a nuclear war. The hazard of escalation to strategic nuclear war would be moderate, although no national leader could dismiss this possibility. Conventional defense would diminish doubts about America's willingness to fight to defend Europe; presumably, the American people would not be faced with their own destruction as the price of defending Europe.

While few strategists challenged the merits of conventional defense (as remains the case today), the astronomical cost of such a response posed a seemingly impossible obstacle. Therefore, American strategists turned briefly to another alternative, the Multinational Nuclear Force (MLF).

Multinational Nuclear Force

The MLF was born out of Europe's concern that America would not honor its commitment to defend Europe. The Soviet Union's capacity to retaliate against American cities, which became a reality around 1960, gave rise to these apprehensions. The Eisenhower administration, in the waning days of reliance upon nuclear retaliation, devised the MLF to allay Europe's fears. Essentially, the MLF consisted of a sea-borne nuclear force jointly manned by crews from all the NATO countries. The concept foundered, however, on the rocks of such essential questions as when the weapons would be fired and who would have authority to launch them. The United States, which was to provide all the nuclear firepower, did not want to lose control of these decisions, since MLF launches could provoke nuclear retaliation against American soil. Without a decisive voice in such questions, Europe quickly lost interest in the MLF, and the concept slipped below the surface.

The demise of the MLF still left unanswered the question of how to defend Europe. By late in the first year of the Kennedy administration, key planners turned once again to the conventional option. Cost studies were undertaken. The more conservative estimates called for at least a 20% increase in the defense budgets of Western countries. Such expenditures were necessary to raise the 100 divisions said to be needed. (At the time, NATO fielded 25 divisions, 22 of them American, of which 16 were active and six were priority National Guard units.) The 16 active American divisions totaled 960,000 men. None of the NATO countries was prepared to spend the increased sums called for.

Strategic Arms Policy

While the Kennedy administration elected to supplement the nation's strategic arsenal with the forces described above, the need persisted for a doctrine to govern the use of strategic weapons. While strategic weapons do not lend themselves to easy definition, they generally refer to long-range, high-yield nuclear weapons. Such weapons are intended primarily not to affect the outcome of a particular battle but rather to diminish the enemy's capacity to prosecute a war. The three principal strategic systems are long-range bombers, land-based intercontinental ballistic missiles (ICBMs), and sea-launched intercontinental ballistic missiles (SLBMs).

As these three systems developed, American planners were faced with two questions: (1) How much destructive power did the United States require? (2) How should the country apportion this power among the three systems?

The answer to the second question has always been affected to some extent by interservice rivalry. At the onset of the Kennedy administration, the Air Force was building bombers and ICBMs, and the Navy was constructing SLBMs. Neither service paid much regard to what the other service was doing, nor did either service entertain a considered conception of how much total destructive power the nation needed.

The three major strategic systems are sometimes referred to as the strategic triad. Each leg of this triad has distinctive advantages and drawbacks. Bombers are vulnerable to attack until they are airborne. At that point they are still somewhat vulnerable to air defense. Airplanes have the unique advantage that they can be recalled after launch. Bombers were the most accurate of the three systems during the Kennedy years. ICBMs are far more secure than bombers before launch, especially if the missiles are placed in hardened underground silos. (Such missiles are growing less secure today against accurate ICBMs. Under Kennedy, Soviet missiles could not destroy hardened ICBMs except by a chance direct hit.) SLBMs are the most secure of the three legs. Thus, they provide the best guarantee of a second-strike capability. Until the 1980s, however, SLBMs were much less accurate than the other two systems. Furthermore, communicating with submerged submarines was not so easy during the Kennedy years, so this leg did not lend itself to as much flexibility as the other two. Maintaining all three systems would give the nation the advantages of each and offer the greatest range of options. This continues to be American policy.

Decisions made during the Kennedy administration about levels of destructive power and the apportionment of this power among the three legs of the triad have influenced force levels to the present day. The term used to describe the destructive power needed by American strategic forces is "assured destruction."

Assured Destruction

Defense Secretary McNamara and his assistants pondered the question of how much damage, inflicted by American forces, would dissuade the Soviet Union from attacking the United States. Must America be capable of wiping out the entire Soviet population? Must America be able to level every building in the Soviet Union? Would half the population and half the structures suffice to deter an attack? McNamara's recommendation, accepted by Kennedy, was that the United States should have the capacity to destroy 20–25% of the Soviet population and 50% of the country's industrial production (Enthoven and Smith, 1971). This capability was termed "assured destruction." It should be emphasized that America was to have this capability after absorbing a Soviet first strike. Presumably, no rational Soviet leader would attack the United States knowing that such a price must be paid.

Force Levels

Assured destruction set a target in terms of mission. But how many missiles and bombs were needed to accomplish that mission? The answer to this question is always open to debate, as Soviet defense capabilities remain in flux, as do American offensive capabilities. To complicate matters further, achieving assured destruction was not the only consideration governing procurement. Kennedy was concerned that he might appear weak to Khrushchev, especially after Kennedy's decision not to support the Bay of Pigs invaders with American air strikes and to leave the Berlin Wall standing. Kennedy also appreciated the fact that Soviet leaders might view his youthfulness and inexperience as an invitation to undertake risks. *Sputnik* had also left the world with the impression that the Soviets were ahead in strategic missiles. In setting force levels, therefore, Kennedy and his advisers went to extra lengths to avoid the appearance of weakness. This outlook no doubt contributed to the procurement of more force than necessary to achieve assured destruction. Kennedy also wanted to deal from a position of strength. Regardless of how many missiles and bombs were needed for assured destruction, Kennedy wanted to have more of these weapons than the Soviets had. Thus, the world—including the Soviets—would see that America was maintaining its strategic vitality. Setting force levels therefore depended to some extent on how many missiles and bombs the Soviets had. In fact, Washington did not know. The best intelligence source, the U-2 spy-plane, had stopped flying after Gary Powers' abortive flight in May, 1960. Reconnaissance satellites were not operational at the outset of the Kennedy administration, although they were under development. What was known was that the Soviets had the productive capacity to build large numbers of strategic weapons. Kennedy did not want to be surprised by the sudden discovery that the Soviets had been taking advantage of their productive capacity and had outbuilt the United States. Therefore, when setting force levels, he instructed McNamara to take into account not only the best estimate of actual Soviet deployments but also a consideration of potential Soviet deployments. This method of force planning could hardly fail to alarm the Soviets. If the Russians were prepared to see the Americans match their strategic forces, they could hardly feel comfortable about American superiority. American construction of weapons to meet *potential* Soviet deployment might well appear threatening on Washington's part. Might not the Americans be masking other, more aggressive intentions? American actions were also bound to derail arms control. In view of Washington's procurement of more strategic weapons than it needed to offset Soviet deployments, the Soviets might reasonably have questioned America's stated desire for limiting arms.

One other influence on American procurement was the efforts of arms manufacturers and their allies in Congress and elsewhere to produce arms for the sake of private gain. Such a factor remains a constant if unquantifiable element in the arms equation.

Ultimately, discussions about force planning come down to numbers. Governments must decide how many weapons to build. So it is with each new president.

When Kennedy came into office, he reviewed Eisenhower's target levels for strategic weapons. These levels described not existing deployments but levels of deployment deemed desirable for the near future. Eisenhower had determined that the country needed 19 missile-firing submarines and 450 Minuteman ICBMs. Kennedy raised these levels to 41 submarines carrying 16 missiles each and 1,000 Minuteman missiles. Kennedy also placed half of the nation's 1,500 intercontinental bombers on 15-minute runway alert, meaning they could take off between the time of warning of a Soviet attack and the arrival of Soviet warheads. Kennedy devoted part of the 1961 supplemental defense budget to accelerating procurement of two older ICBMs, Titan and Atlas, that had started under Eisenhower as well as the newer Minuteman and Polaris. Titan and Atlas were in the initial stages of deployment when Kennedy took office. Minuteman and Polaris were still in the development stage. Titan and Atlas were both liquid-fueled, which meant that they had to be loaded with fuel after the order to launch was given. This greatly extended response time. Furthermore, these missiles were deployed above ground, making them easy targets. Minuteman and Polaris, in contrast, were solid-fuel missiles, which meant they carried their fuel in advance. Thus, these missiles could be launched on short notice. (Later, Atlas missiles were dismantled. Fifty-four Titans were retained, in part because their payloads are larger than those of Minuteman.) By late 1961, the 1,500-mile-range Polaris was ready for deployment. Kennedy phased out the B-47 bomber and replaced it with the B-52.

By October, 1962, approximately the halfway point of the Kennedy administration, American and Soviet strategic deployments were those shown in

Table 3-1. By every measure, the United States was comfortably ahead. Yet, as we have seen, Kennedy set force targets much higher than those shown in Table 3-1. In part, these seemingly unnecessarily high levels were due to the expectation of large-scale Soviet deployments and uncertain information about force levels existing at the time. A strategic forces gap in reverse had clearly materialized.

Table 3-1: American and Soviet Strategic Forces, October 1962

	Soviet Union	United States
ICBMs	75 (approx.)	100 Minutemen I (approx.)
		90 Atlas
		_36_ Titan
		226
SLBMs	0	144 Polaris missiles in 9 Polaris submarines
Long-range bombers	70 Bears	600 B-52s (approx.)
	_120_ Bisons	_750_ B-47s (approx.)
	190	1,350

SOURCE: Richard Smoke, *National Security and the Nuclear Dilemma* (2nd ed.: New York: Random House, 1987), p. 112.

What could Kremlin leaders have thought when they contemplated the figures in Table 3-1 and contrasted them with Kennedy's avowal to embrace arms limitation and to fabricate weapons only for purposes of deterrence? Would such an imbalance be acceptable to an American president? The Soviets reacted with a massive weapons buildup. Kennedy's drive for superiority only provoked the Russians to construct additional weapons, resulting in less security for the United States but at a much higher cost. Kennedy's emphasis on military preparedness also dampened prospects for arms control. Facing such inferiority in strategic forces, the Soviets could hardly be expected to display enthusiasm for curbing their arms. Indeed, they reacted much as President Reagan did upon entering office, proclaiming that America had fallen behind and must at least catch up to the Soviets in armaments before considering arms limitation. In looking back, Secretary McNamara said, "The blunt fact is that if we had had more accurate information about planned Soviet strategic forces we simply would not have needed to build as large a nuclear arsenal as we have today." He added that American superiority in ICBMs (in 1967) was "both greater than we had originally planned, and is in fact more than we require" (Quoted in Ambrose, 1980, p. 252). A study completed in 1968 revealed that the United States could destroy nearly half the Soviet population and 80% of its industry, far exceeding the requirements of assured destruction (Enthoven and Smith, 1971).

With the benefit of hindsight, we might ask why Washington did not accept its marked superiority in the early 1960s and consider increasing its arsenal only if the Soviets did the same. By the fall of 1961, American spy satellites were adequate to detect a significant strategic buildup. Washington's worst-case planning was excessive and led to diminished American security at higher cost. There is little evidence the country learned much from this episode. In response to expected Soviet ABM deployments, the United States built and deployed MIRV, a missile with many warheads. MIRV greatly increased the number of warheads deployed by each side and dramatically heightened the vulnerability of each side's land-based deterrent. The expected Soviet ABM deployments were aborted by the ABM Treaty of 1972.

Controlled Response

Despite the most minute precautions, nuclear war could occur. Controlled response was a concept, adopted by the Kennedy administration, that sought to save civilian lives by sparing cities and to prevent escalation of low-level nuclear fighting to an all-out nuclear exchange. America's nuclear response would be "controlled." Secretary McNamara described controlled response in his June, 1962, commencement address at the University of Michigan (*Department of State Bulletin*, July 9, 1962, pp. 64–69). McNamara explained that in case a conflict should go nuclear, American strategy would be to strike Soviet military forces while avoiding Soviet cities. Hopefully, this tactic would encourage the Soviets to avoid American cities. Furthermore, he declared, the United States would not launch all of its nuclear weapons in a single spasm response; instead, the response would be controlled. The United States would fire a few nuclear weapons deemed necessary for successful prosecution of the conflict. The remainder of the arsenal would be reserved in case of need. Ultimately, Washington might decide to strike Soviet cities, and weapons would be reserved for that purpose, but hopefully the conflict would terminate before reaching such a stage.

Controlled response required a large array of invulnerable accurate weapons, as well as secure command and control. In contrast, McNamara explained how the military situation might evolve if America's strategic weapons were vulnerable to a Soviet strike. Should a crisis intensify, the Soviets might conclude that the United States was about to use nuclear weapons. If the Soviets could destroy these weapons on the ground, they might have every incentive to do so. Pentagon planners, of course, would realize what the Soviets were thinking, and would therefore issue orders to launch. The Soviets would try to beat the Americans to the punch. According to this scenario, an intense U.S.-Soviet crisis could rapidly spiral to nuclear war. If, on the other hand, American weapons were invulnerable to a Soviet strike, the Soviets would have no incentive to preempt, and the United States would be under no pressure to launch a full salvo to beat Soviet preemption. Washington could "control" its nuclear response.

In a sense, controlled response represented a form of flexible response within the nuclear spectrum. The proper mix of weapons would give the president an alternative between full-throated nuclear war and total avoidance of nuclear weapons. One variation of controlled response began with a limited Soviet nuclear strike. Since a large proportion of American weapons would survive, Washington could respond by destroying remaining Soviet weapons. An exchange of cities would be avoided. (At the time, the Soviet strategic arsenal consisted of bombers and vulnerable missiles deployed above ground or in semi-hardened silos.)

President Kennedy accepted much of the reasoning underlying controlled response. Studies undertaken by Secretary McNamara revealed that America's strategic forces, which consisted at the time mostly of 1500 intercontinental bombers stationed at some 60 bases, were growing increasingly vulnerable to the anticipated Soviet increase in ICBMs. The command and control system was also less than secure from attack. Most of these facilities were scarcely protected and were housed at or near SAC bases or major cities. Communications links were vulnerable. If the Soviets initiated an assault by neutralizing America's command and control system, Washington would find itself unable to orchestrate a response of any kind. America's bombers, missiles and submarines would be awaiting orders that would never arrive. In 1961, President Kennedy ordered that America's strategic forces be made less vulnerable, so that he could capitalize on controlled response if such a situation ever arose. He directed a shift from the vulnerable, liquid-fueled Atlas and Titan strategic missiles to the relatively invulnerable solid-fueled Minuteman and Polaris. As we have seen, he also ordered an acceleration of these two missile programs, and he increased the number of bombers on runway alert. He also expanded efforts to protect the command and control system, including the establishment of an airborne command center. Kennedy also phased out highly vulnerable, intermediate-range ballistic missiles placed around the Soviet periphery. These "use 'em or lose 'em" weapons could spark a Soviet first strike in case of a crisis. Snark, Thor, Jupiter and Regulus eventually wound up on the scrap heap. The targeting policy of avoiding cities and concentrating on military forces was incorporated into the nation's SIOP—Single Integrated Operations Plan—the master plan for American operations in time of general nuclear war.

Controlled response had its share of critics. To begin with, mutual city-avoidance called for a degree of joint policy calibration in the midst of war that some strategists called unrealistic. The policy also rested upon a degree of rationality during wartime that critics questioned. Policy-makers would also have to possess information that was more complete and accurate than is usually the case during combat. Many strategic targets are located so close to cities, or in the midst of populated areas, that striking such targets would be tantamount to a counter-cities strategy. Some critics pointed out that the second-strike capability required by controlled response was also a first-strike capability. In other words, if the United States could destroy Soviet weapons in a retaliatory strike, Washington could also neutralize Soviet weapons in a surprise attack. Once the United States gained that capability, might not the Soviets launch early in a crisis, for fear of losing all their weapons on the ground? Realizing this Soviet concern, the United States might launch a surprise attack before Moscow suspected it was coming. The spiral of instability was renewed. From an arms control standpoint, controlled response upset some critics, because it made nuclear war more acceptable. A war that left weapons in ruins but spared cities did not seem totally unthinkable. Finally, controlled response called for a substantial increase in armaments, as demonstrated by the strategic programs that Kennedy accelerated. The president remained unconvinced by these considerations, and controlled response became part of the military doctrine adopted by the Kennedy administration.

Stable Deterrence

The concept of stable deterrence began to attract the attention of strategic thinkers during the time Kennedy presided over the country. Stable deterrence refers to a situation in which the likelihood of utilizing nuclear weapons is low. The key to stable deterrence lies in invulnerable weapons. If country A can destroy country B's weapons before launch, then in a crisis A would have some incentive for a crippling surprise attack. B, realizing this, would be motivated to launch early. Such a situation is highly unstable. If, on the other hand, B's weapons are invulnerable, A would have no motivation for a surprise attack. Thus, stable deterrence depends on the existence of invulnerable weapons, preferably by both sides. (If A has invulnerable weapons but B does not, B might—in a moment of extreme crisis—launch its weapons in the irrational hope of taking down as much of A as possible.)

The very weapons needed for controlled response also provided the underpinning for stable deterrence. These weapons included the solid-fueled Minuteman ICBM, which could be emplaced in hardened underground silos, and Polaris SLBMs, which the Soviets could not locate. Bombers on 15-minute runway alert would also avoid destruction in a Soviet first strike. Secure command and control further contributed to the country's second-strike capability. By the mid-1960s, the United States had a secure second-strike force. The Soviets followed in short order. The balance of terror was in place.

Arms control advocates were divided over the desirability of stable deterrence. Many moderate arms controllers accepted stable deterrence as the optimal superpower relationship one could expect to achieve. Disarmament proponents denounced the concept, because it rested on the perpetuation of nuclear weapons. Representatives from both camps cautioned that stable deterrence might not hold against the irrationality or panic that war sometimes induces. They also lamented the risk of accidental or unauthorized launch. In addition, the continued reliance on nuclear weapons by the world's two largest military powers would encourage other states to emulate them; proliferation of nuclear weapons would follow. In time, most arms control enthusiasts came to accept the view, enunciated by Kennedy's science adviser Jerome Wiesner, that stable deterrence was desirable because it might promote an atmosphere conducive to arms cuts.

Resumption of Testing

A voluntary ban on nuclear testing was in effect when Kennedy took office. By the late summer of 1961, Khrushchev needed a diplomatic victory. The Soviet leader was troubled by America's spurt forward in the strategic arms race. The West was holding firm in Berlin. Khrushchev thought he could score a success at home and abroad by dramatically boosting the yield of his biggest missiles. This would require testing. On August 30, 1961, Khrushchev announced an end to the three-year test moratorium. During the fall, the Soviets conducted a series of tests, climaxed by a much heralded 58-megaton blast. This explosion, 3,000 times more powerful than the one that leveled Hiroshima, was intended to restore Moscow's position as the leading nuclear power. Although a 58-megaton bomb was too powerful to have any discernable military use, it was a mighty propaganda blast.

Kennedy was just as sensitive to appearances as Khrushchev. According to Kennedy's bipolar world vision, which mirrored Khrushchev's, the struggle for world supremacy would largely depend on the third world. These countries were presumably watching the superpowers. No third world leader would seek to align himself with the weaker of the superpowers. In this race for supremacy, appearances were all-important. Kennedy felt he could not allow the world to perceive that the Russians were vaulting ahead in the arms race, regardless of whether or not the United States had a military need to develop new weapons through testing.

Kennedy was personally repelled by a resumption of testing. He believed a renewed round of testing would poison the atmosphere and propel the arms race to new heights. Nevertheless, he felt he had to resume testing in order to avoid the appearance of weakness (Schlesinger, 1965). The Joint Chiefs of Staff and Secretary McNamara encouraged Kennedy to order renewed tests. Kennedy was particularly opposed to atmospheric testing because of radioactive fallout. In September he adopted a compromise position, ordering a series of underground tests but proscribing explosions in the atmosphere. The president was convinced that America was ahead in strategic weapons, based on greater numbers and more accurate and reliable delivery systems. As the Russians continued to test through the fall, including some blasts in the atmosphere, Kennedy's domestic critics hounded him to match the Kremlin's efforts. Kennedy declared, "Personally, I hate the idea of resuming atmospheric tests" (Quoted in Schlesinger, 1965, p. 489). Still, many in the national security community voiced fears that the Russians, through the larger tests that could be conducted in the atmosphere, were positioning themselves for a great leap forward in strategic weaponry over the next two to three years, especially in the all-important yield-to-weight ratio.

Kennedy was persuaded to resume atmospheric testing by his conviction that, in world opinion, Moscow was moving ahead of the United States. In March, 1962, Kennedy announced that America would resume atmospheric testing, coupling his directive with an offer to desist if the Soviets halted all future tests. Moscow declined the invitation. In April, the president directed that the United States resume atmospheric testing. A series of 30 blasts followed.

In retrospect, it is clear that Kennedy placed a great deal of emphasis on military preparedness. Upon entering office, he was spurred by the alleged missile gap to augment American strategic forces, putting some of the fiscal 1961 supplemental defense appropriation to this purpose. However, the largest boost in military preparedness sprang from the doctrine of flexible response. This doctrine required major increases in the nation's conventional and counter-insurgency capabilities, including airlift and sealift. These programs required massive increases in military spending. In the area of strategic arms, Kennedy's concern with assured destruction, controlled response and stable deterrence occasioned sizeable military outlays. The chief executive procured two costly new missile systems, Minuteman and Polaris, to replace the vulnerable, liquid-fueled Titan and Atlas rockets. In part, procurement levels were determined by inflated estimates of future Soviet weapons acquisitions, giving the United States a larger strategic arsenal than needed for assured destruction. Finally, the resumption of nuclear testing, motivated primarily by the desire not to appear weak before world opinion, lent momentum to military preparedness under Kennedy.

Kennedy's world view had much to do with such an emphasis upon military preparedness. Kennedy believed the United States and the Soviet Union were locked in a struggle for world supremacy. In this contest, the United States had to meet all of its commitments, under penalty of appearing to vacillate. Eisenhower shared this bipolar world view, but he expected the threat of massive nuclear retaliation to dissuade communist expansion. Kennedy rejected this military doctrine and replaced it with one he deemed more effective, but one that absorbed huge cash outlays.

Like all chief executives in recent decades, Kennedy had an interest in limiting arms. To this alternative means of assuring national security we now turn.

ARMS CONTROL

While both Eisenhower and Kennedy dreamed of moving towards a disarmed world, Kennedy was more concerned than Eisenhower with taking the first small steps that might lead to that destination. If Eisenhower formulated arms control initiatives with the goal of effecting general and complete disarmament, Kennedy thought smaller but perhaps wiser. Of course, Kennedy had the advantage of seeing how many impediments lay in the path of general and complete disarmament. The outlook of Kennedy, indeed, of most leaders in Washington and Moscow, was sobered by how close the world had approached nuclear war over Cuba. It is likely that the urgency of derailing the fast-moving arms race appeared more immediate to Kennedy than to either of his predecessors.

One of Kennedy's favorite sayings was Winston Churchill's statement, "We arm to parley." Kennedy believed that a mighty American arsenal would induce the Soviets to consider arms reduction, since the Kremlin could entertain no hope of overcoming the United States militarily. It is far from clear, however, that Kremlin leaders perceived the vast military buildup undertaken by Kennedy, from conventional forces to strategic weaponry, as evidence of a desire to "parley." It is just as conceivable that Moscow viewed this buildup, in conjunction with the attempt to unseat Castro and the accretion of forces in Indochina, as a trumpet of aggressiveness rather than a call for arms control. The likelihood of such a perception is heightened when one considers that Kennedy's force targets lay well beyond Soviet programmed force levels.

Be that as it may, Kennedy sought to incorporate into strategic procurement policy certain choices that would enhance the stability of the strategic standoff. These decisions did not depend on explicit agreements with the Soviets; they were strictly unilateral. As we saw in the preceding section, Kennedy eliminated "soft" intercontinental and intermediate range missiles useful only in a first strike. These missiles were destabilizing, because they provided the Soviets with a strong incentive to eliminate them before launch. Such missiles increased the likelihood that a crisis would move rapidly toward a nuclear exchange. Kennedy also improved the command and control system, reducing the likelihood of accidental or unauthorized launch and enhancing the nation's capacity to respond in case of attack. Whether these steps, when set against expanding force levels, persuaded the Kremlin of American wishes for cooperation and arms control is far from certain.

The Kennedy years did not see a wide assortment of negotiations to reduce arms levels. This may have been due to Kennedy's conviction that his first priority lay in augmenting American forces in preparation to "parley." An assassin's bullet cut short whatever plans he may have had to engage the Soviets in arms reduction negotiations.

Executive Decision-Making: ACDA

Symbolizing his interest in arms control, Kennedy revived the post of presidential disarmament adviser, originally created and abolished by Eisenhower. Kennedy deliberately appointed a political conservative, John J. McCloy, to this position, in order to deflect accusations of softness (a perennial concern of Democratic presidents). A leading light of the Republican Party, McCloy had overseen the American occupation of Germany and had served with the Pentagon, the Ford Foundation and the Chase Manhattan Bank. Other important participants in arms control deliberations were Jerome Weisner and Carl Kaysen (science advisers), United Nations Ambassador Adlai Stevenson, Leland Haworth and Glenn Seaborg from the Atomic Energy Commission, Secretary of State Rusk, Secretary McNamara, Roswell Gilpatrick and John McNaughton from Defense, and the Joint Chiefs of Staff.

At the same time, some in Congress, particularly Senator Hubert H. Humphrey, were concerned that arms control was getting short shrift, no matter who resided in the White House. Humphrey took the lead in establishing a new agency, the Arms Control and Disarmament Agency (ACDA), whose primary responsibility would be to provide advice on arms control policy. The existence of such an organization would at least ensure that arms control considerations were voiced in policy deliberations. In September, 1961, Congress established ACDA. At the outset, Kennedy wished the new unit to be located in the Executive Office, an indication of his personal interest in arms control. He was persuaded, however, to place ACDA at State, inasmuch as Kennedy hoped—in vain, it turned out—that the State Department would take a commanding role in setting foreign policy. ACDA continues as a semi-autonomous body within the State Department, receiving overall policy guidance from State but largely free to act independently within those guidelines.

Shortly after ACDA came into being, McCloy decided to return to private life. Kennedy replaced him with William Foster, another political conservative with a business background. Foster, who had led the American delegation to the 1958 Geneva meeting on the prevention of surprise attack, became the first director of ACDA.

U.S.-Soviet Joint Statement

One of the first products to emerge from McCloy's efforts was a Joint Statement of Agreed Principles for Disarmament Negotiations. Washington and Moscow issued the statement following months of diplomatic wrangling between McCloy and Soviet Deputy Foreign Minister V. A. Zorin. Looking back, one might say the statement was "full of sound and fury, signifying nothing." The statement was laced with pious banalities and served the propaganda needs of each nation, much in the manner of disarmament declarations proclaimed in the 1950s. In the Joint Statement, the United States accepted the Soviet call for general and complete disarmament as the guiding principle of future arms talks. Nations would retain only enough force to maintain internal order. The Soviets, in turn, accepted two conditions put forth by McCloy. The total elimination of arms would not occur in one fell swoop but would proceed by stages "under such strict and effective international control as would provide firm assurance that all parties are honoring their obligations." Secondly, progress toward general and complete disarmament would go hand-in-hand with the development of international peacekeeping institutions centered in the United Nations. It has never been confirmed that the Joint Statement was ever consulted by the two countries in future policy decisions.

Eighteen Nation Disarmament Committee

In 1961 Moscow and Washington began talks on revising the principal multilateral disarmament body, the ten-nation, Geneva-based disarmament unit attached to the United Nations. By the beginning of the 1960s, the number of colonies that gained independence had grown and were swelling the ranks of the United Nations. These nations wanted a say in disarmament matters. Accordingly, the two superpowers agreed to establish the Eighteen Nation Disarmament Committee (ENDC). The ENDC included the ten members of the previous body, mostly from Europe, as well as eight neutral nations. In May, 1962, the ENDC held its first session in Geneva. For several years the ENDC served as the principal multilateral forum for disarmament negotiations. In 1969 it was enlarged to 26 states and its name was changed. The United States and the Soviet Union co-chaired the ENDC.

One of the first matters considered by the ENDC was a complex scheme for general and complete disarmament submitted by the United States. The convoluted plan called for three stages toward disarmament. While nations were disarming, peace-keeping institutions would be established and international law would be strengthened. Elaborate linkages connected all facets of the plan; implementation of one stage depended on successful completion of other stages.

Like most plans for total disarmament, the American proposal was extensively debated at the ENDC and then set aside without any consensus to adopt it.

Hot Line

The hot line was the first concrete achievement of the Kennedy administration in the area of arms control. Strictly speaking, it could be argued that mention of the hot line does not belong in a discussion of arms control. After all, it did not result in the limitation of arms. However, the hot line was part of an effort to impart a greater degree of stability to the superpower relationship. For that reason, discussion of the subject is perhaps not out of place.

Installation of the hot line was a direct outgrowth of the Cuban missile crisis. In the course of that episode, leaders of the two giants had several occasions to communicate with each other. Generally, each communication took about four hours. This time included coding, transmission, decoding, translation, and diplomatic presentation from the sender's embassy to the recipient government. In the wake of the missile crisis, leaders on both sides realized that an unintended war might result through a misunderstanding. Rapid communication could save the day. On previous occasions, Washington had proposed a direct communications link between Washington and Moscow. The Soviet Union refused to accept this except as part of total disarmament. In April, 1963, just half a year after Cuba, the Kremlin signaled its willingness to discuss such a link. On June 20, the two parties signed the Memorandum of Understanding between the United States and the Union of Soviet Socialist Republics Regarding the Establishment of a Direct Communications Link, informally known as the hot line.

Contrary to popular belief, the hot line is not a telephone connection. A telephone was rejected because verbal exchanges can be less than precise. Leaders may entertain different recollections of what they said and heard. The heads of government also wished to avoid sending clues to their reactions by tone of voice, inflection, and the like. Instead of a telephone, a teletype connection was selected. Printed messages, it was felt, allowed for more exactness and permitted time for reflection before giving a reply. In 1971, the hot line was improved by adding satellite communication circuits to the existing cable links.

While the extent of use of the hot line remains classified, it is known that the link was used during the Middle East wars of 1967 and 1973.

Limited Test Ban Treaty

The quest for a prohibition on all nuclear tests is the longest-running of all arms control negotiations. Proponents of such an accord regard it as one of the most significant measures that can be taken to slow the arms race. Nations will not place new weapons in their arsenals without first testing them. Therefore, a test halt would amount to a weapons halt. It is true that a comprehensive test ban would do nothing to eliminate existing weapons. However, it would go a long way toward stopping the development of new weapons, and it would discourage the proliferation of nuclear weapons.

President Kennedy made known his views on nuclear testing as early as 1956, when he said the United States should take the lead in halting nuclear tests. As a senator in 1959, he opposed Governor Rockefeller's call to resume underground testing. During the 1960 campaign, Kennedy promised not to be the first to resume atmospheric testing and not to test underground until exhausting all reasonable chances for a test ban agreement. At his first presidential news conference, Kennedy announced his appointment of a team to prepare a new bargaining position and draft treaty to ban nuclear tests.

Recall that a testing moratorium was in effect when Kennedy took office. In the spring of 1961, Kennedy sent Arthur H. Dean to Geneva as head of a delegation to try to negotiate a test ban treaty. The Soviets, however, hardened the position they had taken before the U-2 incident blew the previous negotiations out of the water. The Soviets now insisted upon a three-party directorate to manage the test ban regime and linked a test ban to progress on general and complete disarmament. The three-sided control body—United States, Soviet Union, and a neutral country—would give the Soviets a veto, a condition unacceptable to Washington. (The Soviets, it appears, lost faith in the impartiality of a neutral, after United Nations Secretary-General Dag Hammerskjold took, in Soviet eyes, a decidedly pro-Western position during the United Nations intervention in the Congo.)

As the Geneva negotiations showed no signs of progress, pressure to resume testing intensified within each superpower. Soviet generals and scientists sought tests to improve the yield-to-weight ratio of their warheads; they also warned that on-site inspections would confirm the absence of a missile gap. The Soviets also noted that another Western power, France, was conducting tests. In the United States, numerous conservative voices called for new tests. Like their Soviet counterparts, the Pentagon had designs for improved warheads and wanted to test them. Certain scientists complained that American technical capacities were withering, while no test ban treaty was in sight. In August, 1961, the Joint Chiefs of Staff urged that testing be resumed immediately, a position supported by the Joint Committee on Atomic Energy. Yielding in part to such pressure, Kennedy in August ordered preparations for underground testing but ordered no tests until all hopes for a treaty were exhausted.

On August 30 the Soviets conducted a test in the atmosphere. The test moratorium had been broken. Kennedy felt deceived, because preparations for such a test must have been in progress for weeks, while Soviet negotiators were still active in Geneva. During the next two months the Soviets conducted at least 30 tests, nearly all in the atmosphere, and some in the multi-megaton range. (The Soviets boasted of a 100-megaton blast.)

Kennedy felt he had no choice but to respond in kind. On September 5 he ordered resumption of underground testing. He also called on the Soviets to stop atmospheric testing, in order to prevent radioactive fallout. The Kremlin ignored Kennedy's plea.

As the two superpowers conducted tests, pressure began to mount in the United States for a resumption of testing in the atmosphere. Kennedy hoped to avoid this, as he was sensitive to warnings by scientists about the harmful effects of fallout. In response to demands from some of the Joint Chiefs for an immediate resumption of atmospheric testing, Kennedy ordered a study of the Soviet tests, which had ended in early November. The scientists who conducted the study found that the Russians had made important progress in developing more destructive warheads at lower weights. They warned that if the Soviets conducted another series of atmospheric tests, they could make some perilous breakthroughs unless the United States caught up through atmospheric testing of its own. On March 2 Kennedy announced that the United States would resume atmospheric testing. The first test occurred April 25. Kennedy's vision of a world free from nuclear testing was rapidly dissipating.

"'Tis an ill wind that blows no good." Such a gust emanated from Cuba in October, 1962. The missile crisis, which brought the world so close to nuclear war, also acted as a great spur to talks that culminated in the Limited Test Ban Treaty. The war scare had no little effect on President Kennedy. According to Schlesinger (1965), Kennedy's feelings

> underwent a qualitative change after Cuba: a world in which nations threatened each other with nuclear weapons now seemed to him not just an irrational but an intolerable and impossible world. Cuba thus made vivid the sense that all humanity had an interest in the question of nuclear war—an interest far above those national and ideological interests which had once seemed ultimate (p. 893).

In the aftermath of Cuba, the test ban negotiations took on a new vitality. At first, the diplomats focused their efforts on a total test ban. The Soviets, building on proposals tabled in previous talks, suggested that verification rest on automatic seismic devices to be located in each country. The Soviets also offered two or three on-site inspections each year. The inspection issue proved most contentious. In response to the Soviet offer, Washington wanted eight to ten yearly inspections in each country. The talks approached an impasse.

In a commencement address at American University in early June, 1963, Kennedy tried to give the talks a boost. After calling for a re-examination of American attitudes toward the cold war arms competition, Kennedy announced that the United States was halting atmospheric tests unless the Soviets resumed them. Moscow reacted warmly to this conciliatory speech.

In the summer a new round of talks began. Under Secretary of State W. Averell Harriman led the American delegation. Disagreement over on-site inspection persisted, rendering a comprehensive test ban out of the question. However, negotiators from the United Kingdom, United States and the Soviet Union did agree on the prohibition of nuclear testing in the atmosphere, under water, and in outer space. In these three environments, violations could be detected by "national technical means." The Limited Test Ban Treaty (LTBT) was signed August 5, 1963, in Moscow. Since then, over 100 countries have signed, including India but not France or China.

Kennedy's struggle was far from over, for now the battle for ratification was to begin. This struggle was no easy affair, for opinion on the treaty was sharply divided. Those who favored the treaty stressed its contribution to reducing fallout, curbing the proliferation of nuclear weapons, and improving the prospects for settling differences with the Soviet Union. The strongest argument made by treaty proponents was that the treaty would retard the arms spiral by limiting the development of new weapons. Those opposed to the treaty felt that military preparedness was a higher priority than arms control. Former Air Force Chief of Staff General Thomas D. White maintained that true security against an aggressive foe lay in nuclear superiority; nuclear testing was needed to achieve this. Scientist Edward Teller, former AEC Chairman Louis Strauss, and former JCS Chairman Admiral Arthur Radford stated that the country needed new and improved nuclear weapons, which could be perfected only by testing. Other treaty opponents insisted atmospheric tests were necessary to improve yield-to-weight ratios for warheads (as the Russians had just done), to develop a "pure" fusion weapon that would produce no fallout (for use in Europe), and to gather more information about the effects of nuclear explosions. Scientists wanted to investigate the effects of air bursts on radar, communications systems, and the operation of anti-ballistic missile systems (then entering early stages of development).

President Kennedy took a very active role in promoting the treaty. While negotiations were still in progress, he dispatched Secretary Rusk to Capitol Hill to brief key committees. The president brought a bipartisan group of senators to Moscow for the treaty-signing ceremony. The day after the treaty was initialed, he made a televised address to drum up public support. He met with individual senators to encourage them to vote for the agreement. In press conferences he touted the virtues of the accord.

One of the most effective supporters of the treaty during the Senate hearings was Secretary McNamara. In any treaty involving weapons, the views of the defense secretary count heavily. In his testimony before the Senate Foreign Relations Committee, McNamara argued that the treaty served American interests by promising to freeze American strategic superiority. This approach was bound to intrigue senators who entertained doubts about the agreement for security reasons. McNamara explained that the Soviets were ahead in high-yield nuclear weapons. The United States, he went on, had no need to match the Soviets in this regard; with greater accuracy, the United States could accomplish more by continuing to rely on lower-yield strategic weapons such as Minuteman and Polaris. Besides, such weapons were easier to harden and disperse than Russia's gigantic missiles. Furthermore, the United States had many more warheads than its adversary, the existing force numbering in excess of 500 Titans, Atlas, Minutemen and Polaris. Without additional testing other than underground, the United States could achieve its target level of 1,700 warheads by 1966, the secretary said. This would give the United States an overwhelming advantage over the USSR. Furthermore, more than 500 SAC bombers remained on quick-reaction alert, McNamara said, far in excess of the Soviet fleet. In addition, the United States was deploying large numbers of tactical nuclear weapons, whose yield extended from the sub-kiloton level to several hundred kilotons, McNamara stated. After painting such a rosy picture of American strategic superiority, McNamara asked what effect the treaty would have on this balance. "I can say that most of the factors will not be affected at all—not accuracy of missiles, not variety of systems, not their dispersal or mobility, and not numbers" (Quoted in Kaufmann, 1964, p. 152). McNamara conceded that the treaty could inhibit development of high-yield weapons, which require atmospheric testing. The secretary went on to say that he saw no need to develop such weapons. It would be preferable to saturate defenses with a greater number of lower-yield weapons, he said. "I can state with full confidence that the absence from our arsenal of a bomb greater than the one we can build under the treaty will not impair the effectiveness of our strategic forces," McNamara said (Kaufmann, 1964, p. 154). Rather, he want on, the treaty would help freeze American superiority. "By limiting Soviet testing to the underground environment, where testing is more difficult and more expensive, and where the United States has substantially more experience, we can at least retard Soviet progress and prolong the duration of our technological superiority" (Kaufmann, 1964, p. 159). McNamara testified that the treaty would further serve American security by slowing the spread of nuclear weapons. Such proliferation would jeopardize American security by increasing the likelihood of accidental war, boosting the risk that a regional nuclear war could draw in the great powers, and producing destabilizing shifts in regional power balances.

> Since testing underground is not only more costly but also more difficult and time-consuming, the proposed treaty would retard progress in weapons development in cases where the added cost and other factors were not sufficient to preclude it altogether. One of the great advantages of this treaty is that it will have this effect of retarding the spread of nuclear weapons (Kaufmann, 1964, p. 164).

The Joint Chiefs of Staff were not as enthusiastic as Secretary McNamara in their support of the treaty. Speaking through their chairman, General Maxwell D. Taylor, they expressed "the fear of a euphoria in the West which will eventually reduce our vigilance" (Schlesinger, 1965, p. 912). As the price of their support for the treaty, the JCS demanded the continuation of underground testing, a readiness to resume atmospheric testing on short notice, the strengthening of detection capabilities, and the maintenance of nuclear laboratories. Kennedy assented. On September 24, 1963, the Senate approved the treaty, 80–19.

The Treaty Banning Nuclear Weapons Tests in the Atmosphere, in Outer Space, and Under Water, as the test ban treaty was officially known, was the signal achievement of the Kennedy administration in the area of arms control. To many, the pact has proved a disappointment. It was the hope of treaty supporters that the test ban, limited as it was, would slow the development of new nuclear weapons. Before the treaty, most tests were conducted in the atmosphere. There was considerable uncertainty about how much could be learned about weapons from testing underground. It has turned out that a great deal can be learned. The LTBT has had no perceptible effect on slowing the arms race. Indeed, the treaty has served more to protect the environment than to impede the arms race. Radioactive fallout and its attendant health hazards have been markedly reduced.

4

JOHNSON

The administration of Lyndon B. Johnson began with the crack of a rifle in Dallas on November 22, 1963. From the beginning of his tenure in the White House, President Johnson determined to carry on the policies of his slain predecessor. "As *Air Force One* carried us swiftly back to Washington after the tragedy in Dallas, I made a solemn private vow: I would devote every hour of every day during the remainder of John Kennedy's unfulfilled term to achieving the goals he had set" (Johnson, 1971, p. 42). Unlike Kennedy or Eisenhower, Johnson did not enter the presidency with his own mandate. The Johnson administration differed from its predecessors in another respect. While every administration confronts a varied palette of issues and problems, the Johnson years saw what amounted to an obsession with a single issue, Vietnam. Particularly after 1965, the War in Indochina loomed as a towering peak on the Johnson landscape, in effect casting all other issues in deep shadow. Accordingly, Johnson and his principal assistants devoted enormous quantities of time and emotional energy to Vietnam. Inevitably, some of the other problems with which a president must deal received less attention than they merited.

While one can speak of differences between the presidencies of Kennedy and Johnson, an extremely strong link between them was forged by continuity in personnel. In the national security areas, both Secretary of State Dean Rusk and Secretary of Defense Robert McNamara stayed on board. Many of the undersecretaries and assistant secretaries in all the departments and agencies bridged the two administrations.

THE DOMESTIC SETTING

A little less than twelve months after Johnson ascended to the presidency, he gained the opportunity to garner his own mandate from the American people. The 1964 elections turned largely on the Vietnam war. Republican candidate Senator Barry Goldwater of Arizona urged the United States to exert further effort to bring about victory. Proclaiming that "extremism in the defense of liberty is no vice," Goldwater said he would approve whatever the Joint Chiefs recommended to secure victory, including using nuclear weapons. He also suggested carrying the war to North Vietnam, starting with bombing raids. At the time, no American combat troops were in Vietnam, and America's role was limited to military and economic assistance. In what was to become a never-ending underestimation of measures needed to defeat the communists, Johnson felt that the United States was doing just about all that was required to prevail. At most, he said, Washington would have to increase its assistance. He challenged Goldwater's notion of bombing North Vietnam, saying it would widen the war and perhaps bring in American troops. "We are not going to send American boys nine or ten thousand miles away from home to do what Asian boys ought to be doing for themselves," Johnson proclaimed. In 1968, when over one-half million American troops found themselves slogging through the rice paddies of Indochina, Johnson was to rue these words. In 1964, however, Johnson campaigned on the promise to keep the war limited and keep Americans out. At the same time, he promised a host of social reforms that came to be known as the Great Society. Johnson won the election by a landslide.

In 1964 and 1965, Johnson busied himself with enacting into law the social programs designed by John F. Kennedy and augmented by his own ideas. Foreign policy took a back seat. The Great Society sprang from the New Deal, Franklin Roosevelt's amalgam of social programs that had captured Johnson's imagination when he first came to Washington in the 1930s. A centerpiece of the Great Society was uplifting the poor, an effort dubbed the "war on poverty."

> Harry Truman used to say that 13 or 14 million Americans had their interests represented in Washington, but that the rest of the people had to depend on the President of the United States. That is how I felt about the 35 million American poor. They had no voice and no champion. Whatever the cost, I was determined to represent them (Johnson, 1971, p. 7).

The Economic Opportunity Act, signed into law in August, 1964, was the opening legislative salvo of the war on poverty. This law created the Job Corps, which provided work on federal projects to unemployed persons. The war on poverty embraced many facets, including job training for unskilled people, aid to schools, medical care for the poor, increased Social Security payments to the elderly poor, and housing programs.

The Great Society went beyond combatting poverty to tackle the problem of equal opportunity. Such landmark laws as the Civil Rights Act of 1968 greatly broadened the access of all Americans to housing, use of public facilities and transportation, and voting. In his early years, Johnson devoted prodigious amounts of time and energy to the passage of this legislation. Once Congress enacted the bills, the executive branch faced the challenge of enforcing them, often in the face of a resistant public. By the mid-1960s, though, the Vietnam war was absorbing more and more of Johnson's attention. Many of the over 500 social programs created by Great Society legislation languished due to lack of vigor in implementation and enforcement. The Great Society was one of the casualties of the Vietnam War. Johnson's successor, Richard M. Nixon, no friend of Great Society initiatives, allowed many of these programs to expire.

The 1960s were marked by violence not only overseas but also at home. Such measures as the Civil Rights Act of 1964 and the Voting Rights Act of 1965 fueled hopes that did not quickly translate into expanded opportunities and rights for black Americans. Their expectations heightened, many black Americans felt a renewed sense of frustration. This frustration first made itself felt in August, 1965, in the Watts district of Los Angeles. Blacks went on a rampage, burning and looting much of the area. Watts was the first of over one hundred urban riots that occurred during the summers of 1965, 1966, and 1967. In addition to Watts, Newark (New Jersey) and Detroit saw some of the worst destruction. To quell the disturbance in Detroit in July, 1967, Johnson had to send in paratroopers and federalize the Michigan National Guard. These disturbances took over 225 lives, left 4,000 people wounded, and caused $112 billion in property damage.

The country was also horrified by two political assassinations in 1968. On April 4, Martin Luther King was shot, sparking a large-scale riot in Washington and outbreaks in 40 other cities. The passage of the controversial Open Housing Act one week later did little to suppress the anger felt by many black and white Americans. On June 5, an assassin's bullet claimed the life of Robert Kennedy on the eve of his victory in the California primary. By that time, Johnson had removed himself as a candidate, and Kennedy had emerged as the Democratic Party's front-runner.

These killings, the urban riots and the steady procession of coffins emanating from Southeast Asia combined to produce a backlash that had much to do with the victory of Republican Richard Nixon in 1968.

THE INTERNATIONAL CONTEXT

One of the earliest achievements of the Johnson administration in the overseas area was the signature of a Consular Convention with the Soviet Union on June 1, 1964. This agreement, which provided for the establishment of consulates in each country, gave the American government speedy access to citizens arrested in the Soviet Union and strengthened the government's ability to protect American visitors to that country. Because some Senators feared the Soviets would use consulates as centers for spying, the Senate did not ratify the agreement until three years later.

In October, 1964, the Politburo ousted Premier Khrushchev. His duties were assumed by Alexei Kosygin, who became premier, and Leonid Brezhnev, who became general secretary of the Communist Party. In time, the latter figure came to overshadow the premier.

April, 1965, presented Johnson with his first foreign policy crisis. The Dominican Republic had experienced a lengthy period of tenuous stability, stretching back to 1916 when American Marines took control. In that year, Rafael Trujillo seized control by rigging an election, and he conducted a brutal dictatorship until his assassination in 1961. Thereafter, a series of governments attempted to oversee the country with only moderate success.

On April 24, 1965, a group of young army officers who supported leftist Juan Bosch toppled the government of Donald Reid Cabral, a conservative supported by Washington. As masses poured into the streets, fighting and disorder reigned. Johnson, fearing for the lives of American citizens, dispatched 500 Marines to the island republic. Saving American lives was not the president's only concern, however. Johnson shared the bipolar, zero-sum view of the world taken by many of his generation. He viewed Juan Bosch and his supporters as being linked with Castro and the Kremlin in a Manichean battle for world supremacy with the United States. Declaring that the "American nations cannot, must not, and will not permit the establishment of another Communist government in the Western Hemisphere," Johnson sent 23,000 additional Marines to Santo Domingo. This action was taken on the basis of what was later shown to be a highly questionable cable from Ambassador W. Tapley Bennett warning that communists might take over the government. This assertion was based on a list of 58 communists or pro-communists among the supporters of Juan Bosch. The Marines restored order and prevented Bosch from taking over. In May, a peacekeeping force from the Organization of American States (OAS) replaced American Marines. In 1966, moderate rightist Joaquin Balaguer defeated Bosch in a presidential election.

In Latin America, many people asked why the United States acted unilaterally in violation of the OAS Charter, which prohibits intervention "directly or indirectly, for any reason whatever, in the internal or external affairs of any other state." Johnson could have awaited OAS action. The fact is that Johnson had little faith in the organization, reportedly asserting that "the OAS couldn't pour piss out of a boot if the instructions were written on the heel." In any event, Johnson feared that communists would take over unless he acted swiftly.

Although Johnson and his advisers took a bipolar view of the world, the fault lines separating East from West were beginning to move. In particular, monolithic communism was fragmenting. The Soviet Union, asserting its claim to be the undisputed leader of the communist world, could no longer count on unquestioning obedience from all other communist states. East Europeans sensed some scope for raising differences with Moscow. The Soviet economic model was losing its gloss. Two indications that the communist bloc was shattering appeared in China and Czechoslovakia.

Long-simmering antagonisms between the two communist giants flared into the open in the 1960s. For a century, China had bristled with resentment of Czarist seizure of Chinese borderlands in the nineteenth century. The Chinese also felt slighted by the minimal assistance Stalin provided during the communist struggle for power after World War II. In the 1960s, the Chinese openly challenged the Soviets on two counts, strategy against capitalist countries and leadership of world communism. In matters of strategy, the Chinese insisted

Moscow was too conservative and timid in opposing capitalism. While the Soviets insisted that a final nuclear showdown was suicidal and warned of the necessity to avoid reckless behavior that could precipitate war, Beijing insisted communism must take risks to bring about the ultimate triumph over capitalism. Because a final East-West showdown was out of the question, Moscow said the struggle between the two blocs must take place in the third world. Here, Moscow's strategy was to support non-communist governments in their efforts to break free of Western domination. The objective of this strategy was to leave the West isolated and debilitated. The Chinese denounced this strategy, challenging Moscow's vision that nationalist governments in the third world would ever make common cause with communism. Instead, Beijing urged support for communist parties in the nonaligned countries. Only communist regimes in the third world were reliable allies in the struggle against capitalism, insisted China. For its part, Moscow accused Beijing of recklessness.

The second challenge to Moscow concerned leadership of the communist world. Ever since 1917, the Soviet Union had stood out as the unquestioned leader of communism. In all respects, the Soviet Union dwarfed any other communist country. With one-fourth of the world's population and sizeable territory, China found itself in a position to challenge Soviet domination. Beijing called for an equal say in formulating the strategy and tactics to be employed by communism against the West. Soviet communists, not used to sharing power at home or abroad, predictably balked, accusing China of aiding Western imperialism by dividing communist ranks.

These forces were only beginning to emerge during the Johnson interregnum. Their permanence was far from clear. Some Westerners even argued that the Sino-Soviet dispute was deliberately concocted to throw the West off guard. Nixon realized the significance of these changes by opening ties with China; Carter formalized diplomatic relations with the Asian power. Johnson was too committed to a bipolar world view to take account of these epochal developments. Chinese assistance to the Vietnamese communists further blinded him to the possibilities of a changing world.

A second sign that monolithic communism was fragmenting made itself visible in Czechoslovakia. Just as Brezhnev and Kosygin were leaning toward Stalin's governing style, relying more and more on centralized economic planning and curbing the right of dissent, the Czech regime of Alexander Dubcek was moving in the opposite direction. In the summer of 1968, Czechs were talking of leaving the Warsaw Pact and allowing non-communist parties to organize and run candidates for office. Political dissent gained free scope. The Soviets feared that a failure to clamp down would signal other satellite states that they too had freedom to travel their own paths, even if these paths diverged from the communist road. Soviet leaders also feared that the millions of people inside the Soviet Union, who chafed under communist rule and nationalist suppression, might perceive an opportunity to challenge the supremacy of the Soviet communist party. Accordingly, in August, Soviet and East European forces invaded Czechoslovakia, deposed Dubcek, and replaced him with a reliable old-line Marxist. In justifying the intervention, Brezhnev asserted that socialist nations had the right to save one of their fellows from "world imperialism." This so-called Brezhnev Doctrine bore a striking resemblance to the rationale voiced by President Johnson in justifying the landing of American Marines in the Dominican Republic. Neither superpower, it seems, was prepared to allow ideological heresy within its own self-assigned sphere of influence.

The Eastern bloc was not the only coalition to display fissures. The Western alliance was never as tightly integrated as its Eastern counterpart. The voicing of disagreement in the Atlantic Alliance was not seen as insubordination or heresy, as it was in the East. In February, 1966, however, General Charles de Gaulle announced that France would no longer participate in NATO's military affairs. Although France did not withdraw from the alliance, France pulled out all ground, air and naval forces. De Gaulle also insisted that NATO remove its military headquarters from Paris, and that the United States remove its military bases from French soil. De Gaulle was reacting to Washington's tendency to make unilateral decisions for the alliance in its entirety, rather than consulting with its alliance partners. The French leader also suffered from an inflated vision of France's standing in the Western alliance and the world as a whole. In any event, France's withdrawal from military participation in the Western alliance complicated efforts to plan for the defense of Western Europe.

The Middle East does not go for long without a major upheaval, and such a one occurred in June, 1967. Fearing an attack from their Arab foes, the Israelis struck first with disarming air raids. By the time the Six Day War drew to a close, Israel had seized the Sinai peninsula, East Jerusalem, the West Bank of the Jordan River, and the Golan Heights along the border with Syria. During the fighting, Israel mistook the American intelligence-gathering ship U.S.S. *Liberty* for an enemy vessel and sank it, causing the loss of several American lives. Washington accepted Israel's apology for this unfortunate incident.

In that same month, Johnson met with his counterpart, Alexei Kosygin, at Glassboro, New Jersey. At this inconclusive meeting, the two leaders appeared to be at cross purposes. Previously, Washington had sent Moscow proposals to open talks on controlling strategic offensive missiles as well as anti-ballistic defensive missiles. When Johnson raised these issues at the commencement of the summit, Kosygin abruptly switched the topic to the Middle East. "This became a pattern during both days of our talks," Johnson noted. "Each time I mentioned missiles, Kosygin talked about Arabs and Israelis" (Johnson, 1971, p. 483). Discussions on the Middle East were contentious, Kosygin insisting that Israel withdraw to her pre-1967 borders. The two leaders did agree to have their foreign ministers resolve, in the near future, differences on an agreed draft treaty to curb the spread of nuclear weapons. Congruence was achieved in August.

Korea is another tension area in world affairs. In January, 1968, North Korea presented Johnson with one of the major challenges of his presidency. The North Koreans seized the American intelligence vessel U.S.S. *Pueblo* and towed it into port along with its crew of 82 men. Fearing that the use of force would endanger the lives of the crewmen, Johnson elected to use diplomacy. In December, 1968, the crewmen returned home.

Finally, there are indications that toward the close of the Johnson administration, both Soviet and American leaders were prepared to move off the collision course of East-West hostility toward an improvement of relations. For Washington's part, a strong motivation was to persuade the Soviets to curb their assistance to North Vietnam. Moscow was Hanoi's chief supplier, and the war was draining the Great Society and sinking Johnson's presidency. In the Soviet Union, an enormous military buildup during the 1960s was sapping economic growth. Both sides had come to the realization, not yet accepted by China, that a final showdown was mutually suicidal, and that somehow or other they must adjust to the idea that they would be sharing the planet for a long time to come. This spirit of cooperation was responsible for the Glassboro summit. However, the North Vietnamese Tet Offensive in February, 1968, and the Soviet invasion of Czechoslovakia in August of that year interrupted the relaxation of tension. Detente, as this relaxation came to be known, had to await the accession of Nixon to the White House.

VIETNAM

Every president focuses on some problems more than others, but few presidents have been as consumed with a single issue as Johnson was with Vietnam. Toward the conclusion of his tenure, Johnson and his aides were so immersed in Vietnam that they had little time or energy left for other matters. These matters included military preparedness and arms control, both of which received short shrift.

An exhaustive account of America's struggle in Vietnam exceeds the scope of this study. Our objective here will be the very limited one of describing some of the high points of American involvement, in order to demonstrate Vietnam's impact on military preparedness and the control of arms.

When President Kennedy died, 16,000 American military advisers were in South Vietnam. Washington was supplying Saigon with large doses of military and economic aid. No American troops were engaged in sustained combat.

Johnson and most of his advisers shared the outlook that brought about American involvement in Vietnam going back to support of France's efforts there in the early 1950s. In Johnson's mind, Vietnam was the appropriate place to take a stand against what he perceived to be a communist attempt to take over all of Southeast Asia and then move toward American shores. In this assessment, he was no doubt encouraged by Secretary of Defense McNamara's prediction, made shortly after Johnson assumed the presidency, that all American forces would be out by the end of 1965 (Johnson, 1971, p. 134). This was only the first of innumerable predictions by the American military that turned out to be wildly optimistic. In line with the concept of monolithic communism—which we have seen was actually crumbling—Johnson (1971) wrote,

> Hanoi was not alone in its policy of aggression....We had to be concerned not only about Vietnam but about the entire region....It became increasingly clear that Ho Chi Minh's military campaign against South Vietnam was part of a larger, much more ambitious strategy being conducted by the Communists (p. 134).

China, seen to be in league with the Soviet Union, was very much on the president's mind. Johnson and others perceived a pattern of bellicosity in Beijing's behavior. In October, 1964, China conducted its first nuclear explosion. In September of the following year, General Lin Piao, second in command to Chairman Mao, gave a well-publicized speech in which he asserted China would heartily support wars of national liberation. Communist influence was rising in Indonesia, Laos and Cambodia. North Korea was training North Vietnamese fighter pilots. To use Johnson's (1971) words:

> Thus what we saw taking shape rapidly was a Djakarta-Hanoi-Peking-Pyongyang axis, with Cambodia probably to be brought in as a junior partner and Laos to be merely absorbed by the North Vietnamese and Chinese (p. 136).

If America withdrew from South Vietnam and that country fell, "the entire region would then have been ripe for the plucking.... Clearly the decision we were making," Johnson continued, "would determine not merely the fate of Vietnam but also the shape of Asia for many years to come" (p. 136). In Johnson's eyes, the stakes were not even limited to Asia:

> If we ran out on Southeast Asia, I could see trouble ahead in every part of the globe—not just in Asia but in the Middle East and in Europe, in Africa and in Latin America. I was convinced that our retreat from this challenge would open the path to World War III (pp. 147–48).

Walt Rostow, the president's special assistant for national security, voiced another rationale widely shared by members of the Johnson administration.

> It is on this spot [Vietnam] that we have to break the liberation war—Chinese type. If we don't break it here we shall have to face it again in Thailand, Venezuela, elsewhere. Vietnam is a clear testing ground for our policy in the world (Ambrose, 1980, p. 287).

In other words, Vietnam provided a laboratory in which America could demonstrate that wars of insurgency don't work.

For the above reasons, Johnson continued Kennedy's policy of supporting the Saigon regime. In July, 1964, Johnson increased the number of American military advisers to 21,000. Like Kennedy, Johnson opposed a neutral settlement with a coalition government in Saigon. Both men viewed that outcome as a sure path to takeover of the country by the well-organized and ruthless communists. Throughout the many tortuous attempts over the next few years to work out a diplomatic settlement, Johnson was to oppose Hanoi's several calls for a cease-fire and negotiations. Despite Johnson's continuing offer to negotiate "with no prior conditions," Johnson really did impose prior conditions, namely, the withdrawal by Hanoi of all its forces from Vietnam and the absence of communist participation in Saigon's government. If the stakes in Vietnam were not just Asia but the entire world, Johnson insisted that the only acceptable outcome in Vietnam was complete victory.

America's military involvement in Vietnam, soon to burgeon to over half a million troops, was made possible by Kennedy's alteration of American military doctrine from massive retaliation to flexible response. The latter concept called for the creation of airlift, sealift, counter-insurgency troops, and the nonnuclear equipment they would need to fight in the jungle.

One month after Johnson increased the number of American advisers in Vietnam, an incident occurred that was to have a lasting effect on American military intervention. When President Johnson received reports that two American destroyers had been attacked in the Gulf of Tonkin by North Vietnamese patrol boats, he introduced in Congress the text of a resolution that had been sitting in a White House safe for weeks, awaiting a pretext for action. In introducing the Tonkin Gulf Resolution, Johnson accused Hanoi of committing open aggression on the high seas. According to the president's account, the American ships had been cruising innocently in international waters when assaulted by the North Vietnamese. The resolution amounted to a blank check for the chief executive to wage war in Southeast Asia. Devoid of a time limit, the resolution gave the president authority to use "all necessary measures" to "repel any armed attack" against American forces. The document also gave the president power to "prevent further aggression" and take "all necessary steps" to protect any nation covered by the Southeast Asia Treaty (SEATO) that might request assistance. In the emotionally charged atmosphere following reports of the North Vietnamese attacks, the Tonkin Gulf Resolution passed the House 416–0 and the Senate 88–2. Even before Congress voted on the resolution, Johnson had ordered retaliatory air strikes, under his authority as commander-in-chief of the armed forces, against North Vietnamese naval facilities on shore. This measure marked the first direct American attack upon North Vietnamese soil.

Subsequent congressional hearings revealed considerable obfuscation and less than forthright communication at the time the president reported the naval attacks. Much doubt remains whether the second reported attack ever occurred, and even whether the first alleged attack took place. The American ships suffered no damage, nor did any sailors see any North Vietnamese ships. Evidence for the existence of the vessels was based on radar. It is possible, however, that a stormy nighttime sea, not hostile vessels, accounted for the radar showings. Furthermore, the two American destroyers said to be the targets of the attacks were hardly cruising innocently. Rather, they were relaying intelligence, gathered electronically, to South Vietnamese commandos who were conducting assaults against North Vietnam.

Later, when anti-war demonstrators protested that American participation in the war was unconstitutional, because Congress had not declared war, the White House proclaimed that the Tonkin Gulf Resolution was the functional equivalent of a war declaration. Perhaps it should be added that, while Congress never did declare war, it always could have passed legislation cutting off funds and calling for a cessation of American involvement. In 1970, Congress repealed the Gulf of Tonkin Resolution, but this act had no more than symbolic value.

In early 1965, Johnson sent American troops to Vietnam to protect airbases and other facilities used in support of South Vietnamese forces. In February, Viet Cong troops attacked the American barracks at Pleiku airbase and American helicopters stationed nearby. Nine Americans died and over 100 were wounded. The communists destroyed 5 aircraft and damaged 15 others. In response, Johnson ordered the commencement of sustained bombing of North Vietnam. It was hoped that bombing would reduce the infiltration of men and supplies from the North to the South, heighten South Vietnamese morale, and damage Hanoi's willingness to fight. The bombing failed to achieve these objectives.

On April 7, 1965, Johnson made a highly publicized effort to move the Vietnam struggle from the battlefield to the conference table. In a televised address at John Hopkins University, Johnson proclaimed that Washington was prepared for unconditional discussions. In the same breath, however, he called for an independent South Vietnam "securely guaranteed and able to shape its own relationships to all others—free from outside interference—tied to no alliance—a military base for no other country." From Hanoi's viewpoint, such statements were preconditions. North Vietnam's objective was the absorption of South Vietnam into a unified Vietnam controlled by Hanoi. There was little ground for negotiation. Each side still entertained hopes of winning the war. Hanoi characterized Johnson's speech as "full of lies and deceptions." The next day, America carried out particularly intense bombing raids over North Vietnam.

By the summer of 1965, it was clear that the air war against North Vietnam was not having its intended effects. Men and equipment continued to move south. North Vietnam was not merely replacing its losses but sending whole new fighting units down the Ho Chi Minh Trail. Morale in the South was no higher, and Northern willingness to fight failed to decline.

As the communists stepped up their military activity, Johnson authorized the dispatch of additional American troops. In June, he broadened the rules of engagement, allowing American troops to go beyond perimeter defense of

American installations to seek out and destroy enemy troop concentrations.

In order to block Hanoi's control of South Vietnam, Johnson sent increasing numbers of American troops. By July, 1965, the total reached 125,000. Three years later the figure peaked at 525,000.

As the months went by, the fighting intensified. Toward late 1967–early 1968, the Pentagon released assessments asserting that North Vietnamese was tiring of the war, and that American efforts would soon bear fruit. Then, in February, 1968, came Tet. In a surprise country-wide offensive, the communists struck 36 of South Vietnam's provincial capitals, including Saigon. The communists hoped to spark an uprising of the South Vietnamese people or at least to persuade them to demand that their government join in a coalition with southern communists. Neither occurred. Instead, the communists lost 45,000 men and were forced to regroup for several months before resuming the offensive.

Johnson (1971) called Tet "the most disastrous Communist defeat of the war in Vietnam" (p. 383). In fact, the Tet offensive turned out to be the most disastrous defeat of the war for the Americans. It is true that Hanoi failed to achieve its immediate objectives. However, North Vietnam achieved something far more significant, although no one realized it at the time. The ability of the communists to mount a nationwide operation, even to the point of penetrating the American embassy compound in Saigon, demonstrated to the American people that the Pentagon's glowing reports of imminent victory were unfounded. The prospect seemed to be for an indefinite interval of fighting, resulting in the loss of additional American lives. Not long after Tet, the American commander in Vietnam, General William Westmoreland, requested an additional 206,000 American troops. This request seemed to substantiate the suspicion in American cities that the war was far from over. Johnson rejected Westmoreland's request, thus beginning the slow and tortuous winding down of American involvement. The last American soldier was not to leave until 1973.

On March 31, 1968, Johnson announced that he would not be a candidate for the Democratic nomination, so that he could devote his full attention to bringing the war to a successful conclusion. The president, already consumed by the war, also announced that, to induce Hanoi to negotiate, he was halting bombing north of the 20th Parallel. This decision spared three-fourths of North Vietnam from American air assaults.

Hanoi was still licking its wounds from the losses it suffered at Tet. On April 3, North Vietnam announced its willingness to talk. Although the announcement cheered many, discussions moved at a glacial pace. While bombs and bullets were flying in Vietnam, representatives from the United States and North Vietnam took five weeks to agree on a site for the negotiations. Paris was chosen. Actual negotiations opened May 10. As the talks dragged on without yielding agreement, the fighting in Vietnam continued apace. In the hope of moving the stalled talks and of boosting the electoral fortunes of the Democratic candidate, Hubert H. Humphrey, Johnson in late October announced the cessation of all bombing of North Vietnam. Little changed in Paris. One week later the American people elected a new president, Richard M. Nixon.

MILITARY PREPAREDNESS

One of the consequences of the Johnson administration's consuming involvement in the Vietnam war was a lack of initiative in strategic planning. In essence, the Johnson administration followed the strategic outlines set forth under Kennedy. Linking the two administrations was Secretary of Defense Robert McNamara.

In the area of strategic doctrine, Johnson and McNamara pursued two fundamental concepts, assured destruction and damage limitation.

Assured Destruction

As explained in the previous chapter, assured destruction means that the United States has the capacity to cause unacceptable levels of destruction of Soviet people and industry, even after absorbing an all-out attack by Moscow. Presumably, such a capability would deter any rational Kremlin leader from attacking the United States. Assured destruction capability rules out any possibility of a disarming first strike by the Soviets.

To determine the level of forces needed for an assured destruction capability, McNamara and his assistants applied a new technique known as systems analysis. Using computers, they compared the capacity of both sides' strategic forces to inflict damage, taking into account such factors as survivability, penetrability and reliability. According to one who participated in such force planning, McNamara felt that not only was it important to achieve assured destruction capability, but it was also crucial that the Soviets perceive that America possessed this capability. This latter requirement drove procurement more than the military needs of assured destruction. It was eventually decided that the following force levels were sufficient to guarantee assured destruction and to convince the Kremlin that the United States possessed this capability:

- 1,000 Minuteman ICBMs;
- 54 Titan II ICBMs;
- 656 SLBMs carried on 41 Polaris submarines;
- 600 B-52 long-range bombers.

Several older strategic systems were deactivated, since they were regarded as extraneous to the mission of assured destruction. Earlier Titan I and Atlas ICBMs were destroyed; the B-70 bomber program was abandoned; the nation's fleet of B-47 bombers was gradually deactivated; and intermediate-range

Chapter 4: Johnson

missiles such as Jupiter and Thor were removed from Europe. During the Johnson years, the Pentagon succeeded in building up to the strategic force levels set out above.

In establishing these force levels, DOD leaned toward worst-case planning, a not uncommon practice in military establishments worldwide. The Pentagon assumed Soviet weapons would be highly reliable, and that American systems would operate toward the low end of the reliability scale. Furthermore, each leg of the triad—bombers, ICBMs and SLBMs—was constructed so as to achieve assured destruction independent of the others. The reasons for such caution were as follows. High American force levels would strengthen the deterrent by complicating Soviet counter-force planning. America would have assured destruction even if up to two legs should collapse in combat. Should Soviet engineers achieve a technological breakthrough that could neutralize one or even two legs, Washington would still maintain assured destruction.

While such worst-case planning might have reassured Pentagon planners, how must American force levels have appeared to the generals working in the Soviet ministry of defense? Given their mistrust of the United States, Soviet defense officials must have regarded America's strategic forces as highly threatening. The Soviets could find support for such suspicions in the realization that the United States was well ahead in strategic weaponry at the onset of the Kennedy administration, yet Washington continued to build still further. Might not Soviet leaders have posed a question often heard in American circles: Is not the other side building far beyond what it needs for defense?

It goes without saying that America's strategic buildup more than offset efforts to achieve arms control in strategic weaponry. Indeed, the Johnson years prefigure the first administration of Ronald Reagan. In both cases, the chief executive perceived a strong need to build up military forces. Arms control took a back seat, perhaps to be offered a seat closer to the front at a later time.

According to Richard Garwin and Hans Bethe (1968), scientists extensively involved in strategic weaponry for many years, the United States had achieved assured destruction over the Soviet Union by the last year of the Johnson administration. At the same time, the Soviets became convinced of the merits of the doctrine and adopted it themselves. The Soviets also were determined to match American strategic forces, especially after their humiliation in the Cuban missile crisis of 1962. In consequence, the Soviets engaged in a massive military construction program, while the United States held steady at the force levels already cited. Garwin and Bethe, citing DOD statistics, observe that by October, 1967, the Soviets had 720 ICBMs, 30 SLBMs (missiles, not boats) and 155 long-range bombers. Thus, by the close of the Johnson administration, each side possessed assured destruction over the other. Mutual assured destruction (MAD) had taken hold.

Damage Limitation

While never assigned as high a priority as assured destruction, damage limitation was assiduously pursued during the early Johnson years. The objective of damage limitation was to restrict the extent of damage to the United States in case war occurred. Damage limitation can be achieved either by reliance on bomb shelters and anti-ballistic missiles (defense) or through the use of strategic weapons to destroy enemy weapons (offense). The Johnson administration elected the latter, planning to destroy Soviet missiles and bombers on the ground or—in the case of bombers—as they approached American territory. As the Johnson administration began, the low level of Soviet strategic weaponry made it seem possible to destroy enough of their weapons to significantly reduce damage to the United States in case of attack. In 1964, Soviet strategic forces consisted of 250 intercontinental bombers, less than 200 ICBMs, and a small number of submarines armed with SLBMs (Schlesinger, 1965, p. 502). One of the rationales offered for developing MIRV—to be described later—is that it would enhance damage limitation. MIRV would markedly increase the number of offensive warheads in the American arsenal, greatly improving the ratio of American warheads to Soviet missile silos and airfields.

The American force levels deemed necessary for assured destruction were also considered adequate for damage limitation. To achieve these force levels, annual spending for strategic arms during the Kennedy-Johnson years averaged around $25 billion (in 1974 dollars), approximately 30% of non-Vietnam military spending.

As a military objective, damage limitation reached its zenith in 1964. Thereafter, while rhetorical homage was paid to the concept, defense planners realized that the goal was stretching beyond reach. As we shall see shortly, the Soviet Union undertook a vast military buildup during the 1960s, in part to match American forces. The hardening of Soviet silos, following the American practice, degraded the chances of destroying Soviet missiles on the ground. By the close of the decade, the Soviets possessed too many bombers and missiles, especially SLBMs, to render damage limitation a meaningful objective. The United States decided it had no alternative other than to bare its throat to Soviet fangs, while brandishing fangs of its own to deter a Soviet strike.

MIRV

One of the most far-reaching weapons developments during the Johnson years was the multiple independently targeted re-entry vehicle, or MIRV. This weapons system, later copied by the Soviets, has accounted for a vast increase in the number of strategic warheads in the superpower arsenals. Naturally, this has severely complicated the task of arms control. Indeed, the decision to develop MIRV represents a clear choice of military preparedness over arms

Chapter 4: Johnson

control as a means of assuring national security.

According to a physicist long involved in the design of nuclear weapons, the concept of MIRV was born shortly after the Soviets launched their first satellite in October, 1957 (York, 1973). The Defense Department formed a committee, composed of several DOD elements plus representatives from industry, research groups and consulting firms, to determine whether the designers of offensive missiles should consider the possibility that the adversary could construct anti-missile missiles. In deciding that this was a possibility, the committee discussed measures the offense might use to counteract anti-missile missiles. Some of the methods mentioned in a theoretical context over thirty years ago are employed today, including decoys, chaff, and radar blackouts produced by thermonuclear explosions in the upper atmosphere. One other idea discussed by the committee was overwhelming the defense with a multitude of warheads. To achieve this, one missile would carry several warheads.

By the time Johnson took office, defense officials were troubled by reports of Soviet anti-missile activity. In 1964, Moscow displayed its Galosh interceptor missile. Intelligence reports indicated the Soviets were constructing an ABM complex around Moscow. Might not the Kremlin decide to build a nationwide ABM system? Some defense officials saw the precursor of such a system in the extensive Tallinn air defense system in place to protect the entire Soviet Union against intruding aircraft. Some specialists believed this system could be upgraded to fire anti-ballistic missiles. At the same time, a number of prominent Soviet military spokesmen publicly touted the desirability of an ABM defense and claimed the Soviet Union was making great strides in this area. Should the Soviets succeed, they would find themselves at a tremendous advantage over the United States.

Defense planning requires several years' lead time. Often, seven to ten years elapse between conceptualization of a weapon and actual deployment. In response to the feared Soviet deployment of a large-scale ABM system, the United States began to work on MIRV. A DOD study designated PEN-X demonstrated that a MIRV capability would enable the United States to penetrate any projected Soviet ABM defense (Kahan, 1975, pp. 99–101). In 1964 development of MIRV was officially authorized.

The earliest MIRV efforts differed significantly from what was to be the final product. The A-3 warhead for the Polaris SLBM actually consisted of three warheads, each with a yield of 200 kt. All three warheads were to be fired at a single target, arriving in a cluster pattern. This concept was known as MRV, for multiple re-entry vehicles. The warheads could penetrate early Soviet ABMs, because the offensive warheads would land sufficiently far apart. It was realized that more advanced Soviet ABMs would be able to take out all three warheads. One could not solve this problem by increasing the separation of the warheads, because then not all would fall inside the target area. The answer was MIRV.

Much of the technology utilized in MIRV was developed in the successful effort to devise a missile that could place more than one satellite into orbit. If a missile could release more than a single satellite, why could it not release more than a single warhead? In August, 1968, MIRV was first tested on Poseidon SLBMs (successor to Polaris) and Minuteman III ICBMs. (Later that month Moscow tested a three-warhead MIRV on its SS-9 ICBM.) The United States deployed MIRV on Poseidon SLBMs in 1971. The Poseidon missile carries twice the payload of the Polaris A-3 and can carry up to 14 independently targeted warheads. In practice, most Poseidon missiles were equipped with 10 warheads, each possessing a yield of 50 kt. Poseidon's range was 2,500 miles. The Navy is currently replacing Poseidon with Trident. Each Minuteman III missile in the Air Force's fleet carries three 200-kt warheads (being reduced to one warhead by 2003).

From the standpoint of military capability, MIRV is far superior to MRV. In actuality, MRV has no advantage over a single warhead, except that it allows one to scatter weapons over the target area. In contrast, MIRV greatly expands the number of targets that can be hit. Because each warhead is independently targeted, MIRV allows one to target many more objectives without building more missiles. Alternatively, one can aim several warheads at a single target, thereby enhancing the likelihood of destroying it. What's more, all this can be done at little additional cost, whereas the construction of a vast number of additional missiles would be extremely expensive. MIRV offered an affordable means of overwhelming the projected Soviet ABM system. MIRV also satisfied another objective of the Johnson administration, namely, to stay ahead of the Soviets in numbers of warheads (Kahan, 1975). At that time, history had not yet taught that such efforts are short-sighted, as the adversary is not prone to accept a position of inferiority. The Soviets were already demonstrating this in numbers of offensive missiles, taking great pains to catch up after the debacle in Cuba in 1962. While McNamara began to see this pattern, Johnson, more responsive to political pressures, was determined to remain ahead of the Soviets.

A successful MIRV program would clearly contribute to meeting the goals of assured destruction and damage limitation. More warheads translate into additional cities and industrial installations that can be destroyed. More warheads also allow for the targeting of stationary Soviet weapons. Furthermore, as warheads grew in accuracy, even missiles in hardened silos stood a chance of being destroyed.

From the time planners conceptualized MIRV, some defense specialists questioned the idea. Herbert Scoville, Jr., and George W. Rathjens argued that MIRV could be destabilizing. If MIRV could contribute to damage limitation by destroying the enemy's offensive weapons, MIRV could lay the basis for a successful surprise attack. Advocates of this point of view maintained that MIRV was therefore provocative and threatening. In a crisis, where nuclear war is seen as imminent but not inevitable, MIRV could precipitate a nuclear exchange. By allowing the initiator to destroy some of the enemy's ICBMs, MIRV would confer an advantage (damage limitation). The other side, knowing this, might elect to launch before the first side fires. The first side, aware of this inclination, might rush into a launch at the earliest possible moment, before all alternatives to avoiding nuclear war were exhausted. Thus, it was argued, MIRV makes nuclear war more likely in a crisis.

MIRV advocates questioned this analysis. They said that the temptation to launch a pre-emptive strike would be nil. In such a strike, the chances of knocking out the opponent's entire ICBM force would be minuscule. If the enemy could manage to place even a few warheads on target, the results would be catastrophic. Even granting that MIRV worked perfectly and knocked out the opponent's entire ICBM force, the adversary would still have SLBMs and some bombers left for retaliation. In consequence, MIRV champions alleged, it would be suicidal to try to use MIRV to limit damage in a crisis. Leaders would seek to avoid a nuclear exchange at all costs, with or without MIRV.

While most analysts view MIRV as the antithesis of arms control, there is some evidence that MIRV contributed to the signing of the ABM Treaty in 1972. According to scientist Herbert York (1973), McNamara cited the Soviet MIRV capability as a strong reason for not deploying a full-scale ABM system. Possibly, the Soviets agreed to an ABM treaty because they too realized that MIRV could overwhelm their ABM system.

Although MIRV was developed to overwhelm the country-wide ABM that Washington feared Moscow was preparing to construct, the Soviets never did build such a system. To the contrary, the Soviets signed the ABM Treaty in 1972. As Jerome Kahan (1975) observes, America's deployment of MIRV represents worst-case planning at its extreme. Could not Washington have designed and even tested MIRV but then delayed deployment until there was evidence that the Kremlin was fabricating an extended ABM? Herbert York (1973) contends that MIRV had already broken free of such rational considerations. "The decision to deploy MIRVs was made all but inevitable by the decision to develop them ... the deployment of MIRVs was debated after the development decisions were made" (p. 26).

The MIRV controversy, generally confined to the corridors of the Pentagon and think tanks, surfaced before the public during the 1968 election. In his failed bid for the Democratic nomination, Senator Eugene McCarthy came out strongly against MIRV, emphasizing the previously mentioned arguments that MIRV was destabilizing. Obviously, the senator's viewpoint did not carry the day.

Soviet Military Policy

As we have seen, the United States undertook an extensive military buildup beginning with Kennedy's decision to opt for flexible response over massive retaliation. Flexible response called for sizable increases in conventional weapons, military manpower, airlift and sealift capabilities, as well as support facilities and command and control systems to back up the newly expanded fighting forces. Flexible response also called for the creation of counterinsurgency capabilities. During the Johnson presidency, the United States surged forward in the deployment of strategic systems. After reaching its targets of 1,054 ICBMs, 656 SLBMs and some 600 long-range bombers, the United States took a great leap forward in destructive power with the development of MIRV. These programs demonstrate that both Kennedy and Johnson placed more faith in military preparedness than arms control to attain national security.

It would be more than surprising if the Soviet Union remained quiescent while America augmented its arsenal. At the time Kennedy took office, Moscow found itself in a highly disadvantageous position with respect to strategic weapons. (Knowing the truth about actual Soviet deployments, Khrushchev must have been puzzled, to say the least, by Kennedy's accusation of a missile gap in the 1960 campaign.) Moscow made extensive efforts to catch up to American strategic deployments.

The Soviets had good reason to undertake such a military buildup. Kennedy's flexible response doctrine threatened the one area where the Soviets were clearly superior, namely, conventional forces. In the middle of 1961, Washington revealed the capacity to locate and target Soviet bombers and its small missile force (Kahan, 1975). This must have aroused fears in the Kremlin that Washington could undertake a disarming first strike. America's strategic superiority doubtless played an important role in the Kremlin's retreat in the 1962 Cuban missile crisis. Under challenge from Beijing for leadership of the communist world, the Kremlin could hardly promote the communist cause under the handicap of strategic inferiority to the United States.

It is conceivable that Khrushchev hoped to avoid the astronomical cost of matching America's strategic arsenal by placing medium-range nuclear missiles in Cuba. In any case, pressure from the United States closed out this option. Accordingly, Moscow was compelled to undertake a strategic buildup if it wished to attain parity with the United States. Khrushchev ordered an increase in the production rate of SS-7 ICBMs, accelerated the development of the more advanced SS-9 and SS-11 hardened ICBMs, and called for the development of Polaris-type missile-launching submarines and the Galosh ABM interceptor missile. However, the Soviet leader did not hasten to deploy his new weapons. The military's displeasure over the slow pace of deployment was no doubt one of the reasons—though probably not the most important one—behind Khrushchev's ouster in late 1964. The new leadership team of Brezhnev and Kosygin did not hesitate to deploy the additional weapons. From the end of 1964 to 1966, the number of deployed Soviet ICBMs rose from 200 to 340. In the following year the total jumped to 730. By late 1968, the Soviets were approaching parity with the United States (Smoke, 1987, p. 125). In 1968, the

Kremlin started to deploy its new SLBMs. By the end of 1969, Soviet and American strategic forces totaled as follows:

Table 4-1: American and Soviet Strategic Forces, 1969

	Soviet Union	United States	
ICBMs	1,200	1,054	(1,000 Minutemen and 54 Titans)
SLBMs	230	656	(41 Polaris subs carrying 16 missiles each)
Long-range bombers	70 (Bears and Bisons)	540	

SOURCE: Richard Smoke, *National Security and the Nuclear Dilemma* (2nd ed.: New York: Random House, 1987), p. 126. Smoke's figures are based on *Strategic Survey, 1969* (London: Institute of Strategic Studies).

Just as Moscow was catching up to the United States, the latter spurted ahead by placing multiple warheads on its missiles. The Soviets too followed this practice, leading to the situation of parity in numbers of strategic warheads today.

From the foregoing it is clear that Moscow, like Washington, was placing its faith in military preparedness, not arms control, to assure national security. There is another side to this coin, however. In the waning months of the Johnson administration, leaders in both Washington and Moscow began to perceive the hopelessness of gaining lasting strategic superiority over the other superpower. There was also a dim mutual recognition that added weaponry was not augmenting national security despite the astronomical cost of new military hardware. Thus, the idea of limiting strategic weapons began to gain in appeal, especially once the two sides approached parity. As we shall see in a later section of this chapter, the two superpowers were prepared to discuss strategic arms limitation in the summer of 1968. The Soviet invasion of Czechoslovakia derailed these talks for a year.

Finally, Soviet military policy occasioned reduced emphasis in Washington on damage limitation. As the Kremlin deployed increasing numbers of strategic weapons, particularly SLBMs, American targeters began to give up hope of destroying these weapons before launch. Accordingly, the Pentagon devoted more emphasis to assured destruction than to damage limitation.

By the time Johnson left office, the Soviet Union, like the United States, enjoyed an assured destruction capability. Now neither side had an incentive to launch a surprise attack against the other. A certain measure of strategic stability was setting in. This promoted a positive atmosphere for opening discussions on controlling strategic arms.

Battle over the ABM

During the late 1960s, considerable controversy swirled around the question whether the United States should deploy an anti-ballistic missile (ABM) system. Interest in missile defense arose from concern over Soviet deployment of Galosh ABMs around Moscow, the Soviet strategic buildup during the latter half of the 1960s, and China's explosion of a nuclear device in 1964. Enthusiasm for constructing an ABM system was centered in Congress and the Joint Chiefs.

Analysts foresaw three alternative roles for an ABM. The first two of these roles were consistent with damage limitation. In one scheme, a thick nationwide ABM system would protect American cities, presumably against a Soviet assault. The second conception was designed to protect population centers against a Chinese attack. Inasmuch as China had only a skeletal attack capability, an anti-Chinese ABM system could be much less extensive. The third role was more consistent with assured destruction than damage limitation. In this conception, ABMs would protect Minuteman silos, thereby assuring that these ICBMs would survive an attack and inflict destruction upon the perpetrator. The first and to a lesser extent the second role disturbed some strategists, because they menaced the stability of deterrence. After all, if the United States could blunt a Soviet second strike, Washington could attack the Soviet Union with impunity. In the midst of an intense crisis, the Soviets might launch a preemptive attack, figuring that Washington was bound to attack anyway.

When ABM discussions first entered the public realm, support gathered behind the first conception above. In the public mind, protecting cities and industry is what defense is all about. McNamara and some others argued vociferously against this role. McNamara seriously doubted whether any ABM system could significantly reduce the extent of damage produced by an all-out Soviet attack. McNamara and his supporters were also convinced that a so-called "thick" ABM system would diminish strategic stability, as described above. McNamara, in fact, was opposed to the construction of any type of ABM system. Not only did he doubt the technology, but he was convinced that the Soviets and perhaps others would react by constructing additional offensive warheads. (Indeed, this is exactly how Washington behaved in reaction to fears of a Soviet ABM. Recall that this fear led to the development of MIRV.) Pro-ABM sentiment from the public, Congress, the White House and the Joint Chiefs forced McNamara to give in, and so in September, 1967, McNamara announced that the United States would build a "light" anti-Chinese ABM envisioned in the second of the three roles described above.

In an interview in *Life* magazine, McNamara explained the rationale behind the decision (Stolley, 1967). The Chinese, he said, might deploy a small force of ICBMs in the not-too-distant future. In the event of a tense confrontation, the Chinese might assume the United States would seek to destroy their small, exposed ICBM force. In order to obtain some advantage from their missiles, the Chinese might launch them at American shores. A thin ABM would be able to blunt such a modest attack. Secondly, by negating such an attack, Washington would be in a position to assure its friends in Asia that America would not be dissuaded from supporting them for fear of a Chinese nuclear riposte. McNamara went on to explain that the ABM was not designed to defend American cities against a Soviet attack. "If we deployed a defense that could greatly reduce our expected casualties, the Soviets could and would respond by increasing the size of their offensive forces—just as we have done in response to their system. In the end we would be no more secure" (Stolley, 1967, p. 28a). The system would, however, help protect ICBMs against Soviet attack, and the system would protect the American population against an accidental launch of a missile by any nuclear power, McNamara explained.

The American ABM system, known as Sentinel, was to be based at a dozen sites with a total of 1,000 launchers. Two types of missile were involved, each tipped with a nuclear warhead. The Spartan would intercept incoming warheads at a distance of a few hundred kilometers (one kilometer equals 0.6 miles). Warheads that got through the Spartan defense would be targeted by the much shorter-range Sprint ABM. The system was to be operational by the early 1970s.

Like MIRV, the decision to go forward with an ABM system represents a nod toward military preparedness over arms control as a means of enhancing national security. Also like MIRV, the ABM decision was arguably premature. Many experts on China contended that a Chinese ICBM threat was years away. There was plenty of time, they said, to put an ABM in place as the Chinese threat grew imminent; meanwhile, the Pentagon could test and perfect ABM components but not deploy them. Others argued that the best defense against a Chinese ICBM threat was the fear of retaliation by American missiles.

Like the projected nationwide Soviet ABM system against which MIRV was designed, the Chinese threat never materialized. Sentinel, like MIRV, was an example of extreme worst-case planning. It appears that the country got caught up in some sort of "ABM fever," against which cooler heads could not prevail. There was even talk of "an ABM gap" in relation to the Soviet Union.

The "thin" ABM system Washington had chosen did little to calm Soviet suspicions about American motives. Moscow was aware that a thin system could "gain weight." Such doubts were fed by statements like that of Gen. Earle G. Wheeler, Chief of Staff of the Army, who stated that Sentinel was just the beginning of a much larger ABM complex (Newhouse, 1973, pp. 96–97). While the Soviet reaction is undocumented, one can speculate that Moscow took little comfort from the American decision to deploy ABM. Already, the United States was ahead in offensive weapons. Now, Washington felt the need to construct an ABM system that, even in its thin version, was more elaborate than the Soviet Galosh. At the very least, the announcement that the United States was about to build an ABM system must have silenced Soviet foes of MIRV.

ARMS CONTROL

Not long after assuming the presidency and gathering the reins of government in hand, Johnson turned to arms control. In a letter to Khrushchev dated January 18, 1964, Johnson set forth his main objectives in the area of arms control:

- prevent the spread of nuclear weapons;
- end the production of fissionable material for weapons;
- transfer a large quantity of fissionable material away from arms production to peaceful purposes;
- ban all nuclear weapons tests;
- place limitations on nuclear weapons systems;
- reduce the risk of war by accident or design; and
- move toward general and complete disarmament. (Seaborg, 1987, pp. 7–8).

In his memoirs, Johnson (1971) said he considered slowing and ending the arms race "the most critical issue in Soviet-American relations" (p. 479). Despite these professions of high principle, Johnson made arms control a much lower priority than prosecution of the war in Asia, with the result that arms control accomplishments during his administration were less substantial than his letter to Khrushchev foretold.

Within the executive branch, high-level decisions on arms control were made by a Committee of Principals. Chaired by Secretary of State Rusk, the Committee included the ACDA director, secretary of defense, chairman of the Joint Chiefs of Staff, directors of CIA and USIA, chairman of the Atomic Energy Commission, administrator of NASA, and the president's national security and science advisors. Backstopping this group was a Committee of Deputies, which represented the same organizations at one level down. Adrian Fisher, ACDA's deputy director, chaired this body. Most disagreements were settled here, so by the time an issue reached the Committee of Principals, agreement was already forged.

The first concrete effort by the Johnson administration in the arms control area concerned the production of fissionable material. Stimulated by a letter from Khrushchev urging the great powers to set an example in controlling weapons, Johnson announced in his 1964 State of the Union Address that the United States was shutting down four plutonium piles and closing a number of non-military installations. Stating his intention to cut the production of enriched uranium suitable for bomb purposes by 25%, Johnson invited his Soviet counterpart to do likewise. Further exchanges by letter between the two leaders followed during the spring, but these communications came to nothing. Washington had a strong interest in a mutual cutback. The United States had a much larger stockpile of fissionable material and could afford to reduce production without limiting weapons it wanted to fabricate. The Soviets were in the course of conducting a major military buildup to catch the United States. Consequently, Moscow was not prepared to stem production of the material it needed for new warheads and bombs.

The standoff in Cuba gave rise to discussions of a nuclear weapons free zone (NWFZ) in Latin America. During the missile crisis, as we have observed, Moscow brought approximately 20 nuclear warheads into Cuba. In November, 1962, several Latin American countries drafted a treaty to make the continent a NWFZ. Four years later the Treaty of Tlatelolco was finalized, and the next year it was signed by all the states in the region except Cuba and Guyana. It was not until the early 1990s that Argentina and Brazil agreed to be bound by the treaty.

The Treaty of Tlatelolco stipulates that signatories will use nuclear materials and facilities for peaceful purposes only. The signatories may not test, use, produce or acquire nuclear weapons, or permit the storage or deployment of nuclear weapons by other states on their territory. Two protocols govern relations with external countries. Protocol I calls on outside states with territory in the region to place that territory under treaty restrictions. Great Britain and the Netherlands readily assented. At first Washington hesitated, observing that the limitation would apply to Puerto Rico, the Virgin Islands and the Guantanamo naval base in Cuba. Years later the United States approved the protocol, stating that it interpreted the protocol as allowing the transit of nuclear weapons through these areas.

Protocol II calls on nuclear weapons states to respect the denuclearization of Latin America and not to use or threaten to use nuclear weapons against any treaty state. The five states known to possess nuclear weapons accepted the protocol. As a warning to the Kremlin, the United States accompanied its signature with a formal statement that it would consider an armed attack by a treaty state, assisted by a nuclear weapons state, against any other treaty state to be a violation of that treaty state's obligation under the treaty.

Not long after President Kennedy signed the Limited Test Ban Treaty in 1963, negotiations began on an agreement to keep nuclear weapons out of outer space. These talks resulted in the Outer Space Treaty, signed in 1967. The treaty prohibits placing into orbit or on the moon or other celestial bodies any weapon of mass destruction. It is worth observing that the treaty does not forbid the militarization of outer space in any form. Military communication satellites and military reconnaissance satellites are just two military uses of outer space permitted by the agreement. The placement of non-nuclear weapons in outer space would not violate the treaty.

Like the Seabed treaty that was to follow some years later, the Tlatelolco Treaty and the Outer Space Treaty succeeded in closing off areas of nuclear arms competition before arms races started. In all three cases, agreement was attainable because none of the nuclear weapons powers had any immediate intention to place weapons of mass destruction in the proscribed regions. Locating nuclear weapons in outer space or on the seabed would be enormously expensive and of dubious utility. Before dismissing such agreements as meaningless, however, one must pause to consider that in the absence of such accords, the major powers would be forced to work on the applicable technologies if only to ensure that a rival did not get there first and exploit its advantages. Still, one cannot help observing that these agreements had no perceptible impact on arms competition. No power found itself constrained to give up any weapons system it had planned to build. Thus, the arms control achievements described thus far must be considered of only limited significance.

Such was not the case for the Nuclear Non-Proliferation Treaty, the outstanding arms control agreement of the Johnson years. America's interest in controlling the spread of nuclear weapons extends back to the secrecy surrounding the Manhattan Project and was carried forward in the Baruch Proposal and the safeguards provisions of Atoms-for-Peace. The French atomic explosion of 1960, followed by the Chinese detonation in 1964, lent new urgency to the subject. Kennedy was a strong believer in controlling proliferation, and he initiated discussions with Moscow on the subject in 1962. However, Kennedy harbored another objective that the Soviets insisted was the very opposite of nonproliferation. This goal was to give the West Europeans a sense that they had a share in NATO's nuclear decisions. To satisfy Western Europe's wishes on this count, Washington devised the MLF, described in the previous chapter. From the outset, Moscow displayed intense opposition to the MLF, primarily because it gave West Germany a say in NATO's nuclear decision-making. Because every proposal for non-proliferation tabled by Washington allowed for the creation of MLF, little progress was achieved toward a draft treaty to control the spread of nuclear weapons. It was only when the Europeans themselves showed little interest in MLF and Washington officially dropped it in 1965 that prospects for a non-proliferation agreement brightened. By 1967 the superpowers, working primarily through the ENDC, had agreed on a draft treaty.

The draft treaty thereupon encountered unexpected opposition from a number of non-nuclear weapons states (NNWS). In essence, these states complained, as they do to this day, that the treaty asks them to forswear the most powerful and prestigious weapons without offering them anything in return. Some saw the treaty as a poorly disguised scheme to perpetuate the predominant influence of the nuclear weapons states. An additional year of negotiation was required to satisfy the needs of the more vocal NNWS such as Brazil, Mexico, India and Canada.

Article I of the treaty put to rest Soviet fears about West Germany. The article prohibits transfer of nuclear weapons not only to NNWS but to any association of them; this provision would apply to NATO. The Soviets thereby achieved their primary non-proliferation objective. Other provisions were included to meet the demands of the NNWS. The nuclear powers agreed to help NNWS conduct nuclear explosions for peaceful purposes (such as digging canals or creating a lakebed behind a dam) and work toward the cessation of nuclear testing and reduction and elimination of their own nuclear arsenals. To give the NNWS some say over the future of the global nuclear regime, the treaty calls for a review conference every five years as well as an expiration limit of 25 years. (At the review conferences held thus far, the NNWS have berated the nuclear weapons states for glacial progress in reducing their arsenals and for conducting over 1,500 nuclear tests since the treaty.)

On July 1, 1968, the Nuclear Non-Proliferation Treaty (NPT) was signed. Today, nearly 150 nations have ratified the treaty or agreed to abide by its provisions. This high number lends substance to the global norm of controlling the spread of nuclear weapons. However, a number of states believed capable of fabricating nuclear weapons have not signed, including India, Israel, and Pakistan. Furthermore, as the case of Iraq reveals, adhering to the NPT provides no iron-clad guarantee that a country is not seeking to develop nuclear weapons. Given continued international rivalries and the refusal of the nuclear weapons states to renounce their most potent arms, an omission that reinforces the value of nuclear weapons, there seems little cause for complacency that nuclear weapons will not spread.

The NPT undoubtedly serves America's security interests. The country stands to benefit from having as few potential nuclear adversaries as possible. Should Washington decide to intervene militarily in another country, it would be far easier to make that decision regarding a non-nuclear as opposed to a nuclear nation. Statistically, an increase in the number of nuclear weapons countries boosts the probability of nuclear war; given Washington's worldwide commitments, the United States might find it difficult to abstain from such conflicts. If nuclear weapons confer diplomatic influence—as the NNWS maintain, although there is disagreement on this score—then Washington derives benefits from restricting membership in the nuclear club.

As time has evolved, strategic arms negotiations have become the touchstone of the U.S.-Soviet relationship. The groundwork for strategic arms control was laid during the Johnson administration.

At the dawn of the 1960s, neither great power showed much interest in controlling strategic weapons. The United States was more interested in filling the alleged missile gap than in emptying its weapons coffers. Shortly after the Kennedy administration had ensconced itself in office, satellite information revealed the missile gap to be a myth. As we have seen, the DOD then developed production targets based not on what weapons the Soviets actually possessed but on the quantity and quality of weapons the Soviets were capable of producing. This kind of worst-case planning led to an American inventory swollen beyond actual need. When Johnson took office, the United States enjoyed a comfortable lead over the Soviet Union in strategic weapons. It was in this context that Washington proposed a strategic weapons "freeze" to the Eighteen Nation Disarmament Commission in January, 1964. The American proposal called for a freeze on the number and characteristics of strategic nuclear offensive and defensive delivery vehicles, which included anti-ballistic missiles, long-range bombers and long-range missiles. Deployments would be restricted to existing levels. While countries could build replacements, the new items could not incorporate technological improvements over the old. Verification included on-site inspection of declared manufacturing plants, spot checks of facilities where clandestine production was suspected, and procedures to be agreed upon to guard against prohibited missile tests. Given Washington's existing 4–1 superiority over the Soviets in strategic weapons, one can understand America's interest in such an accord. For the very same reason, however, the Soviets rejected the American initiative. The Soviets also voiced their traditional objection to on-site inspection. According to an American official closely involved in these negotiations, the United States itself was not willing to accept such on-site inspection. However, the American delegation felt confident in tabling such a proposal in the certain knowledge that the Soviets would reject it (Newhouse, 1973, pp. 69–70). This would place the onus for blocking arms control squarely on Moscow. The Soviets had yet another concern, West Germany. Always distrustful of Teutonic capabilities, the Soviets hesitated to entertain a weapons freeze until they had some assurance that West Germany would not become a nuclear power. The Non-Proliferation Treaty of 1968 calmed Soviet anxieties on this count.

The Soviets responded to Washington's initiative with a plan to reduce offensive missiles to very low levels, while at the same time allowing extensive ABM deployments to protect people and weapons. Washington turned down this proposal because it lacked adequate inspection provisions, and because America's strategic doctrine called for high levels of offensive weapons in order to bring about assured destruction and damage limitation. The United States was also reluctant to forego its advantage in offensive weapons.

In the same year the United States proposed "bomber bonfires." Washington offered to destroy its fleet of B-47 medium-range bombers if the Soviets would subject their TU-16 Badgers to the same treatment. However, when Moscow had learned that the United States was planning to deactivate its B-47s anyway, it rejected the American proposal. The Soviets also valued their Badgers as a deterrent to West European, especially West German, aggression. Washington did indeed destroy its B-47s, on the ground that they were superfluous. When the Soviets then proposed the elimination of all bombers, a category in which the United States was markedly ahead, Washington said no.

For the next three years, strategic arms control took a back seat. Washington's growing involvement in Vietnam had a tendency to drive out other concerns. In both Washington and Moscow, the arms control focus shifted toward non-proliferation, where some promise of success was in the offing.

Prodded by McNamara, a firm believer in arms restraint, Johnson wrote to Kosygin in January 1967 to sound the latter's willingness to discuss limiting strategic arms, especially ABMs. McNamara greatly feared that an ABM race would spur an offensive missile race, leading to reduced security at much greater cost. The defense secretary was also aware that intense domestic political pressures from Congress and the public were at work on Johnson to build an ABM system. Kosygin agreed to discuss strategic arms limitation, but he was vague about a starting date and specific topics for negotiation. At the Glassboro, New Jersey, summit held in June, 1967, Johnson again tried to pin down a starting date for arms discussions, but Kosygin remained evasive. It took another 12 months for Moscow to agree to a starting date for talks. By that time, Johnson felt he could no longer resist political pressure to build a limited ABM system to offset the Soviet system and so announced Sentinel. Why did it take the Soviets so long to respond to Washington's offer? Perhaps Moscow wanted time to construct additional weapons so it could negotiate from near parity. Alternatively, bureaucratic in-fighting might have delayed formulation of an agreed Soviet position. At any rate, at the July, 1968, signing of the Non-Proliferation Treaty, Moscow and Washington announced that they would begin negotiations to reduce strategic arms. A summit meeting was scheduled for October, when each side was to present an opening position.

American officials scrambled to formulate a proposal. Previously, Washington had taken the stance that the surest way to limit arms was to restrict production. This called for on-site inspection of production facilities, something the Soviets would not accept and about which many Americans entertained serious reservations. Who knows what technical information Soviet inspectors might glean from their observation posts inside American plants? With the advent of satellites, Washington began to think in terms of checking deployment, which could be observed from the heavens, as opposed to production. While some cheating might be possible, any meaningful breakthrough seemed unlikely. This was the approach taken in Washington during the summer of 1968 and in the SALT negotiations that followed. This new approach contributed significantly to the first SALT agreement, signed in 1972.

During August, the Committee of Principals submitted a negotiating proposal to Johnson, who accepted it. The proposal called for a freeze on the number of strategic missiles deployed and a ceiling on ABM launchers, with equal numbers of the latter for both sides. Land-mobile missiles were banned. The two powers could not construct missile silos so as to make possible the replacement of existing missiles by larger ones. The proposal contained no qualitative limits, such as restrictions on improved accuracy, larger warhead yield, or numbers of warheads that could be carried on a single missile.

Given near parity in numbers of missiles and America's lead in warheads and MIRV technology, such a proposal did no harm to American interests.

On August 20, Soviet and East European armies invaded Czechoslovakia, putting an end to Prague's flirtation with open government. Johnson concluded that the international environment was not ripe for a summit and called off the October meeting. Now it was Moscow's turn to press for arms negotiations, perhaps to dampen the worldwide condemnation of its invasion. In late November, Washington informed Moscow of its willingness to hold a summit just before Christmas. The Soviets suddenly cooled to the idea. Johnson (1971) wrote, "I had a strong feeling that they were encouraged in that view by people who were very close to the Nixon camp" (p. 490). Strategic arms talks had to await the Nixon administration.

5

NIXON/FORD

THE DOMESTIC SETTING

The 1968 Elections

In the presidential elections of 1968, the Democrats faced a serious handicap, in that the public identified the Democratic Party with the unpopular Vietnam War. The party's image suffered another blow at the national convention in Chicago. Here, anti-war protesters sought to impress their views on party regulars by conducting street demonstrations outside the meeting hall. When the Chicago police turned their nightsticks upon the demonstrators, television cameras treated the nation to nightly scenes of disorder and violence. Regardless of who was principally at fault, unruly protesters or violence-prone police, many members of the public associated the Democratic Party with disorder and hooliganism.

The Vietnam War played a significant role in the election. By the fall of 1968, most Americans wished a cessation of the war. Doves, however, found themselves without a candidate. Vice-President Humphrey was tarred with loyal support for Johnson's war policies. Republican standard-bearer Richard M. Nixon was a traditional hawk, a position reinforced by his statement of intention on October 27 "to restore our objective of clear-cut military superiority" over the Soviet Union. Running on a third-party ticket, Alabama Governor George Wallace offered to "bomb North Vietnam back to the Stone Age." Nixon tantalized doves by asserting that he entertained a "secret plan" to end the war, a plan that he never revealed during the election.

It will be recalled that peace negotiations had commenced in May. By November, the parties had agreed to nothing beyond the shape of the negotiating table—an issue that masked the real question of what roles would be played in the talks by the Saigon regime and the Vietcong. Humphrey hinted to voters that he was at heart a dove, but he could not come out and say so while still vice-president. In a last-ditch effort to boost Humphrey's prospects, Johnson declared on October 31, five days preceding the election, a cessation of "all air, naval and artillery bombardment of North Vietnam." The action did improve Humphrey's popularity, but it came too late. Nixon won with 43.4% of the popular vote to Humphrey's 42.7%. Wallace captured 13.5%.

Anti-War Movement

Until the American withdrawal from Vietnam in 1973, the anti-war movement maintained a steady tattoo of dissonance. Through street demonstrations (such as the Chicago convention), the placing of advertisements in the media, circulation of petitions, occasional destructive activities at weapons sites and laboratories, and electioneering, the movement continually reminded the White House of its opposition to the war.

Criticism of the Vietnam War spread to an attack on the entire defense establishment. In essence, the war protesters called for a reordering of national priorities. In concrete terms, this meant reducing defense spending and transferring the "peace dividend" to spending for social programs. In addition, the anti-war movement identified American weapons and overseas bases as causes of world tension that led to increases in Soviet military spending. If America pulled in its aggressive horns, the argument went, the Soviets and others would feel less threatened and the arms spiral could be reversed. The principal lesson to be learned from Vietnam, the dissidents said, was the necessity for America to draw down its commitments overseas. Cutting military spending would force the country to reduce foreign deployments of troops. Furthermore, these critics asked, since the United States already had enough rockets and bombs to destroy all of humanity many times over, why was it necessary to procure more instruments of death and destruction?

Needless to say, President Nixon and his advisors rejected these arguments. They believed that American power was "not only morally defensible but crucial for the survival of free countries" (Kissinger, 1979, p. 202). Rather than instigating tension, they believed America's overseas deployments were responses to communist aggression. And, with the cessation of fighting in Vietnam, they asserted that America needed to build up strategic and tactical systems that had gotten short shrift during the Indochinese engagement. Kissinger disputed the anti-war movement's assertion that American restraint would generate Soviet restraint. He said,

> The Soviet leaders were likely to interpret such steps less as gestures of conciliation than as weakness.... American abdication would tempt Soviet tendencies toward filling every vacuum; the USSR would accept a stabilization of the arms race only if convinced that it would not be allowed to achieve superiority (p. 203).

The lines were clearly drawn. The White House saw the need to boost military spending, devoting particular attention to defense needs neglected during the Vietnam War. The anti-war movement and its supporters in Congress wished to curb military spending and use the newly available funds to attack social problems. In the early years of the Nixon administration, the movement targeted ABM and MIRV for cuts. In presenting his first defense budget in

February, 1970, Nixon sought to preempt his critics by reducing military spending by $5 billion to $73.5 billion (Kissinger, 1979, p. 213). The strategy did not work; Congress cut the figure by an additional $2.1 billion.

Throughout the Nixon years, the anti-war coalition exerted pressure to reduce military spending and shift the "dividend" to domestic needs. The peace movement thus had an effect on the balance between military preparedness and arms restraint. In effect, the movement served as an anchor that prevented military spending from floating to heights the White House would have preferred.

If the anti-war movement could count few successes among its efforts to reduce arms growth, it could clearly cite the Nixon Doctrine as evidence of its clout. While stopping at Guam in July, 1969, enroute to witness the splashdown of the first men to land on the moon, Nixon announced that henceforward the United States would not fight battles for its allies. Nixon pledged that America would uphold its commitments by providing a shield against direct attack on allies by the Soviet Union or China. Washington would also provide military and economic assistance to allies to fight local wars. However, the United States would not provide the manpower; this an ally must provide for itself.

The Guam statement illustrated Nixon's fine sense of politics. By asserting that America would stand by its commitments, he appealed to American hawks and American allies. The brunt of his statement, however, was directed to the swelling majority that wanted the country to limit overseas military involvement. Fortunately for Nixon, he never was forced to face the question of what to do in case an ally of vital importance proved unable to defend itself without an injection of American troops.

The Resurgence of Congress

Beginning with the presidency of Franklin D. Roosevelt, if not before, the executive branch has dominated the foreign policy process, particularly in the area of national security policy. During Nixon's second term, the legislature took steps to restore the executive-legislative balance as set forth in the Constitution. At the same time, Congress leaned away from military preparedness and in the direction of arms restraint.

A number of factors accounted for the resurgence of Congress. Watergate—to be described shortly—temporarily crippled the presidency, providing an opening for Congress to seize back some of its lost powers. Congress bristled at the arrogant and off-handed way the Nixon administration treated the legislature; the Nixon White House cloaked itself in unprecedented secrecy and made little effort to hide its disregard for contributions from Capitol Hill. A sudden influx of youthful congressmen and congresswomen exhibited little of the traditional legislative deference toward the executive branch. In addition, the postwar consensus on the need to oppose a communist monolith intent on dominating the world had broken down. Many officials with policy-making responsibility doubted Moscow's determination to take over the world and even identified some areas of common ground with Moscow, such as avoiding nuclear war and improving the environment. If the nation were no longer locked in a life-or-death struggle with the Soviets, many members of Congress felt there was little need to defer to an almighty chief executive. Perhaps the most important reason for congressional renascence in foreign policy was the simple fact that the "best and the brightest" in the executive branch had involved the United States in a colossal blunder in Indochina. Such a failure made the White House vulnerable to assault from the other end of Pennsylvania Avenue.

The resurgence of Congress took many forms. The War Powers Act of 1973, passed over Nixon's veto, permitted the president to send troops overseas for no longer than 60 days (extendable to 90 if the president deemed it necessary) unless Congress approved a longer period. That same year, Congress disallowed funding for any additional military action in Cambodia. The Jackson-Vanik Amendment denied the Soviet Union most-favored-nation status, unless Moscow agreed in advance to the emigration of a specified number of Jews. The Stevenson Amendment limited the extent of new Export-Import Bank credits to the Soviet Union. In the summer of 1975, the pro-Israeli Senate blocked the sale of Hawk anti-aircraft missiles to Jordan. The following year, the House banned further covert military aid to the UNITA insurgent movement in Angola. The House and Senate each conducted searching investigations of the nation's intelligence agencies, focusing on covert operations. When President Nixon brought back the SALT agreements from the 1972 summit meeting in Moscow, Congress pored over the documents with exceeding care.

One of the clearest signs of congressional regeneration can be seen in military outlays. Here the Senate was particularly assertive. Throughout the 1970s, defense spending steadily declined. Measured in constant dollars, defense outlays in FY 1979 were 29% lower than they had been in FY 1969. While the 1969 figure includes spending for Vietnam, the decline is significant even discounting this item (Muravchik, 1980, p. 8).

Congressional activism in foreign policy put a brake on the Nixon administration's predilection to use force. The legislature demonstrated a preference for diplomacy and the control of arms.

The 1972 Elections

In 1972 the Democrats nominated Senator George McGovern from South Dakota to challenge Nixon for the presidency. If nothing else, the election provided the American people with a genuine choice. As opposed to the conservative Nixon, McGovern alienated most mainstream Americans by gathering around himself proponents of the counter-culture: gays, hippies and political radicals. The Senator urged immediate withdrawal from Vietnam and a major reduction in the defense budget. He also promised to spend the ensuing "peace dividend" for social programs. Then on October 26, just a few days before the election, North Vietnamese peace negotiator Le Duc Tho announced his willingness to sign an accord. As Kissinger announced that "peace is at hand," McGovern lost his cardinal issue.

Nixon won by the largest electoral majority in the twentieth century up to that time. The Democrats continued to control both houses of Congress.

Watergate and the Ford Administration

The 1972 break-in at Democratic presidential campaign headquarters at the Watergate building aroused little public interest until Congress opened hearings in mid-1973. By the end of the following year, many of Nixon's top assistants had resigned in disgrace. As the House of Representatives was preparing impeachment papers, Nixon himself resigned in August, 1974.

The full story of Watergate has been told in countless volumes. Here, we are interested in the episode's effect on military preparedness and arms control. It would be an error to say the investigation pushed the country in either direction. Instead, Watergate proved a ball and chain, slowing movement in any direction, foreign or domestic. By early 1974 Nixon and his chief aides were devoting almost all their time and attention to coping with the political fallout from the investigation. At the same time, the SALT II negotiations were under way. Because of Watergate, Nixon was less able than he might have been to concentrate on forging a united American position on SALT. Even Henry Kissinger, who by this time was practically running foreign policy, could not totally avoid entanglement in the Watergate investigation. In short, Watergate slowed the arms talks. Kissinger observed, "Watergate prevented the full fruition of the prospects then before us, not only in nurturing U.S.-Soviet relations but more generally in developing a new structure of international relations" (p. 1254).

Nixon was succeeded by Vice-President Gerald Ford. Continuity of key personnel, including Kissinger and the rest of the Cabinet, greatly facilitated a smooth transition.

The Ford administration was largely absorbed in domestic matters. One of Ford's earliest acts, pardon of Nixon for any criminal acts he may have committed while in office, aroused much public controversy. A severe economic recession in 1974–75 captured the attention of the public and government alike. One of the foremost tasks facing Ford, the first president who had never been elected to national office, was restoration of the people's confidence in government. The Watergate scandal, the ongoing Vietnam quagmire, and the investigations of the intelligence community that revealed numerous illegalities—including efforts to assassinate Fidel Castro and Patrice Lumumba of Zaire—had depleted the public's respect for government.

The Nixon policy of detente was also coming under fire. As evidence that detente was not promoting a safer world, opponents of the policy cited the collapse of Vietnam and Cambodia in April, 1975, the advance of Soviet and Cuban-supported forces in Angola, and cavalier disregard of human rights in the Soviet Union. Two former secretaries of defense, Melvin Laird and James Schlesinger, denounced detente. They were joined by California Governor Ronald Reagan, who was preparing to challenge Ford for the 1976 GOP nomination.

The above accumulation of domestic matters occupied much of the Ford administration's attention. It was therefore not a time of significant movement on either arms control or military preparedness.

THE INTERNATIONAL CONTEXT

Relations with the Soviet Union

In his 1969 Inaugural Address, Nixon proclaimed his intention to replace "a period of confrontation" with "an era of negotiation." Both superpowers had incentives to improve relations. Washington hoped to prod Moscow to soften Hanoi's bargaining position and help bring about an acceptable peace in Vietnam. Washington also aspired to exploit the Sino-Soviet rift as a way of gaining bargaining leverage with each nation. For their part, the Soviets sought trade and advanced technology from the West, both needed to modernize their stagnating economy. The Kremlin also wished to place limits on Washington's growing friendliness toward China by offering the United States the prospect of benefits from better relations with Moscow. Clashes with Chinese soldiers along the Ussuri River in 1969 reminded the Soviets of the need to avoid facing two mighty antagonists at the same time. The Soviet Union also wanted to gain Western recognition of Europe's postwar boundaries, which reflected communist gains imposed after World War II. If the United States accepted these boundaries, Moscow reasoned, other Western countries would follow. But to achieve American acceptance, better superpower relations were needed. (The West accepted the boundaries at the 1975 Helsinki Conference, to be described later.)

The drive for improved relations with the Soviet Union reflected rejection of the viewpoint that international politics is a contest between good and evil, with one side destined to triumph in the end. Nixon and Kissinger accepted the fact that one cannot eliminate states with different ideologies. The most one can hope to achieve is to influence the international behavior of such regimes. Since the United States and the Soviet Union were going to share the planet, one should strive, in the nuclear age, to make such coexistence as risk-free as possible. The key to such a strategy, in the minds of American leaders, was a balance of power. Only military parity would deprive either power of hope of overcoming the other.

Detente was the term coined to describe the new superpower relationship. Detente meant relaxation of tensions, not, as some believed, the abolition of differences. "At root, detente was a collaborative effort to regulate certain aspects of the superpower relationship within a larger context of continuing rivalry" (Blacker, 1987, p. 101). Liberals welcomed detente as an obituary for the cold war. They saw it as signifying a decided shift from confrontation to cooperation. Conservatives tended to view detente as a Soviet plot to gain unilateral advantage by negotiating arms pacts unfavorable to the United States and intervening in the affairs of other countries. Still others saw detente as a new strategy of containment; by offering carrots as well as sticks, the United States would give the Soviet Union an incentive to act with moderation. This last explanation seems closest to the concept of detente entertained by Nixon and Kissinger.

In all likelihood, the Soviets also attributed different meanings to detente. The most hawkish of Soviet strategists no doubt saw detente as a framework for making the world safe for continuation of the class struggle. It would not be surprising if other Soviet thinkers attributed to detente meanings that mirrored the various American conceptions.

Central to detente was the idea of linkage, advanced most enthusiastically by Henry Kissinger. According to this concept, all facets of the U.S.-Soviet relationship would be "linked" to each other. Consequently, if the Soviets wished to acquire credits, most-favored-nation status and advanced technology, they would have to act with restraint in southern Africa and Southeast Asia. There is little doubt that the Soviets longed for economic assistance from the West, particularly the United States. As the decade of the 1970s opened, Soviet economic growth rates were declining, particularly in such leading edge sectors as computers, petrochemicals and electronics. Agriculture presented another conundrum for the Soviets. Kissinger hoped to link Moscow's desire for economic assistance to foreign policy restraint. In particular, he hoped to use economic leverage to induce the Soviets to curtail the flow of arms to North Vietnam and to block Soviet meddling in the Middle East.

Linkage, however, was "disjointed" by Congress. The Jackson-Vanik Amendment and the Stevenson Amendment, previously described, deprived Kissinger and Nixon of the economic benefits they planned to dangle before Kremlin decision-makers. When the Soviets realized they were not going to achieve the economic benefits they coveted, they had little incentive to show the restraint called for by the White House.

By the closing days of the Ford administration, detente was in full retreat. Many in the United States were convinced that the Soviets had used detente to take advantage of American moderation. Remarks by Brezhnev at the 25th Communist Party Congress in February, 1976, lent credence to this view. Brezhnev said,

> Detente does not in the least abolish, nor can it abolish or change, the laws of the class struggle. No one can expect that under conditions of detente communists will make peace with capitalist exploitation....We do not conceal that we see in detente a path to the creation of more favorable conditions for peaceful socialist and communist construction (Garthoff, 1985, p. 553).

American critics of detente pointed to Soviet and Cuban support of guerrillas in Angola, the continuing Soviet arms buildup, and Soviet meddling in Ethiopia and the Middle East as evidence that Brezhnev mean what he said. These actions violated the spirit of detente, as the Kremlin seemed intent on achieving unilateral advantage. The Soviets were quick to point out that the United States was guilty of violating detente by freezing Moscow out of Middle East diplomacy following the 1973 war, enacting the Jackson-Vanik Amendment, and publicly denouncing Soviet human rights practices. In retrospect, it appears that each superpower felt that under detente it had the right to forward its interests, but the other superpower did not.

As the 1976 election cycle began, many prominent Americans condemned detente, including former Secretary of Defense James Schlesinger, arms negotiator Paul Nitze, former Chief of Naval Operations Admiral Elmo Zumwalt, and Senator Henry Jackson. Ronald Reagan made a strong bid for the GOP nomination on an anti-detente platform. In order to distance himself from the now unpopular concept, Ford declared that he was abandoning the word detente and henceforth campaigned for a policy of "peace through strength."

The demise of detente was hardly conducive to arms control. The control of arms best flourishes in an environment marked by restraint, consultation, renunciation of unilateral advantage, and cooperation on matters of mutual benefit. The SALT I agreement was a product of such an environment and in turn helped perpetuate it. The failure to achieve a second SALT pact during the Nixon/Ford years was due in part to a worsening of the international environment, and it also accelerated that deterioration. Along with the demise of detente came a renewed emphasis on military preparedness.

In the early years of the Nixon administration, however, detente captured the popular imagination. Concrete form was given to what Nixon dubbed "the new structure of peace" at the May, 1972, summit held in Moscow. The centerpiece of this meeting was the SALT I Treaty, to be described later. The two leaders signed numerous other agreements, which established bilateral cooperation in trade, science and technology, medicine and public health, environmental protection, space exploration, and the avoidance of naval incidents. These pacts gave life to linkage. Supposedly, they would give the Soviets incentives to be cooperative so as not to jeopardize the benefits conferred by these joint efforts. The heads of state achieved a meeting of minds on other issues. Nixon agreed to attend a conference on European security; in return, Brezhnev consented to begin talks on reducing troop levels in Central Europe. Strategic arms talks resumed in November.

One of the items signed at the summit was the Basic Principles of Relations Between the United States of America and the Union of Soviet Socialist Republics. This Basic Principles Agreement was drafted to codify new principles of behavior suggested by the term detente. The pact stated that the two powers will conduct their relations on the "basis of peaceful coexistence" and will try to develop "normal relations based on the principles of sovereignty, equality, noninterference in internal affairs and mutual advantage." In the agreement, the two leaders pledged to forgo efforts to "obtain unilateral advantage at the expense of the other." They also promised to conduct their relations "based on the principle of equality and the renunciation of the use or threat of force." The two heads of state also signified their intention to expand cultural, scientific and other exchanges, work for arms limitation, expand commercial ties, and exchange views.

While the Soviets trumpeted the Basic Principles Agreement as being of historic significance, Nixon and Kissinger attached relatively little importance to it. Pragmatists that they were, the Americans were persuaded that governments will act in their own interests, regardless of written pledges. Subsequently, Washington relied on the agreement not to guide its own actions but as a yardstick to measure Soviet behavior—or rather, misbehavior, as represented by Soviet efforts to achieve unilateral advantage in the Middle East and Angola. There is no evidence that the agreement stopped either power from taking actions that served its interests.

In the summer following the summit, American grain companies contracted with the Soviet Union to sell 400 million bushels of wheat for about $700 million. By the end of the year, the Soviets had purchased over $1 billion in American agricultural products, much of it at prices very favorable to the USSR. In October, 1975, the United States and the Soviet Union signed a long-term grain agreement calling for Soviet purchases of a minimum of 6 million tons of wheat and corn annually for the next five years. Following the Soviet invasion of Afghanistan in December, 1979, President Carter suspended new grain shipments to the Soviet Union. President Reagan, in an effort to provide relief to farmers and earn their political support, allowed new agreements to be concluded.

Building on the momentum of detente and the Moscow summit, Nixon and Brezhnev met again, this time in America in June of 1973. The SALT II negotiations, which had become the centerpiece of detente, were progressing at a snail's pace since their resumption in November, 1972. Inasmuch as the Soviets were on the verge of MIRVing their missiles, they were not anxious to accept limits on offensive weapons. The best the leaders could work out at the summit was a statement of seven vague principles to guide additional SALT talks and the setting of the end of 1974 as the deadline for completing a second agreement on offensive strategic arms. The two leaders also established four new areas of bilateral joint activity, namely, oceanography, transportation, agriculture, and the peaceful uses of atomic energy. Finally, Brezhnev and Nixon initialed an Agreement for the Prevention of Nuclear War. The Kremlin had long been calling for a statement renouncing the use of nuclear weapons. Washington objected, since the defense of Europe is predicated on the use of such weapons. The eight-article agreement signed in 1973 called for "urgent consultations" between the Soviet Union and the United States if relations between them, or between one of them and another country (presumably China), would "appear to involve the risk of nuclear conflict." In actuality, the pact added little to safeguards already accepted by the superpowers. The final communique issued at the conclusion of the summit stated that talks on reducing military forces in Central Europe would open in Vienna October 30. (These talks were known as the Mutual and Balanced Force Reduction talks, or MBFR.) Nixon wanted these negotiations as a counterpart to the European security conference scheduled to begin in July. While devoid of any spectacular achievements, the 1973 summit consolidated detente and symbolized the movement toward cooperation and away from confrontation.

Preserving detente seemed to call for annual meetings between the leaders of the two superpowers. In mid-1974 Brezhnev and Nixon met again, this time in Moscow. By this time, American conservatives, such as Senator Henry Jackson of Washington, were beginning to criticize detente. They pointed to a continuing Soviet military buildup, Soviet efforts to seek unilateral advantage in the 1973 Middle East war (to be discussed forthwith), and Soviet support for the MPLA faction fighting to gain control of Angola. In America, the Watergate hearings cast a dark shadow over the presidency, weakening Nixon's ability to impart vitality to the detente process.

The 1974 summit was one last attempt to preserve detente. The strategic arms talks had made negligible progress. Unable to resolve any of the issues that blocked an accord, the two leaders took the hardly dramatic step of pledging to work toward a ten-year accord to cover the period extending to 1985. The leaders also agreed to reduce the number of sites permitted under the ABM Treaty from two to one. Nixon was encouraged to take this step by the refusal of Congress to appropriate funds for the Washington, D.C. site. The Soviet Union proposed a comprehensive nuclear test ban. Washington refused. The two sides did work out a treaty limiting underground nuclear explosions to 150 kt each. On account of verification questions raised in the United States, the U.S. did not ratify the agreement until the early 1990s. Nixon and Brezhnev agreed that their countries would work on a pact "to overcome the dangers of the use of environmental modification techniques for military purposes." This effort culminated in the Environmental Modification Treaty signed by Jimmy Carter in 1977. In addition, the two sides signed agreements to cooperate in energy, artificial heart research and housing. They also decided to open consulates in Kiev and New York City. Finally, they scheduled an "interim summit" late in the year with the purpose of accelerating agreement on controlling strategic arms.

Before quitting this overview of U.S.-Soviet relations, mention deserves to be made of a subject that was beginning to trouble some American officials toward the end of the Nixon/Ford era. Every year the CIA produces an estimate of Soviet military power. In response to allegations that the CIA had underestimated Soviet military power, CIA Director George Bush in 1976 appointed a group of outside experts to check on the CIA's estimate. This group, dubbed "Team B," included such staunch conservatives as arms negotiator Paul Nitze, Professor Richard E. Pipes of Harvard, and retired General Daniel O. Graham. Team B did indeed confirm suspicions that CIA estimates of Soviet military power were low. This highly publicized exercise contributed to the rising conviction that under detente the United States was falling behind the Soviet Union, and that the latter was using detente as a smokescreen to advance its interests worldwide at America's expense.

China

The most dramatic development in Nixon's foreign policy was the opening toward China, secured during the president's visit to Peking in February, 1972. The China visit reversed over two decades of acrimony between the two powers. Nixon's China initiative was motivated, in part, by the expectation of direct benefits from having relations with China. Nixon hoped, in vain as it turned out, to persuade Peking to reduce its aid to North Vietnam. Visions of a teeming Chinese market for American goods also proved enticing. Nixon further expected the opening to China would heighten Washington's leverage over Moscow. In the words of one Russian, the Chinese represented "one billion axe handles." By implication, Washington might strengthen those axe handles should the Soviets prove obdurate on such issues as limiting strategic weapons, promoting European stability, and refraining from troublesome meddling in the Middle East. Nixon, ever mindful of political fallout, also stood to gain by massive television coverage of the epochal meeting with the Chinese leader Mao Zedong. The Chinese, for their part, sought American support against the Soviet menace, a threat made immediate by Sino-Soviet fighting along the Ussuri and Amur Rivers in 1969.

Taiwan proved to be a major sticking point in the negotiations. Washington maintained a defense treaty with Taiwan, which China regarded as one of its provinces. In a communique issued at the conclusion of the summit, the United States agreed to remove gradually—but not immediately, as China wished—its military forces from the island and not to interfere in any "peaceful settlement" between Peking and Taipei. The communique also explicitly recognized China's claim that Taiwan was a part of China. In essence, Nixon and Mao agreed to set aside the Taiwan issue for later resolution. The matter proved more intractable than expected, however, and full normalization of relations had to await 1979.

Germany

Ever since World War II, a divided Germany and a divided Berlin represented flash points. On more than one occasion, tensions over Germany threatened to erupt into war. In late 1969, Willy Brandt was elected chancellor of West Germany. His foreign policy of *Ostpolitik* sought to generate improved relations with Eastern Europe and the Soviet Union, both of which entertained fears of renewed German aggression. The following year, West Germany signed a nonaggression pact with Moscow. Similar accords with Poland, Czechoslovakia, and East Germany followed in the next few years. In 1971, an accord providing for better communications among the sectors of divided Berlin was signed by the United States, United Kingdom, France and the Soviet Union. This pact, plus a more comprehensive agreement on Berlin signed the following year, defused Germany as an explosive factor in East-West relations. In all probability, the reassurance that these agreements provided contributed to the success of SALT I and the movement toward detente in the 1970s.

Helsinki Accords

Soviet anxieties about Central Europe were further soothed by the Conference on Security and Cooperation in Europe, which began in Helsinki in 1973. For years the Soviets had been pressing for formal ratification of the boundaries of Europe established after World War II. Most particularly, Moscow sought assurance that Germany would remain divided and would not lay claim to any land lost in the east during that conflict. The Kremlin also desired international recognition of land it had seized from eastern Poland during the war. Juridical confirmation of the status quo in Central Europe would also legitimize communist control over the region.

Western interest in an elaborate formal conference for such purposes was grudging at best. At the same time, West Europeans were anxious to dissolve East-West barriers as much as possible in order to increase trade, seen as helpful in reviving sluggish Western economies, and facilitate family visits. The East too favored additional trade, as this might bring it consumer goods and technology from the West. Eventually a package deal was arranged. The West agreed to discuss boundaries if the Soviets would talk about force reductions in Central Europe and human rights.

Virtually all the countries in Europe plus Canada and the United States participated in the 35-nation meeting in Helsinki. The negotiations lasted for two years, culminating in a document known as the Final Act. Like the negotiations themselves, the Final Act was divided into three parts. The first of the three sections or "baskets," as they were called, dealt with national security. Here the

Soviets got their wish, as the conferees accepted existing frontiers in Europe. In addition to reaffirming respect for sovereignty and nonresort to force or the threat of force, the signatories agreed to a so-called "confidence building measure" (CBM). This called for prior notification of any military maneuvers involving 25,000 or more troops. The measure also called for exchange of observers and the prior notification of major military movements. These steps were designed to reduce suspicion that one party might be planning a surprise attack.

The second basket provided for increased cooperation in trade, science, technology and the environment.

Surprisingly, the third basket occasioned the most controversy and led to the greatest number of recriminations following the conference. To obtain Western ratification of territorial boundaries, the Soviets were compelled to agree to respect a set of human rights put forth by the West. These rights included the freer movement of people both within borders and between them, increased family visits and reunifications of family members residing in different countries, cultural exchange, and freedom to disseminate information. Thereafter, the West adopted the Helsinki standards as a yardstick by which to measure the human rights performances of various communist governments. In many cases, the West claimed that the communists failed the test. Time and again, President Jimmy Carter flayed the Soviets for failing to live up to the human rights standards set at Helsinki.

While it is true that the West, and particularly the United States, used basket three criteria to chastise the Soviet bloc, the affirmation of the territorial status quo, so desired by Moscow, did contribute to an easing of suspicions. For this reason, the Helsinki Accords helped fashion an atmosphere that allowed for arms control negotiations (such as SALT II) to continue. Indeed, late in 1973 talks began in Vienna on reducing troops and armaments in Central Europe. These negotiations, known as the Mutual and Balanced Force Reduction talks (MBFR), will be described in a subsequent section.

Middle East War

If the Conference on Security and Cooperation in Europe advanced the spirit of cooperation between East and West, circumstances surrounding the Middle East war of 1973 had just the opposite effect.

It will be recalled that at the 1972 summit, Nixon and Brezhnev initialed the Basic Principles Agreement, which renounced unilateral advantage and called for mutual restraint as well as consultation in the event of incipient crisis. In Washington's eyes, Moscow violated that accord in its handling of events in the Middle East.

Following the 1967 war, during which Israel absorbed much territory at Arab expense, President Anwar Sadat of Egypt vowed to restore the honor of his army and his country by dealing a military defeat to the Israelis. Sadat enlisted the cooperation of Syria, which had lost the Golan Heights to Israel, in planning a military attack on the Jewish state. To achieve victory, however, the Arabs needed additional weapons and equipment. Sadat turned to the Kremlin, which proved more than forthcoming on the supply of such necessities as bridging equipment, ground-to-air missiles, and devastatingly accurate anti-tank missiles. While the Soviets might not have known the date of the surprise attack, they certainly knew a war was coming. The Basic Principles Agreement obligated Moscow to inform Washington of the impending crisis. Moscow said nothing. No doubt, the Soviets hoped to win a foothold in the Middle East in the form of gratitude for providing vital supplies to the victorious Arabs. This bid for unilateral advantage was precisely what the Basic Principles Agreement forbade.

The Egyptian-Syrian attack on Yom Kippur (October 6, 1973), the holiest day in the Jewish calendar, surprised the Israelis and drove them off the Golan Heights and back in the Sinai toward Israel proper. As the stunned Israelis regrouped, the Soviets resupplied their jubilant clients. Israel too needed additional equipment and tapped its traditional source, the United States, which responded with a massive airlift. In contravention of the Basic Principles Agreement, both superpowers once again were dueling through proxies.

The Israeli counterattack drove the Syrians back off the Golan Heights and surrounded 30,000 Egyptian troops that made up the Third Army, spearhead of the Sinai attack. As another Israeli victory appeared in the making, Brezhnev proposed to Washington that both powers send a joint expeditionary force to enforce a cease-fire ordered by the Security Council and rescue Egypt's encircled troops. The Soviet leader added that if the United States demurred, the Soviets would go in alone.

At the time, Nixon was mired in Watergate. Henry Kissinger was the architect of policy. The last thing Kissinger wished to see was American troops in combat with the Israelis; he rejected Moscow's proposal for a joint expedition. He also dreaded a unilateral Soviet military presence in the region. To dissuade the Soviets from intervening, Kissinger convinced Nixon to place American military forces on alert, at the same time warning the Soviets not to send in the seven combat-ready, airborne divisions the CIA reported were prepared to land in the Middle East. The Soviets took the threat seriously and set aside plans to intervene. The Israelis allowed the Third Army to escape back to Egypt. The war was over, with the territorial boundaries approximately back to where they were before the fighting began. Through extensive shuttle diplomacy, Kissinger worked out disengagement agreements between the Israelis and both Egypt and Syria.

The October war made it clear to Washington that, despite the good feeling generated at recent summits and the signing of the Basic Principles Agreement, the Soviets continued to seek unilateral advantage. The Soviets, for their part, entertained the identical image of the U.S., exemplified by Nixon's efforts to bring down the leftist government of Chile. The superpower contest was far from over. A neither-war-nor-peace stand-off prevailed. Soviet conduct during the Middle East war reinforced the position of those who claimed the Soviets were exploiting detente, warned of the perils of arms control, and admonished the United States to keep its powder dry.

Angola

The Angolan episode further soured superpower relations and strengthened those in the United States who advocated a vigilant and potent military force.

After a bloodless coup in 1974 overthrew the Portuguese dictatorship of Marcello Caetano, the new regime elected to grant independence to Angola, Mozambique, and Guinea-Bissau. In Angola three parties based on tribal affiliations vied for power. The situation proved a lightning rod for outside intervention. Much controversy swirls around the question of who intervened first, each superpower accusing the other of being the first to enter the fray. Cuba, China and South Africa also intervened before the Soviet-supported faction, MPLA, finally triumphed. With the certain approval of the Soviets, Cuba dispatched 12,000 soldiers to stiffen MPLA ranks. Moscow sent jet fighters, mortars, rockets, armored cars, and ground-to-air missiles, along with a complement of military advisers. Over strenuous objection from Kissinger, the U.S. Senate, fearing another Vietnam, blocked the continuation of American aid. Communist assistance proved decisive in MPLA's victory.

In the Angolan conflict, both superpowers revealed their willingness to set aside the harmonious spirit enshrined in the Basic Principles Agreement. The Angolan incident seriously frayed the fabric of detente. As Kissinger testified before a congressional committee on January 30, 1976, referring to Soviet actions, "A continuation of actions like those in Angola must threaten the entire web of Soviet-U.S. relations" (Quoted in Garthoff, 1985, p. 549).

Southeast Asia

Events in Southeast Asia, to be discussed more fully in the next section, provided further ammunition to those who argued the United States must avoid the pitfalls of arms control and instead build up military strength. In April, 1975, South Vietnam and Cambodia fell to communist forces. At long last, the Vietnam war was over, the first war in recent memory that America lost.

In May, President Ford found an occasion to demonstrate that the United States was not a paper tiger. Cambodian communist (Khmer Rouge) naval units seized the American cargo ship Mayaguez. Unknown to the White House, the Cambodians freed the American crew. In a misguided effort to rescue the already-released crew, American forces launched an attack in which 40 Americans died. Despite the error, most Americans applauded Ford's tough stance. The Mayaguez episode was the GOP's last opportunity to display resolve in the wake of setbacks in Indochina, Angola and the Middle East (where oil prices had risen by four times following the 1973 war).

VIETNAM

Like his predecessor, Nixon found himself saddled with a war in Southeast Asia. We shall limit concern with Vietnam to the major turning points that had some bearing on the administration's general tilt toward military preparedness or arms control. Overall, America's proxy war against communism heightened a siege mentality in America and hardly facilitated arms control. Nevertheless, SALT I and the Nonproliferation Treaty were concluded during the Vietnam War, muddying the impact of the conflict upon the choice between arms control and military preparedness.

As mentioned previously, Nixon assured voters during the 1968 election campaign that he had a "secret plan" to end the Vietnam war. This plan proved to be Vietnamization. Vietnamization meant that the United States would gradually turn the fighting over to the South Vietnamese, who were playing only an auxiliary military role in the late 1960s. Nixon's secret plan reflected the sober assessment that Johnson's hope of an outright American victory was illusory. Instead, Washington would provide the wherewithal for the Army of South Vietnam (ARVN) to carry on the struggle. Thus, America could claim that it was not deserting its ally. Hopefully, the ARVN would defeat North Vietnamese forces and their southern cadres. As a fallback position, Nixon and his aides hoped that Hanoi could be persuaded to accept a compromise settlement, by making it clear that the communists could not expect to triumph on the battlefield. This assurance was to be conveyed by massive assistance to the ARVN forces as well as the prospect of continued American bombing. Such an outcome would permit the United States to claim that it had achieved the "honorable peace" it had sought. As a worst-case scenario, Saigon might lose the war, but only after a "decent interval" following America's withdrawal. In that unhoped-for event, responsibility for the defeat would rest on the shoulders of Saigon, not Washington.

Vietnamization was also part of the home front campaign against the antiwar movement. As American troops began returning home, and the American body count plummeted, Nixon hoped to defuse the anti-war movement. To be sure, he felt, a small number of radicals would protest the war until the very last cordite fumes drifted away from the battlefield. However, he hoped, the vast "silent majority" would consent to continuing aid to the ARVN. A cynic might say that all Vietnamization achieved was "to change the color of the corpses." Nixon hoped it would give him necessary breathing room to achieve an honorable peace.

Why, it might be asked, did not Nixon simply withdraw American troops and declare an end to American participation in the war, if he so badly desired to terminate America's involvement? No doubt many Americans, perhaps a majority, would have applauded such a move. Nixon and Kissinger, however, were even more concerned with great-power relations than they were with the outcome in Vietnam. Viewing Moscow as an aggressive adversary, Nixon and Kissinger feared that an American military defeat, no how matter artfully papered over, would send a signal to Moscow that America was an easy mark. Once the Kremlin became convinced that "when the going gets tough the Americans get going," Moscow might see opportunities all over the globe to extend its sway. Detente would crumble; Nixon and Kissinger believed that a major reason the Soviets accepted detente was their conviction that they could not prevail in military or political confrontations. Furthermore, China had little interest in a feeble America, for such an ally would be of no assistance in discouraging the Soviets from threatening the Asian giant. Once China lost interest in America, Washington could no longer play the "China card" against the Soviet Union.

These considerations also affected the government's position on military preparedness and arms control. Nixon and Kissinger had little faith in Moscow's forbearance or good will. Should the Kremlin convince itself that America was a vacillating adversary, the Soviets might set aside arms control and bid for military superiority. Such a gambit, of course, would ratchet up the arms race, throwing the United States clearly on the side of military preparedness.

In June, 1969, Nixon announced that he was pulling 25,000 American troops out of South Vietnam. So began the gradual winding down of American involvement in the fighting, an involvement that ended only in January, 1973. As American troops left, Nixon did multiply assistance to the ARVN, as implied by the concept of Vietnamization. American air power continued to pound communist positions up to the very final moment of American's participation in the war.

While Nixon began to reduce America's involvement in Vietnam, he broadened American participation in neighboring Cambodia. In response to a major North Vietnamese offensive in February, 1969, Nixon secretly ordered bombing of communist supply routes in Cambodia. In April of the following year, Nixon hoped to deal a serious blow to the entire communist effort in Indochina by capturing the command headquarters that guided the war effort. This structure, known as COSVN, was said to be based in Cambodia. In his April 30 announcement that American troops had invaded Cambodia, Nixon asserted that the capture of COSVN would bring the war to a conclusion. As it turned out, Americans never did find COSVN, if such a central organization ever existed. The "incursion" brought Cambodia into the war, however, and ultimately resulted in the coming to power of the murderous Pol Pot communist regime. This government was to kill over one million Cambodians before being ousted by the Vietnamese communists.

As the fighting raged in Indochina, the United States and North Vietnam engaged in negotiations, both open and secret, in Paris. In October, 1972, the two sides reached an agreement. Hanoi agreed to return American POWs and to leave the Saigon regime of General Thieu in place. In return, America would end its combat role in Vietnam. There was no meeting of minds concerning the cessation of combat between the rival Vietnamese sides. General Thieu accused Washington of selling him out and refused to accept the agreement. Thieu complained that the proposed settlement left North Vietnamese troops in the South while Americans pulled out; it would be only a matter of time, he said, before Hanoi's divisions took over South Vietnam. Sympathetic to Saigon's objection, Washington sought a commitment from Hanoi to set aside attempts to unseat General Thieu. This demand amounted to a call for Hanoi to abandon its basic war aim, namely, control and unification of all of Vietnam. In reaction, Hanoi denounced the October agreement and walked out of the negotiations. Fierce fighting resumed. In an effort to bring Hanoi back to the negotiating table, Nixon in late December ordered the bombing of civilian areas of Hanoi and its port of Haiphong. The tactic worked. In January, 1973, Washington and Hanoi signed a truce essentially identical to the terms of the October agreement. While Thieu fumed, America withdrew. Although America continued to supply large quantities of military aid to Saigon, the South Vietnamese forces were no match for their communist adversaries. In April, 1975, communist forces marched into Saigon and declared victory. That same month, Pol Pot's Khmer Rouge troops captured Cambodia, where the real slaughter had only begun.

MILITARY PREPAREDNESS

Sufficiency

When Nixon entered office, he directed Kissinger to conduct a sweeping review of defense policy. The inter-agency study concluded that the United States would be unable to attain long-term military superiority over the Soviet Union in strategic weapons. In consequence, the analysis recommended a stance of "sufficiency." Sufficiency turned out to differ little from the Eisenhower policy on strategic weapons. Nixon described the concept in these terms. "In its narrow military sense, it means enough force to inflict a level of damage on a potential aggressor sufficient to deter him from attacking us.... In its broader political sense, sufficiency means the maintenance of forces adequate to prevent us and our allies from being coerced" (Quoted in Freedman, 1983, p. 341). To give operational meaning to sufficiency, the study analyzed the concept in terms of four guidelines:

- U.S. strategic forces must be able to deter by causing unacceptable damage to the U.S.S.R. after absorbing a Soviet strike;
- America's strategic forces must be so configured as not to offer an

attacker any advantage; this would ensure "crisis stability," to be discussed later;
- Without necessarily matching Soviet forces, American strategic forces must not be or appear to be inferior to Soviet forces;
- Strategic defense, including ABM, should protect the U.S. against a small or accidental strike and should contribute to the survivability of deterrent forces.

These guidelines were incorporated into Nixon's strategic planning.

Not everyone agreed with the notion of sufficiency. Those to Nixon's political right called for American superiority, on the ground that only through intimidation could the U.S. prevent the Soviets from expanding their influence. At the outset of Nixon's first term, the Soviets were already ahead of the United States in ICBMs and were in the midst of a crash building program dating from their humiliation in the Cuban missile crisis. The United States led in SLBMs and long-range bombers. (See Table 4-1, page 115, for figures in the military balance.) The Soviets, argued conservatives, were striving for military superiority, and the United States must do the same. Nixon and Kissinger rejected these arguments. As the latter stated at a July, 1974, press conference:

> And one of the questions which we have to ask ourselves as a country is what in the name of God is strategic superiority? What is the significance of it, politically, militarily, operationally, at these levels of numbers? What do you do with it? (Freedman, 1983, p. 363).

Nixon and Kissinger doubted that the United States could use strategic superiority to coerce the Soviets in regional conflicts, because the threat to use nuclear weapons was so tenuous. So long as the United States maintained the security of its assured destruction forces, the nuclear deterrent would serve its purpose. Besides, Nixon was convinced that the Kremlin, unfettered by public calls to restrain military spending, would match America's military efforts. Strategic superiority, even if desirable, was unattainable. Nixon also felt that a drive for superiority would intensify the arms race and worsen U.S.-Soviet relations. Both of these consequences conflicted with Nixon's foreign policy objectives. The president badly wanted a strategic arms control agreement, which an arms race would have made all but impossible. Nixon was also trying to fashion detente, which a quest for superiority would have rendered all but hopeless. Sufficiency, by contrast, was perfectly consistent with detente. Sufficiency also dovetailed with Nixon's arms control objectives. SALT I, for instance, set agreed arms ceilings that gave leaders confidence in the level of arms needed to ensure rough equivalence. Arms control and sufficiency both reinforced each other.

The White House was equally forceful in dismissing the arguments of those who called for finite deterrence or minimum deterrence. These strategists branded Washington as foolish for matching the Soviet arsenal. So long as the United States can inflict unacceptable damage upon the Soviet Union, they said, there was no reason to build additional weapons. Overkill was a foolish waste of resources. In rejecting these arguments, Nixon and Kissinger pointed out that *perception* was all-important. For strict military purposes, the United States did not need to match the Soviets weapon for weapon. From the standpoint of global politics, however, the United States must not be seen to be trailing the Soviets. Should the world adopt that perception, dire events could follow. America's allies might take the imbalance as a sign that the United States was losing its will and would no longer sustain them; hence, some might decide to make peace with the Soviets on the latter's terms. Just as portentous, the Soviets might conclude that America was losing heart in the cold war struggle and be emboldened to intervene in areas vital to the United States. When America did react, an unintended war might result. In the Pentagon's annual report for 1976, Secretary of Defense James Schlesinger expressed this outlook tersely. Strategic equivalence, he said, is important "for symbolic purposes, in large part because the strategic offensive forces have come to be seen by many—however regrettably—as important to the status and stature of a major power." Our allies, he continued, could perceive America's falling behind as indicating "a lack of resolve to uphold our end of the competition and a certain deficiency in staying power. Our own citizens may doubt our capacity to guard the nation's interests" (U.S. Department of Defense, 1976, P. II-7).

The concept of sufficiency left at least two questions unanswered. What indicator should be used to determine sufficiency—number of delivery vehicles? number of warheads and bombs? megatonnage? size of delivery vehicles? troop strength? Secondly, was there any evidence to demonstrate that America's allies or the Soviets regarded minimum deterrence as signifying a lack of resolve? None was ever produced. Nevertheless, defense secretaries Laird and Schlesinger followed McNamara's thinking in maintaining sufficiency and in preserving the strategic triad consisting of ICBMs, SLBMs, and bombers. This triad, it was believed, offered insurance against a Soviet technical breakthrough (which might neutralize any single leg) and the operational failure of any leg. The triad also complicated Soviet force planning, especially efforts to mount a disarming first strike.

Strategic Stability

Along with sufficiency, the Nixon administration sought to achieve strategic stability. This may be defined as a situation that minimizes the likelihood of strategic war between the two superpowers.

Some of Nixon's weapons procurement decisions were based in part on strategic stability. The president rejected a nationwide anti-ballistic missile system not only because most scientists doubted it would work, but also because

Chapter 5: Nixon/Ford

that would neutralize Moscow's deterrent. Strategic stability would diminish once the Soviet Union realized Washington was erecting a nationwide ABM, and during this interval Moscow might be tempted to strike before the defensive system was completed. Deploying the Safeguard ABM in such a manner as to defend ICBM sites *enhanced* stability, as it would reduce any temptation Moscow might experience to launch a disarming first strike. Procurement of the B-1 bomber and the Trident submarine was also based partly on the desire to improve strategic stability. Both weapons systems would increase the survivability of the strategic triad and therefore diminish any hopes Moscow might entertain of neutralizing America's retaliatory forces. The same could be said of efforts to make Minuteman silos less vulnerable to attack through hardening.

Sufficiency and strategic stability were closely related. So long as the Kremlin perceived American forces as approximately equivalent to their own, Moscow was unlikely to think it could win a military victory against the United States. Minimum deterrence might be interpreted as a flagging of resolve. This could entice the Soviets to undertake adventurous actions that Washington would resist, thereby provoking an unintended confrontation. If the United States elected to attain strategic superiority, the Kremlin might read this as an effort to overwhelm the U.S.S.R. at an opportune time; in reaction, the Soviets might launch a pre-emptive strike in a crisis. Strategic superiority was inconsistent with strategic stability.

Did the Soviet Union share the American objectives of sufficiency and strategic stability? Judging from Soviet actions, it is difficult to say. Throughout the late 1960s and 1970s, the Soviets engaged in an extensive strategic building program. This included four new ICBMs, including the SS-17, SS-18 and SS-19—all of which were bigger than Minuteman; two new classes of missile-carrying submarines—Delta and Typhoon; accelerated production of the Backfire long-range bomber; the construction of a "blue water" navy as opposed to their traditional coastal defense force; and an enormous buildup of general purpose forces. Right-wing groups like the Committee for the Present Danger, headed by Paul Nitze, accused the Soviets of acquiring far more military power then they needed for defense. Surely, the Committee asserted, the Kremlin had aggressive purposes in mind. Those on the political left explained the Soviet buildup as a reaction to American military measures. In this view, Soviet augmentation of their missile force was a justifiable reaction to the MIRVing of American missiles. The B-1 bomber and Trident submarine were systems the Soviets felt they needed to match if they were to retain sufficiency. Since the United States possessed a "blue water" navy, the Soviets felt entitled to duplicate this capability. Besides, Soviet submarines and other warships operated at a disadvantage compared with the American navy, in that the latter had the advantage of naval bases in nearly every corner of the globe. To equal America's sea presence, the Soviets needed more ships than the United States. Super-heavy Soviet missiles, such as the SS-18 that has seven times the throw weight of Minuteman III, can be seen either as a sign of Soviet technological backwardness or as evidence of Soviet belligerence. Far behind the United States in miniaturization, the Soviet Union had to construct large warheads and consequently needed large missiles to transport them. Once the Soviets embarked on MIRV, they needed even bigger missiles to carry numbers of bulky warheads. Nevertheless, the sheer destructive power of the Soviet missile arsenal struck dread in the hearts of many Americans. Extensive Soviet efforts to construct an elaborate civil defense network, complete with shelters, food stocks and evacuation plans, convinced some planners that the Soviets were entertaining the idea not only of engaging in a nuclear exchange but of preparing for victory as well. Accelerated Soviet production of armor, short-range nuclear-tipped missiles, tanks, and tactical aircraft persuaded many Americans that the Soviets had designs on Western Europe.

The intent of this extensive Soviet buildup remains elusive. Were the Soviets bent on aggressive moves, these measures were precisely the ones the Kremlin could be expected to take. One must also bear in mind, however, that a certain proportion of Soviet forces were targeted against China. In Europe, the Soviets needed to concern themselves not just with American forces but also with the power of Western Europe. Furthermore, Moscow's Eastern European allies were anything but reliable, so the Kremlin needed to assign some forces to this area. Overall, Soviet military policies during the period remained ambiguous. Possibly, bureaucratic forces inside the Soviet Union tugged policy now this way and now that. Perfect consistency may be too much to ask for in any state that qualifies as a superpower.

MIRV, Trident and B-1

Once the Nixon White House elected to pursue sufficiency, it needed to decide which weapons were required. Among the new systems procured were MIRV, Trident and the B-1 long-range bomber.

As explained in the previous chapter, the multiple independently targeted reentry vehicle (MIRV) was designed to saturate the anticipated ABM system around the periphery of the Soviet Union. In 1970 the United States began to deploy the Minuteman III, each armed with three warheads. Shortly thereafter, the United States replaced the sea-going Polaris with MIRVed Poseidon missiles.

Well before these deployments, it became obvious that the Soviets were *not* constructing a nationwide ABM system. Critics of MIRV urged the administration to drop plans to deploy the new technology. These critics said MIRV was not only unnecessary but also would accelerate the arms race. Nixon refused to budge. He and his aides insisted that MIRV provided an extra margin of safety in case the Soviets, in a surprise strike, destroyed some of America's retaliatory forces; that MIRV expanded the breadth of target coverage; that the Soviets were vigorously developing new missiles; and that in the SALT negotiations, Washington needed to negotiate from a position of strength. Even after the ABM Treaty was signed (1972), restricting each side to two ABM sites, Nixon proceeded with MIRV. Later, the administration contended that MIRV helped make possible the SALT I Treaty on offensive weapons, since the new technology compensated for the Soviet lead in numbers of launchers.

In retrospect, it would seem that MIRV went well beyond the requirements of sufficiency. As predicted, MIRV spurred the Soviets to work on the same technology, thus giving rise to a MIRV arms race. It is true that MIRV gave the U.S. a transitory edge in the strategic arms race. In 1977, for example, the United States possessed 10,000 nuclear warheads to the 4,000 for the Soviet Union. However, in 1973 the Soviets began testing MIRV; before long, the Soviets matched the American arsenal. While the number of weapons possessed by each side went up, the security enjoyed by each superpower declined. Furthermore, the United States soon found itself at a disadvantage. The larger Soviet missiles—the SS-17s, 18s and 19s—could carry more warheads than Minuteman or Poseidon. This situation gave rise to fears, beginning with the Carter administration, that the Soviets could knock out America's ICBM force. This concern led to deployment of the MX missile in super-hardened silos (whose vulnerability remains open to question).

MIRV also lessened strategic stability. Previous to MIRV, one side could destroy the other side's ICBMs only by firing its own missiles at enemy silos, approximately a one-for-one exchange. A pre-emptive counter-force strike gravely depleted the attacker's supply of ICBMs, leaving few missiles to strike cities, industrial centers, and other such targets. After MIRV, one side could destroy the other side's entire ICBM force (making the rash assumption of total accuracy and reliability) and still have enough warheads left to obliterate the other country many times over. In a crisis, this situation gives each side an incentive to launch first, in order to avoid the loss of one's ICBMs. Because the Soviets had (and have) a higher proportion of ICBMs to SLBMs, they face a higher risk than the United States in the MIRV era. Of course, such an analysis omits consideration of SLBMs and bombers, which would restrain any sane leader from hoping to achieve victory simply by knocking out his opponent's ICBMs.

Finally, MIRV compounds the difficulties of arms restraint. It is impossible for either side to tell if the other's missiles are carrying as many warheads as they are able to, based on monitored flight tests. To avoid falling behind, therefore, each side tends to assume that the adversary's missiles are in fact carrying as many warheads as they can and to load that many warheads on its own missiles. This process tends to maximize rather than minimize the number of warheads deployed by both sides.

A second major strategic weapons system procured by the Nixon administration was the Trident submarine. As the Soviets developed a MIRV capability in the 1970s, Secretary of Defense Laird and others in the Pentagon voiced fears that America's ICBM force was becoming at risk. Consequently, they argued, the submarine was growing more important as the backbone of the deterrent. As compared to Poseidon, the Trident was quieter, could operate in deep waters for longer intervals, carried larger and longer-range missiles and carried more of them—24 as opposed to 16. Overall, Trident was less vulnerable than Poseidon, a supreme virtue in an age of ICBM vulnerability. In 1971, the Nixon administration decided to accelerate the Trident program, overriding objections of critics that the vessel was too costly and unnecessary in the absence of evidence that the Soviets could locate and destroy the Poseidon fleet.

The leg of the triad composed of bombers was, in the opinion of the Air Force, growing gimpy. This leg was based on the aging B-52, many of which were nearly as old as their pilots. Rather than further modernizing the B-52, the Nixon administration elected to replace these aircraft with a new intercontinental bomber, the B-1. It was not until the 1990s, however, that the B-1 took its place in America's strategic arsenal. Mechanical difficulties kept most of the fleet grounded. The B-1 failed to participate in the Persian Gulf War. Meanwhile, to increase the survivability of existing long-range bombers, the Air Force dispersed aircraft, reduced time needed for takeoff, installed radars to provide earlier warning of close-in SLBM strikes, and developed air-to-surface missiles to destroy the Soviet Union's vast array of anti-aircraft radars, guns, and surface-to-air missile sites.

Conventional Forces and Tactical Nuclear Forces

The Nixon administration assigned a major role to conventional forces and tactical nuclear forces in the event of a massive Soviet assault against Western Europe or Chinese human wave attacks in Asia. Indeed, many strategists insisted these forces had attained renewed importance in an age of strategic nuclear parity, when each side hesitated to use its most potent weapons. Additionally, conventional forces and battlefield nuclear weapons provided the varied menu of choice called for by flexible response. The 1973 crisis in the Middle East demonstrated the utility of multiple options. It will be recalled that the Soviets threatened to intervene in the Arab-Israeli fighting, and that in response Washington placed American forces on alert. Moscow's military planners were no doubt troubled by uncertainty about what measures Washington might take in reaction to a Soviet incursion, The Soviets decided not to intervene.

Not everyone agreed that these forces should be maintained at such high levels. A movement in Congress, led by Senator Mike Mansfield—later ambassador to Japan—argued that the United States should reduce troop levels in Europe, and that the Europeans themselves should fill the gap. These critics asserted that Europe was no longer recovering from World War II and could afford to spend more for its own defense. Nixon vigorously resisted calls for unilateral troop withdrawals, arguing the U.S. should hold out for *mutual*

U.S.-Soviet withdrawals. (In 1973, Mutual and Balanced Force Reduction talks opened in Vienna to discuss joint withdrawals. It was only in the 1990s that troops began to stream home.)

The Pentagon believed tactical nuclear weapons were particularly important for possible conflict in northeastern Asia. It was assumed that the South Koreans or the Japanese would supply most of the manpower needed to repel an invasion. America was prepared to supply tactical nuclear weapons to help these forces overcome an assault by communist forces that might themselves possess battlefield nuclear weapons.

Tactical nuclear weapons had a special role to play in Europe, where communist general purpose forces from the East greatly outnumbered those deployed by the West. Rejecting declarations of no first use, NATO made no secret of its intention to use battlefield nuclear weapons if the East pushed into Western Europe. It was hoped that the prospect of either stalemate or escalation would deter the Warsaw Pact from attacking.

Henry Kissinger (1979) observes that Europe and America developed a split vision over using nuclear weapons in Europe. Europeans feared that widespread use of nuclear weapons would obliterate the continent they were designed to defend. Consequently, Europeans hoped that, in the event of war, fighting would rapidly boil up to the strategic level, leaving most of Europe unscathed. The United States, hoping to spare itself destruction, preferred that the fighting confine itself to Europe. Thankfully, it has not become necessary to face this question.

Anti-Ballistic Missiles (ABM)

It will be recalled that President Johnson had approved the light, "anti-Chinese" Sentinel ABM system before leaving office. Sentinel was designed to protect the United States against a small number of incoming missiles. When Nixon took office, he immediately commissioned a review of defense policy. Out of this review emerged a new concept for ABM, announced in March, 1969. The new ABM, designated Safeguard, consisted of two components. The first component would protect not cities but ICBM silos. The second would protect the country against an accidental launch or deliberate small-scale attack, possibly from a new nuclear power. Nixon was persuaded by scientists that no ABM could protect cities against a full-scale Soviet attack, as only a miniscule proportion of enemy missiles needed to penetrate the ABM shield to rain untold havoc upon the country. However, if ABM could increase the invulnerability of ICBMs, then ABM would further stabilize deterrence. As the Soviets began work on MIRV, Nixon realized that American ICBM fields would grow increasingly vulnerable, diminishing ABM's utility. This was one of the arguments offered against ABM. Nixon and Kissinger, however, felt that at the very least, they needed an American ABM as a bargaining chip to induce Moscow to sign a treaty limiting ABM, a move crowned by success in the 1972 ABM Treaty.

Congress continued to entertain doubts about the wisdom of constructing ABM. Given the vulnerability of its radars, would the system work? Could the system's computers cope with a massive assault, including dummy warheads, chaff and other penetration aids? Was the expense worthwhile? Even in the absence of ABM, were the Soviets convinced that they could knock out enough American ICBMs to make a disarming first strike feasible? Should Moscow reach the unlikely conclusion that it could take out all ICBMs, wouldn't SLBMs and bombers deter the Soviet Union from attacking? Some contended construction of ABM would spur the Soviets to build more missiles, so as to overcome it. If the Soviets so acted, would not the United States feel compelled to match Soviet construction, resulting in a further intensification of the arms race? A Senate vote to block ABM deployment failed to pass by a single vote. ABM construction began.

Flexible Options

In pondering his choices in the event of the outbreak of nuclear war, Nixon was troubled by a seeming lack of options. "Should a President," he asked (1970), "in the event of a nuclear attack, be left with the single option of ordering the mass destruction of enemy civilians, in the face of the certainty that it would be followed by the mass slaughter of Americans?" (pp. 54–55). In 1971 the NSC staff began to examine this question. Two years later, the concept of flexible options was drafted and received White House blessing. At the same time James Schlesinger became secretary of defense, and he became an ardent advocate of flexible options.

The purpose of flexible options was to strengthen deterrence and neutralize the political coercion of the United States and its allies by their foes. This was to be achieved by giving the president a menu of options within the nuclear spectrum. In a sense, flexible options could be viewed as flexible response within the nuclear realm. Under flexible options, in the event of a foreign crisis or a limited attack by the Soviet Union against the United States, the president would not be restricted to a massive attack against the Soviet Union. Rather, the president would be able to select from "a series of measured responses to aggression which bear some relation to the provocation, have prospects of terminating hostilities before general nuclear war breaks out, and leave some possibility for restoring deterrence," in Schlesinger's words (U.S. Department of Defense, 1975, p. 38). Schlesinger and others cited advantages of this limited nuclear war option. Flexible options would:

- enhance deterrence by threatening a credible response to every level of threat;
- achieve crisis stability by reducing an opponent's incentive to strike first in a critical situation, by holding out the prospect of retaliating in kind;
- limit damage and destruction should deterrence fail;
- reduce the likelihood of all-out war;
- reinforce confidence in America's nuclear guarantee on the part of Japan and Western Europe, by having a variety of credible military responses; the United States would no longer have to risk its own destruction in order to defend allies.

To implement this scheme for resisting aggression without precipitating all-out war, flexible options called for an arsenal of highly accurate, low-yield nuclear weapons. Their targets would include troop concentrations, airfields, logistics facilities, transportation and communication sites, command and control headquarters, nuclear submarine pens—in brief, those capabilities that allow a nation to make war. Population centers would be spared to the extent, albeit limited, that they remained separate from military sites.

Limited nuclear war has never been popular with the American citizenry. Not surprisingly, flexible options gave rise to a chorus of criticism. Opponents proclaimed the doctrine made nuclear war more "thinkable" and therefore more likely. Once started, they said, nuclear fighting could not be contained, as there is no salient "firebreak" once the nuclear continuum has been breached. Many of the targets appropriate for limited nuclear war are located in or near cities; hence, millions of civilians are likely to be killed. Furthermore, critics pointed out, not every weapon will land precisely on target; a slight error could place a warhead in the midst of a city. Even if a warhead lands on target, the enemy may see the strike as a prelude to general war and retaliate in full. Or, the enemy's intelligence might be clouded by the "fog of war," and reports of destruction might be greatly exaggerated. Opponents also observed that there was no evidence that Soviet military doctrine referred to limited nuclear strikes. Therefore, a limited American strike would, in all likelihood, precipitate a full-throated Soviet response. Lastly, opponents insisted, from Moscow's viewpoint flexible options was indistinguishable from a threatening first-strike capability. Could not these surgically accurate weapons be aimed at ICBM silos, airfields, command and control facilities, vital communications links, and leadership bunkers? Indeed, Moscow denounced flexible options as a disguise for a first-strike capability and claimed the concept ran counter to the Agreement on the Prevention of Nuclear War signed at the 1973 summit. Needless to say, these arguments carried little weight with the Nixon administration, which went about implementing the new doctrine.

One and One-Half Wars

When Nixon entered office, the United States adhered to the 2½-war doctrine. This doctrine called for the country to maintain sufficient conventional forces to mount, simultaneously, a 90-day defense of Western Europe against Soviet attack, a sustained defense against an all-out Chinese assault against either South Korea or a southeast Asian nation, and a defense against a military outbreak elsewhere in the third world. To Pentagon planners, it appeared unlikely that the Soviets and the Chinese would act independently. According to the accepted notion of a communist monolith, both states would coordinate their military policies toward the West.

However, the communist world had fragmented. Rather than concerting their actions, the Russians and the Chinese regarded each other as principal rivals. Nixon accepted Kissinger's recommendation that the country shift to a 1½-war doctrine. The prospect of a reduced threat meant that the country needed to maintain adequate conventional forces to meet either a Soviet attack on Europe or a Chinese drive into Asia, plus a contingency in the third world. Kissinger also believed that, should China and Russia mount simultaneous attacks, the entirety of world order would be threatened, in which case it would be unrealistic to plan for a strictly conventional response. Beijing applauded the new doctrine, inasmuch as it signaled America's recognition that China was no longer an appendage of Moscow.

ARMS CONTROL

During the Nixon presidency, there was a flurry of arms control agreements. Nixon relied on arms control to enhance American security far more than did any of his predecessors. For Nixon, arms control—particularly limitations on strategic weapons—constituted the essence of detente. Accordingly, the president placed much emphasis on the arms control process.

The first arms control measure concluded during the Nixon administration resulted from an effort to please those non-nuclear countries that had signed the Non-Proliferation Treaty of 1968. Many of these countries chafed in the knowledge that they had denied themselves the most potent weapons, while the nuclear-weapons states continued to enjoy the advantages associated with possession of such weapons. In order to demonstrate self-restraint, the United States, the United Kingdom and the Soviet Union signed the Seabed Treaty in February, 1971. This treaty calls upon the powers to refrain from emplacing weapons of mass destruction upon the ocean floor beyond the 12-mile zone. Inasmuch as the oceans occupy 70% of the earth's surface, the signatories asserted they were denying themselves considerable advantage.

Cynics observed that the agreement did not constrain any country from carrying out any plans on the drawing boards. Some critics even contended that the agreement merely served to divert discussion from more important issues of arms control, including measures to cut back existing arsenals.

The first arms control measure taken by Nixon to lessen the likelihood of war was modernization of the hotline link between Washington and Moscow. The hotline was originally installed, following the Cuban missile crisis, to reduce the chance of war caused by a communications failure. In September, 1971, the superpowers agreed to supplement the land-based link with a satellite circuit. It was hoped the modification would enable the leaders to communicate in a more direct and secure manner.

That same month the superpowers concluded an agreement to prevent accidental war. Suppose that, during an intense international crisis, a nuclear explosion occurred in the Soviet Union or the United States. Might not the country where the detonation occurred conclude an attack was under way and retaliate in kind? Conceivably, however, the explosion had resulted from a technical malfunction. Unexplained objects appearing on radar screens or apparent interference with early warning systems might also trigger a hostile response. The accidental war agreement commits both sides to consult with one another in the event of an ambiguous or threatening situation, to provide information to each other, and to act so as to clarify or correct the situation. Hopefully, this would reduce the chance of an accidental war stemming from a misunderstanding.

Strategic Arms Limitation Talks (SALT)

The centerpiece of Nixon's arms control policy, indeed, of the entire superstructure of detente, was SALT. These negotiations dovetailed with the most important facets of Nixon's defense policy. Acceptance of sufficiency made SALT possible; equivalent forces would have been out of the question so long as one side sought superiority. SALT contributed to both strategic stability and detente; equivalent forces reduced the likelihood of war and gave evidence of a willingness to coexist. SALT also slowed, if it did not halt, the arms race; accepted ceilings meant that neither side had to procure arms against the maximum potential capability of the other side. This brake on the arms spiral also contributed to detente by reducing suspicions that one side was seeking strategic domination.

The SALT negotiations opened in November, 1969, and concluded three years later at the Moscow summit. At this gathering two agreements were signed, an interim agreement that froze existing levels of offensive strategic weapons and a pact that restricted each side to two ABM sites.

Interim Agreement on Offensive Strategic Weapons

The negotiations leading up to this pact were long and tortuous. We shall examine only a few aspects of the negotiations and focus on the results. (Of the many volumes on SALT, the reader may wish to consult Strobe Talbot, *Deadly Gambits* (New York: Vintage Books, 1985), and John Newhouse, *Cold Dawn* (New York: Holt, Rinehart and Winston, 1973).

One of the earliest disputes in the SALT negotiations concerned the definition of strategic weapon. Each side tabled a definition that would advance its own security. The Soviet Union, faced with an array of weapons stationed in Europe, at sea and on American soil, argued that any weapon that can strike the territory of either superpower should be called strategic. This would include America's nuclear-capable aircraft and medium-range missiles based in Europe and on carriers at sea as well as French and British nuclear missiles and aircraft. The United States enjoys a different geographic situation, being immune from all Soviet weapons except long-range missiles and long-range bombers. According to the Soviet definition of strategic weapons, America's forward-based systems in Europe would be constrained, as would European nuclear systems. However, Soviet medium-range and intermediate-range nuclear missiles, as well as aircraft capable of delivering nuclear weapons to Western Europe, would be excluded, leaving Moscow with a preponderance in that area. In consequence, Washington rejected this definition. The American definition would leave the Soviets threatened by a wide variety of nuclear systems based in Europe and Asia and targeted on Soviet soil. In one of several trade-offs during the talks, the Soviets accepted the American definition. In return, as we shall see, the Soviets were allowed to retain more strategic weapons than the United States. Another part of this compromise was the exclusion of long-range bombers, in which the United States held a substantial lead, from the allowed totals. Furthermore, it was decided that the agreement would remain in force for no more than five years, during which the two sides would work toward additional reductions.

The United States sought to treat "heavy missiles" in a manner that would advance its own security at the expense of the Soviet Union. It will be recalled that the Soviets were compelled to construct oversize missiles in order to transport their large warheads, because the Soviets lagged in the technology of miniaturization. The Soviets also trailed the Americans in accuracy, so they required a larger warhead to be certain of destroying a target. In consequence, the Soviets possessed some 300 land-based heavy missiles capable of delivering much larger warheads than existed in the American arsenal. The United States possessed no heavy missiles. In the SALT negotiations, the United States made strenuous efforts to eliminate heavy missiles. The American side was worried about the day when the Soviets caught up in miniaturization. At that time, they could use their heavy missiles to load many more warheads than Minuteman or Trident could mount. Moscow succeeded in blocking Washington's effort to prohibit heavy missiles; the best Washington could extract was a pledge not to build additional ones. Later, American negotiators were flayed for allowing the Soviets to retain their heavy missiles and thus enjoy a huge advantage in throw weight (weight of payload deliverable upon target).

The United States also tried to gain unilateral advantage concerning ICBMs in general. When the talks opened, the Soviets possessed approximately 20% more ICBMs than did the U.S. These weapons represented the keystone of the Kremlin's deterrent. Washington hoped to fragment that keystone by suggesting reductions in the total number of missiles (ICBMs and SLBMs) possessed by each side by 100 missiles a year over a period of seven years; as each side reduced, it could alter the mix by substituting SLBMs for ICBMs, but not the reverse. Such an arrangement would benefit the United States, whose SLBMs were technically superior to those of the Soviet Union.

MIRV offered an opportunity for both sides to seek unilateral advantage. When the SALT negotiations opened, the United States was well ahead of the Soviet Union in perfecting MIRV. As a means of blocking future MIRV deployments by the Soviets, the United States tried, as we have seen, to reduce the number of Soviet heavy missiles, the very missiles best suited to carry several warheads. In April, 1970, Washington proposed a ban on MIRV testing and deployment, but not production. Such an arrangement would suit American interests, since Washington was on the verge of completing its final tests. Washington could then stockpile MIRV before the Soviets could develop the technology. The Soviets, for their part, countered with an offer to prohibit production and deployment, but not testing. This would allow the Soviets to catch up to the Americans by testing. In the end, no agreement on MIRV was concluded.

What, then, did the two parties agree to? Essentially, they agreed to freeze the number of ICBMs and SLBMs in existence or under construction. During the five years that the agreement was to last, they pledged to work toward the reduction of these weapons. Moscow promised not to increase its stock of heavy missiles. Verification was to be by "national technical means," or satellites, and the two sides agreed not to interfere with such means.

Was SALT a worthwhile agreement? The question can be answered from two perspectives, arms restraint and American security.

From the standpoint of controlling weaponry and making the world safer, SALT came in for heavy criticism. Detractors pointed out that SALT did not eliminate a single weapon. Furthermore, they complained, the agreed-upon ceilings were extraordinarily high—2,300 missiles for the U.S.S.R. and 1,700 for the U.S. Just as important, opponents insisted, was what the agreement omitted. The most telling omission, they said, was MIRV. In the years after SALT, each side assembled approximately 10,000 warheads and bombs without increasing its stock of missiles, all because of MIRV. In addition, no limitations were placed on the *quality* of weapons permitted. In consequence, both sides (the Soviets more so) substituted more accurate and lethal weapons for older ones. Supporters of the agreement countered that the pact was only a first step; weapons reductions would follow in the next stage (expected to be within five years but not realized until the 1990s). Furthermore, they said, the suspicion and enmity that separated the superpowers prevented a more far-reaching agreement in 1972. If the two parties developed a habit of respecting the agreed levels, the resulting trust would permit them to embark on a course of weapons reduction in the near future.

Did the agreement serve American security interests? Here too opinion was divided. President Nixon (1978) touted the pact in the following terms:

> Under this agreement, the United States gave up nothing, because we had no programs that were affected by the freeze. The Soviets, however, had a substantial missile deployment under way. It is not possible to state how extensive that deployment might have been in the absence of the agreement. But had it continued, it would have put us increasingly at a disadvantage in numbers of missiles and would almost certainly have forced us into a costly building program just to maintain the then-current ratio (p. 618).

Administration supporters also observed that SALT did not constrain America's forward based systems or the nuclear arsenals of Great Britain and France. America's technological lead over the Soviets more than made up for the Soviet edge in numbers of missiles. Thanks to MIRV, advocates pointed out, the U.S. possessed many more warheads than the Soviet Union. Furthermore, America was far ahead of the Soviets in long-range bombers (400–150), which were not included in SALT. SALT would help dispel distrust and reinforce detente, advocates said, by allowing each side to stop fabricating additional weapons for fear the other side would do so first. Taking all these considerations into account, they maintained, SALT left American security intact.

Critics howled at the Soviet advantage in numbers of missiles and throw weight after SALT. Because of Soviet heavy missiles, particularly the 300 SS-9s, SALT left the Soviet Union with a throw weight edge of nearly 7–1. The agreement also left Moscow with a 2,300–1,700 edge in the total number of SLBMs and ICBMs. In scrutinizing (and approving) SALT, the Senate went so far as to pass a sense of the Senate resolution demanding that the U.S. press for equal numbers in the next round of negotiations. (SALT II satisfied this condition.) Opponents also pilloried the vague language of the agreement, particularly those clauses that permitted each side to modernize existing missiles. Undoubtedly stretching the spirit of the agreement, if not the letter, the Soviets in the years following SALT substituted greatly improved models for older, more cumbersome missiles. These new missiles were not only more accurate, but they were also capable of carrying numerous warheads. The SS-18, for example, carries up to ten warheads. Those opposed to SALT also pointed out in later years that the agreement did not live up to its billing as a brake on the arms race. Mention has already been made of modernized ICBMs and SLBMs that entered the Soviet arsenal in the 1970s. In 1974 the Kremlin deployed a new long-range bomber, code-named Backfire. Moscow also deployed a vastly improved intermediate range missile in Europe, the SS-20, and continued to upgrade its general purpose forces. This continuing military buildup led many Americans to see detente as a screen behind which Moscow was striving for unilateral advantage. Ronald Reagan, running for president in 1980, gave voice to these suspicions.

Anti-Ballistic Missile Treaty

The second agreement signed in Moscow was the ABM Treaty. Anti-ballistic missiles were threatening to undo strategic stability. The Soviets had already erected ABM installations around Moscow and were about to upgrade them. Strategists on both sides realized that if one party could perfect an ABM defense, it could strike its opponent and ward off retaliation. Whoever got there first would enjoy a tremendous advantage, but at the same time strategic stability would decline.

It will be recalled that Premier Kosygin rebuffed Secretary McNamara's efforts to discuss ABM limitations at the Glassboro summit in 1967. At that time, the Russian leader asserted that missile defense is not a cause of the arms race but rather saves lives. By 1972 the Soviets had reversed course and initialed the ABM Treaty.

This agreement limited each party to 200 launchers, which could be divided equally between two sites, the nation's capital and an ICBM field. The parties promised not to construct a nationwide ABM system. A follow-on agreement signed at the June, 1974, summit limited each side to a single ABM site. The Soviets elected to defend Moscow. The United States started to construct a site to defend ICBMs at Grand Forks, North Dakota, but eventually concluded that no shield could protect the missiles. Accordingly, Washington never finished work on the site. The radars remain standing as ghostly monuments to a flawed technology.

The ABM Treaty represented a towering peak amidst the gently rolling hills of arms limitation efforts to date. By forswearing missile defense, the superpowers aborted a race to overwhelm each other's defenses with clouds of additional offensive missiles. Indeed, the ABM Treaty facilitated conclusion of the interim agreement on offensive weapons; neither side felt the need to increase stocks of offensive missiles to saturate missile defenses. The ABM Treaty saved both sides considerable sums that would have been needed to erect and modernize missile defenses. As opposed to the interim agreement on offensive weapons, the ABM Treaty included qualitative restrictions. The parties agreed to refrain from the development, testing or deployment of ABM systems or components on the sea, in the air or space, or on mobile surface vehicles. The precise meaning of this provision came into question when President Reagan proposed a space-based ABM system known as the Strategic Defense Initiative, or Star Wars. Of signal importance, the ABM Treaty reinforces mutual deterrence through a mutual baring of throats. To put it differently, neither side can hope to attack the other and escape devastating retaliation. Some American strategists have identified an advantage accruing to the United States as a result of the treaty. Since the Soviets have placed 75–80% of their strategic megatonnage in ICBMs, while the United States has vested only 25–30% in ICBMs, the treaty leaves the Soviet strategic force more vulnerable to attack. No one has yet figured out how to capitalize on this supposed advantage, however.

While the two SALT agreements mark major milestones along the path of arms control, they did, in an indirect way, contribute to the accumulation of military hardware. Defense Secretary Laird and the Joint Chiefs of Staff took the formal position that the SALT agreements were in America's interest, *provided* the country undertake to modernize its strategic forces. In particular, they insisted on (and received) approval for a new bomber (B-1) and submarine (Trident). This was not the first occasion when the price of an arms accord proved to be the acquisition of additional weapons.

Vladivostok

Not long after the ink dried on the SALT agreements, the two sides began work on the next phase of controlling offensive arms. These negotiations proved much more contentious than expected. The Soviets raised a number of concerns they had set aside in negotiating the Interim Agreement. Since the United States was far ahead in numbers of long-range bombers, Moscow wanted these aircraft to be counted as part of the total number of strategic delivery vehicles. The Kremlin also revived the question of America's forward-based systems, which were capable of striking Soviet territory, as well as French and British nuclear systems, also targeted on the Soviet Union. Washington agreed to count bombers in the strategic totals but not the forward-based systems. These, Washington argued, were designed to blunt attacks against Western Europe, Korea, and other tension areas around the Soviet periphery, not to strike at Soviet vitals. Concerning British and French nuclear weapons, the United States insisted it lacked standing to negotiate for these countries. Additionally, Washington said that to bring these countries into the negotiations would so complicate the talks as to make agreement all but impossible. These issues were to delay agreement for several years.

In March, 1973, Washington tabled a proposal that included bombers in strategic totals. At the same time, Washington bid for unilateral advantage by attacking the one area where the Soviets were ahead, namely, ICBMs. The American proposal called for equal ceilings on ICBMs and ICBM throw weight. This would have required the Soviets to dismantle most of their heaviest missiles or for the Soviets to stand still while America built about 300 heavy missiles. The Kremlin showed little interest. Two months later, just before the June, 1973, summit, Washington floated another proposal. Recognizing earlier

Chapter 5: Nixon/Ford

Soviet objections, the United States dropped the provisions for equal ceilings on ICBMs and ICBM throw weight, proposed a combined total of 2.350 ICBMs, SLBMs, and bombers, and suggested a freeze on MIRV testing and deployment. This last provision would have frozen Soviet inferiority in MIRV technology. At this date, the United States had already deployed 350 Minuteman III missiles with three warheads each, while the Soviets had yet to test their first MIRV. Moscow turned down the offer. Fractious negotiations continued, interrupted by Watergate. Finally, the two sides were able to strike an agreement, which was finalized by General-Secretary Brezhnev and President Ford at Vladivostok in November, 1974.

The two leaders met not to sign a treaty but rather to lay out guidelines for a second SALT agreement they hoped would be finalized soon and last for another decade. (Another five years were to pass before SALT II was concluded.) These guidelines were embodied in the Vladivostok Accord, under which each power was entitled to 2,400 strategic launchers. This figure included ICBMs, SLBMs and bombers. Of this total, 1,320 launchers could be MIRVed. While forward-based systems were not included, the Soviets did achieve their goal of limiting bombers and were permitted to retain their heavy missiles. The equal aggregates satisfied the Senate's demand for equivalence.

Contrary to expectations, subsequent negotiations leading toward SALT II proved extremely difficult. Two issues bedeviled the talks. Should the new Soviet bomber, the Backfire, be counted in the 2,400 total (as the Pentagon insisted), or did it lack intercontinental range (as the Soviets claimed)? Should air-launched cruise missiles attached to bombers be counted separately to make up the 2,400 total (the Kremlin view), or did these weapons fall outside the meaning of strategic (the American position)? In the next chapter we shall continue to trace the discussions concerning strategic weapons.

Biological Weapons Convention

Numerous other arms control agreements were concluded during the Nixon administration. None of them, however, was as central as SALT. The first agreement we shall examine is the Biological Weapons Convention, completed in 1972.

The Geneva Protocol of 1925, concluded in reaction to the widespread use of chemical weapons in World War I, outlawed the use but not the production or stockpiling of chemical and biological weapons (CBW). Sporadic interest in a tighter prohibition intensified following the death in 1968 of some 6,000 sheep in Utah resulting from a nerve gas leak from a military installation. This effort was given a boost when the Conference of the Committee on Disarmament (CCD), the United Nations arms control forum, assigned a high priority to an improved CBW agreement. Multilateral negotiations commenced.

A major impediment to such an accord had been the linkage of chemical weapons and biological weapons. While chemical weapons had proved themselves as a viable military tool, biological weapons posed as many risks to the user as to the target. Epidemics can spread back to the originating country. The extent of biological infection, even within the target country, cannot be controlled, resulting in the suffering of many innocent people. Biological weapons, in contrast to chemical weapons, are not suitable for battlefield use. In 1969, President Nixon, convinced of the disutility of biological weapons, announced that the United States would not use biological weapons under any circumstances, was suspending further development of biological weapons, and would destroy existing stockpiles. The following year Nixon extended the proscription to deadly toxins, which are byproducts of bacteriological growth. Nixon's actions lent momentum to the negotiations at the CCD, and in April, 1972, the Biological Weapons Convention was opened for signature.

The Convention prohibits the development, production and stockpiling of biological weapons and requires the destruction of existing stockpiles. This was the first postwar arms pact that called for the elimination of weapons. The Convention contains no provisions for inspection or enforcement and no sanctions for violations. The Western powers, traditionally adamant about verification, made an exception in this case, due to the inherent limitations of biological weapons. Any party to the treaty that suspects a violation may complain to the United Nations Security Council; each party agreed to submit to Security Council investigations. In 1974 the Senate approved the Biological Weapons Convention as well as the Geneva Protocol (never previously accepted by the U.S.). One year later the government announced the destruction of biological weapons stockpiles.

While the Biological Weapons Convention clearly represents a nod in the direction of arms control, even disarmament, it has had no noticeable effect on the military policy of any country. The disadvantages of biological weapons are so widely recognized that no country had plans to use them. However, the Convention allowed the United States to abandon work on biological weapons, confident that no other country was likely to make a technological breakout and gain a sudden advantage. (In the 1980s, the U.S. raised a question about Soviet violation of the Convention, after an extensive outbreak of anthrax in the Soviet city of Sverdlosk. The Soviets attributed the outbreak to rotten meat. Later, Moscow admitted that it had been developing biological weapons at the site.)

Other Arms Control Agreements

While notan arms control compact, strictly speaking, the Agreement on the Prevention of Nuclear War, signed at the 1973 summit, merits mention at this juncture. The superpowers stated that "an objective of their policies is to remove the danger of nuclear war." In the event of the imminent danger of nuclear war between themselves or between one of them and another country, the two parties agreed to conduct "urgent consultations" with each other. They also pledged to act so as to avoid "a dangerous exacerbation of their relations" and "to avoid military confrontations." The Soviets, who attached considerable significance to the document, regarded it as an extension of the Basic Principles Agreement of the preceding year. There is little evidence that either party ever incorporated either of these two pacts in their policy planning. The concords contributed to the spirit of detente but also to its demise, when it appeared that both sides violated the agreements when politically opportune. Later, in writing about the 1973 agreement, Kissinger commented, "I doubt whether the result was worth the effort" (Quoted in Garthoff, 1985, p. 343). More directly related to the subject of arms control were the Mutual and Balanced Force Reduction negotiations (MBFR) that opened in October, 1973. Recently concluded treaties between West Germany and the Soviet Union, Poland and East Germany, affirming existing borders, helped establish suitable political preconditions for these talks on force reductions in Europe. The White House welcomed these efforts as a way to forestall unilateral American troop reductions in Europe, subject of the perennial Mansfield Resolution in the Senate. With the onset of these talks, Nixon argued that the U.S. must keep its troops in Europe as a bargaining chip to bring about *mutual* reductions. (This was not the first time a country used arms control discussions as a pretext for *maintaining* arms levels.) At first, Moscow was cool to the idea of such talks. The Soviets consented, however, when the West insisted on the negotiations as a precondition for discussions on territorial boundaries and human rights so desired by the Kremlin and soon afterward to open in Helsinki.

Western interest in MBFR stemmed from anxiety over surprise attack from the East, given the enormous firepower and high state of readiness of Soviet troops stationed in Eastern Europe. It was hoped that the combination of reduced Soviet strength, the stationing of NATO observers in Eastern Europe, and prior notification of troop movements would lessen the danger of surprise attack. Mutual troop withdrawals would also reinforce detente.

The MBFR talks lasted over a decade and were eventually abandoned without having produced results. From the outset, geographical asymmetries dogged the discussions. Soviet troops eliminated from Eastern Europe could withdraw to western Russia, from which they could readily return. American forces would have to travel 3,000 miles across the Atlantic Ocean. Troop counts also bedeviled the talks. NATO refused to accept the Warsaw Pact count of its own troops in Europe, insisting the Pact was deliberately undercounting. Still another divisive issue was the extent of reductions. The West demanded that the Pact reduce its forces by a greater amount than NATO cuts, since the Pact had so many more forces to begin with (an assertion the Pact refused to accept). Instead, the Pact called for equal reductions, which would still leave it with the capacity to overwhelm the West in a surprise attack (given Western troop counts). Differences arose over whose forces should be reduced. The

United States, viewing the threat to Europe as coming mainly from the Soviet Union, proposed initial cuts of only American and Soviet troops. A second phase would deal with European demobilization. The Soviets, their eyes cast with suspicion upon West Germany, preferred a single phase to cover both superpower and European troop reductions. At times the talks focused on manpower reductions only, while at other intervals the various parties—up to 19 countries participated at one time or another—discussed withdrawals of armaments. The East never showed enthusiasm for the confidence-building measures suggested by NATO, including observers to accompany large troops movements and the right to conduct periodic inspections in Central Europe. In the late 1980s, the MBFR talks were superseded by other forums to discuss many of the same issues.

One final area of arms negotiations concerned nuclear testing. Since the Limited Test Ban Treaty of 1963, which outlawed all nuclear tests except those underground, discussions on a comprehensive ban had been sputtering along with little progress. At the 1974 summit in Moscow, Nixon and Brezhnev initialed the Threshold Test Ban Treaty (TTBT). This agreement prohibited underground tests in excess of 150 kilotons (approximately ten times the explosive force of the Hiroshima bomb). While no provision was made for on-site inspection, the parties did agree to specify test areas, exchange data on geological characteristics of these areas, and exchange data on two blasts in each test area so seismic devices could be calibrated to measure future tests. Peaceful nuclear explosions were exempted, the parties agreeing to conduct separate negotiations on this issue.

Arms control advocates criticized the TTBT's threshold, which they said was so high as to be non-restrictive. With improved accuracy, there was no need to fabricate warheads with a yield of 150 kt. Critics also complained that the exemption for peaceful explosions provided a loophole for other countries to test. Indeed, India claimed that its 1974 nuclear test was for peaceful purposes. The fact remains, however, that regardless of its motivation, a nuclear blast is a nuclear blast, and a country can exploit that technology for peaceful or martial ends. After signing the TTBT, the executive branch elected not to submit it to the Senate until the signing of an agreement on peaceful nuclear explosions.

Such a treaty was concluded by President Ford two years later. The Peaceful Nuclear Explosions Treaty (PNET) limited peaceful nuclear explosions—such as for digging dams or diverting a riverbed—to 150 kt. The parties agreed that any blast outside regular military test sites would be subject to on-site inspection, in order to ensure that the explosion was not a military test in disguise. The country conducting the peaceful detonation was obliged to inform the other party in advance so it could arrange to send observers.

After President Ford sent the two treaties to the Senate for approval, they became enmeshed in the downward spiral of superpower animosity as well as uncertainty over verification. It was only in the 1990s that the Senate approved

Chapter 5: Nixon/Ford

the agreements.

Richard Nixon fabricated his political career largely on the basis of fighting communism. One might well expect that once he became president, he would combat communism with every available means, particularly military force. It would seem consistent with his past words and actions to emphasize military preparedness over arms control.

Ironically, however, Nixon involved himself in more arms control initiatives than any president in American history. Nixon's interest in arms control sprang not from any new-found love for the citadel of world communism, but rather from his highly attuned sense of pragmatism. Nixon realized that the Kremlin would not allow the United States to sprint ahead militarily; memories of the Cuban missile crisis were still fresh. In consequence, Nixon accepted military sufficiency instead of superiority. Recognizing the dangers posed by nuclear armaments, Nixon also endorsed strategic stability, meaning a superpower relationship that minimized the likelihood war, because neither side could hope to gain advantage from the outcome.

Of course, sufficiency and strategic stability required a certain degree of military preparedness. Nixon continued to develop MIRV, even after it became clear that the Soviets were not constructing the nationwide ABM system MIRV was designed to overcome. He also ordered the Trident submarine and B-1 bomber. Nixon assigned important deterrent roles to tactical nuclear weapons and conventional forces, maintaining both in a high state of readiness. In approving flexible options, Nixon broadened the repertoire of the nation's nuclear forces. Military preparedness certainly did not languish in neglect during the Nixon years.

The Nixon administration was notable for the prominence it gave to arms control. SALT suited the administration's strategic aims extremely well. As a result of the interim agreement on offensive weapons, the United States felt confident in estimating Soviet strategic arms levels. These levels provided benchmarks for the achievement of sufficiency. The government did not need to worry about Soviet weapons *potential*, inasmuch as SALT set ceilings. In the absence of these upper limits, the U.S. might have adopted a worst-case stance and built additional weapons against maximum Soviet production capabilities. Such a step would have escalated the arms race and made it much more difficult to determine what was needed to maintain sufficiency. SALT also advanced the goal of strategic stability. Strategic weapons ceilings limited the number of warheads available to take out the opponent's deterrent forces (although MIRV allowed for an expansion of these numbers). The ABM pact removed an important obstacle to the penetration of strategic weapons, ensuring that neither side could expect a desirable outcome from attacking the other.

Detente was a major contributor to the success of arms control during the

Nixon years. A joint acceptance of coexistence, the offspring of nuclear weapons, as well as a determination to avoid nuclear war, fostered an atmosphere that encouraged agreements such as SALT, the hotline upgrade, the Seabed Treaty, MBFR talks, and the two nuclear testing accords. Combined with sobering realities concerning nuclear war, detente helped promote the Biological Weapons Convention. The Sino-Soviet split, again leavened with detente, made possible the 1½-war doctrine, which represented a nod in the direction of limiting general purpose forces.

In sum, the Nixon/Ford administration, while not neglecting military preparedness, placed more emphasis on arms control than that of any other president—with the possible exception of George Bush.

6

CARTER

THE 1976 ELECTIONS

In the 1976 election between Gerald Ford and Jimmy Carter, foreign policy did not play a paramount role. Carter stressed honesty and efficiency in government, vowing to bring these qualities to his administration if elected. He also asserted that he would balance the budget, reduce unemployment, and devote his attention to other domestic concerns. The former governor of Georgia made much of his distance from official Washington, pointing out that he was no creature of the Washington establishment and was beholden to no special interests. This theme struck a responsive chord with a populace chastened by Watergate and the lengthy parade of GOP officials who were serving time in jail. The Democratic candidate also placed much emphasis on his religious faith and human decency.

In discussing foreign policy, Carter railed against the heavy-handed use of power, particularly military force, by Nixon, Kissinger and Ford. Citing his religious beliefs, Carter vowed to infuse foreign policy with Christian morality. Carter claimed America was too often perceived as an uncaring bully ready to use force at the slightest provocation. Instead, Carter said, the United States must stand for compromise and cooperation. The Democratic front-runner also criticized his predecessors for an obsession with the Soviet Union. Contesting Soviet power, he said, often led Washington to back immoral regimes (as in the Philippines and Nicaragua) and mire itself in areas of marginal strategic import for the United States, as had occurred in Vietnam. Carter called for the United States to allow local forces to work out their disputes without great-power intervention. America's obsession with the Soviet Union, Carter insisted, blinded the country to other international issues of equal or greater significance, including such "global order" issues as pollution, hunger, population growth and poverty. Military power is irrelevant to the solution of such problems. Instead, Carter said, the United States must pool its wealth and technology with other countries to find answers. In this context, he asserted, the East-West struggle had no significance. Carter's concern with these global order matters sprang in part from his religious convictions.

Another foreign policy issue connected with Carter's religious outlook was human rights. Addressing a town meeting in Clinton, Massachusetts, in March,

1977, Carter explained his interest in human rights in the following terms:

> I want to see our country set a standard of morality. I feel very deeply that when people are put in prison without trial and tortured and deprived of basic human rights that the President of the United States ought to have a right to express displeasure and do something about it....I want our country to be the focal point for deep concern about human beings all over the world (Brzezinski, 1983, p. 1244).

In a more lofty tone, Carter's national security adviser, Zbigniew Brzezinski, explained the administration's interest in human rights as follows:

> In international affairs, there seemed to be a moral vacuum. The Carter Administration resolved to make a break with the recent past, to bring the conduct of foreign affairs into line with the nation's political values and ideals, and to revitalize an American image which had been tarnished by the Vietnam experience (Brzezinski, 1983, p. 124).

To inject more emphasis on human rights into foreign policy, Carter created a new position, assistant secretary of state for human rights, and appointed civil rights activist Patricia Derian to that post. He also established a new Interagency Group on Human Rights and Foreign Assistance to examine foreign aid decisions from a human rights standpoint. In November, 1976, while still president-elect, Carter engaged in a flurry of activity to underline his commitment to human rights. He sent a telegram of support to Soviet dissident Vladimir Slepak. The following month, designated Secretary of State Cyrus Vance received exiled Soviet dissident Andre Amalrik. Shortly after his inauguration, Carter received a letter from Andrei Sakharov, Soviet Nobel Peace Prize winner, physicist, and human rights activist, congratulating the new president for his commitment to human rights. Carter replied positively and publicly.

As things turned out, few subjects were to mire President Carter in more controversy than his commitment to human rights. Moscow was outraged at Carter's constant criticisms of Russia's human rights record, even going so far as to clamp down further on human rights activists to demonstrate that Moscow was not cowed by the president's words. From Moscow's viewpoint, American demands for freedom of religion, assembly and political dissent assaulted the fundamental nature of the Soviet regime. Carter's human rights campaign helped cause a deterioration of relations with the Soviet Union. In an indirect sense, then, human rights slowed arms control and reinforced the standoff between two armed camps.

The president also discovered that he could not apply human rights considerations consistently without jeopardizing other American interests. These pragmatic retreats from human rights opened him to accusations of hypocrisy and inconsistency. For example, the shah of Iran imprisoned or tortured some 50,000 political opponents. Despite this fact, on New Year's Eve of 1977,

Carter visited Iran and toasted the shah. Clearly, Iran's importance as America's surrogate in the Persian Gulf persuaded Carter to ignore the shah's egregious human rights abuses. South Korea, another country important to American policy, likewise received little criticism for its human rights violations. Countries that played a lesser role in Washington's foreign policy designs, such as Brazil, Chile and Argentina, came in for more vocal denunciations on account of human rights. Many human rights advocates were angered by Carter's normalization of relations with mainland China, a land where Western concepts of human rights were alien.

There can be little doubt that Carter's foreign policy themes detailed above appealed to most voters. Yet it cannot be said that the election turned on foreign policy. Nor is it accurate to state that Carter received any particular foreign policy mandate from his electoral victory.

As the Carter presidency matured, several themes he had deemed virtues in the campaign came back to haunt the former peanut farmer from Plains, Georgia. For instance, during the campaign Carter turned his lack of Washington experience into an asset, claiming he would be his own man and would introduce fresh air into the clubby political atmosphere of the capital. Once in office, however, this lack of experience, particularly in foreign affairs, led to vacillation in policy. Indeed, one might speak of two Carter presidencies. The first one ended in December, 1979, when the Soviet Union invaded Afghanistan. Up to that point, Carter made strenuous efforts—despite human rights roadblocks—to improve relations with Moscow. After the invasion of Afghanistan, Carter renounced hope of striking a *modus vivendi* with the Soviets and adopted a policy of confrontation. Carter's split vision in foreign policy was reflected in the appointment of his two most influential advisers. Secretary of State Vance and National Security Adviser Brzezinski, as well as President Carter, believed that policy toward the Soviet Union should represent a blend of competition and cooperation. However, Vance and Brzezinski differed markedly on where the emphasis should lie. While Brzezinski viewed the United States and the Soviet Union as locked in a titanic struggle for global influence, Vance strained to identify areas of cooperation. Rather than integrating these opposing viewpoints, Carter veered from one to the other. During the "first Carter presidency," Vance's influence was ascendant. Following the Soviet move into Afghanistan, Brzezinski moved to the forefront (and Vance eventually resigned).

Another supposed "virtue" in Carter's campaign was his promise to be frugal in the application of military power, a stance he contrasted to his "trigger-happy" predecessors. Carter's reluctance to utilize armed force echoes a familiar theme in American foreign policy. From the founding of the Republic, Americans have identified military power and *realpolitik* with the scheming chanceries of the Old World. As a shining city upon a hill, America would achieve its noble purposes without recourse to shot and shell. In the eyes of many practiced diplomats, this American attitude smacks of naivete. Carter's refusal to intervene in such regional disputes as Angola, Nicaragua and the Horn of Africa persuaded many that America was losing interest in the world beyond its own borders. It is at least arguable that the Soviets viewed Carter's ambivalence toward military power as an opportunity to intervene with impunity in Afghanistan and elsewhere.

Jimmy Carter assumed office amidst the breakdown of America's consensus regarding the containment of communism. Up to the period of detente—beginning in the late 1960s—Americans were united in the opposition to Soviet expansion. The fracturing of the communist world, particularly the Sino-Soviet split; the conclusion of bilateral pacts such as SALT I; and America's hapless adventure in Vietnam led many Americans to question the urgency of opposing communism in every remote corner of the world. Yet certain events of the early 1970s alerted segments of the public to the dangers posed by this alien ideology. Most important, perhaps, was the steady Soviet armaments buildup dating from the Cuban missile crisis. Communist intervention in Angola, Ethiopia and South Yemen also reinforced the notion that the so-called free world must circle its wagons against communism.

Jimmy Carter was affected by and also reflected this ambivalent attitude toward communism. His appointment of Cyrus Vance and Paul Warnke (as head of the Arms Control and Disarmament Agency) represented a nod toward cooperation with the Soviets. His appointment of Zbignicw Brzezinski reflected the hard-line approach. There is much evidence that Carter himself inclined toward the dovish position upon taking office but lurched into the hard-line camp following the Soviet invasion of Afghanistan in December, 1979.

THE INTERNATIONAL CONTEXT

Carter's efforts to negotiate a new treaty with Panama illustrate how differently he viewed world politics compared with his *realpolitik* predecessors, particularly Kissinger. Refusing to view all international politics through an East-West prism, Carter identified with the vast majority of Panamanians who saw American control of the Canal Zone as an affront to national pride. In the ten-mile wide Zone, America behaved like a swaggering colonial power complete with monocle and baton. American law, administered by American courts, prevailed. Americans ran all the business enterprise. Throughout Latin America, Washington's stance on a new treaty with Panama was seen as a litmus test of America's willingness to allow Latin Americans to guide their own affairs.

Following Panamanian riots in 1964, resulting in Panamanian and American fatalities, President Johnson inaugurated negotiations aimed at the return of the Canal to Panama. Although progress ensued over the years, it was Jimmy Carter's energetic efforts that finally produced an accord. The new agreement would turn control of the Canal over to Panama in the year 2000.

Conservatives railed at the new treaty, insisting that America must retain control of the waterway for strategic purposes. They added that American control of the Canal symbolized American power, which seemed already on the decline in such places as Iran, Southeast Asia and the Horn of Africa. It is high time, they asserted, for America to stand tall and assert itself. Carter disagreed. Supercarriers and large tankers were too big to pass through the Canal, reducing its strategic significance. More important, in Carter's mind, was the need to express sympathy for the nationalistic aspirations of Panamanians and, through them, the entire third world. East-West relations were not paramount.

In the U.S. Senate, Carter waged a battle-royal to persuade the required two-thirds majority to approve the treaty. In April, 1978, the Senate assented by only one vote more than the requisite number. Denizens of the third world hailed the United States for its new-found identification with their aspirations. Latin Americans were particularly enthusiastic in their praise.

A dispute in the Horn of Africa provided a laboratory for examining the erosion of consensus over the containment of communism. As Russia's closest ally in Africa, Somalia had granted the Soviets a strategic naval base at Berbera. Soviet gratitude took the form of arms shipments. In 1977, Somali troops joined those of the Western Somali Liberation Front in an effort to detach an area known as the Ogaden from Ethiopia. The Somalis claimed that the region was populated primarily by Somalis and rightfully belonged to Somalia.

Inasmuch as Ethiopia is ten times larger than Somalia, Moscow shifted its support to Addis Ababa. The Soviets sent Ethiopia $1 billion in military supplies and 1,000 advisers. Cuba despatched 20,000 advisers and troops. Soviet and Cuban intervention placed pressure on Carter to respond. Hardliners such as Brzezinski and the Pentagon called for American counteraction. Otherwise, they said, the Soviets would gain control of the southern entrance to the Red Sea, which led to Suez and Israel, and would find themselves in a position to menace oil tankers exiting the Persian Gulf. America's failure to respond, they added, would be taken as a sign of weakness that would encourage Soviet adventurism and dishearten pro-Western allies. Secretary Vance, by contrast, insisted the problem was in essence an indigenous one. Local parties should be left to settle matters on their own. American involvement would place the country atop the identical slippery slope that resulted in massive American participation in Vietnam. To the charge that American forbearance would not necessarily lead to a similar Soviet reaction, Vance replied that Moscow would prove no more able to establish a permanent foothold in Ethiopia than they had been in Egypt or the Sudan. Nationalism would eventually drive the Soviets out. Carter was swayed by his secretary of state and refrained from intervening. While the United States and the Soviets did not come to blows over the Horn, the episode did help to poison superpower relations and no doubt retarded progress in arms control and reinforced those in Washington who favored additional military preparedness.

Perhaps Carter's brightest moment in foreign policy occurred in connection with the Middle East. In the hope of breaking the perennial Arab-Israeli impasse, President Anwar Sadat of Egypt stunned the world by offering to go to Israel to negotiate a peace accord. The offer signified willingness to recognize Israel, the first such initiative from an Arab state. In November, 1977, Sadat stated his desire for peace in an historic address to the Israeli parliament. Peace, however, did not arrive. Fearing for its security, Israel refused to meet Sadat's conditions, namely, Israeli withdrawal from territory seized during the 1967 war, including East Jerusalem, and formation of a Palestinian state. Israel's offer to allow Palestinian self-rule under Israeli sovereignty did not satisfy the Egyptian president. To break the diplomatic logjam, Carter invited both Sadat and Israeli Prime Minister Menachim Begin to the presidential retreat at Camp David. Twelve days of contentious and sometimes belligerent bargaining laid the groundwork for a formal peace treaty between Egypt and Israel, concluded in March, 1979. President Carter played a central role in bringing about agreement, including a post-Camp David trip to the Middle East to help resolve remaining differences. The treaty called for Israel to return the Sinai Peninsula to Egypt and for the establishment of diplomatic relations between the two countries. While the treaty failed to sever the Gordian knot of Arab-Israeli conflict, many hailed Carter for bringing the two primary protagonists to a limited accord.

Americans with vivid memories of the Vietnam war were roused to anger when Vietnam invaded Cambodia in December, 1978, to depose the brutal regime of Pol Pot. The Khmer Rouge movement that he headed had executed over one million Cambodians. Echoing his decision in the Horn of Africa, Carter elected not to intervene. Hard-line anti-communists were appalled.

The following year China invaded Vietnam as punishment for deposing Pol Pot (whom China supported) and for expelling some Chinese from Vietnam. Again Carter was urged (such as by GOP presidential hopeful Senator Howard Baker) to "do something." Carter refused, not wanting to jeopardize ties with China, with whom Washington had normalized relations January 1, 1979.

Of all of Carter's foreign policy initiatives, none was to have a greater impact on arms control and military preparedness than relations with China. Toward the end of 1978, the tortuous negotiations for a second SALT accord were practically completed. Over Vance's objection, Carter announced on December 15 that the United States and China would normalize relations January 1, 1979. This gambit represented a victory for Brzezinski, who explained:

> Normalization of relations with China was a key strategic goal of the new Administration. We were convinced that a genuinely cooperative relationship between Washington and Beijing would greatly enhance the stability of the Far East and that, more generally, it would be to U.S. advantage in the global competition with the Soviet Union (Brzezinski, 1983, p. 196).

In more pointed words, Brzezinski (1983) noted, "U.S.-Chinese collaboration could be valuable in helping Moscow understand the value of restraint and reciprocity" (p. 196).

As Vance had feared, the Soviets perceived improved Sino-American relations as a spear aimed at the Kremlin. To demonstrate their displeasure, the Soviets raised secondary issues (concerning cruise missiles and the encryption of telemetry) at the SALT negotiations, thereby delaying final agreement by about six months. This interval proved crucial, because the Soviets invaded Afghanistan before the Senate could complete its deliberations on the treaty. As a result of Moscow's incursion, Carter withdrew the treaty from Senate consideration, and the United States never approved the accord. Without the delay, the Senate might have approved the treaty before Afghanistan. (More on these matters in a subsequent section of this chapter.)

On January 1, 1979, normalization took effect. Carter announced that the two nations would exchange ambassadors. Washington agreed to abrogate its 1954 security treaty with Taiwan and withdraw diplomatic recognition from the island. American trade and travel restriction to the mainland were lifted. A new era in American-Chinese relations began.

Following the Soviet invasion of Afghanistan in December, 1979, Washington began to deal its "China card." To signal American displeasure, Secretary of Defense Harold Brown visited China in January, 1980. The trip symbolized closer Sino-American collaboration against the Soviet Union. Later that month, Congress approved most-favored-nation status for China, a favor pointedly denied to the Soviet Union. During the remainder of the year, Sino-American relations broadened. More than 1,000 Chinese delegations visited the United States, while some 60,000 Americans journeyed to China. Significantly, military delegations from the two countries exchanged visits. Trade rose to $5 billion, exceeding American trade with Russia for the first time. Washington liberalized restrictions on the sale to China of certain military support items, such as air defense radars, transport helicopters, long-distance communications equipment and electronic countermeasure devices.

There is no question that Moscow was miffed at the warming of relations between its most bitter rival and the United States. We have already seen the effect of the new relationship upon SALT. In general terms, American cooperation with China aggravated the deterioration in superpower relations begun by the Soviet military buildup and communist intervention in Africa and Afghanistan. It can therefore be concluded that Washington's new ties with China impeded arms control and contributed to military preparedness.

The greatest foreign policy disaster of the Carter administration occurred in Iran. Following Britain's withdrawal from the Middle East, Iran under the shah served as America's gendarme in the oil-rich Persian Gulf. A loyal ally of America, the shah proved a prime customer for American military hardware, opposed the advance of communism, called for moderation in OPEC councils, refused to join the Middle Eastern embargo of oil to the United States following the 1973 war, backed Egypt's efforts to make peace with Israel, and allowed the United States to place electronic listening posts in his country to monitor Soviet missile tests. At the same time, the shah alienated successive segments of Iranian society by his despotic rule and rapid Westernization of a traditional Islamic nation. As angry crowds took to the streets to denounce the shah, Carter, following the noninterventionist bent he had displayed in Africa and Southeast Asia, and doubting the United States could block a highly popular revolution, offered nothing more than words of encouragement to the beleaguered monarch. This proved insufficient, and in January, 1979, the shah fled his country. In November, the United States admitted the shah, diagnosed as suffering from cancer, for medical treatment. This action spurred Iranian militants, with a blessing from the new ruler, Ayatollah Ruhollah Khomeini, to invade the American embassy and seize the inhabitants as hostages. Nightly news broadcasts showed Iranians pouring into the streets to denounce the "great Satan," as they called the United States. The world's greatest power seemed pitiful and helpless before these affronts. In the spring of 1980, the Pentagon mounted an attempt to rescue the hostages. This effort ended in ignominious failure, as helicopters malfunctioned and one of them crashed into a refueling plane in the desert. This debacle only underlined America's seeming weakness and humiliation. Iran held the hostages over a year, releasing them on the very day that Ronald Reagan was inaugurated as president.

The Iranian episode contributed to military preparedness by compounding sentiment in the United States that the country must build up its strength. Although it remains unclear what Washington could have done to sustain the shah, except for an elaborate military intervention the population would have probably rejected, the perception of American weakness was pervasive. Ronald Reagan capitalized on this feeling during the 1980 election campaign. After he was elected, he undertook extensive measures to add to America's arsenal. The Iranian episode left the United States feeling insufficiently secure to contemplate extensive arms control.

If American flirtation with China led the Soviets to throw metal filings into the mechanism of arms control, the Russian invasion of Afghanistan spelled the end of arms control for the Carter administration. In December, 1979, 85,000 Soviet troops crossed into Afghanistan to prop up a faltering socialist regime. Perhaps Moscow expected a Western reaction no stronger than the denunciations that followed communist intervention in Angola or Ethiopia. The incursion into Afghanistan, however, came after a series of untoward actions in response to which the Carter administration had acted with restraint. These events included communist intervention in the Horn of Africa, Vietnam's invasion of Cambodia, China's attack on Vietnam, seizure of American hostages in Teheran, and a Soviet strategic buildup. In an election year, Carter sought to defang critics who accused him of weakness.

In an address to the nation on January 4, 1980, Carter specified a series of measures to demonstrate the United States would not conduct business as usual with the aggressors. The president announced postponement of the opening of consulates in Kiev and New York City, deferment of most economic and cultural exchanges under consideration, curtailment of Russian fishing privileges in American waters, a ban on licensing high technology or strategic items for sale to the Soviet Union, and a grain embargo. Over the next several weeks, Carter prohibited American athletes from participating in the 1980 Moscow Olympics (and urged other countries to pull out as well), suspended export licenses covering $150 million in goods, and revoked licenses for the export of spare computer parts for the Kama River truck plant in the Soviet Union.

In a television interview shortly after the invasion, Carter summed up his reaction as follows: "This action of the Soviets has made a more dramatic change in my own opinion of what the Soviets' ultimate goals are than anything they've done in the previous time I've been in office" (Garthoff, 1985, p. 950). Hard-line critics of the president were aghast at Carter's alleged naivete.

The Soviet invasion of Afghanistan marked a turning point in the Carter presidency. No longer did Carter call for downgrading the centrality of U.S.-Soviet relations. Superpower relations now rose paramount over ties with the third world and "global order" issues. In remarks to members of Congress on January 8, 1980, Carter offered the wildly exaggerated opinion that "the Soviet invasion of Afghanistan is the greatest threat to peace since the Second World War" (*Weekly Compilation of Presidential Documents*, 1980, pp. 40–41). He went on to make the questionable statement that "our own Nation's security was directly threatened."

The impact of the invasion upon arms control was swift and direct. Realizing that the Senate would not approve the SALT II treaty, Carter asked the legislature to postpone consideration of the document. Subsequently, President Reagan sought to renegotiate it, without success. Negotiations continued into the Bush administration.

The invasion's effect on military preparation was not long in coming. In his State of the Union Address on January 23, 1980, President Carter declared that "an attempt by any outside force to gain control of the Persian Gulf region will be regarded as an assault on the vital interests of the United States of America, and such an assault will be repelled by any means necessary, including military force" (Quoted in Garthoff, 1985, p. 954). This statement has since been labeled the Carter Doctrine. The president then called for a 5% increase in military spending after inflation for fiscal year 1981 and reinstated registration for the draft. Covert aid to Afghan resistors began to flow. Despite evidence that Pakistan was seeking the components to fabricate a nuclear weapon—in direct opposition to one of Carter's foreign policy objectives—the president approved an increase in military and economic aid to that country to "defend its independence and its national security against the seriously increased threat it now faces from the north." Planning soon began for a Rapid Deployment Force that could be rushed to the Persian Gulf at a moment's notice. Negotiations to demilitarize the Indian Ocean and to curb conventional arms transfers were superseded by the buildup of the American Navy in the Indian Ocean/Persian Gulf region and heightened arms transfers to Pakistan, Egypt, Saudi Arabia and other friendly states in the area. Clearly, the invasion of Afghanistan propelled the Carter administration to stress military preparedness over arms control.

Was Carter's response to the invasion appropriate? If one assumes that the Soviets were preparing to move beyond Afghanistan toward the Persian Gulf, then Carter's actions were well chosen. It is conceivable that Moscow had this step in mind but drew back in the face of America's strong response. The absence of any subsequent Soviet moves in the direction of the Gulf, however, suggests that the Kremlin's motives were more limited. In all likelihood, Moscow sought only to consolidate its socialist backyard, which was being threatened by upheaval in Kabul. Moscow may have felt that laxness in disciplining the Afghans would signal softness to their ethnic cousins in the Soviet Union, resulting in attempts to break away from the Soviet state. The Kremlin may also have feared that a disintegrating Afghanistan might drift into the Western camp, placing the adversary at the Soviet Union's back door. All these possible motivations form a constellation of a defensive nature. If these were the genuine Soviet reasons for the invasion, as seems the case, then Carter's reaction was greatly exaggerated. At the very least, the president might have made a more measured response and then waited to see what developed.

According to a seasoned observer (Garthoff, 1985), Moscow interpreted the Carter Doctrine and attendant military preparations as a pretext to dismantle detente, accelerate the arms race, establish a position in the Persian Gulf (not a traditional area of American military presence), and mount a general offensive against the Soviet Union. This represents a grievous misreading of the American intent, reflecting a similar misjudgment of Soviet intentions on the part of the United States. In any event, the invasion of Afghanistan spelled the demise of both detente and arms control and led to greater military preparedness. In this respect, the Reagan presidency had its origins in early 1980.

MILITARY PREPAREDNESS

During the election campaign, Carter pilloried his predecessors for overemphasizing military force as the bedrock of diplomacy. The Georgian pledged to reduce reliance on force and, accordingly, to cut back military spending.

Upon assuming office, the new president commissioned a comprehensive assessment of the U.S.-Soviet relationship, including the military balance. This study, known as PRM-10, resulted in a presidential directive (PD-18) that called for the maintenance of "essential equivalence" in strategic weapons and reaffirmed a secure retaliatory capability as the foundation of American security.

Inasmuch as the Soviets continued to accumulate additional weapons, this decision called on the United States to do likewise. Accordingly, Carter jettisoned his promise to reduce spending on strategic weapons.

The Strategic Balance

The Soviet military buildup with which Carter had to contend included the following:

- Backfire bomber, which some military experts said could reach America's shores;
- MIRV technology;
- 3 new ICBMs (SS-17, 18, 19) larger than the American Minuteman;
- 2 new types of SLBM;
- SS-20 medium-range missile.

In his final report to Congress in January, 1977, outgoing Defense Secretary Donald Rumsfield said the Soviets had boosted military spending 4–5% annually during the first half of the 1970s.

There was widespread disagreement within the American military community concerning the implications of the Soviet buildup. The most outspoken response emanated from the Committee on the Present Danger, headed by longtime defense expert Paul Nitze (primary author of NSC-68 under Truman). The "present danger" that troubled the Committee was ICBM vulnerability. For several years, the number of American ICBMs had held steady at 1,054 (1,000 Minutemen and 54 Titans). Meanwhile, the number of Soviet warheads available to destroy these missiles continued to grow, as did the accuracy of Soviet ICBMs. MIRV technology, introduced by the United States, gave a significant boost to the total number of Soviet warheads. Approximately three-fourths of Soviet warheads were mounted on ICBMs, now sufficiently accurate to destroy American ICBM silos. The U.S. could not claim a similar capability against Soviet ICBMs, since two-thirds of American warheads were placed on SLBMs, which were not sufficiently accurate to knock out ground-based silos. In sum, the U.S. had more silos to target with fewer ICBMs, while the Soviets had fewer silos to target with more ICBMs. Moscow could allocate six ICBM warheads to each American silo. Assuming only moderate accuracy for the Soviet missiles, there was a good chance of destroying the American ICBM force. Moscow would still have enough warheads left to destroy the United States.

The Committee on the Present Danger also set forth an alternative if no less satisfactory scenario. A successful Soviet first strike against American ICBM silos would inevitably kill millions of Americans, many through fallout. Using bombers and SLBMs, the President could order retaliation against Soviet cities. But would he, since the Kremlin could in turn eradicate American cities? Even if the dreaded first strike never came, the existing strategic situation would greatly benefit Moscow, the Committee insisted. The Soviet advantage would embolden them in regional contests around the world, eventually leading to a large increase in Soviet influence at America's expense. In the Committee's eyes, the appropriate American response to Russia's ICBM advantage was obvious—construct more ICBMs.

Not all defense analysts shared the Committee's dire views. Less well-funded (and therefore less visible) analysts observed that at the time Carter took office, the U.S. led the Soviet Union in total number of strategic warheads 8,500–4,000 (increased to 9,200–4,000 by 1980) (Garthoff, 1985). This would certainly give the Soviets pause before striking the United States. Any Soviet planner contemplating a strike against American ICBMs would have to consider a number of uncertainties. Might not the president order a launch-on-warning retaliatory strike against the Soviet Union? Even if the president waited out a Soviet attack, might he not retaliate in anger even at the risk of a Soviet counter-city strike? And what about French and British nuclear forces? If the destruction of a single American city would be regarded as the single greatest catastrophe ever to befall the country, could not the same be said of the Soviet Union? The greater likelihood would be the annihilation of several cities, dwarfing the loss of life sustained in World War II. Surely, critics of the Committee asserted, no sane Soviet leader would risk such a debacle. Furthermore, these critics said, the very reason for locating the bulk of American strategic forces at sea was to place them beyond the reach of Soviet power, thus maximizing deterrence. Fear of SLBM retaliation would continue to deter a Soviet strike, the critics maintained; there was no need to augment the ICBM force. For these reasons, there was no reason for America to retreat in regional conflicts, and indeed critics observed there was no sign the U.S. was behaving in that manner. Still other critics of the Committee questioned the vaunted accuracy of newer Soviet ICBMs. In a pre-planned single flight across the east-west Soviet test range, a missile might prove accurate. However, the critics said, no missile had ever been tested on a north-south trajectory over the North Pole; might not electro-magnetic forces disrupt flight paths? The explosions of the first Soviet missiles to land would destroy second and third wave missiles. Some missiles would misfire or wander off course. In sum, in the excitement of war, the Soviets could not hope to duplicate the accuracy of calmly organized test firings; many American ICBMs would survive. Knowing this, the Soviets would never launch the first strike feared by the Committee.

While it remains impossible to state with certainty the motivations underlying the Soviet strategic buildup, one may speculate. Is it not at least possible that the Kremlin entertained the mirror image of the Committee on the Present Danger? It seems not inconceivable that the Soviets viewed American acquisition of MIRV—rendered unnecessary by the ABM Treaty—as a drive for a counterforce capability and a means of intimidating the Soviet Union in

Chapter 6: Carter

regional struggles. While two-thirds of American warheads remained on submarines beyond the reach of Soviet power, three-fourths of Moscow's warheads sat in underground silos that were becoming increasingly vulnerable to American missiles growing in accuracy, especially with the introduction of the Mark 12A warhead. The Soviets might also have been alarmed by official estimates of the growth in Soviet military spending, which were later found to be inflated by approximately 100%. While the U.S. attributed the error to faulty intelligence, the Soviets might have interpreted the difference as a deliberate falsification of data to justify a drive for military superiority. Soviet misgivings might also have been heightened by the Carter administration's decisions to deploy not only Pershing II intermediate-range missiles and ground-launched cruise missiles in Europe, but also the MX ICBM, and to reaffirm a limited warfighting capability (all to be discussed later in this chapter).

Back in the United States, pressures from the Committee on the Present Danger and like-minded interest groups succeeded in overturning Carter's campaign pledge to cut military spending and de-emphasize military force. Those on the conservative side of the political spectrum persuaded the American people that the Soviets were seeking strategic superiority and unilateral advantage in the third world, in violation of the spirit (if not the letter) of SALT and detente. The president soon found himself approving various weapons systems deemed necessary to blunt domestic criticism and maintain the essential equivalence called for in PD-18.

One of the most controversial such weapons systems was the MX ICBM. Capable of mounting 10 highly accurate warheads, the MX was chosen by the Carter administration as the new ICBM permitted by the SALT II treaty, then in its final stages of negotiation. Opponents of deployment said the new missile was an ideal first-strike weapon, since it was sufficiently accurate to destroy Soviet ICBM silos. The Soviets, they added, would perceive the missile in that light; deployment would increase tension. Furthermore, critics could find no rationale for deploying additional ICBMs, since they would be vulnerable to a Soviet strike. Carter, however, was swayed by those who argued that the United States must match the Soviet strategic buildup, including its capacity to threaten American ICBMs. Senator Majority Leader Robert Byrd and Senator Sam Nunn, both influential Democrats, announced they would not approve SALT II unless the U.S. broadened its defense efforts (Brzezinski, 1983). (This episode represents an interesting illustration of how an arms control treaty can give rise to the acquisition of additional arms.) Finding some merit in the contention of critics that the MX would be vulnerable, the Defense Department wrestled with various basing modes to decrease vulnerability, including underground railways, over-the-highway trucks, and ships on inland waterways. Domestic political opposition torpedoed all these schemes, and eventually the Pentagon placed the missiles in "super-hardened" underground silos. A direct Soviet hit could destroy these silos.

As a further concession to the hard-liners, Carter approved the Trident II submarine armed with D-5 SLBM warheads. This vessel, programmed to enter the fleet in the 1990s, combined increased invulnerability with precision counterforce capability, compared to earlier SLBMs. Again, some critics complained that the high accuracy of the undersea missiles would fuel Kremlin fears that the U.S. was seeking a first-strike capability.

One of the most controversial elements of military preparedness under Carter was the "countervailing strategy." This doctrine represented a reaffirmation and broadening of the "flexible options" package devised under Secretary of Defense James Schlesinger (see preceding chapter). This concept, it will be recalled, was designed to provide the U.S. with a range of military options, nuclear and non-nuclear, in case fighting broke out between the superpowers. Advocates of the countervailing strategy claimed that the doctrine would (1) enhance deterrence by offering a credible response to a variety of possible threats; (2) promote crisis stability by reducing an adversary's incentive to strike first in a crisis, through a believable threat to respond in kind; (3) limit escalation, damage and destruction in case deterrence failed; and (4) cement alliance cohesion by reinforcing faith among America's allies that the United States would respond in case of attack, since a limited American response would not automatically precipitate retaliation against America's homeland. Some of the doctrine's supporters also claimed it would enable the United States to win in case a limited nuclear war broke out. In signing PD-59 in July, 1980, which signified approval of the countervailing strategy, Carter broadened Schlesinger's flexible options by increasing the number of pre-planned military alternatives, augmenting the re-targeting of missiles, and improving the accuracy of nuclear weapons. In the last-mentioned respect, deployment of the Mark 12-A warhead with the NS-20 guidance system on 300 Minuteman III missiles gave the country a counterforce capability against enemy ICBM silos and other hardened targets.

As might be expected, the Soviets denounced the countervailing strategy, claiming it was in actuality a war-fighting doctrine, not a war-deterring doctrine. Moscow also saw the concept as an attempt to intimidate the U.S.S.R. during a crisis by threatening low-level nuclear war.

Domestic critics also lashed PD-59, stressing the practical difficulties in implementation. These critics cited the absence of adequate attack assessment capability, re-targeting capability, secure command, communication and control, accurate and immediate intelligence on the status and disposition of Soviet forces, and continuing communication with Soviet leaders required to facilitate restraint. Once war erupted, Washington would not even be likely to know where Soviet leaders would be hiding. During the fighting, a good portion of each side's intelligence and military communications networks would probably be destroyed, making it all but impossible for either party to calibrate military moves so as to keep a war limited. Even assuming flawless accuracy (a rare occurrence in war), so many military targets are situated in or near civilian targets that it would be difficult to distinguish a limited strike from the first wave of an all-out attack. Would not the receiving party retaliate massively before it is too late? Even if not, the number of civilian deaths likely to result from fallout would make it difficult to exercise restraint. Indeed, one of the problems in waging a limited nuclear war is ensuring that the enemy understands one's intentions. Might not the enemy perceive a limited nuclear strike as a sign of cowardice instead of controlled restraint? Alternatively, the adversary might not see the strike as restraint at all. This could result from the enemy's faulty intelligence about what really had occurred at some distant location or from the occurrence of more damage than originally intended, perhaps the result of a malfunctioning guidance system or unexpected fallout. Critics went on to point out that all these factors would be complicated by the possibility that France and Great Britain, not to mention China, might launch some of their nuclear weapons. In brief, critics warned that any limited nuclear war would rapidly boil up to a full-fledged nuclear exchange. While these views seemed consistent with those held by Carter at the outset of his presidency, the president had made a decided tilt toward military preparedness over arms control by the close of his term.

NATO

If the newly installed President Carter believed his predecessors had obsessed too much over superpower relations and nuclear weapons, he also felt that the GOP had devoted insufficient attention to strengthening NATO, particularly the alliance's conventional weapons. Carter was concerned about a steady buildup of the Warsaw Pact's conventional forces, tactical nuclear weapons, and long-range theater nuclear forces in Europe. Accordingly, during 1977–1978, the United States increased its forces in Europe by 35,000 men and women, augmented its stores of arms and equipment prepositioned in Europe, increased the number of SLBMs available to meet an emergency in Europe from 80 Polaris missiles to 400 Poseidon warheads, and doubled the number of F-111 long-range fighter bombers capable of delivering nuclear weapons deep into Soviet territory in all weather from 80 to 164. Washington also decided to replace Pershing I missiles with an extended range version and to develop a ground-launched cruise missile of intermediate range. In approving these systems, Washington was particularly mindful of the new Soviet SS-20 missile. This weapon was mobile, highly accurate, and carried three warheads capable of hitting almost any target in Western Europe.

Other NATO leaders shared Washington's concerns. These heads of government came to Washington for an important summit meeting in May, 1978. At this gathering they approved a Long-Term Defense Program, which called for a minimum of 3% increase after inflation of the defense budgets of all NATO countries (a goal that few of them met). The Program also called for the upgrading of NATO's overall military efforts, particularly conventional forces, reinforcement capabilities and theater nuclear weapons.

When Carter entered office, NATO was growing seriously concerned about the Warsaw Pact's decided edge in troops and armor. At the same time, American weapons scientists were working on an "enhanced radiation" weapon, or neutron bomb. Compared to other nuclear weapons, the neutron bomb relied on radiation rather than blast and fire to destroy its target; fallout was also reduced. In highly urbanized, densely populated Western Europe, this weapon offered the prospect of sparing more structures and civilians than other nuclear weapons (hence the nickname "real estate bomb"). Furthermore, the bomb's relatively low level of radiation would enable Western troops to occupy, after a short interval, sectors where the weapon had been detonated. Proponents (mostly Americans) argued vigorously for deployment. Many in Europe were less enthusiastic about the weapon. Some suspected the bomb as yet another attempt by the U.S. to ensure that if an East-West conflict erupted, the fighting would be confined to Europe. In contrast to more destructive nuclear weapons, the enhanced radiation weapon would be less likely to precipitate a Soviet response against United States soil. If a war were to occur, these Europeans preferred that the superpowers slug it out and spare Europe. Other opponents argued that because the weapon was so effective against an armored attack, early use was likely. Thus, the neutron bomb would rapidly shift a conventional war to the nuclear level. In the heat of battle, the Soviets could not be expected to distinguish between enhanced radiation weapons and other nuclear weapons. Rapid escalation would follow the use of the neutron bomb. Thus, the most heated discussion concerning the neutron bomb revolved around the question of whether it would enhance deterrence or make resort to nuclear weapons more likely once conventional war began. After a lengthy debate along these lines, NATO elected to deploy the weapon.

Reaction in Europe was intense and vitriolic, especially in West Germany, locus of heavy devastation in case of war. No European government seemed anxious to field the weapon. In April, 1978, Carter abruptly decided to defer production and deployment. German Chancellor Helmut Schmidt felt a combination of embarrassment and fury. At considerable political expense, he had twisted the arms of his colleagues to gain approval for the weapon, largely at Carter's urging. Now the president left him "dangling in the wind." Carter's reversal appeared impulsive and unwarranted, particularly in the wake of earlier statements about the weapon's necessity. Commentators pointed to the decision as evidence of Carter's vacillation on defense. As Brzezinski (1983) candidly commented, the affair was a "major setback in U.S.-European relations, particularly in our relations with West Germany" (p. 301).

NATO found itself troubled not only by the Warsaw Pact's advantage in armor and troops but also by a new generation of intermediate-range nuclear forces (INF), specifically the SS-20 missile. As described above, the SS-20, first deployed in 1976, was mobile, highly accurate, carried three nuclear warheads, and could reach all of Western Europe from deployment sites in western Russia. The SS-20 could be used against military targets or cities. Moscow introduced the SS-20 to replace SS-4s and 5s deployed in the late 1950s and early 1960s. These cumbersome liquid-fueled missiles required several hours to prepare for launch. Situated on open pads, they were highly vulnerable.

NATO possessed nothing *exactly* comparable to the SS-20. Obsolete Thor and Jupiter missiles had been withdrawn. Pershing missiles carried nuclear warheads, but they lacked the mobility, range and accuracy of the SS-20. The Pact's seeming clear advantage in INF threatened NATO. Many in the West feared that the Pact could overwhelm NATO with troops and armor, and then hold off a tactical nuclear response by threatening to unleash its SS-20s. Superpower strategic parity would discourage the United States from acting to reverse the onslaught. In the event that the United States surprised the Soviets with a limited strategic strike, an unintended full-scale war might eventuate.

The Soviets, to be sure, saw the situation differently. In their eyes, the SS-20 was needed to *match* NATO nuclear superiority in Europe. As Moscow pointed out, many NATO aircraft stationed in Europe and at sea were capable of carrying nuclear bombs and rockets. Britain possessed 64 missiles with three warheads each on submarines, and France had 18 land-based missiles as well as 80 SLBMs on five boats. Both countries also possessed long-range nuclear bombers. All the above weapons were targeted against the Soviet Union and its allies. Moscow refused to accept NATO's contention that these weapons should not be counted in NATO-Warsaw Pact totals, because they remained under British and French control and were not automatically available to NATO commanders.

NATO remained divided on how to respond to the SS-20. Belgium and the Netherlands recommended limiting the weapon through arms control. The U.S. and West Germany favored military deployments to offset the SS-20. European opponents warned that use of INF to defend Europe would only destroy it. American opponents of this position noted that a decision not to offset the SS-20 would spur the Europeans to increase their conventional forces so NATO need not resort to nuclear weapons. Still other foes of offsetting deployments found merit in the Soviet contention that NATO already had the capacity to destroy targets in Eastern Europe and western Russia. Those who doubted the possibility of limited nuclear war contended that American strategic weapons would do the job reserved for INF, so the latter could be dispensed with. INF advocates cited the importance of coupling the United States to Europe by emplacing American weapons on European soil. These weapons would then act as a "plate glass window," ensuring that any fighting in Europe would involve the U.S. This position was attacked by those who said America was already linked to Europe by the presence of 300,000 troops, not to mention a web of military installations and economic, social and financial ties.

In December, 1979, NATO elected to pursue a two-track policy. The alliance called on the United States to engage the Soviets in arms control negotiations to eliminate the SS-20. As the talks progressed, NATO would plan for deployment of two offsetting weapons, the Pershing II and the ground-launched cruise missile (GLCM). If the U.S.-Soviet negotiations succeeded, NATO would scrap deployment of the Pershing IIs and GLCMs.

Rapid Deployment Force

The Persian Gulf was also the subject of military preparedness during the Carter presidency. The early inter-agency study of the U.S.-Soviet strategic balance (PRM-10) concluded, among other things, that the Persian Gulf was both vital and vulnerable, and that the United States should be prepared militarily to protect its interests there by creating a rapid strike force. PD-18, approved by Carter in August, 1977, called for establishment of a "deployment force of light divisions with strategic mobility" for global contingencies, possibly in the Persian Gulf or Korea (Brzezinski, 1983). The administration took no action, however, until the Soviet thrust into Afghanistan focused attention on the Persian Gulf. There began a scramble to fabricate a rapid deployment force and military facilities in the Middle East and North Africa. A Rapid Deployment Joint Task Force was established in March, 1980, at MacDill Air Force Base in Florida. Within a year, the Pentagon assigned to it four Army divisions (approximately 100,000 troops) and associated airlift, sealift and logistical capabilities. Equipment was prepositioned on land and on ships. Later in 1980, the Rapid Deployment Force (RDF) began to conduct joint operations with several Middle Eastern countries.

Acquiring facilities in the area proved no easy task. Many states in the region resented America's support of Israel and identified the United States with earlier colonial exploitation of the Middle East. Nevertheless, Washington did gain access to Masirah Island, near the Persian Gulf, as well as Berbera in Somalia, Mombasa in Kenya, and Ras Banas in southeastern Egypt.

Critics of the RDF concept ridiculed the meager extent of bases America might use in case of conflict near the Gulf. They insisted the United States could not begin to position enough troops there to blunt a serious Soviet drive. Defenders of the RDF accepted this contention but argued that the RDF need do no more than place a small contingent of forces in front of a Russian advance. That would guarantee superpower combat, a condition likely to deter a Soviet attack in the first place, RDF advocates claimed. The Reagan administration took measures to broaden the capabilities of the RDF during the 1980s.

ARMS CONTROL

Throughout the 1976 campaign, Carter stressed his desire to replace power politics, so closely associated with Henry Kissinger, with military

Chapter 6: Carter

restraint. In his acceptance speech in January, 1977, the new chief executive (1982) said, "We pledge perseverance and wisdom in our efforts to limit the world's armaments to those necessary for each nation's own domestic safety. We will move this year a step toward our ultimate goal—the elimination of all nuclear weapons from this earth" (p. 20). Cyrus Vance (1983) noted Carter's

> profound commitment to reversing, not simply curbing, the upward spiral of nuclear weapons. As much as any other president since World War II, Carter was repelled by the irrationality of piling up thousands upon thousands of unimaginably destructive nuclear weapons in both sides' arsenals.... He was convinced that rational men should start moving seriously and at once toward reducing the terrible danger of nuclear weapons (p. 51).

Carter signaled his own desire to control arms during his first meeting with Soviet Ambassador Anatoly Dobrynin on February 1, 1977. The president (1982) told Dobrynin that he (Carter) wanted to proceed on SALT, and he suggested negotiations on prior notification of long-range missile tests, a comprehensive test ban, demilitarization of the Indian Ocean, and sharp cutbacks in nuclear weapons.

When Carter entered office, an active arms control agenda was in place. Washington and Moscow had agreed to most provisions of a second SALT treaty, while negotiations on reducing troops in Europe (MBFR) were deadlocked. Two nuclear testing treaties, the Threshold Test Ban Treaty and the Peaceful Nuclear Explosions Treaty, had been signed but not ratified. During Vance's journey to Moscow in March, 1977, to work on SALT, he and his Soviet counterpart agreed to establish eight working groups on arms restraint. Not exactly negotiating bodies, these working groups could be characterized as bilateral study groups. Hopefully, each would give rise to an agreement some time in the future. Working groups were established for each of the following: comprehensive test ban, curbing anti-satellite weapons, demilitarizing the Indian Ocean, prior notification of test-firings of long-range missiles, conventional arms transfers, banning radiological weapons, chemical warfare, and civil defense. Except for the groups on civil defense and test-firings of long-range missiles, the working groups began meeting after a brief interval. Washington and Moscow also agreed to discuss nuclear proliferation and revitalize the MBFR talks. As we shall see in the ensuing pages, most of these initiatives, announced with so much hope, fizzled out by the end of Carter's term. The president failed to display the tenacity to sustain these efforts in the face of opposition within his own bureaucracy. The Soviet invasion of Afghanistan drove the final nail into the coffin of arms control.

SALT II

As we noted earlier, a second SALT agreement was near completion. However, President Carter was no more pleased with the agreement he had inherited than was President Reagan four years later. Strongly committed to arms control, Carter felt that the pact worked out under President Ford, based on the Vladivostok accords, did not go nearly far enough in reducing strategic weapons. In the spring of 1977, top foreign policy officials developed a new package for Secretary Vance to present at his March, 1977, meeting in Moscow. The new proposal consisted of the following elements:

- decrease overall aggregate strategic launchers from 2,400 (Vladivostok level) to 1,800–2,000;
- decrease number of MIRVed missiles from 1,320 (Vladivostok level) to 1,100–1,200;
- reduce number of modern heavy missiles to 150 (no reductions called for at Vladivostok);
- cut MIRVed ICBMs to 550;
- ban development, testing and deployment of new types of ICBM, including mobile ICBMs;
- limit the number of annual ICBM and SLBM test-firings to 6 each;
- ban all cruise missiles with range in excess of 2,500 kilometers;
- limit air-launched cruise missiles with 600–2,500 kilometer range to heavy bombers;
- eliminate the Soviet Backfire bomber from the aggregate total, provided Moscow gave assurances it would not extend the aircraft's range.

With this proposal, Carter hoped to move beyond the incremental reductions accepted at Vladivostok and take a giant step in the direction of arms restraint. The Soviet reaction was immediate and sharp. Moscow flatly rejected the American offer. Apparently, the Kremlin's response was based upon two considerations, one procedural and the other substantive.

In procedural terms, the Soviets regarded Vance's offer as an unwarranted and unexpected turning back on an agreement (Vladivostok) that had been all but finalized. Moscow preferred to wrap up the Vladivostok limits and then consider further reductions. The Soviets also were angry because Washington released its proposal publicly instead of following the customary procedure of informing Moscow first. Reflecting on these events, Vance (1983) hypothesizes that Moscow rejected the deep cuts because the Politburo had tortuously agreed to the Vladivostok limits, and re-thinking the matter was a gargantuan challenge.

Substantively, Vance's package invited the Soviets to make much more far-reaching cuts than required by the U.S. The explanation for this imbalance lay in the asymmetry of strategic weapons. As we have seen, the Soviets placed a much greater proportion of their warheads on ICBMs than did the Americans. Therefore, ICBM reductions degraded the Soviet arsenal more than the American arsenal. For instance, Vance's proposals called for the Soviets to reduce the number of heavy missiles from 308 to 150; the United States, lacking heavy missiles, needed to make no equivalent reductions. Russia would have to eliminate 400–500 planned ICBMs equipped with MIRV; the United States, none. The only system the U.S. would have to forgo was the MX missile, which was not yet even built. Furthermore, Vance's offer said nothing about limits on American forward-based-systems, so worrisome to Moscow. Thus, the Kremlin viewed the American proposals as seeking unilateral advantage.

President Carter's early denunciations of the Soviet Union for its human rights practices also did not incline Moscow to cast Vance's offer in a favorable light.

On the matter of SALT, Vance returned to Washington empty-handed. Shortly thereafter, negotiations resumed, largely on the basis of the Vladivostok accord. Two issues impeded agreement, cruise missiles and the Backfire bomber.

In the mid-1970s, the United States was well ahead of the Soviet Union in cruise missile technology. Moscow demanded that any cruise missiles with ranges exceeding 600 kilometers (about 375 miles) be included in the total number of permitted strategic launchers. The United States refused, on the ground that these weapons were not intended for strategic purposes.

The Soviets began to deploy the supersonic Backfire bomber around 1974. Washington insisted Backfire was a strategic weapon and should be counted in the permitted aggregate total. Moscow demurred, noting that the aircraft carried insufficient fuel to allow a bombing run from Russia to America and then back to Russia. Washington countered that the Soviets could refuel the aircraft in flight, allowing it to return. Alternatively, said the U.S., the Backfire could land in Cuba after completing its bombing run over American territory.

Agreement on these issues proved elusive. Meanwhile, Washington continued to put forth proposals that Moscow regarded as one-sided. For example, the U.S. suggested reducing heavy missiles (possessed only by Moscow) to 190 instead of 150 as proposed in March, 1977. Washington also offered a moratorium on the MIRVing of large (smaller than heavy) ICBMs. The Soviets rejected both proposals.

The negotiations continued in an atmosphere of deteriorating superpower relations. Moscow continued to raise objections to Carter's human rights denunciations. America regarded Moscow's involvement in the fighting between Ethiopia and Somalia as aggressive and in violation of the spirit of cooperation. Washington continued to harbor suspicions about the intent behind the deployment of SS-20s and new generations of strategic systems. The Soviets took particular exception to the normalization of relations between Washington and Beijing, announced in December, 1978. Brzezinski had made no secret of his plans to use this new friendship as a lever against the U.S.S.R.

The spreading acrimony between the superpowers delayed final agreement on SALT until June, 1979. That month, Brezhnev and Carter journeyed to

Vienna and initialed the pact.

The following month, the Senate Foreign Relations Committee opened hearings on the treaty. In the midst of these deliberations, there occurred a trivial incident that got blown all out of proportion and caused a delay fatal to the SALT II treaty. The episode illustrates the hazards (unavoidable in a democracy) of allowing domestic political considerations to affect foreign policy.

Preparing to run for re-election in Idaho, Democratic Senator Frank Church, chairman of the Foreign Relations Committee, was sensitive to accusations of being soft on communism. On August 30, Church announced at a press conference that American intelligence had confirmed the existence of a Soviet combat brigade of ground forces in Cuba, numbering 2,300–3,000 men. The senator condemned the Soviets and called on Carter to demand withdrawal of these forces. Speaking for the administration, Vance declared at a September 5 press conference that "we regard this as a very serious matter affecting our relations with the Soviet Union" (Quoted in Garthoff, 1985, p. 829). The administration, overreacting to a situation that contained no threat, branded the presence of the Soviet brigade in Cuba as "unacceptable." Not wishing to be bullied by Washington, the Soviets refused to withdraw the brigade. A diplomatic impasse was at hand. Finally, on October 1, Carter resolved the episode by beating a retreat. In a televised address, he said he had extracted Soviet agreement not to enlarge the unit or give it additional capabilities. He also detailed certain steps the United States would take to ensure the brigade would present no threat (which it didn't anyway).

Insignificant in itself, the incident of the Cuban brigade poisoned U.S.-Soviet relations and interrupted Senate consideration of SALT for a crucial month. Treaty opponents cited the presence of the brigade, which violated no previous understanding, as evidence that the Soviets were taking advantage of detente and were not a fit partner for an arms control pact. The incident also stirred resentment in Moscow, which could find no basis for the American excitement over troops that offered no threat whatsoever. Had the incident not occurred, it is more than possible that the Senate would have approved the SALT II treaty before the Soviet invasion of Afghanistan in December, 1979. The anti-Soviet feeling that swept Congress in the wake of that invasion led Carter to withdraw the treaty from Senate consideration.

Since debate over the merits of the treaty extended into the Reagan administration, we shall postpone our consideration of that topic until the next chapter.

Conventional Arms Transfers

In line with his desire to downgrade the role of force, Carter instructed Vance to discuss conventional arms transfers (CAT) with the Soviets during his March, 1977, trip to Moscow. A study group on CAT was established during this meeting. Two months later Carter gave an indication of his feelings about arms transfers, pledging that henceforth arms transfers would be viewed as "an exceptional foreign policy implement," and that the burden of persuasion would "be on those who favor a particular arms sale, rather than on those who oppose it."

Substantive discussions commenced in December and lasted for one year before collapsing, Under the best of circumstances, it is doubtful whether agreement could have been achieved, inasmuch as other suppliers would probably have jumped in to fill gaps left by U.S.-Soviet restraint. The circumstances were far from ideal, however, as superpower relations began to fray due to disputes over human rights and intervention in the third world. Nevertheless, initial talks gave rise to a certain degree of optimism by the close of the second round in May, 1978. At this point, State and ACDA split on negotiating strategy. As originally conceived (primarily by the State Department), the CAT talks were part of a broader effort to temper superpower competition in the third world. In State's view, the two parties should try to reach agreement on certain areas of the globe where the superpowers would exercise circumscription in transferring weapons. The U.S. suggested Latin America and sub-Saharan Africa as promising regions, since they received only a modicum of outside arms to begin with. Moscow agreed and proposed West Asia (including Iran) and East Asia (including China and the Koreas) as well. The Soviet suggestion was consistent with Russia's long-standing desire to keep hostile forces distant from its borders, but it clashed with America's containment policy. Besides, Washington did not wish to name China as an object of arms control at a time of delicate normalization negotiations. Iran too was not an auspicious choice for the United States, inasmuch as the long-standing American ally was experiencing grave internal upheavals connected with the demise of the shah. Despite these differences, the talks proceeded.

In the meanwhile, ACDA proposed that the two governments adopt a list of *weapons* not to be transferred, instead of focusing on *areas* for the exercise of restraint. As agreement on regions proved elusive, Carter backed ACDA's approach. Moscow showed little enthusiasm for the shift in America's position. Washington itself was losing interest in the discussions, as Carter felt the need to demonstrate firmness in the face of Soviet and Cuban meddling in such places as Angola, the Horn of Africa and Yemen. One year after the CAT talks began, they expired without result.

B-1 Bomber and ASAT

Carter's efforts to de-emphasize military force were proving more than a challenge in the SALT and CAT forums. In June, 1977, though, the president made a unilateral decision in the direction of arms control. The Pentagon had been lobbying with vigor for a new bomber to replace the aging B-52. Many

B-52 aircraft were older than the pilots who flew them. President Ford had approved development of a state-of-the-art strategic bomber designated B-1. Carter reversed this decision in favor of modernizing the B-52 fleet and equipping it with thousands of air-launched cruise missiles (ALCM). Armed with such weapons, B-52s could fly up to the periphery of Soviet air space and launch their ALCMs against targets inside Soviet territory. Among many considerations behind this decision, cost-effectiveness was one. Cost estimates for the B-1 were soaring. Political conservatives cited Carter's decision as evidence that Carter was soft on defense and was guilty of unilateral disarmament. At the very least, they said, Carter should have demanded an equivalent step from Moscow.

Just before leaving office, President Ford approved a two-track policy concerning anti-satellite (ASAT) weapons. This decision directed the Defense Department to develop an ASAT capability while at the same time to explore the possibility of an ASAT accord with the Soviet Union.

Satellites were rapidly becoming the standard means of military communication for both superpowers. A "decapitation" strike against satellites would effectively prevent the target government from receiving battle assessments from field commanders and from communicating orders to these commanders. Satellites were also crucial tools of military intelligence.

American interest in ASAT sprang from Soviet efforts to develop an ASAT capability. From 1968–1971 and from 1976–1977, Moscow had tested a clumsy ASAT missile. While most of these tests (9 of 13) had resulted in failure (Garthoff, 1985), Washington feared that the Soviets might achieve a breakthrough that could give them a decisive advantage in time of war. Mutual deterrence would best be served if neither side attained an ASAT capability. Should one or both superpowers gain such a capability, it might be tempted to exploit it in time of tension and thereby precipitate a war. A moratorium on ASAT would have to be mutual if it were to materialize at all.

Carter was particularly anxious to devise a mutual ASAT ban, an idea he proposed to Brezhnev in a letter sent the month after the presidential inauguration. As a result of Vance's Moscow trip in March, 1977, an ASAT working group was established. The American government then undertook a study of space policy and decided to continue work on ASAT while opening discussions on a mutual prohibition.

Talks began in May, 1978, and continued intermittently through June, 1979, when they adjourned without success. Like most other arms control initiatives, this one fell prey to the growing acrimony in superpower relations. During the talks, the Soviets suspended their ASAT tests in a gesture of good will. The United States pressed for a short-term moratorium on testing, until its own program was ready to be tested, a good example of the use of arms control to halt the opposition's progress while one is playing catch-up. The Soviets preferred a long-term or indefinite suspension of tests. One can speculate that the

Soviets took this position, which would seem to negate their lead, because they doubted their system held much promise and/or they expected the U.S. would develop a superior system. Before the talks adjourned, the two sides were close to agreement on no-first-use and were discussing a prohibition on testing and deployment. After the invasion of Afghanistan, the talks did not resume.

Comprehensive Test Ban

Carter signified his enthusiasm for a comprehensive test ban by publicly calling for an agreement only four days following his inauguration. In June, 1977, the U.S., U.K., and the U.S.S.R. opened negotiations on the subject. The talks proceeded smoothly. In November, the Soviets made a concession, as Brezhnev abandoned reservations allowing the parties to conduct peaceful nuclear explosions. The Soviets had shown an interest in such explosions for purposes of digging dams, rechanneling rivers, and the like. The Soviets also agreed to accept Washington's suggestion that verification be carried out by national seismic stations on each other's territory, supplemented by on-site challenge inspections. The parties also agreed to limit a ban to 3–5 years. The Soviets preferred this because France and China were not participating in the talks and could conceivably achieve a technological breakthrough. The U.S. delegation's adoption of this position reflected influence by those opposed to a CTB, namely, the departments of energy and defense and the Joint Chiefs of Staff. These groups pressed for a short-term pact so that stockpiled weapons could be tested for reliability and weapons laboratories would remain in operation.

Starting in 1978, the influence of hard-liners in the Carter administration began to grow. This influence was apparent as the U.S. continually hardened its position in the CTB negotiations. The American delegation insisted that the treaty be renegotiated at expiration, instead of being automatically extended, as the Soviets preferred. Washington's position reflected the hard-liners' contention that more testing would be required. Then the U.S. insisted that seismographs to be situated in the U.S.S.R. be fabricated in the United States. Next, the U.S. called for real-time satellite reports from these seismic stations.

The continued alterations in the American position raised doubts in the Kremlin about American sincerity. These reservations proved well-founded, as Carter's early enthusiasm gave way to hesitation fueled by hawks in his administration and troublesome Soviet foreign adventurousness described earlier. In September, 1978, Carter redefined "comprehensive" to allow for a small number of tests. Not long thereafter, the delegations declared a recess. Following Afghanistan, the talks did not resume.

Radiological and Chemical Weapons

Radiological weapons produce harm primarily through the spread of radioactive substances. A working group established after Vance's March, 1977, trip to Moscow began working on an agreement to limit these weapons. In mid-1979 the two parties produced a draft agreement, which they then sent to the United Nations Committee on Disarmament (CD). The CD considered the agreement and suggested dropping the clause excluding nuclear weapons, adding a prohibition against attacking nuclear facilities with conventional weapons, reaffirming the right to use nuclear energy for peaceful purposes, and transferring monitoring responsibility from the Security Council to the General Assembly. By the time Carter left office, these matters had yet to be resolved and were carried over to the Reagan administration.

The working group on chemical weapons also managed to produce a draft agreement that went to the CD. Verification presents a particular difficulty here, because chemicals that might be used for military purposes have perfectly legitimate civilian uses (such as in pesticides). Therefore, any prohibition must be directed not toward the production of such chemicals but to their placement in weapons. The CD had yet to resolve the issue by the end of Carter's term.

Indian Ocean Arms Control

In 1977, the Indian Ocean region appeared to offer a good prospect for military restraint, inasmuch as neither superpower maintained a large military presence there. A working group set up during Vance's March, 1977, trip to Moscow began to discuss Carter's stated goal to demilitarize the Indian Ocean.

In October, the United States tabled a proposal calling for the U.S. and the Soviet Union to refrain from significantly upgrading its naval strength in the Indian Ocean or substantially altering previous patterns of military deployments there. Under these rules, the Soviet Union could maintain their deployment of 18–20 vessels, one-third to one-half combatants. The U.S. could continue its complement of three ships—two destroyers and a command vessel—on station and could send three task forces (including an aircraft carrier) a year into the Indian Ocean for visits lasting 35–65 days. Neither superpower would acquire new bases or expand existing military facilities in the Indian Ocean area.

As might be expected, not all elements in the U.S. government shared Carter's enthusiasm to place constraints on military deployments in that part of the world. Citing Russia's hovering land presence north of the Indian Ocean, the JCS and some other elements in the Defense Department argued that naval arms control would have no effect on Moscow's capacity to intervene. The Kremlin could mass troops on the borders of Turkey and Iran, and it could unleash bombers against other Indian Ocean states. The Soviets might also direct their Cuban surrogates, unrestrained by any treaty, to alter the status quo. Critics also referred to the need to protect American interests regardless of the Soviet Union. "The necessity for being present and manifestly prepared to provide such protection would exist even were there no Soviet maritime presence at all

Chapter 6: Carter 191

in the Indian Ocean," said Rear Admiral (retired) Robert J. Hanks (Quoted in Stivers, 1981–1982, p. 132). Hanks had in mind the need to rescue hostages endangered by revolutionary upheaval, protect Western shipping against terrorists and others, and provide a show of force in support of pro-Western governments. Since the Navy was the ideal instrument for these tasks, Hanks warned against limiting nautical forces in the Indian Ocean.

Those who favored an accord claimed that America held a decisive upper hand when a task force was present in the Indian Ocean. Thus an agreement would not only freeze Soviet inferiority but also stand in the way of a Soviet military buildup, including air bases. Reinforcing America's advantage was the presence of Australian and British warships in the Indian Ocean. Advocates of an agreement also doubted the U.S. could wield the influence referred to by Hanks with just a few ships. It must be added that those who favored an accord were thinking beyond the Indian Ocean to the broader U.S.-Soviet relationship. An agreement on the Indian Ocean would pave the way for superpower restraint in other regions; detente would receive a boost.

The prospects for demilitarizing the Indian Ocean were shattered by events in Africa in late 1977 and 1978. Soviet/Cuban aid to Angola, Mozambique and Ethiopia strengthened the position of Washington hawks, who in turn persuaded Carter to suspend the talks. The overthrow of the shah and seizure of American hostages convinced the president that the time was not opportune for curbing American military capabilities in the Indian Ocean. Efforts to demilitarize the Indian Ocean expired.

Nuclear Proliferation

A former nuclear engineer, Jimmy Carter understood and cared deeply about the spread of nuclear weapons. The most likely route to the proliferation of nuclear weapons was nuclear energy. Plutonium produced by the burning of uranium in nuclear reactors could be used as the fuel for a nuclear weapon. Uranium enriched beyond its natural state could also be used for this purpose. In order to curb the spread of nuclear weapons, therefore, Carter sought the cooperation of nuclear allies in restricting the dissemination of such technology.

Carter's efforts inevitably led to disputes with other nuclear suppliers. England, France and West Germany hoped to finance their nuclear energy programs, in part, by selling reprocessing plants and other lucrative technology abroad. Washington managed to antagonize West Germany and Brazil by seeking (unsuccessfully) to halt the export of a reprocessing plant from the former to the latter.

In April, 1977, Carter formally announced his administration's nonproliferation policy. The thrust of this policy was to minimize the accumulation of nuclear weapons fuel from nuclear energy programs. Carter declared that the United States would defer indefinitely commercial reprocessing, restructure the

American breeder reactor program, and redirect nuclear R&D funding toward the exploration of safer methodologies.

Closely tied to Carter's policy was a three-year international study known as the International Nuclear Fuel Cycle Evaluation (INFCE). Over 500 experts from some 50 countries met starting in late 1977 to consider the consequences of nuclear energy programs. Their report, issued in February, 1980, affirmed the Carter administration's fears about the weapons implications of nuclear energy. However, the document did not persuade countries to turn away from the quest for more nuclear energy.

Congress too took an interest in controlling the spread of nuclear weapons. In 1978 the legislature passed the Nuclear Non-Proliferation Act. This bill set criteria for licensing the export of nuclear material and technology and proscribed such exports to any country that refused to accept international safeguards on all its nuclear plants. While the president could waive these restrictions in face of national security, Congress could override such waivers.

Applying the Act proved no simple task, as represented by the case of India. Under a 1963 accord, the U.S. contracted to supply India with fuel for its safeguarded nuclear reactor at Tarapur. When India refused to accept international safeguards on all its nuclear facilities, as required by the 1978 legislation, the Nuclear Regulatory Commission denied a license to export fuel to Tarapur. This decision seemed to reflect Carter's preference on matters of nuclear proliferation. However, Carter reversed the NRC's decision. The episode illustrates how easily one foreign policy objective can conflict with others. Carter felt duty-bound to honor the earlier contract. He also feared India would abolish safeguards at Tarapur if the U.S. ceased to supply fuel. Finally, in the wake of Moscow's invasion of Afghanistan, the administration sought cooperative relations with all states in the region. While the House of Representatives overrode Carter's decision, the Senate did not, and the sale went through.

It must be added that the accidents at Three Mile Island and Chernobyl led to a precipitous decline in interest in nuclear energy worldwide.

Intermediate-Range Nuclear Forces

It will be recalled that, largely in response to Moscow's deployment of SS-20 missiles, NATO adopted in December, 1979, a two-track policy regarding intermediate-range nuclear forces (INF). One track consisted of engaging the Soviets in negotiations to halt or reverse INF deployments. The second track called for the stationing of 108 Pershing IIs and 464 GLCMs by NATO while the talks proceeded. Here we shall be interested primarily in the first track.

Moscow was particularly worried about the Pershing II missile, because its flight-time to target was only 6–10 minutes. This brief interval made the weapon ideal for a first strike, since it could without warning destroy many Warsaw Pact command, communication, control and intelligence facilities. The

Soviets also viewed the missile as in violation of the spirit of SALT, since the missile could strike strategic targets inside the U.S.S.R., while the SS-20 was incapable of such a mission against the United States.

The INF negotiations commenced at a most untimely moment, not long after the Soviet invasion of Afghanistan. As we have seen, this act infected the entire corpus of cooperative activities between the superpowers.

The first round of talks, lasting from mid-October to mid-November, 1980, found the two sides far apart. The American position, worked out in previous discussion with its NATO partners, called for restricting the talks to Soviet and American land-based INF missiles: SS-4s, SS-5s, SS-20s, Pershings, and GLCMs. The Soviets sought broader talks. They insisted deployment of the SS-20 was only in reaction to the vast array of NATO nuclear systems on land, at sea and in the air. Thus, Moscow wanted to include all NATO INF, not just those deployed by the United States. Moscow's definition of INF included all Western forward-based nuclear systems, including nuclear-capable bombers based on land and sea. Moscow also took exception to Washington's demand that the INF talks include Soviet systems deployed in the Far East well out of Europe's range. Washington maintained that Moscow could transfer these systems to Europe, so they should be included. The Soviets also proposed lower levels for American than Soviet INF, on the ground that Moscow needed to offset not just American nuclear systems but those of France and Great Britain as well. Other than defining their positions, the two parties achieved no progress during this first round of talks. Negotiations resumed in 1982 after Carter left the White House.

One final arms control accomplishment need detain us here. In the early 1970s, the U.S. Senate, spurred by Sen. Claiborne Pell of Rhode Island, took up the question of modifying the environment for hostile purposes. Such action could include inducing a tidal wave or altering the weather to ruin a country's agriculture. At their last summit, Nixon and Brezhnev agreed to negotiate a ban on such behavior. In 1974 the Soviets proposed in the General Assembly a broad ban on environmental modification. Negotiations moved to the CCD the following year, and agreement was announced in 1976. The draft treaty prohibited only those actions that were "widespread, long-lasting or severe." In 1979 the Senate approved the Environmental Modification Treaty.

Despite his fervent embrace of arms control at the outset of his administration, Carter's accomplishments were modest. He did conclude a second SALT agreement, but he elected to withdraw it from Senate consideration in order to save himself from the embarrassment of almost certain defeat. Efforts to control conventional arms transfers, limit anti-satellite weapons, terminate all nuclear testing, curb radiological and chemical weapons, demilitarize the Indian Ocean, and limit INF proved abortive. The president did cancel the B-1 bomber and the neutron bomb, and the Environmental Modification Treaty was finalized on his watch. In toting up the arms control achievements of the Carter administration, it is only fair to say that both superpowers respected the provisions of SALT II (with a few minor exceptions) while seeking to negotiate a subsequent pact. Yet, arms control enthusiasts were sorely disappointed at the meager results achieved by the Carter administration.

To everyone's surprise, friends of military preparedness found much to applaud during the Carter years. At the outset, Carter pledged to de-emphasize the obsession with military force that he said characterized his predecessors. He accepted the doctrine of strategic equivalence. In his view, however, maintaining parity called for approval of the MX ICBM and the Trident SLBM. In signing off on PD-59, which detailed the countervailing strategy, Carter significantly broadened America's nuclear arsenal. Approval of NATO's decision to deploy INF had a similar effect. Establishment of the Rapid Deployment Force called for an expansion of the country's conventional forces, particularly airlift and sealift capabilities.

As has been mentioned on many occasions, the decline of detente and the Soviet invasion of Afghanistan had much to do with deflecting Carter from his initial course of emphasizing arms control over military preparedness. Carter's successor was to continue this stress on military preparedness.

7
REAGAN

THE 1980 ELECTIONS

In 1980 voters enjoyed a genuine choice between the two major presidential candidates. Jimmy Carter ran on his record, an accumulation of achievements and failures that many citizens found unsatisfactory. Americans felt pistol-whipped by high inflation and low productivity. Many citizens also felt that Carter had allowed the nation to grow weak and suffer humiliation at the hands of countries most Americans regarded—perhaps erroneously—as inferior. The most notable such instance was Iran, whose Islamic fundamentalist government held over 500 Americans hostage for 444 days. A rescue attempt that sputtered in the desert merely added to Carter's image as a vacillating leader. Embroidering this image of America as a faltering giant were the defeat in Vietnam, Carter's retreat on the Russian brigade in Cuba, inaction in the Horn of Africa and Washington's inability to pry Soviet troops out of Afghanistan.

Jimmy Carter unwittingly contributed to his own demise in magnifying the significance of certain events. The Soviet brigade in Cuba represented scarcely a pinprick in America's side. It certainly did not warrant statements that the presence of the brigade was unacceptable, a position from which Carter was forced to retreat. Neither the seizure of American hostages in Teheran nor the Soviet invasion of Afghanistan challenged fundamental American interests. Carter magnified both of these events, which America was powerless to prevent, all out of proportion and thereby fed his image of impotence.

Ronald Reagan rode onto the national political stage at the very time when many Americans longed for a decisive and tough leader. Seizing upon this yearning, Reagan masterfully utilized the media to persuade the country that he would restore national greatness. The former governor of California vowed that he would revitalize the nation's military power. He insisted that America must cease coddling left-leaning third world countries that nourished themselves on morsels of criticism aimed at America. Most of all, Reagan promised to face down the Soviet Union. In Reagan's eyes, Russia was an expansionist state that would stop at nothing to advance its interests. Every gain for the Soviets represented a loss for America, Reagan insisted. The GOP challenger made no secret of his contempt for past efforts to ease superpower tensions and reach for accords to limit arms. On account of Moscow's expansionist ambitions and totalitarian nature, he explained, there was virtually no basis for accommodation with the Soviet Union. Reagan criticized past arms control agreements, especially SALT II, as harmful to American interests and pledged to build up the country's arsenal. In setting aside the goals of easing tensions with the Soviet Union and controlling nuclear arms, Reagan in effect repudiated almost forty years of American foreign policy. Nevertheless, many Americans were swayed by his accusation that under Carter America had grown feeble, and that the country must harden its military muscle.

Domestically, Reagan also sought to repeal several decades of accepted policy. Reagan came down hard on what he termed the gargantuan size of government. Not only was big government expensive, he said, but more importantly, it stifled individual initiative and strangled the economy. A government safety net for all individuals, he claimed, discouraged citizens from taking the high-flying risks that had propelled the country forward until the New Deal. Government had entangled business in so many regulations that it could no longer churn out the products and technologies that had made America the world's foremost economic power. Reagan promised that, if elected, he would "get big government off the people's backs."

When the polls finally closed in November, 1980, Ronald Reagan carried the day. The Republicans were in control in the Senate, but the Democrats retained control of the House of Representatives. In the 1986 mid-term election, the Democrats captured the Senate while retaining dominance in the House. So it remained throughout the Reagan presidency.

THE REAGAN ADMINISTRATION

The leading policy-makers in the Reagan administration, including the president himself, were singularly unversed in foreign policy, with the exception of Secretary of State Alexander M. Haig. Furthermore, many of these personalities were interested much more in domestic politics than in foreign affairs. Toward the beginning, Reagan's staff was nearly obsessed with image-building. Seeking to restore respect to the office of president, they took great pains to fabricate Reagan's image as strong and tough, a virile leader. The president and his aides also believed that revitalizing the economy was urgent, while foreign policy could be set aside for a time. The world, however, was not content to wait. Foreign policy questions called for answers. Unfamiliarity with a topic does not necessarily serve to prevent individuals from forming views, sometimes strong ones, on that topic. Let us try to gauge the ideas of a handful of leading policy-makers toward the Soviet Union, arms control and military preparedness.

"Where presidents from Truman to Carter saw the cold war as a power struggle, Reagan saw it as a holy war" (Schlesinger, 1987/88, p. 265). In other words, the president viewed U.S.-Soviet relations not as a challenge to be managed but rather as a life-and-death struggle between the forces of good and evil. Soviet values and beliefs were so antithetical to those held by the majority of Americans that no purpose was to be served by trying to bridge the superpower gap. Seeking agreements with Moscow was virtually pointless, since the Soviets would sign only those pacts that would confer upon themselves unilateral advantage. The two powers shared no common goals, since the object of each was the annihilation of the other. It was this outlook that led Reagan to state that the Soviet Union is "the focus of evil in the modern world" and that "the Soviet Union underlies all the unrest that is going on" in the world. In Reagan's eyes, the proper way to meet this threat was not through a search for common ground but with military strength. Arms control could only weaken America's resolve. Thus, at the outset of his presidency, Reagan all but abandoned efforts to negotiate agreements with Moscow and set about strengthening America's military might. As we shall see, Reagan oversaw the largest accumulation of arms in the nation's peacetime history. This led one observer to remark that during the president's first term, his foreign policy consisted primarily of swelling the arms budget (LeFeber, 1985).

Curiously, while the president's rhetoric crackled with ideological and confrontational phrases, his actions belied a hesitation to engage the Soviets in direct clashes. It seems that the more pragmatic views of his secretaries of state—first Haig and then George P. Shultz—submerged Reagan's instinct to throw down the gauntlet at Moscow's feet. In his second term, Reagan moved toward unilateral rhetorical disarmament and displayed traditional moderation in his actions. Gone were references to Moscow as the implacable enemy. Conservatives were horrified to witness the president smiling and bantering with General Secretary Mikhail Gorbachev at a series of summit conferences. Indeed, by the conclusion of his presidency, Reagan's reversal of course toward the Soviet Union proved no less dramatic than his predecessor's change in direction after the invasion of Afghanistan. Still, it seems fair to conclude that for most of his presidency, Reagan adopted an extremely hostile outlook toward the Soviet Union, and that he emphasized military preparedness far above arms control.

The only member of Reagan's inner circle to possess previous foreign policy experience, Secretary of State Alexander M. Haig, Jr., served on Henry Kissinger's White House staff from 1969–1973. Haig shared Reagan's outlook toward the Soviet Union, but he also possessed a sober realization that the two superpowers were bound to share the planet far into the future. Therefore, he believed it was necessary to work out some rules of international conduct or limits to their competition, if they were to avoid blowing themselves up some day. Thus, Haig acted as a brake on Reagan's ideological momentum. The secretary of state sought to compel the Soviet Union to accept "restraint and reciprocity" in its international behavior. In a passage that evokes the draught of containment sweetened with a twist of optimism, Haig (1984) wrote:

> The Soviet Union, as Reagan came to office, was in an expansionist period, but already ... the point of excess had been reached. America and the West might wait for this historical phenomenon to subside, but we and our friends could not wait in idleness. We must do what we could ... to arrest Soviet imperialism by confronting it, by containing it ... and, when it was in harmony with international stability and the cause of freedom, by joining with the Soviets to make one small peace after another in the countless places where they have made their small and deadly and unnecessary wars (p. 107).

Haig (1984) clearly shared his boss' view that Moscow was expansionist.

> Like the assiduous students of tactics and vulnerabilities that they are, the Russians would send out a probe—now in Angola, again in Ethiopia, finally in El Salvador—to test the strength of Western determination. Finding the line unmanned, or only thinly held, they would exploit the gap. From unstable situations of this kind, routs develop. It was time to close the breach and hold the line (p. 95).

At the same time, the secretary of state was more optimistic than his chief that the two superpowers could find enough common ground to avoid a final showdown.

In mid-1982, Haig was eased out of the Cabinet for his insistence on playing the "vicar" of foreign policy. This conception of his role differed from that held by other leading members of the administration, men who distrusted his ambition. (Haig had made an unsuccessful bid for the 1980 GOP nomination.) Haig's successor, George P. Shultz, exerted an even more pragmatic and moderating influence over the president's ideological instincts.

If restraining forces emanated from Foggy Bottom, the same could not be said for the Pentagon. Secretary of Defense Caspar W. Weinberger, together with some of his civilian assistants (notably Richard N. Perle and Fred C. Ikle), mirrored Reagan's ideological outlook and readiness to engage the Soviet Union in geopolitical confrontation across the globe. Weinberger (1987) wrote,

> The European experience before World War II bears a remarkable resemblance to the present, especially in some of the attitudes that ascribe solely peaceful and defensive intentions to the Soviet Union's military buildup. If it is not careful, the democratic West might one day find itself in the same dangerously weak position that the Allies were in when Germany attacked in 1939 (p. 12).

As late as the spring of 1988 he said,

> Just because General Secretary Gorbachev wears a smile and dresses fashionably does not mean there is any fundamental change in Soviet goals.

* * *

Chapter 7: Reagan 199

> ...no general secretary will be allowed to alter in any fundamental way the *never-changing* Soviet goals of world domination, or the nature of the Soviet regime. (italics added)
>
> * * *
>
> The West's decade-long [referring to the 1970s] reduction of military expenditures, and its good-faith effort to achieve stabilizing arms control, had been answered by unremitting Soviet actions increasing its military capabilities. The West could not allow the military balance to swing further in favor of the Soviets (Weinberger, 1988, pp. 700–703).

As might be expected, Reagan often received conflicting advice from the departments of State and Defense. As his tenure in office advanced, Reagan's own sense of pragmatism, joined with moderating advice from State, generally overcame his ideological predispositions, reinforced by Defense. Nevertheless, the entire thrust of the Reagan administration was to view the Soviet Union as hostile, aggressive and dangerous. This outlook inclined American policy markedly in favor of military preparedness over arms control. Some (including the early Reagan) deemed Moscow an unfit partner for any agreement, based on the godless totalitarian nature of the Soviet system. Against such a foe, the safest course was to accumulate military power, a cardinal objective of the Reagan administration. This preference was reinforced, as we shall see, by a perception that the United States had fallen behind the Soviets in military might.

THE INTERNATIONAL CONTEXT

As mentioned previously, the leading priorities of the new administration lay in the domestic realm, not foreign affairs. The president also set out to lower taxes and shrink the size of government. He also deemed it important to restore the self-confidence of the nation in the wake of humiliations at the hands of the Iranians, the Russians and the Vietnamese. Reagan also sought to revive confidence in American institutions, especially the presidency. Historians may well place the principal achievements of the Reagan administration in these areas. Reagan did preside over a healthy boost in American pride and prestige (and consequently influence) during his eight years in office. These achievements were somewhat dimmed, however, by the Iran/Contra scandal of his second term.

Regardless of preferences, no president can ignore foreign affairs for long, and so Reagan was compelled to deal with the world around him. To an even greater extent than Nixon, Reagan placed the Soviet Union at the vortex of American foreign policy. In direct contrast to Jimmy Carter, Reagan paid little heed to "global order" issues and the third world, except as a battleground with Moscow.

It will be recalled that U.S.-Soviet relations plummeted during the last year of the Carter administration, following Carter's overreaction to the invasion of Afghanistan. Reagan entered office with no particular desire to patch up relations. Indeed, his hatred and distrust of communist Russia led him to concentrate on gathering military strength rather than seeking compromise settlements. The state of U.S.-Soviet relations was reflected in Secretary Haig's first meeting with Soviet Ambassador Anatoly Dobrynin. Haig (1984) explained, "At this early stage there was nothing substantive to talk about, nothing to negotiate, until the U.S.S.R. began to demonstrate its willingness to behave like a responsible power" (p. 105). The Soviets, in other words, had to reform; nothing different was required of America. At this icy encounter, Haig complained about Soviet actions in Africa and Afghanistan as well as support for Cuban interventions in Angola and Ethiopia. He warned Moscow to stay out of Poland, where the communist government was uttering threatening statements against the Solidarity trade union, which represented a threat to communist control of the country. Haig also complained about the transshipment of Soviet arms through Nicaragua to leftist insurgents in El Salvador. Needless to say, there was no meeting of minds between the two diplomats.

In April, 1980, Reagan lifted the grain embargo that Carter had imposed against the Soviet Union as a penalty for invading Afghanistan. This action made hardly a blip on the screen of U.S.-Soviet relations, as Moscow understood (properly) Reagan's action as an effort to ease the plight of American farmers and a response to political pressures from farm belt legislators. Besides, Reagan's inflammatory rhetoric about the Soviet Union submerged any goodwill that the lifting of the embargo might have created.

Relations with the Soviet Union took a downward dive toward the close of 1983 with the destruction of Korean Airliner 007. When the civilian aircraft with 269 persons aboard strayed off course over Soviet territory, a Soviet interceptor dispatched a missile into the body of the airplane, sending it plunging into the ocean. There were no survivors. Without waiting for any explanation from the Kremlin, Reagan vitriolically denounced the Soviet action, claiming that the heartless Soviet leaders knew from the outset that the innocent aircraft had unintentionally wandered off course. Later investigation revealed that the Soviets suspected the airplane was engaged on an intelligence mission to collect information on Soviet air defenses (since KAL 007 had strayed over highly sensitive Soviet military installations). While there is no evidence that the Kremlin perception was accurate, some mysteries surround the incident to this day. Why did the Korean pilot fail to respond to warnings by the pilot of the aircraft that eventually shot it down? Did not American surveillance reveal that a civilian airliner was lost over Soviet military facilities, and, if so, why didn't someone alert the pilot? In any event, the haste and intensity with which Washington denounced the Soviet action only confirmed Soviet suspicions that Washington held little interest in dialogue and compromise and instead preferred confrontation. Over the next few weeks, each side used the incident as a pretext for

Chapter 7: Reagan 201

making extremely negative remarks about the other. U.S.-Soviet relations were as chilly as they had been since the onset of the cold war. (In December, 1990, the Kremlin officially apologized to South Korea for downing the airliner.)

Two other events in 1983 brought superpower relations to their nadir. In March, President Reagan gave his noted "Star Wars" speech, which Moscow digested with extreme discomfort. (See the section of this chapter on military preparedness for a discussion of this speech.) Partly on account of the president's insistence on going ahead with this defensive system, the Soviets stormed out of recently resuscitated arms limitation talks. The dialogue between Washington and Moscow fell silent.

Inside the Soviet Union, the turbulence that accompanies unscheduled leadership changes contributed to paralysis in foreign policy. In November, 1982, the weak and doddering Brezhnev died, to be succeeded by the equally sclerotic Yuri Andropov. A little more than a year later, he passed away and was followed by Konstantin Chernenko. It was only in March, 1985, when Mikhail Gorbachev succeeded at the helm, that the Soviet Union had a vigorous leader who promised to remain in office for a substantial period of time.

However, it should not be concluded that in the absence of this revolving door of leadership, U.S.-Soviet relations would have been much better. The Soviet leadership, noting Reagan's 1983 outbursts designating the Soviet Union as "the focus of all evil" and an "evil empire," seems to have concluded that Washington had lost interest in cooperative relations and was embracing confrontation. In September, 1983, Andropov read a statement on Soviet radio and television describing the policy of the Reagan administration as "a militarist course that represents a serious threat to peace. Its essence is to try to ensure a dominating position in the world for the United States of America without regard for the interests of other states and peoples" (Garthoff, 1985, p. 1015). The Kremlin, it seems, concluded that the United States had made a fundamental shift in its foreign policy beginning in the final year of the Carter administration and extending into the Reagan presidency. As explained by Garthoff (1985), this alteration consisted of the following elements:

- abandonment of detente;
- a military buildup including deployment of intermediate-range nuclear missiles in Europe and ballistic missile defenses (Star Wars) and a quantum jump in military spending for all purposes;
- alteration in military doctrine from pure deterrence or war prevention to nuclear war fighting, marked by Carter's approval of PD-59 and Reagan's embrace of that doctrine;
- abandonment of arms control signaled by Carter's withdrawal of SALT II from Senate consideration and extended by Reagan's denunciations of arms control and tardiness in engaging the Soviets in strategic arms talks; and

- enthusiastic reliance on paramilitary tactics against leftist movements in the third world, including El Salvador, Nicaragua, Grenada, Afghanistan, Cambodia, Ethiopia, Angola and Mozambique.

By the end of 1983, each superpower entertained a mirror image of the other as seeking confrontation over detente and military advantage over arms restraint.

Not long after, U.S.-Soviet relations began to bounce back to their more normal condition, which consisted of a mixture of hostility and cooperation. This may have been due in part to a conviction in Washington that the nation had succeeded in restoring its military strength and could therefore deal as an equal partner with the Soviet Union. The approach of presidential elections may also have induced some moderation in American policy. Additionally, Washington may have come to realize that Moscow had shown considerable restraint in its external behavior during Reagan's first term. The moderating tones of Secretary Shultz and a new national security adviser, Robert McFarlane, were sounding louder in policy deliberations. No doubt the most substantial reason for the improvement in superpower relations was the arrival of Mikhail Gorbachev as master of the Kremlin. It gradually became clear that the energetic new leader wished to liberate the Soviet Union from its costly links to revolutionary movements around the world. Gorbachev proved to be the first Soviet leader to elevate economic vitality to top priority, symbolized by his embrace of *perestroika*. One means of strengthening the economy was to reduce the approximately 15% of GNP that flowed to the military. Accordingly, Gorbachev developed a genuine interest in arms control. The new leader's outlook amounted to a turning away from foreign policy adventures. Gorbachev displayed no taste for taking on new commitments overseas that would drain away resources from the ailing Soviet economy. Such preferences could not help pleasing the Reagan administration, which had viewed Moscow as expansionist in the extreme. More than any other factor, the accession of Gorbachev made a significant improvement in U.S.-Soviet relations possible.

Can hardliners in Washington substantiate their claim that it was primarily American toughness, as displayed by Reagan, that brought the Soviets around? Those who nod in the affirmative insist Reagan's strong-willed rhetoric and military buildup persuaded the Kremlin that it had no hope of winning the cold war. In consequence, Moscow gave up. In all likelihood, American resolve did lend credence to those Soviet policy-makers who argued for the need to divert energy and resources away from global confrontation. However, it required a leader like Gorbachev to realize that economic stagnation, an ossified bureaucracy and severe ethnic strife threatened to shred the very fabric of the Soviet Union and therefore required immediate attention. Regardless of America's stance, these overriding problems were bound to dominate the attention of Soviet policy-makers sooner or later.

The Geneva summit held in November, 1985, provided concrete evidence of the upturn in superpower relations. At this two-day get-acquainted session, Reagan and Gorbachev gained the opportunity to take each other's measure and commit themselves to future get-togethers. While they reached no agreements on arms control—they had not expected to reach any— they did agree on the general principle of reducing strategic arms by 50%, and they issued instructions to their teams of experts to work for such an accord. More important than this somewhat vague and distant aspiration was the cordial spirit that prevailed, a stark contrast to the frosty relationship that had existed between Reagan and previous Soviet leaders (whom Reagan never met). The two presidents developed a feeling of personal rapport and committed themselves to meet again in 1986 and 1987.

The 1986 summit occurred in October in Reykjavic, Iceland. At this hastily arranged meeting, President Reagan proposed the abolition of all Soviet and American strategic missiles within ten years. This suggestion provoked a storm of astonishment within the community of strategic analysts, inasmuch as America relied primarily on strategic missiles to protect the country against attack. Allies in Europe were also aghast, since they too relied on American missiles to dissuade Moscow from assaulting Western Europe. In addition, the allies felt they should have been consulted before Washington made such a proposal. Apparently, the president let himself get carried away by his vision of SDI, which in his view—shared by very few—would by itself protect the country. The chairman of the House Committee on Foreign Affairs, Dante B. Fascell, observed (1987), "To bargain away America's deterrent shield today for the hypothesis that SDI will be cost-effective, functional and deployable sometime in the near future, not to mention within ten years, would be the height of folly" (p. 743). In any event, Gorbachev conditioned his acceptance of Reagan's proposal on Reagan's willingness to extend the ABM Treaty (which prohibited such defenses as SDI) for another ten years and to refrain from developing and testing any SDI components outside the laboratory. Since this would shatter Reagan's dream of shielding the nation with missile defense, he refused. The summit adjourned without result.

As the Reagan administration moved toward its waning months, it became increasingly clear that Gorbachev was intent on transforming the Soviet state in the direction of economic liberalization and political openness, two values with much appeal to Americans. To make available resources for *perestroika*, Moscow agreed to withdraw from Afghanistan. The Soviets also indicated they were prepared to let Eastern Europe go its own way, and they applied pressure upon Cuba to remove its forces from southern Angola in order to promote a settlement in Namibia. These measures signaled a willingness by Moscow to renounce its ambition to promote global revolution. This perception could not but contribute to warmer feelings between the United States and the Soviet Union. At the end of 1987 the two leaders, now on almost familial terms, initialed a treaty to eliminate intermediate-range nuclear forces. It was hoped that the two powers would soon sign a strategic arms treaty, but by the time they met for the last time in the spring of 1988, negotiators were unable to agree. At this final gathering, held in Moscow May 29–June 2, Reagan and Gorbachev approved nine agreements on such subjects as student exchanges, fisheries, nuclear power research, maritime search and rescue, transportation and radio navigation. While welcome, these pacts did not approach the significance of a strategic arms treaty, and many observers were disappointed in the results of the summit.

A review of U.S.-Soviet ties during the Reagan years reveals a turnabout as remarkable as that under Jimmy Carter. At the commencement of the Reagan presidency, superpower relations moved toward their all-time low, only to vault upward by the close of 1988. Observers were beginning to relegate the phrase "cold war" to history.

In the early years of the Reagan administration, American relations with Russia were complicated by events in Poland. In the early 1970s, the Polish government borrowed heavily from Western banks to build heavy industry and upgrade technology. By Reagan's election, the Poles owed some $20 billion, yet the economy failed to advance as hoped for. When the communist government introduced a tight austerity program, angry workers formed a new organization, Solidarity, and demanded the right to strike and to vote in open democratic elections. The Roman Catholic Church offered its support. Solidarity represented a grave threat to communist control not only in Poland but throughout the Soviet realm. If Solidarity could get away with challenging the communist monopoly of power, the entire communist house could come crashing down. In a geopolitical context, Poland provided the corridor through which a succession of Western armies had invaded Russia. Only communist control, in Kremlin eyes, could block another assault. The Soviet Union, in brief, had strong reason to maintain communist control over Poland.

With encouragement from Moscow, Polish authorities in December, 1981, declared martial law and arrested Solidarity's leaders, except for the highly visible Lech Walesa. To dissuade Poles from rising up against these measures, Moscow assembled a large military force on the Polish border. These repressive measures angered Washington and contributed to the deterioration in U.S.-Soviet relations detailed earlier. To punish Poland and Russia, Reagan prohibited new credits and exports to Poland and imposed economic sanctions against Moscow, including suspension of Aeroflot service to American airports, deferral of talks on a new long-term grain commitment, a halt to the issuance of or renewal of export licenses for electronic equipment and computers, and a stay of export licenses for certain oil and gas equipment, including pipelayers. Along with its NATO allies, the United States called for the lifting of martial law in Poland, the release of political prisoners, and a dialogue among the government, Solidarity and the Catholic Church. For some time the situation remained frozen, but eventually the Polish government complied with Western demands. Reagan relaxed some of the sanctions against Poland in 1984 and removed them entirely by 1987. Democratic elections not long after left Solidarity in control of the country.

Washington's prohibition on the shipment of pipelaying equipment to Moscow led to a minor flap in the Western alliance. Reagan's ban occurred at the same time that a number of West European countries had contracted to purchase Soviet natural gas as an alternative to fragile supplies of Middle Eastern oil. Washington strongly opposed this arrangement, arguing that it would provide the Soviets with hard currency and render Europe dangerously dependent on its Soviet foe. At this juncture Washington sought to aggravate Soviet economic difficulties, thereby forcing Russia to divert resources from military to civilian purposes. The restriction on exporting pipelaying machinery to Russia had the effect of blocking construction of the pipeline. Washington took the additional measure of prohibiting European subsidiaries of American corporations, as well as European firms operating under license from American corporations, from selling such equipment to the Soviets. The Europeans were furious. Once Washington realized the restrictions were harming allied ties more than the Soviet Union, the United States retreated and lifted the restrictions on European companies.

Much more so than its predecessor, the Reagan administration focused on the Soviet Union and Europe, while slighting the third world. To the degree that Reagan devoted attention to the vast ring of developing nations that stretched around the world, he did so in terms of East-West conflict. That is to say, Reagan deemed most of these nations as insignificant in their own right. They took on importance primarily as tiltyards between the United States and the Soviet Union. This orientation often produced a blind spot that obscured the way third world nations felt about each other. For example, one stunningly unsuccessful effort by the Reagan administration was to tool a belt of Middle Eastern countries, which eyed each other with great suspicion, into a barrier against Soviet expansion southward. These countries displayed no interest whatever in signing on to Washington's cold war schemes. The Reagan administration had no patience with the anti-American rhetoric of many developing countries. As a staunch believer in free enterprise, Reagan had little use for the government-controlled economies of many developing countries. As opposed to the Carter administration, Reagan was determined to confront and face down third world regimes hostile to the United States. In response to third world pleas for a new international economic order and additional foreign aid, Reagan advised them to adopt a market economy as the remedy for their economic woes. He took the same view of the world's poor as he did of the American poor, namely, that they were undeserving and should work harder. The president had little appreciation for the fact that American prosperity was in part tied to the well-being of developing countries. As a group, they represented a larger market for American exports than Europe and Japan combined, but economically declining nations of the third world could afford to purchase few American goods. The third world also supplied such crucial strategic minerals as tin, natural rubber, oil, and bauxite. The hundreds of billions of dollars owed by developing nations to Western banks rendered the latter much more dependent on the prosperity of the former than the president realized.

Reagan's refusal to recognize indigenous forces in the third world was well expressed in a campaign speech in June, 1980. "Let's not delude ourselves," he said. "The Soviet Union underlies all the unrest that is going on. If they weren't engaged in this game of dominoes, there wouldn't be any hot spots in the world" (Quoted in LaFeber, 1985, p. 301). Nowhere did the president apply this viewpoint more fully than in Latin America. El Salvador is a country the size of New Jersey and contains 5 million people. Wracked by chronic poverty and a tradition of political oppression, El Salvador was experiencing a leftist revolution when Reagan entered office. The new administration's view of the situation was well expressed by Secretary Haig (1984).

> ... grave as its economic plight may be, El Salvador was not merely a local problem. It was also a regional problem that threatened the stability of all of Central America, including the Panama Canal and Mexico and Guatemala with their vast oil reserves. And it was a global issue because it represented the interjection of the war of national liberation into the Western Hemisphere (p. 118).

It was the regional and global dimension that the Reagan administration emphasized. Despite government-associated death squads which killed 40,000 civilians between 1979–1984 (LaFeber, 1985), and only a modicum of social or economic reforms, Washington supplied the regime with military and economic aid. In the absence of such assistance, the White House maintained, communist revolutionaries sponsored by Russia, managed by Cuba, and supplied through Nicaragua, would take over and export their revolution to neighboring countries. The Asian dominoes now spoke in a Spanish tongue. Critics of the president's policy insisted the primary cause of unrest was not communist meddling but local economic and social problems that the communists exploited. The best solution, opponents of the president's policy continued, was not to help the government fight the insurgents but to insist that the government clear away the underlying problems that fueled popular resentment. Sustaining the existing government without insisting upon reforms only served to compound the country's difficulties and generate more communist recruits, critics said. Reagan remained unconvinced. The civil war persisted throughout his term in office, settling into a stalemate between the conservative government and the leftist guerilas.

In neighboring Nicaragua, the Reagan administration revealed its tendency to equate Soviet *support* of third world countries with Soviet *control* of their governments. This confusion was facilitated by the White House's tendency to view all leftist movements in the third world as the product of Soviet geopolitical manipulation, not indigenous grievances. Overthrowing the Marxist government of Nicaragua became one of the foremost foreign policy objectives of the Reagan administration. Only two days after entering office, Reagan froze economic aid to the Sandinista regime. Not long after, Reagan authorized a campaign to unseat the government by supporting pro-American revolutionaries known as the *contras*. Claiming that the Sandinistas acted as the conduit for supplying weapons to the leftist insurgents in El Salvador, Reagan directed the CIA to arm and train the *contras*. Among the more controversial activities undertaken by the CIA were the publication of a manual instructing *contras* on assassination of Sandinista officials and the mining of Nicaraguan harbors. The latter act led Congress to order the cut-off of funding for the *contras*. Not long after, Lt. Col. Oliver North of the National Security Council staff began to arrange secret funding for the *contras* from private sources. Eventually, North illegally used the proceeds from arms sales to Iran to sustain the *contras*. The *contras* failed to overthrow the Sandinista regime militarily. In elections held in February, 1990, however, Violeta Barrios de Chamorro defeated Sandinista President Daniel Ortega Saavedra, and a new regime took over.

In a related action, the Reagan administration forcefully overthrew the government of the island country of Grenada, population 110,000, as a signal of firmness to leftists throughout the Western Hemisphere. The American invasion was precipitated by the overthrow of the Marxist government by a pro-Soviet faction in late 1983. On the pretext that 1,000 American medical students were in danger, American military forces landed on the island and replaced the government with one more to its liking. American troops encountered several hundred Cuban construction soldiers as well as Soviet, North Korean and East German personnel. Sizeable caches of arms were also unearthed.

Another third world country that Reagan identified as under Moscow's thumb was Libya. Four months after entering office, Reagan ordered the closing of the Libyan embassy in Washington, on the ground that President Qaddafi used it as a support base for terrorism. Relations between the two countries quickly soured, fueled by an intense personal dislike between Qaddafi and Reagan. In August, 1981, two American jets shot down a pair of Libyan fighters to contest Qaddafi's claim of control over the Gulf of Sidra. Citing Tripoli's continuing support for terrorism, allegedly abetted by Moscow, the United States dispatched aircraft to bomb Qaddafi's headquarters and various military facilities in Libya. Thereafter, the dictator's visible support for terrorism subsided.

Elsewhere in the third world, Reagan actively opposed Marxist regimes with ties to the Soviet Union. The United States gave "overt/covert" support to insurgents in Afghanistan, Angola, Cambodia, Ethiopia and other countries deemed to be in the Soviet camp. Some pundits dubbed American paramilitary aid to anti-Marxist revolutionaries the "Reagan Doctrine."

Toward the sunset of the Reagan administration, the Soviet-American geopolitical confrontation in the third world began to wane. Not long after coming to power in 1985, Gorbachev gave evidence of seeking to draw down Soviet commitments to far-flung allies. In the interest of diverting funds to economic revival, Gorbachev pulled Soviet forces out of Afghanistan and proved forthcoming on settling such third world disputes as those in Angola, Namibia and Cambodia. The Soviet president erected no barriers to a cease-fire in the war between Iran and Iraq. Moscow had ceased soliciting new clients in the third world. Doctrinaire communists were horrified to witness the leader of the world's strongest communist country turning his back on global revolution. Soviet-American cooperation in settling various third world conflicts most certainly contributed to the marked improvement in relations between the superpowers at the end of the Reagan administration. While the countries managed to sign no arms control accord other than the INF Treaty, the improvement in their relations across the globe helped clear a path for a strategic arms treaty during the Bush presidency.

MILITARY PREPAREDNESS

Throughout the 1980 election campaign, Reagan lamented the fact that Carter had allowed the United States to fall behind the Soviet Union militarily. Secretary Haig (1984) summed up the administration's view of this dire situation in the following words:

> In the 1970s, the Soviets deployed an entirely new generation of land-based strategic missiles, three new submarine systems, and a new intercontinental bomber. In the same period, the megatonnage of American weapons was cut in half. America deployed no new ICBMs, no new ballistic missile submarines, no new bombers. Real U.S. defense spending shrank by 22 percent. The Army was reduced by three divisions and the number of Navy ships declined by half. During the Vietnam War, substantial proportions of U.S. defense expenditures were diverted to pay the operating expenses of the conflict, rather than being budgeted for overall force improvement (p. 221).

A decade earlier, Moscow saw itself in precisely the identical position, that is, dangerously trailing in military preparedness. Just as Reagan vowed to rectify the balance (if not over-correct to achieve American superiority), the Soviet Union in the 1970s felt it had no choice other than to catch up to the United States. The two countries were locked in a classic arms spiral.

During the decade prior to Reagan's election, Moscow engaged in a veritable feeding frenzy of weapons building. Moscow knew it was well behind America in MIRV technology, which dramatically boosted the firepower of a given number of missiles. The American Polaris and Minuteman II were technologically superior to their Soviet counterparts. While American B-52 and

FB-111 long-range bombers were targeted on the Soviet Union, Moscow had no aircraft that could reach American soil. The American navy had unquestioned control of the world's oceans.

If the Soviets wished to retain superpower status and advance the cause of Marxism around the globe, they had little choice other than to match American military strength. Accordingly, throughout the 1970s Moscow devoted enormous sums to military spending, outdistancing the United States even though the Soviet GNP was less than one-half that of the U.S. To be sure, Soviet citizens paid dearly for this spending spree in terms of reduced living standards.

Moscow augmented its capabilities in both strategic forces and general purpose forces. Three gargantuan new ICBMs—designated SS-17, 18, and 19—entered the Soviet arsenal. The SS-18, the largest of the three, especially troubled the U.S. This missile could carry three times the payload of America's Minuteman III. While the latter carried three warheads, the new Soviet projectile carried eight, each of which was larger than any single Minuteman warhead.

In actuality, the mammoth size of the new Soviet missiles was traceable to technical backwardness in miniaturization. Unable to fabricate modest-size warheads that carried high yields, Moscow was compelled to construct outsize missiles to carry their heavy payloads. To the U.S., however, the sheer magnitude of the new Soviet missiles appeared threatening. Looking to the future, some strategists observed that when the Soviets mastered the technology of miniaturization, the new Soviet missiles could carry so many warheads that the front end would resemble a porcupine.

At sea the Russians also churned forward. In the early 1970s, Moscow relied on a relatively primitive SLBM with a range of 1,750 miles, roughly comparable to America's early Polaris. By the middle of the decade, the Soviets had begun to deploy a new submarine, known as Delta-class, that carried a new improved missile with a range approximating 5,000 miles. At the dawn of the 1980s, Moscow MIRVed its SLBMs and was constructing the largest submarine in the world, the Typhoon-class.

The Soviets also invested huge amounts in general purpose forces, augmenting inventories in practically every category of weapon and support equipment. Moscow significantly boosted its stock of tactical aircraft, short-range missiles with nuclear warheads, armor and ships. By the time Reagan took office, the Soviet armed forces had more weapons than the U.S. in many categories. Particularly troublesome was the Soviet lead of 2–1 in numbers of tactical aircraft and 4–1 in tanks and armored personnel carriers. Furthermore, Soviet weapons were no longer technologically inferior to American equipment.

While Moscow's substantial investment in military preparedness was undeniable, the military significance of Russia's swelling arsenal was far from clear. Between one-fourth and one-fifth of Soviet forces were deployed along the extensive border with China; these forces, some argued, should not be included in calculating U.S.-Soviet force balances. In a general war, the United

States would gain assistance from European allies. The Soviets might have to *divert* forces to police their Warsaw Pact allies. Weapons comparisons could be misleading. In battle, tanks would not necessarily square off against each other. A more useful gauge would be one side's tanks versus the other side's anti-tank weapons, an area where the West was decidedly ahead. Nevertheless, Soviet numerical advantages left Western strategists uneasy not only about the outcome of a war but also about underlying Soviet intentions. Was all that equipment necessary strictly for defense?

No less troublesome was the situation at sea. The United States had practically taken for granted its control of the world's oceans. Aside from coastal defense, the Soviet navy offered little challenge to America's mighty armada. During the 1970s the Soviets constructed a "blue water" navy. Frenetic Soviet shipbuilding gave the Russians a 1.5–1.0 advantage in numbers of combat ships—surface plus submarine—by 1980. In the capacity to bring great power to bear at long distances, large aircraft carriers gave the United States unquestioned advantage. The Soviets had only three carriers, each of them much smaller than the typical American vessel. Nevertheless, Russian shipbuilding efforts led Western strategists to inquire why the Soviets were so intent on increasing their naval power. Such a large navy was not needed for defense. The Soviets had no need for a global navy to protect shipping, such as oil routes, or to reinforce allies in time of war. The Russians had always been a land power, and most of their strategic interests remained accessible by land. It was difficult to avoid the conclusion that the Soviet Union built such a large navy in preparation for exerting Soviet power and influence at far distances from their shores.

President Reagan and his top aides had no hesitation in their determination to rectify a military balance they felt had lurched to Moscow's advantage. Indeed, accumulating more military equipment became one of the new administration's leading priorities. Until this was accomplished, Reagan and his team expressed little interest in controlling the weapons of war through negotiations.

Reagan's military buildup can be measured in terms of both dollars and equipment. Let us first examine military spending.

Following the end of American involvement in Vietnam in 1973, America's defense budget began to decline. In 1976, Ford began a gradual increase in military spending, a trend followed by Carter, mostly for conventional forces. Reagan greatly accelerated this spending increase. Shortly after entering office, he requested $32 billion above Carter's request for that fiscal year; Congress gave its consent. These funds were primarily for existing programs, not new weapons systems. In January, 1982, Reagan unveiled an ambitious five-year defense plan. The president announced his intention to spend $1.6 trillion during this interval.

Practically no area of procurement escaped this orgy of military spending. With the exception of ballistic missile defense—to be examined later—President Reagan introduced no major modifications in American military doctrine. Instead, he sought to assure the integrity of existing military doctrine by heightening the Pentagon's capacity to carry out existing missions. In the next few pages, we shall highlight the most important targets of increased military spending.

In October, 1981, the Reagan administration revealed its plans for strategic weapons. The Pentagon announced its intention to accelerate development and production of various strategic systems already under way in the Carter years, including the Trident submarine, cruise missiles (which performed so effectively in the Persian Gulf War of 1991), and the MX and Trident missiles. Plans were also announced for developing a new strategic bomber, designated Stealth (an allusion to its radar-evading properties). The administration's strategic plans also embraced four new elements: increasing funds for civil defense; upgrading air defense (partly in reaction to a new Soviet bomber, Blackjack, under development); improving command, communication and control, so the nation's leadership could communicate in war with strategic commanders, including submarine commanders; and reviving the B-1 bomber canceled by Carter. The Pentagon requested 100 of these, to be known as B-1B, which would become available in the mid-1980s. The Stealth bomber would enter inventory in the 1990s. With B-52s about to be equipped with cruise missiles, some critics wondered whether the B-1B (a $35 billion program) was truly necessary. (The Air Force acquired the last of the 100 B-1Bs in 1988. From the beginning, the plane suffered from major problems such as leaks from fuel tanks, ineffective systems for jamming enemy radar, and engine failures. During the 1991 Persian Gulf War, the airplane sat grounded due to chronic engine troubles.)

One of the most controversial weapons advanced during the Reagan years was the MX missile. Conceptualization of this ICBM began nearly a decade before Reagan's election. As the Soviets pressed ahead with modernization of strategic weapons, the U.S. Air Force voiced fears that increasingly accurate Soviet ICBMs would be able to pulverize American ICBMs in their silos. The Air Force proposed a new ICBM, one that would remain invulnerable because it would be mobile. Preliminary development began in 1973. The new missile was designated MX for "missile experimental." It was designed to carry ten warheads accurate enough to hit Soviet ICBM silos. In late 1979, Carter approved development and deployment of 100 MX missiles. Reagan inherited the MX and immediately accelerated the program.

The MX generated controversy on two counts, deployment mode and mission. In order to render the missile invulnerable to Soviet attack, the Carter administration favored placing it on railway cars that would constantly travel underground in the southwestern United States. Should the need arise, the missile trains would stop at designated launching points to fire the missiles. Public opposition by citizens in the affected areas killed this deployment mode. Critics cited astronomical costs and environmental damage as well. The Pentagon conducted an extensive search for a feasible way to deploy the MX in a mobile manner. Experts suggested that the missiles be placed on trucks that traversed interstate highways or on ships that plied inland waterways. Public opposition blocked all such proposals. The Reagan administration then devised the idea of "densepack." The 100 missiles would be housed in hardened underground silos spaced 500 yards apart. Should the Soviets attack the missile field, explosions from incoming Soviet missiles would destroy follow-on missiles. Only a few MX would be damaged. The remainder could retaliate against the Soviet Union. Skeptical that this scheme would work, Congress approved continued funding for the MX but directed the Pentagon to come up with a better means of deployment. To resolve this issue, Reagan appointed a high level commission under Brent Scowcroft, Kissinger's successor as national security adviser under President Ford, to examine basing alternatives. After exhaustive study, the Scowcroft Commission recommended in 1983 that the MX be placed in existing Minuteman silos that would be super-hardened. The Commission expressed its confidence that the entirety of the U.S. deterrent would dissuade Moscow from launching an attack. The blue-ribbon commission also suggested that the U.S. deploy the MX primarily as a bargaining chip for future arms talks and rely upon a single-warhead missile as America's primary land-based deterrent in the 1990s. Critics howled that this deployment mode defeated the original purpose of the new missile, which was to evade Soviet attack by way of mobility. They also contended that silo-basing would invite a pre-emptive Soviet strike. In the event of a crisis, the Soviets would be tempted to attack the vulnerable MX missiles in order to forestall an attack by the deadly accurate MX on Soviet ICBMs. A mutual hair-trigger situation would arise from silo deployment, in this view, possibly leading to a nuclear war nobody wanted. Congress, however, accepted the Scowcroft Commission's recommendation and voted funds to deploy 50 MX missiles in existing silos.

    The second controversial facet of the MX concerned its mission. The MX was considerably more accurate than Minuteman III. Armed with ten warheads each, the force of 100 MX ordered by Reagan had the potential to wipe out all Soviet ICBMs, the backbone of their defense. Bellicose utterances by Reagan in his early years in the White House persuaded some critics, not to mention the Soviets, that the president might be tempted to launch the highly accurate MX in a disarming first strike. Critics also insisted the MX was unnecessary from the start. The Kremlin could never count on destroying the entire force of Minutemen, they said. And, even if Moscow could achieve such an unlikely feat, Moscow would have to face retaliation from America's fleet of missile-carrying submarines and long-range bombers. Some strategists went so far as to recommend that the United States simply abandon the ICBM leg of the triad. Despite the energy with which critics set forth these arguments, they did not carry the day.

    At the same time these debates whipsawed strategic planners, a flurry of

Chapter 7: Reagan 213

interest was generated by the Scowcroft Commission's proposal to deploy a single-warhead, mobile ICBM, dubbed "Midgetman." The Commission maintained that if both superpowers substituted such a missile for their MIRVed ICBMs, the strategic relationship would return to the more stable situation that had prevailed in the 1960s. Because of mobility, Midgetmen would be invulnerable. This invulnerability would be heightened by the fact that neither side would have enough warheads to threaten the other side's Midgetman force (given the abolition of MIRV). Aside from the difficulties that mobility creates for counting and verification, the Midgetman proposal could not withstand the momentum propelling both sides' strategic weapons programs. The proposal quietly slipped below the surface.

Reagan also continued deployment of the Trident submarine. Originally approved by Nixon and then developed under Ford and Carter, the first Trident slid off the ways in 1979. Reagan planned to deploy 12 of the boats. As long as a football field, each Trident boat carries 24 C-4 missiles with eight warheads and a range of 4,600 miles. As a symptom of the growth in the destructive power of strategic weaponry, two Tridents carry as much destructive power as the entire American missile force at the time of the Cuban missile crisis. Since the Soviet Union contains only 218 cities with a population in excess of 100,000, America's Trident fleet alone could readily inflict the degree of destruction called for by the doctrine of deterrence (lending support to those who argue for abandonment of ICBMs). A new improved SLBM, known as the D-5, is being developed to replace the C-4 missile in the Trident fleet. With a range of 6,000 miles, the D-5 can strike Soviet territory from nearly any spot beneath the world's oceans.

Under Reagan, the United States deployed a fourth strategic weapons system, the cruise missile. Unlike ballistic missiles, which ascend to high altitudes and plunge downwards at breakneck speed, cruise missiles hug the ground or water on the way to their targets. The United States first experimented with cruise missiles in the early 1950s and actually placed some into service. Because these missiles had a very short range and were not fully reliable, the country abandoned them at the time. Today's cruise missiles can travel thousands of miles and are deadly accurate. They can be launched from platforms on land, sea or air. Difficult to spot on radar, because of their ground-hugging trajectory, cruise missiles can be fitted with conventional, chemical or nuclear warheads. Sea-launched Tomahawk cruise missiles performed with great effectiveness in their first combat test in the 1991 Persian Gulf War. Cruise missiles can extend the range and utility of B-52 and FB-111 bombers, as they enable the aircraft to remain far from their targets (and thus avoid air-defense systems) while launching their deadly cargo.

There is no question that the Reagan administration achieved its goal of expanding and modernizing the nation's strategic weapons. Top-of-the-line weapons that joined the strategic inventory under Reagan included the MX

ICBM, Trident submarine, B-1B and Stealth bombers, and cruise missiles.

The president's determination to upgrade the nation's military forces did not stop with strategic weapons. He also set out to expand and improve tactical nuclear and conventional forces.

Under Reagan, the Pentagon reaffirmed its willingness to engage the Soviets in limited nuclear warfare. As expressed by Secretary of Defense Weinberger (1987), "America faces an adversary with a different strategic outlook from its own—an adversary that, while understanding the destructive potential of nuclear weapons, still plans to fight and win should either a nuclear or a conventional war break out" (p. 5). In the event of limited nuclear war, the Pentagon called for a quantity and mix of tactical nuclear weapons that would enable the United States to "prevail." Reagan elaborated on Carter's "countervailing strategy' (see chapter 6) by appending to it the notion of horizontal escalation. According to this concept, if warfare with the Soviets erupted in one theater, the U.S. might engage Soviet forces not only at the locus of aggression but elsewhere as well.

To provide the wherewithal to wage limited nuclear war, Reagan proceeded with plans, concluded under Carter, to deploy 108 Pershing II and 464 ground-launched cruise missiles (GLCMs). It will be recalled that NATO decided to emplace these weapons in Europe in response to Soviet deployment of SS-20 missiles, while at the same time engaging the Soviets in negotiations to eliminate these weapons. From the onset of NATO's deployments, some security analysts questioned whether NATO needed these missiles, given the Alliance's formidable array of nuclear-capable forward-based systems at sea and in the air. (These were the very systems Moscow said it was only matching in deploying the SS-20.) From Washington's perspective, deploying ground-based intermediate-range missiles in Europe was as important for political as for military reasons. The Pentagon was anxious to "couple" American strategic forces to the defense of Europe. This determination sprang from perennial uncertainty in Western Europe and the Soviet Union concerning America's willingness to launch its strategic weapons to defend Europe, since such action would invite crippling Soviet retaliation against the United States. Supposedly, launching intermediate-range nuclear weapons from Europe would be less hazardous for America, since the appropriate Soviet response would be to engage Western forces in Europe; America would be spared. Accordingly, some said, a European-based American response would be more credible and therefore have greater deterrent effect upon Moscow. Additionally, as Reagan's national security adviser Robert McFarlane put it (1988), once limited nuclear war were under way, Washington's decision to escalate (if necessary) to strategic war would be "less anguishing." Not only would this knowledge presumably dissuade Russia from attacking Europe, but it would also tie in or "couple" American strategic forces to the defense of the continent. When confronted with the notion that a Soviet attack on Western Europe appeared highly unlikely, some proponents of coupling agreed. However, they went on to say, a Russia confident that America would not commit its strategic forces to the defense of Europe might exert political pressure on European states, resulting in their "Finlandization." Such a tactic, if successful, would fragment Western unity.

Skeptics continued to raise familiar arguments against the likelihood of keeping a nuclear war limited (see chapter 6). They also questioned the necessity of deploying the GLCMs and Pershings in light of the fact that by the mid-1990s, the U.S. would be likely to possess up to 4,000 highly accurate warheads mounted on the MX and Trident II. These weapons could be targeted against missile staging areas, ICBM silos, bunkers sheltering leaders, command and communications and intelligence facilities, and other targets associated with limited nuclear war. Still other INF opponents asked how the West could ever expect to terminate a war with an enemy leadership lying dead in a bunker destroyed by an intermediate-range nuclear weapon.

Despite these arguments, the Reagan administration went forward with GLCM and Pershing deployments, beginning in late 1983.

In yet another nod toward military preparedness, Reagan in late 1981 reversed Carter and announced plans to deploy the neutron bomb in Europe.

President Reagan also added measurably to the nation's conventional forces. Much of the funding that would normally be utilized for this purpose was expended on the Vietnam war. In Reagan's view, Carter had neglected the need to augment non-nuclear forces. The GOP leader gave particular attention to the Navy. Encouraged by especially forceful secretaries of the Navy, Reagan set his sights on a 600-ship fleet, including an increase in the number of carrier battle groups from 12 to 15. Under Reagan, the Navy also acquired a more aggressive mission. In the event of hostilities with the Soviet Union, hunter-killer submarines would enter the Barents Sea to attack Soviet submarines and naval bases on the Kola Peninsula. Carrier-based aircraft would strike naval and air bases at Kola and Sakhalin Island. Such attacks, it was hoped, would relieve pressure on the central front—presumably Europe—and also destroy so many nuclear bombers and submarines as to alter the nuclear balance in favor of the United States. The Navy, along with the Air Force, has primary responsibility for conducting what was known as the horizontal response. Should fighting erupt in one theater, American forces might choose to retaliate in another theater of equal value to the Soviets. To be sure, such a mission called for a strong navy.

Delighted with their president's relish for military spending, all the services put in for augmented forces and modernization of weapons. The Army proposed a 28-division force, of which 18 would be active duty and receive new tanks, new infantry fighting vehicles, and new attack helicopters. The Marines called for sealift capabilities for an additional brigade. Vying with the Navy for the largest chunk of the expended military dollar, the Air Force hoped to increase its active and reserve fighter and attack wings from $36\frac{1}{2}$ to 44 and to double the capacity of its intercontinental airlift.

While the armed services did not obtain all the items on their wish lists, they did acquire a significant portion of them. The following table reflects the magnitude of increase in conventional military forces that the Pentagon achieved under Reagan.

Table 7-1: Conventional Weapons Procurement Under Reagan

Weapons	Numbers Purchased 1981–1987
Aircraft, fixed wing, combat	2,973
Aircraft, fixed wing, airlift	276
Rotary aircraft	1,748
Tactical missiles	214,899
Combatant ships	91
Tanks and Combat Vehicles	
Heavy	9,747
Light	2,985
Other	3,476

SOURCE: Lawrence J. Korb, "The Reagan Defense Budget and Program: The Buildup That Collapsed," in David Boaz, ed., *Assessing the Reagan Years* (Washington: The Cato Institute, 1988), p. 92.

Among the munitions procured under Reagan may be found the precision-guided missiles and bombs and other weapons that performed so impressively during the Persian Gulf War. These weapons included the Patriot surface-to-air missile, Hellfire anti-tank missile launched by Apache attack helicopters, Tomahawk cruise missile, M1A1 tank, Bradley fighting vehicle, F-117 Stealth fighter-bomber, and other high-performance aircraft.

In addition to increasing and modernizing equipment, the armed services under Reagan boosted readiness, measured by such criteria as flying hours, steaming days and days of combat training. Stocks of war reserve munitions and material also rose.

Unquestionably, the most controversial element of Reagan's defense program was the Strategic Defense Initiative (SDI), dubbed "Star Wars" by the media and ballistic missile defense by military strategists. The president stunned the world when he announced at the end of a nationally televised address on March 23, 1983, his scheme to render nuclear weapons obsolete by erecting an

Chapter 7: Reagan 217

impenetrable "shield" around the country. In a single stroke, Reagan declared his intention to abandon deterrence, the military doctrine relied upon since World War II to protect the country's security. Reagan even suggested the U.S. might share SDI technology with the Soviets, a dramatic counterpoint to the fact that some items sold in Radio Shack stores were banned from sale to Moscow. Not long after the speech, the White House revealed its plan to spend $26 billion over five years for SDI research and testing. It was far from clear when actual construction of SDI would begin, if ever, or what technologies would underpin it. For the remainder of his presidency, Reagan displayed unswerving determination to push ahead with research and testing in the hope of perfecting SDI.

The president's speech generated a firestorm of debate. SDI proponents echoed the president's plea to move away from a military doctrine, deterrence, that conditioned the country's security on the threat to incinerate tens of millions of innocent people. They also reiterated the many ways in which deterrence could result in war, such as by an accidental or unauthorized launch or the action of a madman with his finger on the button. So long as the superpowers continued to rely on nuclear weapons, advocates of ballistic missile defense said, other countries would follow suit, leading to a highly dangerous proliferated world.

Critics attacked SDI primarily on two fronts, feasibility and strategic stability.

Scientists who questioned the concept's feasibility observed that in every configuration of SDI, innumerable radars, launchers, space-age guns, battle management stations and computers must perform flawlessly within minutes for the very first time. The sheer magnitude and complexity of the enterprise gives pause to many technically knowledgeable people. Not only must the system work perfectly, but it must do so in a wartime environment where the enemy will make every effort to destroy components and fool sensors with dummy warheads, chaff and other means. Opponents further noted that SDI is intended to blunt only ballistic missiles, not cruise missiles or bombers. A determined enemy could also bring in missiles on trucks or ships. With only a small portion of the success enjoyed by narcotics traffickers in smuggling goods into the country, a nuclear foe could wreak untold destruction upon American cities even if SDI worked perfectly.

Defenders of Star Wars reply that naysayers always debunk seemingly impossible technical feats, such as landing a person on the moon. Some SDI supporters concede that the system is not likely to work with 100% effectiveness, but they contend that America should build it anyway. Defense Secretary Weinberger (1987) insisted that SDI would yield great benefits:

> It would enhance deterrence by complicating the USSR's ability to gain a decisive advantage by initiating conflict. The uncertainty introduced by the

loss of an unknown number of missiles seriously would erode its planners' ability to time an attack and assign forces adequately. More important, it would severely restrict the confidence level Soviet leaders could have in a first strike designed to disable Western retaliatory forces and essential communication links ... and thus would enhance deterrence and save lives (p. 17).

In this view, SDI would not replace deterrence but rather reinforce it. A notable variation of this is known as silo-defense. Here, SDI would not try to shield the entire country—a seemingly impossible task—nor even American cities, but rather American ICBMs and other war-making capabilities! Far from rendering nuclear weapons obsolete, SDI would only make them more secure. Presumably this would disabuse the Soviets—or anyone else—of any notion that they could disarm America in a surprise first strike. Even a relatively imperfect SDI could advance this objective, since only a few MIRVed ICBMs need survive to deter an adversary from attacking. Advocates of SDI add that it serves the national interest by shooting down the few missiles a terrorist group or maddened dictator might hurl at the United States.

A second issue raised by Star Wars is strategic stability. This may be defined as the likelihood that a war will occur. Would SDI raise or lower the prospects of war? Proponents of SDI argue that it would lower the prospects of war for reasons already stated. Detractors reach the opposite conclusion. Suppose, they suggest, that SDI's undefended, space-based components are vulnerable to destruction. In a tense crisis, the very vulnerability of these components would tempt the Soviets to attack them, thus precipitating a nuclear exchange. Alternatively, Washington might choose to utilize ballistic missile defense in an *offensive* mode. Should the U.S. succeed in building a defensive shield, it could threaten Moscow with war without needing to worry about retaliation. Even an imperfect SDI could achieve this, since America's first strike with highly accurate weapons would leave the Soviets with only a handful of missiles to launch in return. Realizing this situation would come about, Moscow might seek to destroy Star Wars in the process of construction. Again, a nuclear war might eventuate.

Despite considerable skepticism in Congress and elsewhere, Reagan persuaded the legislature to appropriate for SDI $1.6 billion in fiscal 1985, $2.9 billion in FY 1986, and $3.5 billion in FY 1987.

ARMS CONTROL

Of all the presidents covered in this study, Reagan displayed the least interest in arms control. Reagan's view of the Soviet Union as inherently evil precluded the notion that the United States could sign mutually advantageous agreements with Moscow. Strength and determination, not compromise, was the proper formula for dealing with an expansionist totalitarian regime, Reagan

Chapter 7: Reagan 219

believed. Ever since the SALT I agreement of 1972, the Soviets had modernized and expanded their strategic arsenal. At the same time, the Kremlin sponsored insurrectionary behavior from Angola to Cambodia and Ethiopia to El Salvador. The Reagan administration was convinced that Moscow used arms control as a way to lull the West while it reached for military superiority and expanded its global influence. Given this outlook, it is hardly surprising that Reagan and his top assistants assigned arms control a low priority while they concentrated on increasing the nation's military resources.

Strategic Arms

When Reagan entered office, he inherited a strategic arms pact, SALT II, that he considered fatally flawed. In the wake of Russia's invasion of Afghanistan, Carter withdrew the treaty from Senate consideration. Having signed the document, the Soviets were prepared to see the treaty enter into force.

The SALT II treaty was a lengthy and complicated document, running to over 10,000 words. The essential provisions were as follows:

- each country was limited to a total of 2,400 strategic nuclear delivery vehicles, a figure that was to decline to 2,250 by 1985;
- of this total, each side was limited to 1,350 MIRVed ICBMs, MIRVed SLBMs, and bombers equipped with long-range cruise missiles;
- of this total, each side was limited to 1,200 MIRVed ICBMs and MIRVed SLBMs;
- of this total, each side was limited to 820 MIRVed ICBMs;
- each side could construct no more than one new type ICBM, and it could carry no more than 10 warheads;
- neither side could build additional "heavy " ICBMs (the U.S. had none);
- new SLBMs may carry no more than 14 warheads;
- verification would be by national technical means (meaning satellites primarily);
- a protocol to the treaty prohibited the deployment of mobile ICBMs until the end of 1981.

During the 1980 presidential campaign, Reagan stated that the treaty prejudiced American interests and required renegotiation. (Nevertheless, he abided by the essentials of the agreement.) The president voiced three principal objections to SALT II. Of primary importance, the treaty allowed the Soviets a 3–1 advantage in throw weight. Throw weight, it will be recalled, refers to the size of the payload a missile can deliver on target. The Soviet Union's gigantic ICBMs, the SS-17, 18 and 19, were each bigger than the largest American missile, the Minuteman. As explained earlier, Washington feared that these missiles, when

MIRVed, would enable Russia to knock out America's ICBM silos, thereby negating the country's most accurate and reliable missiles. Reagan was intent on renegotiating the treaty so as to eliminate Moscow's approximately 308 "heavy" missiles, as the 17s, 18s and 19s were called. (The U.S. never did construct any heavy missiles.)

Reflecting a debate that arose during the drafting of the treaty, Reagan felt the agreement also disadvantaged the U.S. by not including Russia's Backfire bomber in the Soviet totals. The Soviets continued to insist that the aircraft was suited only for tactical missions, and that it could not carry its bomb load all the way to America's shores and then return to Russia. Washington demurred, claiming that with in-flight refueling the Backfire could carry out strategic missions. Even without in-flight refueling, Washington said, the Backfire could drop its load on American soil and then land in Cuba. The Reagan administration was not satisfied with a separate exchange of letters (not part of the treaty) between Carter and Brezhnev that stated that Moscow would not deploy the bomber in the far North (closest to American territory), would not produce the airplane above the then current rate (estimated by the U.S. at 30 per year), and would not equip the aircraft with probes for mid-air refueling.

The third factor that troubled the Reagan administration concerned verification. Given the new administration's near-total absence of trust of Russia, Reagan demanded abnormally high levels of verification. In the opinion of some national security specialists, certain facets of the treaty could not be verified to the required degree.

One factor that bothered arms control enthusiasts but not did overly trouble the Reagan administration was the complaint that SALT II barely restrained the arms race. The permitted ceilings were so high that they restrained neither party, these critics asserted. Furthermore, they said, the treaty placed few qualitative restrictions on the arms race and did not call for the destruction of a single strategic weapons system in the arsenal of either side. Indeed, the agreement allowed each side to build one *new* ICBM.

Supporters of SALT II recognized that the agreement was not without deficiencies. However, they stated, the agreement was the best that could be achieved at the time, given the extreme rivalry and suspicion existing between the superpowers. They also insisted the treaty served American interests. SALT II must be seen as part of a lengthy process, they said, in which each side must convince itself that the other abides by treaties. Once a modicum of trust accumulates, or verification methods improve, the two parties can move on to meaningful weapons reductions. In his address to Congress upon his return from signing the SALT treaty, President Carter (1982) remarked, "SALT II is the absolutely indispensable precondition for moving on to much deeper and more significant cuts under SALT III" (p. 262).

SALT II advocates regarded Reagan's complaint about throw weight imbalance as overstated. Even in the highly unlikely event the Soviets could cripple the ICBM leg of the triad, they said, the other two legs contain three-fourths of America's warheads and bombs and would crush Russia. Knowing this, Moscow would never be so foolish as to launch a surprise attack on American ICBMs. Besides, SALT supporters added, Moscow could hardly count on every one of its warheads landing on target; fratricide might destroy some incoming warheads; and America might launch some of its ICBMs on warning, leaving nothing but empty holes for Russian warheads to strike. Besides, SALT proponents added, the U.S. makes up for the Soviet throw weight edge by significant American advantages in total numbers of warheads and bombs, missile accuracy, reliability, and numbers and capability of heavy bombers.

Regarding verification, scientists who supported SALT II asserted that the Reagan administration was calling for artificially high levels of verification as a means of torpedoing the treaty. Only a sustained program of cheating would yield advantages. Before the Soviets cheated enough to gain any military advantage, advocates said, American satellites and other listening devices would detect the violations.

Treaty proponents went on to argue that the pact enabled the Pentagon to engage in rational force planning, since the treaty set an upper limit to Soviet forces. The Soviets could easily exceed the SALT limits using existing assembly lines, whereas the U.S. had no plans to increase its stocks of existing strategic weapons; thus, the agreement prevented a not improbable spurt in Soviet strategic weaponry. In the words of Zbigniew Brzezinski (1983), President Carter's national security adviser, "The SALT agreement ... was in the American interest, for it imposed stricter limits on the Soviet side at a time when it had genuine momentum in its military buildup" (pp. 343–44). The treaty would not prevent the U.S. from carrying out its plans to add new strategic weapons (the MX ICBM and the highly accurate Trident SLBM); the Pershing II intermediate-range nuclear missile slated for deployment in Europe; and thousands of air, sea, and ground-launched cruise missiles. The U.S. was and remains far ahead of Russia in cruise missile technology. Limiting the number of warheads on new missiles restricted Moscow's capacity to exploit the enormous lifting power of its heavy missiles by adding warheads. The eventual limit of 2,250 missiles and bombers would require the Soviets to dismantle some 250 launchers, while the U.S. would not need to eliminate any.

In sum, backers of SALT asserted that the treaty served American interests. Reagan and his advisers, however, remained unconvinced. They stuck to their determination to revise SALT II.

Doing so, however, was far from the top of the new administration's agenda. The president and his aides busied themselves with fulfilling pledges to reduce the size of government, cut taxes, and augment the country's military strength.

The president's inaction on arms control did not go unnoticed. Peace activists in America and Europe were worried by bellicose statements emanating from the White House and the Pentagon, by America's military buildup, and by the president's stated belief in the possibility of limited nuclear war. In 1981–1983, the peace movement in America gathered considerable publicity and support. Among its demands were an immediate freeze on the development, testing, production and deployment of additional nuclear weapons and delivery systems. In the 1982 congressional elections, freeze resolutions were on the ballots in 11 states; in 10 states the resolution passed. In May of the following year, the House of Representatives passed a resolution calling for a nuclear freeze. The Reagan administration spoke out vigorously against a freeze, arguing that the only thing it would freeze was American military inferiority. Partly to deflate the freeze movement, Reagan offered in May, 1982, in a speech given at his alma mater, Eureka College in Illinois, to commence strategic arms talks with the Soviet Union. At the same time he renamed the negotiations START, for strategic arms *reduction* talks. The president also outlined a new American position. This proposal well illustrates the use of arms control to seek advantage over one's adversary. Reagan's offer included the following limits for each party:

- total of 850 ICBMs and SLBMs;
- 5,000 ballistic missile warheads, no more than 2,500 of which could be land-based.

Both countries possessed over 850 ICBMs and SLBMs. However, since the Soviets fielded more missiles than the U.S., the first provision would have compelled Moscow to make greater reductions than Washington. More pointedly, the 2,500 limit on land-based warheads would have forced the Soviets to reduce their ICBM warhead stock by 60%, while the U.S. could *add* 350 warheads! This reflects the Soviet choice to place about three-fourths of their warheads on land-based missiles, while the U.S. spread its warheads more evenly among all three components of the triad. Reagan's offer said nothing about two areas where the U.S. enjoyed a firm lead, cruise missiles and strategic bombers. Nor did Reagan's statement curtail planned improvements in America's strategic arsenal—the MX, B-1 bomber, and Trident.

While decidedly one-sided, the American proposal generated considerable interest. The proposal was innovative in restricting warheads; previous proposals had focused on missiles and aircraft, not warheads. Never before had such far-reaching reductions been proposed in official negotiations. The ceiling of 5,000 warheads called on each side to reduce by approximately one-third.

Secretary Brezhnev welcomed Washington's bid to resume strategic arms negotiations, but he flatly rejected the specifics of Reagan's proposal. On June 29, 1982, the START talks opened. The Russians entered the discussions prepared to fine-tune the SALT II agreement that Reagan had rejected. Washington offered a slightly modified version of Reagan's 1982 proposal. A cavernous gulf separated the two sides. The talks continued until November, 1983, when the Russians walked out in reaction to NATO's deployment in Europe of ground-launched cruise missiles and Pershing IIs. The Kremlin claimed that the Western deployments revealed the lack of genuine interest in arms restraint. Reagan countered that the U.S. was more than willing to discuss the subjects, but that the Russians had walked away. Arms control lay dead in the water.

Reagan's re-election in 1984 spoiled any hopes the Russians might have entertained that they would face a new, less intractable president. Moscow agreed to resume arms control talks, which opened in March, 1985. That same year the Soviets had a new leader of their own, Mikhail Gorbachev. By this time the arms control agenda had grown more complex. Three areas of military activity required resolution: strategic nuclear weapons, intermediate-range nuclear weapons, and defensive and space-based weapons. The last-named item arose following Reagan's Star Wars speech. The Russians adamantly opposed the Strategic Defense Initiative. Rather than fold the three areas of discussions into a single forum, the two sides agreed to conduct separate parallel talks for each issue. We shall reserve the question of intermediate-range missiles for the next section and here concentrate on the other two.

From the outset of the new round of negotiations, Moscow devoted great effort to blocking SDI. At first the Kremlin said cancellation of SDI was a precondition for discussing reductions in offensive arms. Then Moscow retreated to the position that cancellation could be part of an agreement on offensive weapons. At the November, 1985, summit at Geneva, Gorbachev and Reagan agreed in principle to reduce offensive arms by 50%, a startling breakthrough, but Gorbachev insisted that the U.S. restrict SDI activity to laboratory research. Reagan refused, and no agreement was concluded.

Meanwhile, in May, 1986, Reagan declared that beginning that autumn, the U.S. would no longer consider itself bound by SALT II limits, due to alleged Soviet cheating. In November, the U.S. exceeded SALT II restrictions by deploying its 131st bomber equipped with cruise missiles. For all practical purposes, this action amounted to no more than a symbolic gesture and did little damage to strategic arms negotiations.

The talks proceeded at a glacial pace and failed to culminate in a treaty by the time Reagan left office. The two sides did manage to agree on the following numerical limits for each party:

- 4,900 ballistic missile warheads;
- 6,000 ballistic missile warheads + ALCMs + non-ALCM-carrying

bombers (a reduction of 25–30%);
- 1,600 ballistic missiles + bombers + cruise missile carriers;
- 154 heavy missiles carrying no more than 1,540 warheads (a 50% cut).

In contrast to SALT I and II, these negotiations embraced both delivery vehicles (missiles and aircraft) and warheads. In that respect, the talks recognized the criticism that launcher limits were practically meaningless so long as each side could load additional warheads on permitted launch vehicles.

In an effort to bridge existing differences, Reagan and Gorbachev held one last summit in Moscow in late May–early June, 1988. There was an outside chance the two leaders could finalize an agreement. However, when they adjourned without a treaty, they acknowledged that "serious differences remain on important issues."

What were these differences?

One of the indisputable barriers that separated the two sides was the enmity with which each viewed the other. It is well documented that many leading members of the Reagan administration, including the chief executive himself, were convinced that the Soviets habitually used arms control to seek unilateral advantage—consider Reagan's criticisms of SALT II—not to constrain the likelihood of war. No doubt many Kremlin officials mirrored this view of the U.S. Numerous American policy-makers believed the Kremlin deemed nuclear war as winnable. In consequence, these officials felt the U.S. must maintain a warfighting capability within the nuclear spectrum. Clearly, this insistence on retaining a large and varied nuclear arsenal impeded arms control. Uncertainty concerning an adversary's intentions also interferes with arms control. Enmity and distrust only magnify this uncertainty and lead each side to assume the worst. Against this possibility, a healthy arsenal is often seen as the best guarantee of national security. In such a perceptual cocoon, each party tends to see the other's arms control proposals not as efforts to fashion a safer world but as a trick to gain unilateral advantage. There is always enough data to sustain this argument or at least to prevent anyone from demonstrating its falsity. Only during the Bush administration did Washington begin to revise its appraisal of Soviet intentions, thereby clearing the way for the historic START arms control agreement signed in 1991 and even deeper cuts in strategic arms agreed to the following year.

There were, of course, more specific obstacles to agreement in 1988. Most important was the question of SDI. Moscow continued to precondition strategic arms control on strict SDI limitations. The Soviets apparently feared that the U.S. was using SDI to gain unilateral advantage by combining force modernization (sword) with ballistic missile defense (shield). This would give the United States a first-strike capability or at least the confidence to bully the Soviet Union during international crises. Moscow was unwilling to limit its offensive weapons while the U.S. proceeded to construct SDI, believing a large quantity of offensive weapons was necessary to saturate and overcome SDI. For the most part, the effort to block SDI took the form of insisting that Washington restrict SDI activity to laboratory research. Any testing of components in space, the Kremlin maintained, violated the ABM treaty. In late 1985 the Reagan administration announced that it had "reinterpreted" the ABM treaty to allow testing of SDI components in space. The Soviets howled in protest, and even some members of the American team that had negotiated the agreement protested. Two years later the Senate, unpersuaded by the White House's position, blocked funding for any SDI work that conflicted with the traditional interpretation of the treaty. The president, intent on leaving SDI as his legacy to the American people, then sought to set a date for expiration of the ABM treaty. Following that date, SDI testing in space and actual deployment could begin. Washington proposed five years; Moscow, 15. Discussions ensued. By the time Reagan left office, agreement remained elusive.

Questions about Soviet compliance with the provisions of SALT II comprised another major obstacle to a follow-on treaty. The White House voiced frequent and public complaints about a pattern of alleged Soviet violations. The public manner of these accusations poisoned the diplomatic atmosphere and no doubt impeded the arms control process (which was exactly what some of the loudest protesters intended). The SALT II treaty provided for an official channel, the Standing Consultative Commission, for voicing complaints about compliance. The Reagan administration abandoned this forum on the ground that it proved ineffective in inducing the Soviets to modify their behavior.

The most insistent American accusation of Soviet cheating referred to the construction of a large, phased-array radar facility at Krasnoyarsk in central Siberia. The ABM Treaty provides that such radars may be constructed only on a country's periphery and must be oriented outwards. These provisions are designed to insure that the radar could be used only for early warning of a ballistic missile attack and not for the purpose of guiding ABMs to hit incoming warheads. Against the Kremlin's statement that the radar facility was to be used for tracking space vehicles, the Pentagon insisted it was being constructed for battle management purposes prohibited by the treaty. In particular, the Pentagon believed the radar would be used to defend nearby missile fields. Not long after the close of the Reagan administration, the Kremlin agreed that the radar facility did violate the ABM Treaty and halted work on the giant project.

The U.S. also accused the Soviets of constructing two new ICBMs, in violation of the SALT II limit of one. The missile in question was the SS-25. Moscow insisted this missile was merely an upgraded version of an older missile and hence did not violate the agreement. Washington maintained that the missile contained so many modernized features as to constitute a new weapon. There was no dispute concerning the MIRVed SS-24, which both sides agreed was a new ICBM permitted by the treaty. America's new missile was the MX.

Disagreement also arose over encryption. SALT II obligated both parties not to encode telemetric information during ICBM and SLBM tests, whenever such information was needed to verify compliance with the treaty. Washington said Moscow encoded such information. The Soviet Union insisted it encoded only that information needed to protect military secrets, and that it did not protect information required to verify compliance. Moscow also suggested that the U.S. was using the issue to fish for data on Moscow's military capabilities.

Some in the Reagan administration used these alleged violations to argue against a new strategic arms treaty. What was the sense of signing a treaty, they inquired, if the other side was only going to cheat? Others questioned whether the alleged violations did not amount to differing interpretations of highly technical language in the agreement. If the Soviets were merely stretching the meaning of such terms to their advantage, but not clearly violating any document, then the appropriate response would be to gauge the military significance of such alleged violations against the value of the accord. If Soviet actions had minimal military significance that did not outweigh treaty benefits, then it served the national interest to support the treaty while continuing efforts to resolve disputes. In actuality, it appears that the second view prevailed, despite administration rhetoric that suggested the contrary position.

The question of sea-launched cruise missiles (SLCMs) also helped block a strategic arms agreement. A protocol to SALT II banned SLCM deployments for three years, after which the U.S. began to deploy some. The SLCM is a small, highly accurate, low-flying drone that can carry a conventional, chemical or nuclear warhead. It can be deployed aboard surface ships and submarines. Since the U.S. was ahead of the Soviets in the miniaturized guidance and propulsion systems for cruise missiles, many in the administration wanted to press the American advantage and deploy large quantities of cruise missiles on land, sea and in the air. The Soviets wanted to limit cruise missiles, as they succeeded in doing in the INF negotiations (to be discussed shortly), which banned ground-launched cruise missiles in Europe. At the Reykjavik summit in 1985, the chief of the Soviet general staff argued that ballistic missile reductions were meaningless if the U.S. could surround the U.S.S.R. with nuclear-tipped cruise missiles. Moscow wanted to place low limits on SLCM in a new strategic arms agreement. American military thinkers were divided on the issue. The Navy, which had begun to deploy the weapon, opposed treaty restrictions on SLCM. The Joint Chiefs and Secretary of Defense Frank Carlucci (Weinberger's successor) concurred, arguing that SLCMs were necessary to bolster deterrence in Europe after the INF Treaty prohibited the U.S. from stationing intermediate-range nuclear missiles on the Continent. Paul Nitze, Reagan's senior adviser on arms control, favored a treaty ban on SLCMs while the Soviets were still interested. Those who took this position argued that geographic asymmetries favored the U.S.S.R., while America's technological edge would soon give way. Situated near the coasts, American cities and large military installations offered ideal targets to Soviet SLCMs. Comparable Soviet targets lay inland and were protected by the world's most elaborate defenses. Furthermore, SLCM opponents said, American aircraft carriers and battleships were highly vulnerable to SLCMs. America's naval superiority would melt in the face of Soviet SLCMs armed with nuclear warheads.

In the end, the Navy's position prevailed on Washington's battlefield. (Strikes by SLCMs designated Tomahawk launched the war in the Persian Gulf in early 1991.) The impasse with the Soviets remained unresolved by the end of Reagan's term.

Intermediate Range Nuclear Forces

The sole arms control achievement during the Reagan administration was the INF Treaty, signed in December, 1987. The negotiations that led to this important agreement had their origin in NATO's 1979 decision to deploy intermediate-range nuclear missiles (INF) in Europe, while at the same time engaging the Soviets in negotiations to restrict such weapons. NATO's decision was taken in response to Moscow's deployment of SS-20 missiles in Eastern Europe and western Russia. In reaction to America's plans to place 464 ground-launched cruise missiles (GLCMs) and 108 Pershing II missiles in Europe, large protest demonstrations erupted in Europe, especially West Germany. Partly to quell these outbursts, Reagan in November, 1981, announced his readiness to discuss limitations on the missiles. The president offered to cancel deployment of American missiles, which had not yet begun, if the Soviets withdrew from Europe their 250 SS-20s and 350 older SS-4s and SS-5s. This proposal became known as the "zero option," since it would leave both sides with zero INF.

Negotiations opened but got nowhere. The Russians were quick to reject the zero option. They cited the inequitable condition that they would have to withdraw some 600 missiles, while the U.S. need not take any comparable action. Besides, Moscow averred, it needed the above weapons to balance NATO's tactical nuclear aircraft, sea-launched cruise missiles, and approximately 200 strategic missiles in the possession of France and Great Britain. Moscow also objected to Washington's insistence that the Soviets destroy their INF based in Asia (part of the zero option), on the ground that they could be shifted to Europe. Some Soviet spokespersons echoed Westerners who accused Reagan of introducing the zero option in the confident knowledge that Moscow would reject it; this would give America a green light to deploy INF while claiming it had tried to halt such a development. When, in November, 1983, America began to deploy INF, the Soviets stormed out of the negotiations. They also called off the SALT talks.

With a new leader, Mikhail Gorbachev, in place, Moscow rejoined the arms control negotiating process in 1985. As mentioned earlier, these talks were now divided into three forums: strategic weapons, defense and space issues, and INF.

The INF negotiations proved tortuous. Washington offered some modifications of the zero option, and Moscow floated a variety of proposals that would allow them to retain some INF. At one point, the Soviets offered to keep only enough SS-20s to match the number of missiles fielded by Britain and France. For a time the Russians insisted on including American forward-based aircraft, capable of carrying nuclear weapons, in the American INF count. Eventually the Soviets retreated on all these points and accepted the zero option. At the December, 1987, summit, the INF Treaty was signed.

As the U.S. wanted, the treaty called for the destruction within three years of all American and Soviet nuclear missiles with a range between 500 and 5,500 kilometers (300–3,400 miles). Associated equipment such as launchers and support facilities were also to be destroyed. For the first time an agreement was struck that eliminated an entire category of weapons. The treaty was particularly significant for the precedents it set in the area of verification. Each side agreed to admit the other side's inspectors to witness the destruction of missiles and to station themselves outside plants where such weapons were fabricated to ensure no additional ones were made. The agreement was notable also because the Soviets agreed to eliminate many more weapons than the U.S. (approximately 1,500 for the U.S.S.R. to 350 for the U.S.). Arms control specialists voiced the hope that these precedents might facilitate other agreements, such as efforts to reduce strategic weapons and conventional forces in Europe.

When the INF Treaty was submitted to the Senate, a vigorous debate ensued. Treaty opponents insisted the agreement would make Europe safe for conventional warfare. Because of the risks of retaliation, the U.S. would not be likely to respond with its strategic weapons to a Soviet conventional attack on Europe. Should a conventional war break out, the Warsaw Pact had an enormous numerical advantage in nearly every category of weaponry and would probably prevail. For this very reason, the INF Treaty might tempt the Soviets to strike Europe. Those who favored the agreement rejected this argument. Since Moscow could not be certain the U.S. would refrain from defending Europe with strategic weapons, they said, Moscow would not risk an attack on Europe. Even though the Soviets were ahead in quantities of conventional forces, Western weapons systems were technologically superior, and the Soviets could not count on the support of their East European allies. Taking into account such non-numerical factors as quality of leadership, morale, training, ability to reinforce the battlefront, and command, control and communications abilities, the Joint Chiefs of Staff concluded, in a secret study, that NATO had sufficient conventional strength to make a Soviet attack on Western Europe highly unlikely (*The New York Times*, November 30, 1987). Additionally, the West could soon count on sea-launched cruise missiles and highly accurate D-5 warheads on Trident SLBMs to strike some targets previously assigned to the American INF. Capabilities aside, treaty advocates said, the Soviets gave no evidence of wanting to expand into Western Europe. Rather than take on new foreign commitments, Gorbachev seemed much more concerned with reducing overseas involvements and concentrating on reviving Russia's ailing economy. Some defense-minded treaty supporters hoped the elimination of INF would spur the Europeans to make long-needed increases in conventional forces. A few military analysts, such as Richard Smoke (1987), hailed the INF Treaty for contributing to crisis stability. Crisis stability may be said to exist when, at a time of crisis that might lead to war, governmental leaders face force configurations that encourage calm, unhurried decision-making. Imagine that one or both sides fielded important weapons that are vulnerable to attack, perhaps by accurate missiles. Once fighting erupts, leaders find themselves under pressure to launch these vulnerable weapons for fear of losing them. In this situation, crisis stability evaporates. Crisis stability calls for secure forces, so leaders need not "use them or lose them." Highly accurate missiles such as the SS-20, Pershing II and American GLCM undercut the security of the other side's weapons and consequently negate crisis stability. It is believed that one reason the Cuban Missile Crisis did not culminate in nuclear war was the fact that leaders had ample time to deliberate their responses.

In May, 1988, the Senate approved the INF Treaty.

In the early years of the Reagan administration, there was a flurry of interest in the doctrine of "no first use." This refers to a pledge not to be the first to use nuclear weapons. The subject shot into prominence in the wake of an article published in the Spring, 1982, issue of the prestigious American quarterly *Foreign Affairs* by such luminaries as former national security adviser McGeorge Bundy. No first use challenged NATO's doctrine for the defense of Europe that had been in place for four decades. This doctrine called for the use of nuclear weapons to offset superior Warsaw Pact conventional forces. Bundy *et al.* argued that the nuclear defense of Europe was not credible, because it would destroy the continent, and therefore European leaders would never resort to nuclear weapons. In effect, the authors were saying that NATO's deterrent was a big bluff. To lend credibility to European defense, the authors urged Washington to join the Soviets in a no first use pledge, while NATO/Europe markedly increased its conventional forces. In case of war, the authors contended, Europe would be willing to defend itself with conventional forces. Deterrence would be heightened, and the risk of nuclear war would diminish.

In its quest for added military preparedness, the Reagan administration found this notion anything but palatable. Indeed, Reagan called for augmented conventional forces *in addition to* the nuclear defense of Europe. In rejecting no first use, Secretary of State Haig (1984) said,

> ... deterrence is based on the threat that you will use your weapons and the belief on the part of your adversary that you will do so; if you abandon the threat, you relinquish the power to deter, and you also give the other side the option of waging a large-scale conventional war, or even launching a first strike of its own. Of all solutions, this is the most likely to prod the fatal miscalculation that has haunted the sleep of mankind since the invention of nuclear weapons (p. 233).

Haig offered yet another objection. If the U.S. renounced first use of nuclear weapons, more European countries might elect to go nuclear, accelerating the proliferation of such weapons.

Obviously, the question of no first use turned in large part on the willingness of NATO/Europe to boost defense spending by enormous sums. Western Europe could clearly afford such expenditures; its combined populations and gross national products exceeded that of the Soviet Union. However, European publics gave no indication whatever of a willingness to forsake social welfare programs in order to swell military coffers. Accordingly, the no first use proposal quietly faded away.

Toward the close of the Reagan years, the North Atlantic nations began to move in the direction of reducing their conventional military forces. This stirring culminated in the Conventional Forces in Europe Treaty signed in the second year of the Bush administration. The process got under way with a speech by Gorbachev in April, 1986, in East Berlin. The Soviet president proposed new negotiations for reducing conventional forces in Europe. The MBFR talks that had begun in Vienna in 1973 seemed totally moribund. In this speech and in subsequent remarks, the Soviet leader suggested that the fresh negotiations go beyond MBFR and include both conventional and battlefield nuclear arms—such as artillery shells and landmines—stationed between the Atlantic and the Urals, stretching more than 1,000 kilometers into Soviet territory. In June, 1986, the Warsaw Pact tabled the following reductions:

- each side would reduce military manpower by 100,000–150,000 within 2 years;
- in the early 1990s each side would eliminate ¼ of its remaining troops;
- additional cuts would be made subsequently, eventually to include European neutral countries.

Verification would be carried out not only by national technical means but also through on-site inspections and consultations. Compared to MBFR, Gorbachev was proposing a broadening of both the types of weapons to be reduced and their geographic location. The following year NATO agreed to re-open negotiations, and soon East and West began so-called mandate talks to determine the parameters of the negotiations. In December, 1987, Gorbachev stunned the world by announcing in a speech to the General Assembly his intention to reduce Soviet military forces by 500,000 men or roughly 20%. He also pledged to withdraw from Eastern Europe and western Russia 10,000 tanks, 8,500 artillery pieces and 800 combat aircraft. Furthermore, he said, Soviet forces in Eastern Europe would be reconfigured into a clearly recognizable defensive stance. He promised to take all these measures unilaterally.

Western strategists were quick to point out that even after these reductions, the Warsaw Pact would still greatly outnumber NATO in all these categories of weaponry. Hence, they said, NATO could not afford to reduce its forces. In addition, many in the West greeted Gorbachev's promises with extreme skepticism. These doubts melted, however, as Gorbachev began implementing his words. There can be no doubt that the Soviet leader's actions had an immeasurable effect on the success of the negotiations to reduce conventional forces.

Contributing in a small way to the more harmonious superpower relations that blossomed during the Bush administration was a 1986 agreement regulating the use, if not the level, of conventional arms in Europe. This agreement provided, among other things, that (1) each state give all other signatory states two years' notice in advance of any military exercise involving more than 40,000 troops; (2) each signatory publish a yearly calendar of all out-of-garrison military activities of troops in excess of a certain number; and (3) all signatories must be invited to observe each exercise.

One final area of arms control bears mention. In 1986 the Rarotonga Treaty was opened for signature. This agreement prohibits signatories from dumping nuclear waste or producing or storing nuclear weapons in the South Pacific. The treaty does not restrict the passage of nuclear-powered or nuclear-armed ships in the region. The Soviet Union, China, Australia and various South Pacific states have signed, but so far the United States has refused to do so.

Like Harry Truman and Dwight Eisenhower, Ronald Reagan entered office persuaded that America faced a dire threat from an expansionist Soviet Union. Setting aside arms control, the president concentrated on domestic matters and building up the nation's military capabilities. There can be no question that Reagan emphasized military preparedness over arms control, perhaps more than any chief executive since Truman. During Reagan's second term, however, the world entered a period of convulsive change. A new Soviet leader, Mikhail Gorbachev, concluded that Moscow should set aside any ambition of fomenting worldwide communist revolution and concentrate on repairing the Soviet economy and dealing with restive nationalities. At first it was not clear that Kremlin policies had reversed course. By the conclusion of Reagan's term, however, all but the most iconoclastic of cold warriors agreed that the world was entering a new, post-cold war era. This realization made possible the INF Treaty as well as significant strides toward concluding a strategic arms pact. The growth in American military spending came to a halt. The stage was set for both superpowers to begin dismantling the military infrastructure of the cold war through a series of arms control agreements as well as unilateral measures.

8
BUSH

END OF THE COLD WAR

If the international state system traversed the foothills of change during the closing years of the Reagan administration, it ascended the peaks during the Bush presidency. Due primarily to changes in the Soviet Union, the cold war came to an end. Not only did Gorbachev renounce the long-standing Soviet commitment to global communist revolutions, but the Soviet Union itself fragmented into 15 separate states. Furthermore, Moscow let go its grip on Eastern Europe, where one state after another replaced communist governments with regimes that promised democracy and private enterprise. These cataclysmic changes in global politics contributed to a distinct emphasis during the Bush administration on arms control over military preparedness. We examine some of the more significant alterations in the Soviet Union before tracking President Bush's ventures into arms control and military preparedness.

Demise of the Soviet Union

Seismic alterations in the Soviet political landscape began to occur well before the splintering of the Soviet Union in late 1991. One of the most startling of these transformations was the vote taken on March 13, 1990, by the Third Soviet Congress of People's Deputies, to repeal that provision in the Soviet constitution that guaranteed to the Communist Party of the Soviet Union (CPSU) a monopoly of political power.

The dramatic measure taken by the Congress reflected *glasnost*, or openness, proclaimed by Gorbachev at an earlier time. Indeed, in the elections of March, 1989, for seats in the Congress, two-thirds of the seats were designated "free," meaning that non-communists could run for these positions. In most cases, these candidates trounced their communist opponents. The new legislature then witnessed something not seen in Soviet legislative behavior since the early years of the century, namely, genuine political debate and criticism of the government, including even Gorbachev himself.

In another expression of *glasnost*, the Supreme Soviet on June 12, 1990, approved a law establishing freedom of the press. The following month, Gorbachev ended the CPSU monopoly on radio and television broadcasting. In

October, the Supreme Soviet voted to guarantee religious freedom to all Soviet citizens. Restrictions on emigration were also eased.

Glasnost did not spell the arrival of democracy, but it permitted groups espousing various causes—political and otherwise—to emerge throughout the country. One cause that attracted widespread emotional support was ethnic nationalism. Several ethnic minorities demonstrated for more autonomy. In one of the Soviet Union's 15 republics after another, violent clashes erupted between ethnic minorities. By early 1991, virtually every one of these republics, including even the Russian republic, had voted to secede from the Soviet Union. The Baltic republics, which had never accepted their forced incorporation into the Soviet Union during World War II, were particularly determined to achieve independence.

On the economic front, matters were no less unsettling to the Soviet leadership. Cataracts of statistics demonstrated that the Soviet economy was plunging downward. In a desperate effort to reverse the decline, Gorbachev declared *perestroika*. According to this concept, the state would no longer own and manage all economic enterprise. Private enterprise was permitted. However, there was no agreement on either the scale or pace of transformation to a market economy. Obviously, such a shift would produce volcanic dislocations in Soviet economic life. Complicating the issue was the further downward slide of the Soviet economy since the proclamation of *perestroika*. Soviet citizens were infuriated by *perestroika*'s failure to place more merchandise on the shelves or more food on the counters.

Deprived Soviet consumers were not the only ones incensed by the changes Gorbachev had introduced. Those who believed in Marxism-Leninism as the best guide for Soviet society accused Gorbachev of being a traitor against communism. To halt the free fall of the Soviet Union out of the communist orbit, a number of Soviet leaders, including the head of the KGB, mounted a coup in August, 1991. The plotters managed to seize Gorbachev and place him under house arrest. In Moscow, Russian Republic President Boris Yeltsin courageously defied the conspirators, and consequently the coup collapsed. Communism in the Soviet Union was dead. Following a period of rivalry between Yeltsin and his former mentor Gorbachev, the latter retired from the scene. One of Yeltsin's first acts upon taking power after replacing Gorbachev was to issue a decree banning the Communist Party from Russia and seizing its assets for the state.

In December, the Soviet Union splintered into 15 separate republics. Russia was by far the largest in size and population. In an effort to cement these new countries together, a Commonwealth of Independent States (CIS) was created. The CIS included 11 of the new states that arose out of the ashes of the Soviet Union; the three Baltic republics as well as Georgia elected not to join. It remains far from clear whether the CIS will survive. Power relationships among the members remain murky, including Russia's self-proclaimed prerogative to give direction to the other republics. As of late 1992, the CIS had failed to provide the framework for cooperation it had promised. The CIS has failed to resolve the ethnic conflicts plaguing the former Soviet Union, nor has it fostered significant economic cooperation among the new republics.

Europe

Ever since World War II, domination of Eastern Europe had been one of the bedrock elements of Soviet foreign policy. Aside from the desire to spread communism, Moscow sought control of this region for defensive purposes. Eastern Europe had served as a corridor through which passed the invading armies of Napoleon, the Kaiser and Hitler. If the Soviets had one war aim in World War II, it was to block the recurrence of Western invasions by seizing control of Eastern Europe.

The incorporation of the East European nations into the Soviet orbit is a familiar tale. In 1956 (Hungary) and 1968 (Czechoslovakia), the Red Army resorted to force to maintain the obedience, if not the loyalty, of the East European satellites. In what became known as the Brezhnev Doctrine, Moscow proclaimed that no Socialist state would be permitted to leave the Marxist fold. In subsequent years, Moscow actually granted a good deal of autonomy to these nations, so long as they continued to follow the basic dictates of Marxism-Leninism. Gorbachev, however, severed the cord that tied these states to the Soviet Union. Not long after coming to power, he announced that the states of Eastern Europe were free to chart their own destinies. Before long, movements for democracy and private enterprise arose throughout Eastern Europe. 1989 brought momentous changes. By the close of that year, democratic regimes had replaced communist governments in Hungary, Poland, East Germany, Czechoslovakia, Bulgaria and Rumania. Soviet troops quartered in these nations remained in their barracks as these changes occurred. Soon after, Albania discarded its commmunist mantle, and Yugoslavia shattered into separate warring states.

The most dramatic changes occurred in Germany. On November 9, 1989, the East German government opened the Berlin Wall. That gesture more than any other best symbolized the end of the cold war. In another measure that marked the unraveling of the Iron Curtain, representatives of 42 industrial nations, including the United States, met in Paris in April, 1990, and agreed to create a special bank to aid struggling East European economies. On September 12, 1990, representatives of East and West Germany, the Soviet Union, France, Great Britain and the United States, meeting in Moscow, signed the Final Settlement with Respect to Germany. This document terminated occupation rights stemming from World War II and guaranteed the Oder-Neisse line as the boundary between Germany and Poland. East Germany was now completely free. In October it formally united with West Germany. The newly unified nation remained in NATO, but no Western troops were to be stationed in what had been

East Germany. Soviet troops were permitted to remain in the East until 1994, resulting in the bizarre situation of having Soviet troops in a NATO country!

At a three-day summit meeting in Paris of the Conference on Security and Cooperation in Europe, in November, 1990, leaders of the 22 NATO and Warsaw Pact nations signed a Joint Declaration pledging that their nations are "no longer adversaries." The leaders also signed the Charter of Paris for a New Europe, which declared that "the era of confrontation and division of Europe has ended. We declare that henceforth our relations will be founded on respect and co-operation." The cold war was over.

The Russian military presence in Eastern Europe is ebbing. In early 1991, the Warsaw Pact was dissolved as a military alliance, although some talk prevailed about converting it into an as yet unrealized economic cooperation group of sorts. (The former Soviet Union remains Eastern Europe's principal source of energy and raw materials.) By the summer of 1991, all Russian troops were to be out of Hungary and Czechoslovakia. Moscow wishes to maintain 50,000 troops in Poland until 1994, and the two governments are discussing the matter.

Elsewhere

The Soviets displayed remarkable moderation in the developing world as well. In 1989, Moscow terminated its most costly foreign policy venture since World War II, namely, the invasion of Afghanistan, launched a decade earlier. No doubt the Soviet defeat was aided by the supply to Afghan majahedeen of American weapons, including Stinger and Blowpipe hand-held anti-aircraft missiles. In Cambodia, the Soviets were helpful in working with others to arrange a cease-fire among the Vietnamese-sponsored government and three internal factions opposing it. Similarly, Moscow constructively participated in the complex negotiations that yielded a cease-fire in the 15-year-old civil war in Marxist Angola. In both of these cases, the Soviet Union displayed a willingness to concur in options that might result in the withering away of Marxist regimes. Such an event transpired in Marxist Nicaragua, where democratic elections resulted in the defeat of the Sandinista government by Violetta de Chamorra in early 1990. In the Persian Gulf War of 1991, triggered by Iraq's invasion of oil-rich Kuwait, Russia placed no obstacles in the way of U.S.-led coalition forces. During the cold war, Moscow would surely have acted strongly to block any increase in American influence in that region of the world.

United States-Russian Cooperation

As the epochal events related above were occurring, the leaders of the two superpowers conferred periodically to concert their policies. Bush and Gorbachev held their first meeting aboard ship off the stormy seas near Malta in December, 1989. At this get-acquainted session, interrupted by occasional bouts of seasickness, Bush hinted at a willingness to extend economic assistance to the Soviet Union. Both leaders reaffirmed their determination to reach arms control agreements, and they stated their conviction that the countries of Eastern Europe should be allowed autonomy. German unification was also discussed. The Malta meeting will not be remembered for any precedent-setting agreements. Rather, it permitted the two leaders to become familiar with each other and provided an occasion to confirm the friendly convergence of the two superpowers.

In May–June of the following year, Gorbachev and Bush conducted a more substantial meeting in Washington. During a four-day summit, the two leaders signed over a dozen bilateral accords, including a framework for an agreement on reducing strategic nuclear weapons. This framework called for a ceiling of 6,000 nuclear warheads for each party. Other accords included a pledge to cease production of chemical weapons and to normalize trade.

As the decade of the 1990s unfolded, American interest in the region formerly dominated by the Soviet Union underwent a transition. No longer was blocking aggression from Moscow the principal concern (although, as we shall see, America continued to keep its powder dry). In place of this 45-year objective, the U.S. now elected to assist the new countries in this region to make the transition from communism to democracy and a market economy.

A prime instrument for achieving this goal was economic aid. In November, 1991, President Bush announced a $165 million program in food aid to help the former Soviet republics get through the coming winter. In January of the next year, the U.S. launched "Operation Provide Hope," a plan to send Russia 19,200 tons of food left over from the Persian Gulf War plus excess medical supplies from Defense Department stocks. In April, the Group of Seven major industrial democracies announced a $24 billion assistance program to help stabilize the fledgling market economies of the new republics. The U.S. will contribute about one-quarter of this sum. The aid package includes $18 billion in loans, debt deferral and other financial assistance from international financial institutions to help the countries cover shortages in their balance of payments, plus $6 billion to stabilize the ruble. The president also announced new credits to help Russia and other republics buy U.S. agricultural products, and he called upon Congress to repeal dozens of provisions in U.S. law that limit or ban American business exchanges in the former Soviet Union.

Whether such aid will succeed in enabling the new countries to make the transition to democracy and capitalism remains an open question. Short-term economic sacrifices have strained the patience of citizens throughout the region. Some are turning to extremist demagogues who promise food and jobs immediately. Economic shortages are also exacerbating ethnic tensions, often resulting in bloody clashes. The future political and economic landscape of the former Soviet Union and Eastern Europe defies prediction. American policy, however, remains guided by the principle that the triumph of democracy and free enterprise in these lands would help shape a world in which America could flourish.

Some Americans, including former President Nixon, have criticized Bush for being too stingy to help consolidate and advance the fragile gains made by democracy and capitalism in Eastern Europe and the former Soviet Union. In the election year of 1992, however, the president has found it difficult to win votes by giving money away.

MILITARY PREPAREDNESS

As we have observed before, governmental decisions regarding military preparedness stem in large part from assessments of the threat the country faces.

The monumental changes in the Soviet Union and its eventual collapse were bound to have an effect on Washington's assessment of the military threat posed by the Kremlin. As the decade of the 1990s began to unfold, Washington made some incremental revisions in its estimates of this military threat. Changes in procurement and planning were at first highly gradual, reflecting the caution that gripped the nation's military planners. While these limited changes were disappointing to those who wished to declare the cold war at an end and to disarm precipitously, professional military planners observed that

- the Russians continued to field strategic forces that could destroy American society;
- Russian weapons and military advisers continued to play a role in trouble spots from Cuba to Vietnam; and
- the alterations in Russian behavior were engineered by a single individual who might one day be toppled by conservatives opposed to *perestroika* and *glasnost*.

Yet, even before the Soviet Union disintegrated at the end of 1991, many agreed with Theodore Sorensen (1990) that

> The Soviet threat has not only been contained; it has collapsed. The Soviet empire has disintegrated. Its long-time ideology has been repudiated. Its combat forces are being unilaterally drawn down. Its military alliance is in tatters. Its attraction as a political or economic model or mentor for new and developing nations has vanished. Its ability to invade, arm, subvert, subsidize or even threaten those nations or virtually anyone else has been substantially reduced. Given the grave economic, ethnic, social and political problems that the Soviet Union faces internally, the long-term future of its present form and borders is in doubt (p. 2).

Given these two differing views of the Soviet threat, the Bush administration started out by paring military spending only slightly. In January, 1989, the Reagan administration had submitted its final military budget. It called for a rise in military spending by 2% above inflation. That spring, Secretary of Defense Richard Cheney reduced Reagan's request by 1%, from $306 billion to $296 billion. The revised budget called for a continuation of all strategic programs, including the Midgetman and MX ICBMs, B-2 Stealth bomber, and SDI. After emerging from Congress, SDI received $3.8 billion. Each armed service lost a small number of troops. Congress reduced the ceiling on American troops in Europe by 14,500, equal to the number of persons manning the GLCMs and Pershing IIs that were to be withdrawn anyway. The Army retained its 18 divisions, but the Navy lost a carrier battle group. The Air Force had decided in 1988 to eliminate two of its 27 wings (above figures from Treverton, 1989/90).

As the changes in Moscow appeared less temporary, the Pentagon decided greater military cuts were in order. A study undertaken in the summer of 1990 concluded that once Russia withdrew its forces from Eastern Europe, it would take two years for her to mobilize for an invasion of Western Europe. In consequence, the U.S. could afford to reduce its forces-in-being and still have time to build up if an invasion seemed likely. Accordingly, the U.S. announced a 25% reduction in military forces by 1995. Since the Army and Air Force are oriented primarily toward the defense of Europe, these services were targeted for significant reductions. The Army will lose six of its 18 divisions. The Navy will suffer least of all, due to its importance in dealing with third world trouble spots. As mentioned above, however, the Navy will lose one of its 13 carrier battle groups.

Reflecting these planned reductions, the Pentagon requested $278.3 billion for FY 1992, a figure that did not include unexpected expenses for the Persian Gulf War (*The New York Times*, February 5, 1991).

By the beginning of 1992, the U.S. began to move away from the assumption, unquestioned for nearly half a century, that the principal security threat facing the U.S. emanated from Moscow. More and more military planners found themselves agreeing with the statement made in January, 1992, by CIA Director Robert Gates in testimony before the Senate Armed Services Committee. "The threat to the United States of deliberate attack from that quarter [Russia] has all but disappeared for the foreseeable future," Gates declared (*The Washington Times*, January 23, 1992). Following the collapse of the Soviet Union as an imperial power, U.S. security concerns began a hesitating shift away from fear of expansion by Moscow. Other security concerns long consigned to the background began to move toward center stage. Iraq's missile attacks on Saudi Arabia and Israel during the 1991 Persian Gulf War heightened fears of the spread of weapons of mass destruction. Suppose Iraq had affixed nuclear, chemical or biological warheads to its SCUD missiles. More and more countries were gaining access to medium-range and short-range missiles, and this development presented another security hazard. In the next regional war, might American troops come under attack from such weapons? Terrorism, of course, represented yet another security threat.

Given the new, fluid world situation, military planners were forced to ask questions they had not posed for decades. Which countries should be placed on a U.S. "enemies list"? Who, if anyone, might entertain plans to attack the U.S.? How much military force did the U.S. require?—a perennial question that took on new urgency. A "war of scenarios" began at the Pentagon. Some planners asked such questions as "what if" narco-terrorists sponsored a coup in Panama, or North Korea attacked its southern neighbor.

Some senior officials cited the futility of identifying potential enemies and military outbreaks as the basis for sizing U.S. military forces. Instead, they said, the U.S. needs certain *capabilities* in order to remain a superpower. According to this argument, the U.S. has enduring vital interests, such as the stability of Europe and northeast Asia and access to Persian Gulf oil. The U.S. must field the military capabilities required to protect these vital interests, whatever the source of threats.

For military planners in the Defense Department, these matters are critical, for it is they who are charged with advising the president on the size and nature of the nation's future military forces. This recommendation is expressed in an important document known as Defense Policy Guidance. Revised every two years, the Guidance statement serves as an internal planning tool for the military services on how to prepare their budgets and forces for the years ahead. To a certain extent, the Pentagon's recommendations start from a view of the world security situation.

In a preliminary effort to specify the global security situation facing the United States in the post-cold war era, the Pentagon stated that America's political and military mission was to ensure that no rival superpower emerged in Western Europe, Asia or the territory of the former Soviet Union (*The New York Times*, March 8, 1992). In this unipolar world view, the U.S. would act in a benevolent manner in order to protect the interests of the advanced industrial nations; therefore, they would have no incentive to challenge America's predominant position. Absent from this conception was the notion of collective security that had provided the underpinning for the formation of the United Nations after World War II.

Critics lambasted the Pentagon's vision of America's role in the post-cold war world. They complained that the military's conception made the U.S. the world's policeman and displayed an arrogance of power. In May, 1992, the Defense Department revised its Policy Guidance. The new statement dropped the idea of a one-superpower world and highlighted America's commitment to collective military action (*The New York Times*, May 24, 1992). The new draft appeared to accept leadership by regional allies, such as German or Japan, when their interests were more directly involved than the United States. Still, the U.S. would seek to preserve a leading role in strategic deterrence and regional alliances. The document also preserved the option "to act independently, as necessary, to protect our critical interests."

The new version, intended to provide guidance for the 1994–99 fiscal years, supports the Bush administration's call for a "base force" of 1.6 million uniformed troops. The statement also directs the military to be prepared to fight two regional wars simultaneously (a far cry from the 2½ war strategy at the cold war's height) while maintaining a sizable military presence in Europe.

Even though the cold war is over, and the U.S. intelligence community no longer perceives Moscow as likely to attack the United States, one determinant of the military threat facing the U.S. is the magnitude of Russia's military forces. Military planners cannot disregard a military force as large as Russia's. Potential upheaval could overturn those who favor democracy and a moderate foreign policy and return Russia to her long tradition of imperialism. At the beginning of 1992, Moscow fielded an impressive array of strategic weapons. This arsenal included over 2,300 missiles capable of carrying nearly 9,500 warheads plus 162 long-range bombers equipped with nearly 900 missiles and bombs. In determining U.S. force levels, American planners insisted they could not ignore the Russian arsenal. (The 1991 START agreement and a 1992 arms reduction pact, to be examined soon, reduce the size of both Russian and American strategic forces, but only over the next seven years.)

What of the other 14 republics that comprised the former Soviet Union? Should their military forces be lumped together with those of Russia for purposes of estimating the force the U.S. might face? The new Commonwealth of Independent States (CIS) was supposed to coordinate the military forces of all 15 new states. However, the lance of ethnic resentment rapidly burst this bubble of military cooperation. In April, 1992, Moscow established a separate military force of its own. According to the decree creating this force, the Russian military will decline from its cold war numbers of nearly 4 million to approximately 1.5 million men in uniform. Russia also proclaimed the adoption of a defense-oriented military doctrine to replace the offensive thinking that had predominated under the Soviet Union. It is worth noting that all *strategic* forces stationed throughout the former Soviet Union remain under the control of the Russian military, no matter where these weapons may be located.

With the demise of the Soviet Union and the growing spirit of cooperation between Moscow and the West, many analysts have concluded that military threats from any quarter pose less of a danger to the United States than in the recent past. Non-military hazards to American well-being have nudged their way to the forefront, including pollution, trade imbalances, drugs, refugees, and the degradation of America's technological leadership.

Debates in the aerial realm of philosophy tend to come to ground when the time arrives to allocate funds. This descent occurs annually when the president submits his military spending proposals to Congress. In January, 1992, President Bush submitted a $272.8 billion defense budget for fiscal year 1993, $9.8 billion less than for fiscal year 1992. In several ways, the 1993 proposal signals a reduction in military preparedness. The president had already announced plans to reduce the armed forces to 1.6 million active-duty personnel by the mid-1990s (the new base force), a 25% cut. Two-thirds of the savings in the 1993 military budget are to come from reductions in two costly procurement programs. Orders for the B-2 Stealth bomber were lowered from 75 to 20 airplanes. Some questioned the need for any penetrating bombers in view of the Soviet Union's collapse. The Seawolf hunter-killer submarine program was terminated after construction of a single vessel. Other spending cuts will come from the elimination of some strategic weapons (discussed later under "Arms Control") and the stretching out of other procurement programs. Bush also announced plans to reduce defense spending by 4% in each of the following five years.

Realizing defense spending is on the decline, the Pentagon is shifting to a new procurement strategy. In an effort to keep its technological edge in the face of shrinking budgets, the military will ask contractors to design prototypes but not fabricate multiple copies. In case of war, the Pentagon will place orders for production. Some challenged this plan to put R & D above production, questioning whether the prototypes could be rapidly translated into mass production once a crisis erupts.

Political liberals tore into Bush's military spending proposal as excessive. In the absence of a hot war or a cold war, they asked, why can't defense spending contract much further? The resulting "peace dividend" could then be used to reduced the federal deficit, repair roads and bridges, combat poverty, and the like. The age-old question of how much is enough for defense is not likely to go away anytime soon.

One of the more controversial programs that received funding for fiscal 1993 was SDI. Bush requested over $5 billion for this program. Since Reagan proposed "Star Wars" in 1983, the program has experienced several metamorphoses from protection of cities to protection of retaliatory missiles. The collapse of the Soviet Union raised the question of whether the recession-wracked U.S. needed such a multi-billion-dollar defensive system. In its latest transformation, SDI will no longer be directed against a massive missile attack but will seek to protect the country from a few "rogue missiles" that might be launched by a renegade dictator or that might be fired by accident. This new conception of SDI was given a new name, Global Protection Against Limited Strikes, or GPALS. The Missile Defense Act of 1991 calls for deployment by 1996 of an "ABM Treaty-compliant" defense at a single site, with plans for expansion to additional locations should the ABM Treaty be renegotiated. President Bush remains an enthusiastic supporter of ballistic missile defense, despite critics' claims that no country is likely to attack the U.S., and that a nuclear adversary could circumvent GPALS by placing nuclear bombs on ships, trucks and cruise missiles.

Finally, in a move pregnant with symbolism, U.S. and Russian warships conducted their first joint naval exercise on July 5, 1992. The exercise in the Barents Sea was named Operation Northern Handshake.

ARMS CONTROL

While events always manage to confound prophets, it seems safe to predict that just as Reagan will be noted for military preparedness, Bush will be identified with arms restraint.

To be sure, an inclination toward military preparedness or arms control depends in large measure on one's assessment of external threat. The collapse of the Soviet Union led to a reassessment of the foreign military danger facing the U.S., as described earlier. The resultant downgrading of this menace paved the way for historic reductions in military preparedness and an equally historic array of arms control measures.

The Bush administration displayed characteristic caution in reevaluating the threat from Moscow. This circumspect approach was reflected in the gradual decline in U.S. military spending from the stratospheric heights of the Reagan years, as described above. We have also noted plans to reduce the size of the armed forces by one-quarter.

The most dramatic arms control measures of the Bush presidency concerned strategic weapons.

Strategic Weapons

When Bush entered office in 1989, experts were far from united in their views on the durability of change in the Soviet Union. Some drew plausible scenarios of a successful coup by hard-line communists and the rebirth of Soviet imperialism. Reflecting this uncertainty, negotiations over strategic arms started out haltingly, like a train leaving the station and gingerly picking its way over switches and crosstracks. As the U.S. gained confidence that Gorbachev was sincere in renouncing communist world domination and that he would not be toppled, the negotiations picked up speed. In July, 1991, Moscow and Washington signed the START Treaty. Highballing along, the two powers agreed on still further strategic arms cuts in June, 1992. These epochal developments merit more detailed consideration.

Not long after taking office, Bush opened strategic arms talks with Moscow. The previously noted uncertainty over the future of the Soviet Union and a long legacy of mutual distrust prevented the talks from proceeding other than at a tortuously slow pace. Meeting in Washington in June, 1990, Gorbachev and Bush issued a joint statement in which they committed themselves to finalizing a strategic arms treaty in that year. They also endorsed the objectives of reducing the risk of nuclear war and ensuring strategic stability, transparency (each side's ability to monitor the other's forces), and predictability. In the interest of stability, the two leaders agreed to give priority to retaining highly survivable weapons systems.

As things turned out, the leaders missed their deadline. However, in July,

1991, the United States and the Soviet Union signed a START agreement. Reflecting the complexity of the issues and lingering mistrust, the document runs to over 500 pages. The most important features of the agreement are summarized below:

- Each party will reduce its strategic nuclear arsenal to no more than 6,000 accountable warheads on 1600 deployed delivery vehicles.
- Within these limits, no more than 4900 warheads may be deployed on ballistic missiles, 1540 on heavy ICBMs and 1100 on mobile ICBMs.
- The Soviet Union will cut its SS-18 heavy missiles and the aggregate throw weight of its strategic missiles in half by eliminating 22 SS-18 launchers every year for seven years.
- U.S. heavy bombers may carry no more than 20 long-range air-launched cruise missiles each, and 150 of these bombers will count as carrying only 10.
- Soviet heavy bombers may carry no more than 12 ALCMs each, and 210 of these bombers will count as carrying only 8 each.
- Heavy bombers equipped with bombs and short-range attack missiles will count as carrying one warhead each.

The parties will carry out these reductions in three phases over seven years. The treaty will remain in force for 15 years unless superseded earlier by a subsequent agreement. "Politically binding" agreements, not strictly part of the treaty, will limit sea-launched cruise missiles with ranges over 600 kilometers to 880 for each side; the Soviets will deploy no more than 500 Backfire bombers, and these will not be given intercontinental range.

The treaty embraces various other prohibitions, including

- no flight testing of missiles with re-entry vehicles in excess of the attributed number;
- no rapid reloading of ICBM launchers;
- no air-to-surface ballistic missiles;
- no cruise missiles on naval vessels other than ballistic missile submarines and surface ships;
- no fractional orbital ballistic missiles.

START contains verification measures that dramatically advance each side's capacity to monitor the other's performance. These measures include data exchanges; on-site inspection (OSI) to establish a base-line inventory; OSI of dismantlement and destruction; continuous OSI of critical production and support facilities; short-notice OSI of of existing and former sites for systems covered by the treaty; short notice inspections, in accordance with agreed procedures, of suspect sites; a ban on encryption and other concealment devices; and cooperative measures to enhance observation by satellites.

Because of somewhat peculiar counting rules, START will reduce warhead levels by about one-third, leaving the U.S. with about 8,500 warheads and bombs and the Soviet Union with about 6,500. The treaty promises to increase stability and predictability, decrease arms competition between the superpowers, and improve transparency. From Washington's point of view, a major attraction of the agreement is that it will halve Moscow's SS-18 force and eliminate Soviet advantages in the number of ICBM warheads and throw weight.

START was signed at the very end of the era of U.S.-Soviet antagonism. Despite significant weapons cuts, the high levels of armaments the treaty allows reflect the fear that still prevailed on each side that the other might reverse course and behave aggressively. In the months after START was concluded, dramatic developments took place in the Soviet Union. These events, which we have already described, included the abortive counter-coup by hard-line communists, Yeltsin's displacement of Gorbachev, the extinction and fragmentation of the Soviet Union, and commitments by the emergent republics to implement democracy and free enterprise. (The break-up of the Soviet Union raised the troublesome question of who was responsible for implementing the START Treaty. Strategic weapons were situated in not only Russia but also the new independent states of Ukraine, Bylarus and Kazakhstan. Under a protocol signed in Lisbon in May, 1992, the latter three states agreed to adhere to START and to destroy or turn over to Russia any weapons covered by the treaty.) As a consequence of the changes mentioned above, the relationship between Washington and Moscow shifted markedly from adversarial to cooperative. The new spirit of cordiality was expressed by Bush and Yeltsin—now president of the new Russian Republic—at Camp David in February, 1992. The two statesmen declared, "Russia and the United States do not regard each other as potential adversaries. From now on, the relationship will be characterized by friendship and partnership founded on mutual trust and respect and a common commitment to democracy and economic freedom" (*The New York Times*, February 2, 1992). In case anyone had doubted whether the cold war were truly over, this statement drove a stake through the heart of the conflict.

The growing amity between the U.S. and Russia lubricated the tracks to yet further cuts in strategic weapons. In his State of the Union Address on January 28, 1992, just before his summit with Yeltsin, Bush called for strategic arms cuts that went well beyond those in the as yet unratified START Treaty. Yeltsin countered almost immediately with a speech proposing even deeper reductions. Cordial negotiations thereafter yielded yet another historic arms agreement, concluded at the June, 1992, summit in Washington. The Washington Agreement will

- eliminate all 50 U.S. 10-warhead MX missiles;
- accelerate the elimination of America's 450 2-warhead Minuteman II missiles;

- download America's 500 Minuteman III missiles from 3 warheads each to 1;
- halve the number of warheads on America's D-5 Trident SLBMs from 8 warheads to 4;
- eliminate all of Russia's SS-18 and SS-24 heavy ICBMs;
- impose a ceiling of 3,000–3,500 strategic warheads and bombs on each power by the year 2003; and
- eliminate all MIRVed ICBMs by 2003.

These reductions are to take place in stages, concluding in the year 2003. At this time, each country will limit itself to 1,750 SLBM warheads and may divide the other weapons among bombers, cruise missiles and single-warhead ICBMs. The resulting U.S. and Russian arsenals are likely to conform to the figures in Table 8-1.

Table 8-1: U.S. and Russian Projected Strategic Forces in 2003

	United States	Russia
Total nuclear warheads and bombs	3,500 approx.	3,500 approx.
SLBM warheads	1,728	1,744
ICBMs (1 warhead each)	500	500
Cruise missiles and gravity bombs on long-range bombers	1,250	1,256

The Washington Agreement is remarkable in several ways. The pact reduces U.S. and Russian long-range nuclear weapons by two-thirds, a far more extensive cut than found in previous strategic arms agreements. The ceiling of 3,000–3,500 weapons is interesting in that it expresses a range rather than a precise number. This limit represents a compromise between Bush's proposal of 4,700 (made in his 1992 State of the Union Address) and Yeltsin's startling counter-offer of 2,000–2,500. In reaching the compromise position, the U.S. agreed to eliminate more SLBMs than it had originally wanted, while Russia agreed to scrap more ICBMs than it had first contemplated. The U.S. agreed to eliminate over half of its SLBM warheads. Plans to eliminate all MIRVed

ICBMs are especially noteworthy. These are the most destabilizing weapons, given their accuracy, power, and large numbers. Any country considering a surprise attack would launch these first in the hope of destroying much of the opponent's retaliatory weapons, command and control system, and leadership. Resting in fixed silos, these missiles pose more inviting targets for destruction by a nuclear enemy than single-warhead missiles and thus heighten anxieties about a possible preemptive strike. In the Washington Agreement, the U.S. finally achieved one of the major objectives it had pursued throughout the nuclear era, namely, eradication of Moscow's gargantuan ICBMs. While the U.S. price for this achievement was reduction of its SLBM warheads from 3,840 to 1,750, the latter figure still represents a devastating sea force. One might wonder why Yeltsin agreed to forsake his entire MIRVed ICBM force, the backbone of Russia's nuclear arsenal. Perhaps he felt this was the price he must pay for the substantial economic aid he hoped for to rebuild the shattered Russian economy. In an interesting twist, the U.S. agreed to devote $400 million to help Russia dismantle its missiles and warheads in the years ahead.

The strategic arms agreements just described have generated hopes in some quarters that even deeper cuts can be made. If Russia and the U.S. are no longer enemies, the argument goes, why would either need 3,000–3,500 strategic nuclear warheads and bombs? Why not abolish nuclear weapons entirely?

The new international alignment has prompted military planners to address the question, "How low can you go?" The answer would seem to depend on the purpose one assigns to nuclear arms. If these weapons are to be used exclusively for deterrence, a few hundred might well suffice, as France and Great Britain have concluded. One would need only enough warheads to ensure destruction of some cities and important military targets. Some of these warheads could also be dedicated to the deterrence of a chemical or biological attack.

Another conceivable use for these weapons is war-fighting. A large and varied array of weapons would be required to strike not just cities and industrial sites but also a variety of military targets. These could include troop assembly points; dockyards; fleet concentrations at sea; airbases; power grids; maintenance facilities; and command, control, communications and intelligence networks.

A third use that could be assigned to strategic weapons is insurance. This role in all probability explains why few serious military thinkers since the Baruch Plan of 1946 have recommended elimination of nuclear weapons. No one knows what might happen in the future. Might an imperialistic regime come to power in Russia or somewhere else? Could nuclear-armed China decide to flex its muscles? Might one or more radical dictators in the third world brandish nuclear weapons? Since the future has an annoying habit of defying prediction, most military planners recommend keeping some (not necessarily 3,000–3,500) nuclear weapons on hand just in case.

Still another purpose these weapons can serve is reassurance. America's nuclear arsenal reassures its allies that the U.S. is capable of defending them.

Otherwise, wealthy and technologically advanced allies like Japan and Germany might decide to develop nuclear weapons of their own. America's decision to reduce its nuclear arsenal below an as yet undetermined floor might lead such allies to doubt Washington's will to come to their defense, with the consequence of more national nuclear forces around the world.

Nuclear weapons also play a symbolic role. In today's world, they are the badge of great power status, just as the great steel dreadnoughts were earlier in the century.

The uses of nuclear arms just catalogued are not mutually exclusive. The United States, it would seem, assigns all these purposes to its nuclear arsenal. If all the states that possess nuclear weapons were to negotiate verifiable reductions, then the U.S. could probably realize these objectives at levels in the range of 250 warheads or thereabout. Due to uncertainty about the intentions and capabilities of other states, it is doubtful the U.S. (and probably other nuclear nations as well) would ever descend much below that floor.

Before leaving the strategic area, we should mention one other development at the June, 1992 summit. Bush and Yeltsin agreed to open discussions on strategic defense. No longer foes, the two nations have begun to seek out common ground to defend themselves against missile attacks by third parties. The most likely candidates would be rogue leaders from third world states who sought to dissuade other powers from blocking their aggression or who wanted to engage in some form of nuclear blackmail. With the detachment of so much territory formerly belonging to the Soviet Union, Russia's radar coverage of its territory suffers from broad blind spots. At the Washington summit, the two sides agreed to make arrangements to share data on missile launches worldwide.

In 1992, the U.S. announced it would not resume production of the 475-kiloton W-88 warhead for its Trident II submarines. Enough warheads existed to equip two of the boats in the planned fleet of 18 Tridents. Older, less powerful W-76 warheads will be deployed on the remaining vessels. Bush also stated the U.S. will not resume production of plutonium or highly enriched uranium, the key ingredients in nuclear weapons. The announcement's value was purely symbolic, however, since an abundance of these materials will be available from weapons dismantled pursuant to START and the Washington Agreement. It is noteworthy that Bush did not avail himself of the opportunity to propose an international treaty to halt production of fissile material.

Tactical Nuclear Weapons

Ever since World War II, arms control negotiations have been characterized by painfully slow, tortuous discussions in which every miniscule point was contested. Once Washington and Moscow moved off this collision course, however, a new *process* of arms control appeared, namely, unilateral reductions. Unthinkable during the cold war, these unilateral moves bypass time-consuming haggling over minute details.

President Bush exemplified this tactic with an announcement in September, 1991, that, regardless of what the Soviets do, the U.S. would withdraw all its foreign-based nuclear artillery shells and nuclear warheads for short-range missiles back to U.S. territory, where they would be dismantled or destroyed. The president added that the U.S. would also remove all tactical nuclear weapons, including nuclear cruise missiles, from its surface ships and attack submarines, and that nuclear weapons associated with land-based naval aircraft would similarly be removed for destruction or storage. In effect, the president's message eliminated all U.S. tactical nuclear weapons overseas except bombs and warheads fired from land-based aircraft. The presidential initiative included other unilateral measures as well. Bush stated that all U.S. strategic bombers would be taken off day-to-day alert status and their weapons returned to storage areas; that the U.S. would immediately stand down from alert all ICBMs scheduled for deactivation under START; that the U.S. would abandon efforts to devise mobile basing systems for ICBMs; and that the U.S. was canceling the nuclear short-range attack missile.

In setting forth this package of unilateral initiatives, the president explicitly invited Moscow to follow suit. However, it was equally clear that the steps announced were not contingent on Soviet reciprocity.

As it turned out, however, Moscow was more than willing to comply. Soon after Bush's announcement, Gorbachev agreed to match the U.S. nuclear withdrawals. He also called upon the U.S. to sign a comprehensive nuclear test ban, declare a cessation in production of fissile material, subscribe to a no-first-use policy, and remove all air-launched nuclear bombs from Europe. (In July, 1992, Bush agreed to the second item, as we have mentioned.)

In October, 1991, NATO defense ministers decided to reduce by 50% the number of U.S. and British nuclear bombs launched from aircraft. This move, combined with Bush's earlier announcement, reduced NATO's nuclear arsenal by a whopping 80%. NATO's decision leaves approximately 700 tactical nuclear bombs in Europe.

As a footnote, we might observe that after the splintering of the Soviet Union, many of the country's 17,000 tactical nuclear weapons were located outside of the Russian Republic. By the summer of 1992, all of these had been transferred to Russia for storage or dismantlement.

Europe

For nearly half a century, Europe stood at the vortex of cold war rivalry. Therefore, arms reductions in that region are of particular significance.

We have already referred to the withdrawal of nearly all tactical nuclear weapons from Europe. Such a move reflects a conviction on both sides that they are not likely to be the victims of attack (and that any plans to mount an attack of one's own have been canceled).

On the conventional front, we have noted the Pentagon's plans, finalized in the summer of 1990, to reduce the armed forces by 25%, primarily by disbanding a number of Army and Air Force units designed to defend Europe. This American reduction did not occur in a vacuum. Gorbachev had already begun to make unilateral cuts of 50,000 men and 5,000 tanks from Eastern Europe and had permitted those countries to chart their own non-communist paths. The likelihood of a Soviet assault upon Western Europe receded rapidly during the late 1980s.

These developments were accompanied by vigorous diplomatic efforts. The MBFR talks that had been moving at a languid pace since 1973 were terminated by common consent in early 1989. In March of that year, a new series of negotiations began, known as the Conventional Forces in Europe (CFE) talks. The seven Warsaw Pact states and the 16 members of NATO participated. Progress occurred rapidly, aided by a February, 1990, United States-Soviet understanding (not a formal treaty) limiting each superpower to 195,000 troops in Central Europe. Because of the distance from America to Europe, Washington received permission to station an additional 30,000 troops in Europe outside the central zone.

Troops, however, were not the only concern of military planners. For years NATO had been alarmed by the Warsaw Pact's daunting advantage in tanks, armored personnel carriers, artillery and other heavy equipment. These fears were laid to rest on November 19, 1990, when leaders of NATO and Warsaw Pact nations signed the CFE Treaty. This historic document limited each alliance to 20,000 battle tanks, 20,000 artillery pieces, 30,000 armored combat vehicles, 6,800 combat aircraft, and 2,000 attack helicopters. As part of these totals, each superpower was limited to 13,300 tanks, 13,700 artillery pieces, 20,000 armored combat vehicles, 5,150 combat aircraft, and 1,500 attack helicopters.

The demise of the Warsaw Pact and the disintegration of the Soviet Union played havoc with the CFE Treaty's East European force allocations. In June, 1992, 29 states from NATO, the former Warsaw Pact, and the former Soviet Union, meeting in Oslo, signed a protocol that allows Russia to keep approximately half the weapons assigned to it in the original accord. Six of the new republics are to divide the remainder. Each of the signatory countries must now ratify the agreement.

Other developments occurred that signified the coalescence of a continent divided by nearly a half century of cold war. Just prior to the Oslo meeting, NATO approved the use of its troops and equipment to conduct peacekeeping operations in European conflicts beyond the boundaries of member states, if requested to do so by the CSCE. This preliminary effort to transform NATO from a defensive alliance into a peacekeeping force is part of the alliance's effort to carve out a role and rationale for itself in the post-cold war world. NATO peacekeeping could occur in the Balkans or Eastern Europe, both loci of intense nationalist conflict. At the Oslo meeting, the East European states endorsed NATO's decision, and some of them offered to participate. There was even talk of accepting East European countries into NATO itself!

Russian and American troop levels in Europe are already showing every likelihood of sinking beneath the floor of 195,000 set by Gorbachev and Bush in February, 1990. Russia is in the process of removing its troops from Eastern Europe. Faltering efforts to find housing and jobs for them are slowing the pace of withdrawal. U.S. troop levels in Europe slid from 314,000 in late 1990 to 200,000 in mid-1992; they are slated to reach 150,000 by the end of 1995. It is not inconceivable that the number will drop well below this figure, as many strategists search in vain for a mission for such a large force. Corresponding to the fall in troop levels, the U.S. is planning to close down at least one-third of its military installations in Europe.

Concern over troop levels extends beyond Russia and the U.S. Accordingly, the 29 states that met in Oslo in June, 1992, reconvened in Vienna the following month to conclude an understanding that limits the number of troops they may station in Europe. This non-binding agreement applies to land and air forces in the area between the Ural Mountains and the Atlantic Ocean. According to this understanding, the U.S. may station 250,000 troops in the area; Russia, 1,450,000; Ukraine, 450,000; Germany, 345,000; France, 325,000; and Great Britain, 260,000. In many cases (including the U.S.), these figures are higher than actual troop levels in mid-1992.

It will be recalled (see chapter 2) that President Eisenhower proposed that East and West open their military facilities to aerial surveillance, primarily to allay fears that one side was massing forces for a surprise attack. Such miscalculation could lead to unintended war. This Open Skies proposal plummeted to Earth in the baleful era of cold war hostility. In 1989, Bush resuscitated Eisenhower's proposal and offered it to Gorbachev. After the failed August, 1991, coup in the Soviet Union weakened communist hard-liners and the military, negotiations began in earnest. In May, 1992, the U.S., Russia, Canada and 21 European states initialed the Open Skies Treaty. This pact opens a vast area to aerial inspection—from Vancouver to Vladivostok. It covers all 16 members of NATO and all members of the former Warsaw Pact as well as Russia, Ukraine, Belarus and Georgia. The agreement provides for short-notice surveillance flights over military sites of signatory countries. The treaty is intended to help build confidence in the peaceful intentions of member states by increasing the transparency of their military forces and activities.

Other Areas of Arms Control

Since 1968, the nations of the world have been working to devise a ban on chemical weapons (CW). The 1925 Geneva Protocol bans the *use* of CW but not its development, production or stockpiling. In any case, the Geneva Protocol has not served as an effective barrier to CW use, as demonstrated recently in the Iran-Iraq War. The issue has become particularly grave inasmuch as the Defense Department claims that at least 14 nations outside the former Soviet Union and NATO possess CW, and that ten other nations are actively seeking CW (*The New York Times*, March 10, 1991). The countries listed as "probably possessing" CW include North Korea, Syria, Vietnam, Egypt, Pakistan, Libya, Iran and Iraq. Controlling CW was given added urgency during the 1991 Persian Gulf War. Although the SCUD missiles Iraq fired at Saudi Arabia and Israel were not equipped with chemical warheads, Baghdad showed that the technology for delivering CW was within the grasp of many countries.

As part of his decided nod in the direction of arms control over military preparedness, President Bush has taken a special interest in limiting CW. In September, 1989, President Bush proclaimed, in a speech before the General Assembly, that the U.S. was prepared to reduce its CW stockpile by 80%, if the Soviets agreed to reduce their level to the American level. In April, 1990, both countries announced agreement to lower their CW stocks to 5,000 tons each. At the Washington summit in June, Bush and Gorbachev agreed to terminate production of CW.

Meanwhile, international negotiations held under the auspices of the UN-affiliated Conference on Disarmament managed in mid-1992 to produce a draft Chemical Weapons Convention (CWC). The CWC prohibits not just the use of CW but also its development, production, stockpiling and transfer.

Verification has long been a major bugaboo of a CW treaty. Many chemicals that go into CW have legitimate civilian uses, such as in pesticides, so the production of these substances cannot be outlawed. The only way to tell whether a chemical plant is manufacturing aphid killer or CW is to inspect the facility from within. However, unimpeded entry could easily become a form of industrial espionage. The CWC reflects a compromise on the issue. Inspectors will be given access to a facility within five days of expressing an intent to visit it. Five days, it was felt, would allow for the shrouding of sensitive materials and machinery unrelated to weapons but would not provide sufficient time to hide a weapons program. The treaty also calls for routine visits to factories known to produce dangerous chemicals.

The question of riot-control agents such as tear gas presents difficulties for American negotiators. Almost alone among the countries involved, the U.S. seeks to preserve the right for some combat use of nonlethal agents like tear gas. Washington feels such agents could prove useful in subduing terrorists holding hostages, for instance. The U.S. is currently studying the language in the draft Convention in hope of devising a successful compromise on this issue.

Should the Convention take effect, a United Nations organization to supervise the accord would be set up in The Hague.

To spur completion of the CWC, the U.S. unilaterally decided to forswear the use of CW for any reason, effective once the Convention enters into force. The U.S. also announced that it will, without condition, destroy all of its CW stocks and production facilities within ten years of entry into force of the Convention.

With the end of the cold war, the United States has begun to focus more attention than previously on another security threat, namely, the proliferation of "weapons of mass destruction" (WMD). These weapons consist of nuclear, chemical and biological arms. Since these armaments would most likely be delivered by missiles—though artillery shells and gravity bombs could also be used—missiles are often included in discussion of WMD. We shall follow that practice here.

U.S. efforts to stem the spread of nuclear weapons have taken several dimensions. Washington has taken the lead in reinvigorating efforts to control the transfer of nuclear technology and equipment that could be used to manufacture nuclear weapons. With American prodding, the Nuclear Suppliers Group (NSG) renewed its formal activities in March, 1991. The NSG is composed of over 20 states with the capability of producing the sophisticated items needed in a bomb-making effort. Many of these items also have legitimate uses in civilian nuclear programs and hence are referred to as "dual-use" equipment. In March, 1992, the NSG agreed to an extensive list of dual-use equipment that member states will export only under stringent controls. Members of the NSG also announced they would require non-nuclear weapons states to accept International Atomic Energy Agency (IAEA) safeguards on *all* their nuclear activities as a precondition for any significant new supply. For certain countries of special proliferation concern, such as Libya, North Korea and Iran, the U.S. has virtually banned nuclear cooperation of any kind and has urged other suppliers to do likewise. In an attempt to uncover secret nuclear weapons programs, such as that mounted by Iraq before the Persian Gulf War, the U.S. has supported the IAEA's proposal to conduct surprise inspections of undeclared nuclear facilities. Heretofore, the IAEA has limited its inspections to facilities declared by states that have agreed to adhere to the Nonproliferation Treaty (NPT). (Of course, the IAEA has no authority to inspect sites in non-member states.) The U.S. has also actively encouraged states to adhere to the NPT. Opened for signature in 1968 (see chapter 4), the NPT obliges nuclear weapons states not to transfer such weapons to non-nuclear weapons states and prohibits the latter from seeking to acquire or fabricate nuclear weapons. NPT members also agree to open all their nuclear facilities to inspection by the IAEA. The NPT serves as a cornerstone of the global effort to control nuclear proliferation. Approximately 150 nations have adhered to the NPT. Prompted by the U.S. and other countries, a number of controversial non-NPT states recently agreed to adhere to the treaty, including South Africa, China and France. Argentina and Brazil, while not subscribers to the NPT, signed a full-scope safeguards agreement with the IAEA, thus aborting a potential nuclear arms race in Latin America.

In trying to prevent the spread of nuclear weapons, the Bush administration has devoted special attention to the former Soviet Union. At the beginning of 1992, the countries that once comprised the U.S.S.R. possessed about 27,000 nuclear weapons, ranging from ICBMs to artillery shells. Washington shares the concern of many other states that some of these weapons might fall into the hands of regimes that do not currently possess nuclear weapons. A related concern is that some unemployed nuclear scientists and technicians will agree to help build nuclear weapons in such states in return for lucrative salaries.

A large proportion of these weapons is scheduled for elimination under international treaties like START and INF. This process will be facilitated by pledges already made by the new republics to transfer all their nuclear weapons to Russia for destruction. However, destroying nuclear weapons is neither simple nor inexpensive. To facilitate such dismantlement, the U.S. Congress appropriated $400 million. The U.S. has also offered to send experts to help with transportation and storage as well as actual destruction of the weapons. To help prevent a "brain drain" of Soviet nuclear scientists, the U.S., along with Japan and the European Community, is establishing international science and technology centers in Russia and Ukraine to provide employment for weapons specialists. In 1992, the U.S. said it would contribute $35 million to establishing these new centers.

Despite the measures described above, much concern remains that some of these nuclear weapons and nuclear experts will turn up in renegade states that are willing to pay practically any price for a nuclear capability.

As mentioned before, missiles would seem to be the carrier of choice for delivering nuclear bombs. The Iran-Iraq War in the 1980s, the Falkland Islands War, and the Persian Gulf War of 1991 highlighted the dire prospects for the world of missile proliferation. Third world protagonists in all these conflicts launched missiles at their opponents. Certain countries, such as China and North Korea, are anxious to earn foreign currency by exporting short-range and medium-range missiles. While the oceans insulate American territory from such attacks (for the present), there is a strong likelihood that U.S. military forces engaged in combat overseas will have to contend with missile attacks, perhaps involving chemical or nuclear warheads. American allies such as Israel and South Korea are greatly worried about missile attacks.

To help control the spread of missiles, the U.S. took the lead in setting up the Missile Control Technology Regime (MCTR). The 18 countries which subscribe to the MCTR agree not to export missiles capable of carrying a payload of 500 kilograms (approximately 1,100 pounds) farther than 180 miles. Most countries where such missiles are manufactured have joined. However, the refusal of China, North Korea and a handful of other states to become part of MCTR remains unsettling.

Finally, the issue of nuclear testing merits brief mention. It will be recalled that the Limited Test Ban Treaty of 1963 prohibits all nuclear testing except underground. Ever since, many arms control advocates have called for a comprehensive test ban for the very reason the U.S. has opposed it. Such a treaty would impede the development of improved warheads and bombs. In 1992 President Yeltsin announced a one-year testing moratorium and urged the U.S. to reciprocate. When the Bush administration demurred, Congress gave evidence it might legislate a testing halt. In large part to forestall Congress, the president announced in July, 1992, certain limits on nuclear tests. Henceforward, Bush declared, the U.S. would conduct no more than six tests per year (not much of a reduction from recent years) for the next five years. No more than three of these annual tests will exceed 35 kilotons. Testing will be carried out only to ensure the reliability and safety of existing weapons, not to develop new ones, the president said.

More so than any of his predecessors, President Bush is relying on arms control as opposed to military preparedness to enhance America's security. This stance is due primarily to changes in the Soviet Union initiated by Mikhail Gorbachev and extended by Boris Yeltsin. The splintering of the Soviet Union and Moscow's renunciation of worldwide revolution have reduced America's need to maintain military forces in every corner of the globe. With the demise of the Warsaw Pact and the end of Russia's insistence on dominating Eastern Europe, Washington has started to telescope its military presence in Europe. Similarly, as the threat of a Russian attack upon the United States has all but disappeared, Washington has found renewed hope in joint limitations of strategic arms. Since third world disputes will no longer involve a proxy contest between the superpowers, Washington can afford to scale down military resources for deployment in developing countries.

These dramatic developments have made possible a recent proliferation of arms control agreements. Not only has President Bush reversed his predecessor's upward climb of military spending, but he has also announced a 25% reduction of the nation's military forces. Through unilateral, bilateral and multilateral measures, Bush is in the process of carrying out deep reductions of strategic, tactical and conventional weapons. Scarcely a single weapons system has escaped the pruner's blade.

At the same time, Bush has retained arms for use in those third world regions of intrinsic importance, such as the Persian Gulf and the Caribbean. Future uncertainties also impose a limit on the arms reductions Bush has been prepared to implement. Nevertheless, Bush stands out among post-World War II presidents as the one most reliant on arms control as opposed to military preparedness. Despite the war in the Persian Gulf, it appears that President Bush has ushered in a rather lengthy period that will reveal an emphasis upon arms restraint, not military preparedness, in American foreign policy.

CONCLUSION

The Roman god Janus is portrayed with two heads facing in opposite directions. His chief temple in Rome ran east and west, where the day begins and ends. His month, January, signifies the beginning of the new year and the end of the old.

The image of Janus is relevant to one who would enhance the nation's security. Such an individual might look in two different directions. On one side, the individual sees the traditional method of securing the nation's safety, namely, military preparedness. Down the long corridor of history, national leaders have accumulated weapons, military equipment and soldiers to defend national frontiers. Turning to the other side, the guardian of the nation's security espies arms control. Arms control can enhance a country's security by diminishing military threats. For the custodian of national security, arms control is hardly the opposite of military preparedness; instead, arms control complements military preparedness. Like the god Janus, the chief executive who would increase his country's national security should indeed look in two directions, one view leading to military preparedness and the other toward arms control.

No president has found both visages equally appealing, however. With the exception of Richard Nixon, Jimmy Carter in his "first presidency," and George Bush, every White House occupant starting with Truman has relied on military preparedness more than arms control to enhance national security. Of the first two presidents who placed substantial faith in arms control, Nixon can point to numerous concrete achievements (especially SALT I and the ABM Treaty), while Carter managed to negotiate but two accords, SALT II, on which the Senate never voted, and the environmental modification agreement. George Bush has been responsible for more arms limitation than any other American president.

To be sure, presidents do not select arms control or military preparedness in a vacuum. The prevailing diplomatic atmosphere has a large bearing on which instrument offers more hope of success at a given time. Clearly, cold war hostility served as an impediment to arms control during the administrations of Truman, Eisenhower, Kennedy, Carter (in his "second presidency") and Reagan. Johnson was too distracted by Vietnam to devote much attention to arms control, although the NPT and some regional accords were finalized during his tenure. Had Reagan been willing to confine SDI development to the laboratory, he might well have secured an agreement to reduce strategic warheads and bombs by one-half. During these presidencies, the country went ahead with new military doctrines and weapons programs that dwarfed arms control achievements before the 1990s.

Just as cold war enmity inclined various chief executives toward military preparedness, the end of the cold war provided an opportunity that President Bush seized to restrain arms. The collapse of the Soviet Union and Russia's renunciation of imperialist ambitions led to a host of noteworthy arms control measures, including INF, START, CFE, the Washington Agreement to further reduce strategic forces, and commitments to lower troop levels in Europe. Unilateral steps announced by Washington and Moscow have nearly eliminated tactical nuclear weapons. A Chemical Weapons Convention, if approved (as seems likely), will come close to eliminating these ghastly armaments.

As the world approaches the twenty-first century, the major fault line in global politics gives promise of shifting from the East-West ideological divide to the North-South economic cleft. Nations that once glared daggers at each other across the former chasm appear to find some common ground as they face off against states across the latter fissure. Nearly all southern states, whatever their political coloration, want increased economic assistance and debt relief from their more affluent neighbors to the north. The latter, likewise regardless of political stripe, are joining their wagons together in a circle against a full-scale economic assault. (This is not to say that northern states refuse *any* economic assistance, but they clearly are unwilling to provide the levels requested by the South.) At the same time, there is increased cooperative activity by *all* nations to solve common problems, such as environmental degradation, global warming, health, population growth, proliferation of weapons of mass destruction, and the like.

In such a world, arms would appear to play a less central role than they did in the first 90 years of the twentieth century. To be sure, regional conflicts may well boil up to the level of military engagement. The Middle East and South Asia (India-Pakistan) appear fraught with such danger. Since America's interests are global in scope, the U.S. will need military forces capable of playing an effective part in regional wars. The 1991 Persian Gulf War offers a recent example. However, with the end of the cold war, there seems little need for voluminous quantities of mass destruction weapons. Accordingly, under President Bush, the U.S. has begun to reduce these in concert with Russia. Indeed, as the 1990s unfold, the planet is witnessing the most extensive exercise in arms control in history, with the possible exceptions of the demobilizations following each world war.

While the prospect of nuclear war involving the U.S. grows more remote each day, no one can predict what the future holds. At the conclusion of World War II, to illustrate, most people assumed the threat of aggression had

Conclusion

evaporated; the cold war soon materialized. Such uncertainty places limits on how far down any nation can draw its military stocks. While for the U.S. at least, arms control seems in the ascendant over military preparedness, the latter is unlikely to lose its relevance. Like the great god Janus, the true protector of national security must gaze in two directions.

REFERENCES

Acheson, D. (1969). *Present at the creation.* New York: W. W. Norton.
Adams, S. (1961). *Firsthand report: The story of the Eisenhower administration.* New York: Harper and Brothers.
Allison, G. T. (1971). *Essence of decision.* Boston: Little, Brown.
Alperovitz, G. (1965). *Atomic diplomacy.* New York: Random House.
Ambrose, S. E. (1980). *Rise to globalism: American foreign policy, 1938–1980.* (2nd ed.). New York: Penguin.
Blacker, C. D. (1987). *Reluctant warriors.* New York: W. H. Freeman.
Brzezinski, Z. (1983). *Power and principle.* New York: Farrar, Straus, Giroux.
Carter, J. (1982). *Keeping faith.* New York: Bantam Books.
Divine, R. A. (1976). *Blowing in the wind: The nuclear test ban debate 1954-1960.* Cambridge: Harvard University Press.
Eisenhower, D. D. (1965). *The White House years: Waging peace 1956–1961.* Garden City, N.Y.: Doubleday.
Enthoven, A. C., & Smith, W. K. (1971). *How much is enough?* New York: Harper and Row.
Fascell, D. B. (1987). Congress and arms control. *Foreign Affairs, 65,* 730–749.
Fleming, D. F. (1961). *The cold war and its origins.* Garden City, N.Y.: Doubleday.
Freedman, L. (1983). *The evolution of nuclear strategy.* New York: St. Martin's.
Garthoff, R. L. (1985). *Detente and confrontation: American-Soviet relations from Nixon to Reagan.* Washington: Brookings Institution.
Garwin, R. L., & Bethe, H. (1968). Anti-ballistic missile systems. *Scientific American, 218,* 21–31.
Haig, A. M. (1984). *Caveat.* New York: Macmillan.
Horowitz, D. (1971). *The free world colossus.* New York: Hill and Wang.
Huntington, S. P. (1961). *The common defense: Strategic programs in national politics.* New York: Columbia University Press.
Johnson, L. B. (1971). *The vantage point.* New York: Holt, Rinehart and Winston.
Jones, J. M. (1955). *The fifteen weeks.* New York: Harcourt, Brace and World.

Kahan, J. H. (1975). *Security in the nuclear age.* Washington: The Brookings Institution.
Kaufmann, W. W. (1964). *The McNamara strategy.* New York: Harper and Row.
Kennan. G. F. (1967). *Memoirs 1925-1950.* Boston: Little, Brown.
Killian, J. R. (1977). *Sputnik, scientists, and Eisenhower.* Cambridge: MIT Press.
Kissinger, H. A. (1979). *White House years.* Boston: Little, Brown.
Kolko, G. (1969). *The roots of American foreign policy.* Boston: Beacon Press.
LaFeber, W. (1967). *America, Russia, and the cold war.* New York: John Wiley.
LaFeber, W. (1985). *America, Russia, and the cold war.* (5th ed.). New York: Alfred A. Knopf.
McFarlane, R. C. (1988). Effective strategic policy. *Foreign Affairs, 67,* 33–48.
McNamara, R. (1987). *Blundering into disaster.* New York: Pantheon.
Muravckik, J. (1980). *The Senate and national security: A new mood.* Washington: The Center for Strategic and International Studies: The Washington Papers No. 10.
Newhouse, J. (1973). *Cold dawn.* New York: Holt, Rinehart and Winston.
Nixon, R. M. (1970). *United States foreign policy for the 1970s.* Washington: GPO.
Nixon, R. M. (1978). *RN: The memoirs of Richard Nixon.* New York: Grosset and Dunlop.
Schilling, W. R. (1961). The H-bomb decision: How to decide without actually choosing. *Political Science Quarterly, 76,* 24–46.
Schlesinger, A. M., Jr. (1965). *A thousand days.* Boston: Houghton Mifflin.
Schlesinger, A. M., Jr. (1987/88). A Democrat looks at foreign policy. *Foreign Affairs, 66,* 263–283.
Seaborg, G. T. (1987). *Stemming the tide.* Lexington, MA: D. C. Heath.
Smoke, R. (1987). *National security and the nuclear dilemma.* (2nd. ed.). New York: Random House.
Sorensen, T. C. (1990). Rethinking national security. *Foreign Affairs, 69,* 1–14.
Stivers, W. (1981/82). Doves, hawks and detente. *Foreign Policy, 45,* 126–144.
Stolley, R. B. (1967, September 19). Defense fantasy comes true. *Life.*
Talbot, S. (1985). *Deadly gambits.* New York; Vintage.
Tolchin, M. (1992, January 15). U.S. underestimated Soviet force in Cuba during '62 missile crisis. *The New York Times.*
Treverton, G. F. (1989/90). The defense debate. *Foreign Affairs, 69,* 183–196.
Truman, H. S. (1956). *Years of trial and hope, 1946-1952.* Garden City, N.Y.: Doubleday.

U.S. Department of Defense. (1975). *Annual report, fiscal year 1975*. Washington: GPO.
U.S. Department of Defense. (1976). *Annual report, fiscal year 1976*. Washington: GPO.
Vance, C. (1983). *Hard choices*. New York: Simon and Schuster.
Wadsworth, J. J. (1962). *The price of peace*. New York: Praeger.
Weekly Compilation of Presidential Documents, January 14, 1980.
Weinberger, C. W. (1987). Why offense needs defense. *Foreign Policy, 68*, 3–18.
Weinberger, C. W. (1988). Arms reductions and deterrence. *Foreign Affairs, 66*, 700–719.
Williams, W. A. (1952). *American-Russian relations: 1781–1947*. New York: Holt, Rinehart and Winston.
York, H. T. (1973, November). Multiple-warhead missiles. *Scientific American, 229*, 18–27.

INDEX

ABM (anti-ballistic missiles), 149-150
ABM Treaty, 113, 147, 150, 242; controversy surrounding, 116-118; discussion of, 134, 157-158; effect of, 163; Gorbachev's desire for extension of, 203; Soviet violations of, 225
Acheson, Dean: arms control efforts by, 8, 25, 26; hydrogen bomb and, 22, 223; rearmament of Germany and, 21
Acheson-Lilienthal Report, 8
Adzhubei, Aleksei, 65
Afghan invasion, 133, 171; arms control negotiations and, 172, 173, 183, 194; Carter's administration and, 173-174, 195; effect on U.S.-Soviet relations, 167, 186, 193; events of, 172; relationship between Soviet's view of Carter and, 168; and withdrawal of Soviet troops, 203, 236
African Americans, 99
Agreement on the Prevention of Nuclear War, 134, 151, 160-161
Air Force, U.S.: demobilization following World War II, 3; Eisenhower's goals for, 29; endorsement of hydrogen bomb project by, 23; Truman administration proposals for, 19
Air-launched cruise missiles (ALCM), 188
Air Policy Commission, 17
Albania, 235
Alliance for Progress, 71
Amalrik, Andrei, 166
Ambrose, S. E., 6
Andropov, Yuri, 201
Anglo-Iranian Oil Company, 32
Angola: Carter administration and, 168; communist forces in, 130, 132, 134, 203; covert military aid to UNITA movement in, 128; Soviet assistance in cease-fire arrangements in, 236; superpower conflict over, 139, 191

Antarctic Treaty, 45, 59-60
Antarctica, 59
Anti-satellite (ASAT) weapons, 188
Arbenz, Jacobo Guzman, 34
Argentina: human rights violations in, 167; Treaty of Tlatelolco and, 119
Armed forces, U.S.: for assured destruction, 110; during Bush administration, 239-242, 250; demobilization following World War II, 3; during Reagan administration, 215-216; reduction of, 30
Arms control: across the presidencies, 257-259; during Bush administration, 243-255; during Carter administration, 171, 173, 182-193; during Eisenhower administration, 44-62; Gorbachev's interest in, 202; for Indian Ocean, 190-191; during Johnson administration, 109, 118-124; during Nixon administration, 128, 129, 152-164; during Reagan administration, 202-204, 218-231; Soviet proposals for, 9, 46-47, 49; through restriction of technology, 191-192; during Truman administration, 8, 24-26; U.S. verification scheme for, 26
Arms Control and Disarmament Agency (ACDA), 89, 187
Army of the Rhine, 21
Assured destruction: concept of, 80, 108; levels needed for, 108-109
Aswan Dam, 36
Atlantic Alliance, 102
Atlas ICBM, 41, 44, 81. *See also* Strategic weapons
Atlee, Clement, 8
Atomic energy, 7-8
Atomic Energy Commission (AEC), 8; creation of, 10; nuclear testing and, 55-57; view of hydrogen bomb, 23
Atomic weapons: cabinet meeting in 1945 to discuss, 7; Eisenhower administration

Index

views regarding, 31-32; fear of surprise attack by, 58-59; New Look policy and, 28-32; post-World War II U.S. stockpiles of, 3-4, 10; Truman administration views regarding, 22-24. *See also* Hydrogen bomb; Strategic weapons
Atoms for Peace, 45-47
Austrian State Treaty, 35
Ayatollah Khomeini. *See* Khomeini, Ayatollah Ruhollah

B-1 bombers, 148, 158, 163, 188, 193, 211
B-52 bombers, 187-188
B-70 bombers, 73
B-47 medium-range bombers, 122-123
B-2 Stealth bombers, 242
B-1B bombers, 211
Backfire bomber, 185, 220
Baker, Howard, 170
Balaguer, Joaquin, 100
Ballistic Missile Early Warning System (BMEWS), 41, 43
Baruch, Bernard, 8
Baruch Plan, 8-10, 24, 46, 247
Basic Principles of Relations Between the United States of America and the Union of Soviet Socialist Republics, 133, 137-139, 161
Batista, Fulgencia, 39, 66
Bay of Pigs, 67, 69, 71
Begin, Menachim, 170
Bennett, W. Tapley, 100
Berlin Blockade, 12-13
Berlin crisis: conventional forces and, 75; events of, 67, 68; results of, 69
Berlin Wall, 68, 235
Bethe, Hans, 54, 55, 109
Biological weapons, 159-160
Biological Weapons Convention, 159-160, 164
Boaz, David, 216
Bombers: B-1, 148, 158, 163, 211; B-52, 187-188; B-70, 73; B-47 medium-range, 122-123; B-1B, 211; long-range, 40, 79, 82; shift in emphasis from, 40-41
Bosch, Juan, 100
Brandt, Willy, 136
Brazil: human rights violations in, 167; Treaty of Tlatelolco and, 119
Brezhnev, Leonid I.: and agreement at Vladivostok, 159; and comprehensive test ban negotiations, 189; and Middle East conflict, 138; strategic arms talks with, 132, 134, 185-186, 222-223; view of detente, 131-132
Brezhnev Doctrine, 101, 235
Brinkmanship: Cuban missile crisis and, 69; explanation and illustrations of, 30, 40; nuclear superiority and, 31
Brown, Harold, 171
Brussels Pact, 12, 13
Brzezinski, Zbigniew: Carter appointment of, 168; on human rights, 166; and relations with China, 170-171; on SALT agreement, 221; view of Soviet Union, 167, 169
Bulganin, Nikolai, 35
Bulgaria, 235
Bundy, McGeorge, 229
Bush, George: as CIA director, 135; emphasis on arms control by, 164; interest in banning chemical weapons, 252; meeting in 1989 with Gorbachev, 236-237; support for ballistic missile defense, 242
Bush administration: arms control during, 243-255, 257, 258; assessment of, 255; international situation during, 233-238; military preparedness during, 238-242; military spending during, 238-239, 255; SALT negotiations during, 173
Bylarus, 245
Byrd, Robert, 177
Byrnes, James F., 4, 8, 11

Cabral, Donald Reid, 100
Caetano, Marcello, 139
Cambodia: collapse of, 130, 139; funding for military action in, 128; Khmer Rouge troops capture of, 142; Nixon administration involvement in, 141; Soviet assistance in cease-fire arrangements in, 236; Vietnamese invasion in 1978 of, 170, 172
Camp David Accords, 170
Carter, Jimmy: and 1980 election, 195; and Camp David Accords, 170; election of 1976 of, 165, 168; and human rights issues, 137, 165-166; Iranian hostage crisis and, 172, 191; nonproliferation policy of, 191-192; and Soviet invasion of Afghanistan, 133, 167, 168, 171-174, 183, 186, 195, 200; and use of military power, 167-168; view of arms transfers, 187

Carter administration: arms control during, 171, 173, 182-194, 257; assessment of, 193-195; international situation during, 168-174; military preparedness during, 171-179, 194, 211; military spending during, 173, 210; NATO during, 179-182; relations with Soviet Union, 166
Carter Doctrine, 173, 174
Castro, Fidel: attempt to assassinate, 71, 129; takeover of Cuba by, 39, 66-67
Central Intelligence Agency (CIA): activities in Nicaragua, 207; establishment of, 17; estimation of Soviet military power by, 135
Charter of Paris for a New Europe, 236
Chemical weapons: countries assumed to have, 252; negotiations to limit, 190, 251-252; as viable military tool, 160
Chemical Weapons Convention (CWC), 252-253
Cheney, Richard, 238-239
Chernenko, Konstantin, 201
Chernobyl disaster, 192
Chile: human rights violations in, 167; Nixon administration and, 138
China. *See* People's Republic of China
Church, Frank, 186
Churchill, Winston, 88; plan for Eastern Europe, 6; speech regarding Soviet Union, 4
Civil Rights Act of 1964, 98, 99
Clay, Lucius, 13
Clean bomb, 53
Cold War: end of, 232, 233; evolution of, 10, 259; as impediment to arms control, 257; Reagan's view of, 196-197
Commission for Conventional Armaments, 25
Committee for a Sane Nuclear Policy (SANE), 55
Committee on the Present Danger, 145, 175-177
Commonwealth of Independent States (CIS): coordination of military forces by, 241; creation of, 234-235
Communism: breakdown in U.S. consensus regarding containment of, 168; Kennedy's view of, 65; Republican party view of, 27, 28; Soviets as leaders of, 101; summit conference of 1955 and, 36
Communist Party of the Soviet Union (CPSU), 32, 233
Conference of the Committee on Disarmament (CCD), 159, 193
Conference on Security and Cooperation in Europe, 236
Congress, U.S., resurgence during Nixon administration of, 127-128
Congressional elections: of 1946, 5; of 1982, 222
Consular Convention, 99
Containment: challenges to U.S. policy of, 34; measures to implement, 12; views of, 11-12
Continental air defense, 29
Contras, 199, 207
Controlled response, 83-85
Conventional arms transfers (CAT), 186-187
Conventional forces: debate over, 75-76; Nixon's view of, 163; Reagan's buildup of, 215-216, 230; role in Europe for, 78, 148-149
Conventional Forces in Europe (CFE) Treaty, 230, 250
COSVN, 141
Counter-insurgency, 74
Countervailing strategy, 178
Crisis stability, 229
Cruise missiles, 211, 213
Cuba: Communist takeover in, 39; intervention in Angola, 139, 191, 203; intervention in Ethiopia by, 169, 191; Soviet brigade in, 186, 195; U.S. intervention in, 66
Cuban missile crisis: conventional forces and, 75; discussion of, 68-69, 114, 229; impact of, 72, 109
Cutler, Robert, 52
Czechoslovakia: Communist coup in, 12; democratic regime in, 235; relations with Egypt, 36; removal of Russian troops from, 236; Soviet invasion of, 101-103, 115, 124

Damage limitation, 109
de Chamorro, Violeta, 207, 236
de Gaulle, Charles, 70, 102
Dean, Arthur H., 92
Defense Policy Guidance, 240
Democratic party, Vietnam War identified with, 125
Derian, Patricia, 166
Detente: meaning of, 131; Nixon administration and, 163-164; opposition to policy of, 129-130, 132; views of Soviet acceptance of, 141

Index

Diem, Ngo Dinh, 33-34
Dobrynin, Anatoly, 183, 200
Dominican Republic, 99-101
Dubcek, Alexander, 101
Dulles, John Foster: arms control and, 47, 50-54; Iran and, 32, 33; and Korean truce negotiations, 30-31; relations with Nasser, 36-37; summit conference of 1955 and, 35-36; test bans and, 50-52; Vietnam and, 33, 34; view of communism, 65

East Germany: crisis in 1958 in, 38-39; democratic regime in, 235; unification of, 235-236. *See also* Germany
Eastern Europe: Churchill's plan for, 6; and demise of Soviet Union, 235; end of Soviet control of, 203; Russian military presence in, 236. *See also individual countries*
Egypt: conflicts with Israel, 137-138; impact of Nasser on, 36; and Suez Canal seizure, 36-37
Eighteen Nation Disarmament Committee (ENDC), 90
Eisenhower, Dwight D.: and balanced budget, 27-28; creation of position of special assistance for disarmament by, 45, 60; and doctrine of sufficiency, 42; involvement with NATO, 14, 16-17, 21; at summit conference of 1955, 35-36, 48; view of Third world, 70; view of world by, 64
Eisenhower administration: Antarctic Treaty and, 59-60; arms control during, 44-60, 251, 257; assessment of, 60-62; Atoms for Peace plan of, 45-47; international situation during, 32-40; military preparedness during, 40-44; military spending during, 28-32; New Look of, 28-32; nuclear test bans during, 50-58; Open Skies plan of, 48-50; surprise attack conferences of, 58-59; target levels for strategic weapons of, 81; view of liberation under, 12
Eisenhower Doctrine, 37
El Salvador, 206, 207
Elections. *See* Presidential campaigns/elections; Congressional elections
Encryption, 227
England. *See* Great Britain
Environmental modification, 193
Environmental Modification Treaty, 134, 193, 194

Ethiopia, 169, 191
Europe: buildup of Western defenses in, 20-21; debate over conventional forces in, 75-76, 148-149; demise of Soviet Union and changes in, 235-236; Nixon's view of maintaining troops in, 161; reaction to neutron bomb in, 180; reduction of forces in, 249-251; Truman policy regarding defense of, 16-17. *See also* North Atlantic Treaty Organization; *individual countries*; Warsaw Pact
European Common Market, 70
Export-Import Bank, 128

Falkland Islands War, 254
Farouk, King of Egypt, 36
Fascell, Dante B., 203
Final Act, 136-137
Final Settlement with Respect to Germany, 235
Finletter Report (Air Policy Commission), 17
Flexible options: Carter's use of, 178; critics of, 151; Nixon administration concept of, 150-151
Flexible response: conventional forces and, 74-76; counter-insurgency capabilities and, 74, 114; explanation of doctrine of, 73-74; during Kennedy administration, 114; tactical nuclear weapons and, 77
Ford, Gerald: and agreement at Vladivostok, 159; in election of 1976, 165; signing of Peaceful Nuclear Explosions Treaty by, 162; strategic weapon approvals by, 188
Ford administration: action in Cambodia by, 139-140; detente during, 131; domestic affairs during, 129, 130; military spending during, 210
Foreign policy: Carter's criticisms of previous, 165; emphasis on human rights in, 166; post-World War II, 15-17
Foster, William, 89
France: atomic explosion in, 120; early arms control efforts of, 25, 26; involvement in Vietnam, 24, 33; proposal in 1954 for arms control, 46; relations with NATO, 102; and Suez Canal seizure, 36-37; U.S. aid to, 24

Gaither, H. Rowan, Jr., 42
Gaither Report, 42-44
Garthoff, R. L., 201
Garwin, Richard, 109

Gates, Robert, 239
Geneva Protocol of 1925, 159, 160, 251-252
Germany: post-World War II rearmament of, 21; unification of, 235-236. *See also* West Germany; East Germany
Gilpatric, Roswell, 89
Glasnost, 233, 234
Glassboro, New Jersey, summit (1967), 102, 123, 157
Global Protection Against Limited Strikes (GPALS). *See* Strategic Defense Initiative (SDI)
Goldwater, Barry, 97
Gorbachev, Mikhail, 201; announcement of reduction in military forces by, 231; arms control efforts by, 197, 202-204, 223-224, 228, 229, 243, 249, 255; and demise of Soviet Union, 233-235; profile of, 202; Weinberger's views on, 198-199
Graham, Daniel O., 135
Great Britain: creation of Army of the Rhine by, 21; early arms control efforts of, 25, 26; involvement in Turkey and Greece, 10-11; proposal in 1954 for arms control, 46; and Suez Canal seizure, 36-37; U.S. weapon deals with, 69-70
Great Society, 98
Greece, 10-11
Grenada, 207
Gromyko, Andrei, 8
Ground-launched cruise missiles (GLCM), 182, 214, 215, 223
Guatemala, 34

Haig, Alexander M., Jr.: on El Salvador, 206; foreign policy experience of, 196, 197; meeting with Dobrynin, 200; on military preparedness, 208; on no first use, 230; views on Soviet Union, 197-198
Hanks, Robert J., 191
HARDTACK tests, 56-58
Harriman, Averell, 93
Haworth, Leland, 89
Helsinki Accords, 136-137
Helsinki Conference (1975), 130
Ho Chi Minh, 15, 33
Horn of Africa, 168, 169, 172, 195
Hotline, 69; establishment of, 90-91; during Nixon administration, 153
Humphrey, Hubert H.: as presidential candidate, 107-108, 125; role in arms control, 89

Hungary: democratic regime in, 235; removal of Russian troops from, 236; revolution of 1956 in, 12, 37
Hussein, King of Jordan, 37
Hydrogen bomb, 22-24. *See also* Atomic weapons

ICBMs. *See* Intercontinental ballistic missiles (ICBMs)
Ikle, Fred C., 198
India: nuclear test in, 162; Tarapur nuclear reactor safeguards in, 192
Indian Ocean, attempt to demilitarize, 190-191
Indochina, U.S. involvement in, 15, 33-34, 71
INF. *See* Intermediate-range nuclear forces
INF Treaty, 228-229, 232
Interagency Group on Human Rights and Foreign Assistance, 166
Intercontinental ballistic missiles (ICBMs): monitoring of, 48; negotiations with Russians regarding, 246, 247; negotiations with Soviets regarding, 158-159, 184-185; production of, 43, 54, 81; projections for Soviet, 63; questions regarding, 79; SALT negotiations and, 155; Soviet construction of, 225, 226; U.S. vs. Soviet, 82-84, 175, 176, 209, 246. *See also* Strategic weapons
Intermediate-range nuclear forces (INF), 254; fear of Warsaw Pact's, 180-181; negotiations regarding, 192-193; Soviet-U.S. attempt to eliminate, 203-204, 227-229
International Atomic Energy Agency (IAEA), 46, 253
International Nuclear Fuel Cycle Evaluation (INFCE), 192
International situation: during Bush administration, 233-238; during Carter administration, 168-174; during Eisenhower administration, 32-40; during Johnson administration, 99-103, 168; during Kennedy administration, 66-72; during Reagan administration, 199-208; during Truman administration, 5-15
Iran: banning of nuclear cooperation with, 253; Carter's relationship with, 167, 171-172; hostage crisis in, 172, 191, 195; return of Shah to, 32-33; Soviet occupation of, 7; U.S. power in, 169
Iran-*contra* scandal, 199
Iran-Iraq War, 254

Index

Iraq: nuclear weapons program in, 253; as threat, 239. *See also* Persian Gulf War
IRBMs, 41, 43
Isolationism, 4, 5, 11
Israel: and Camp David Accords, 170; Persian Gulf War and, 239; Six Day War and, 102, 137; Suez Canal seizure and, 36-37; Yom Kippur War and, 138

Jackson, Henry, 132, 134
Jackson-Vanik Amendment, 128, 131, 132
Japan, 14, 24, 254
Jews, Soviet, 128
Job Corps, 98
Johnson, Louis, 22, 23
Johnson, Lyndon: campaign in 1964 of, 98; preoccupation with Vietnam, 103, 108, 257; social program of, 98; takeover of presidency by, 97
Johnson administration: arms control efforts during, 118-124, 257-258; domestic setting in, 97-99; international situation during, 99-103, 168; military preparedness during, 108-118; Vietnam War during, 70, 103-108, 123
Joint Chiefs of Staff, 17
Joint Statement of Agreed Principles for Disarmament Negotiations, 89-90
Jordan: aid to King Hussein in, 37; block of Hawk missile sale to, 128; British troops in, 38
Jupiter missile, 41, 44

Kahan, J. H., 58-59
Kaysen, Carl, 89
Kazakhstan, 245
Kennan, George, 22, 23
Kennedy, John F., 58; arms control views of, 120; election of, 63-64; view of communism, 65; world and domestic outlook of, 64-65
Kennedy, Robert, 99
Kennedy administration: arms control during, 88-96, 257; flexible response doctrine of, 73-76; international situation during, 66-72; military preparedness during, 68, 72-87, 114; military spending during, 68, 72-73; nuclear test ban treaty during, 93-96; nuclear testing during, 86-87, 92-93; strategic arms policy of, 79-86, 108; and Vietnam, 70, 105
Khomeini, Ayatollah Ruhollah, 172

Khrushchev, Nikita: and aborted summit of 1960, 38-39, 58; arms control proposals by, 118, 119; Cuban missile crisis and, 69; East German crisis and, 38-39, 68; Kennedy administration and, 66, 67, 114; overthrow of, 99, 114; and test ban talks, 55, 57, 58
Killian, James, 54, 55
Killian Commission, 41
King, Martin Luther, Jr., 99
King, McKenzie, 8
Kissinger, Henry, 129, 130, 182; 1-' war doctrine and, 152; on Agreement on the Prevention of Nuclear War, 160; Angola conflict and, 139; defense policy study by, 142-143; detente and, 131; Middle East conflict and, 138; view of Soviet Union, 141, 149-150
Kistiakowsky, George B., 54
Korb, Lawrence J., 216
Korean War, 11, 25; military spending during, 16, 18; truce talks of, 30, 33
Kosygin, Alexei: at Glassboro summit, 102, 123, 157; Johnson and, 102, 123; as premier, 99

Laird, Melvin: on SALT agreements, 157; on Trident submarines, 147-148; view of detente, 130
Laos, 67, 71
Latin America: Johnson administration problems with, 99-100; Kennedy administration programs for, 71; as nuclear-free zone, 119
Lebanon, 38
Libya, 207, 253
Lilienthal, David E., 8, 10, 22-23
Limited Test Ban Treaty (LTBT), 69, 93-96, 119, 254-255
Lin Piao, 104
Linkage, 131
Long-range bombers, 40; questions regarding, 79; U.S. vs. Soviet, 82. *See also* Strategic weapons
Long-range missiles: race with Soviets to develop, 54; Soviet testing of, 40-41
Long-Term Defense Program (1978), 179-180
Lumumba, Patrice, 129

Macmillan, Harold, 53, 69
Manchuria, 33
Mansfield, Mike, 148

Mansfield Resolution, 161
Mao Tse-tung, 7, 135
Mark 12-A warhead, 177, 178
Marshall, George C., 12
Marshall Plan, 11, 12
Massive retaliation doctrine, 40, 75-76
Matsu, 34, 38
McCarthy, Eugene, 113
McCloy, John J., 89, 90
McCone, John, 57
McElroy, Neil, 63
McFarlane, Robert, 202, 214
McGovern, George, 128-129
McMahon Act, 10
McNamara, Robert, 64; arms control and, 94-95, 123; as bridge between administrations, 97, 108; on controlled response, 83-84; on military preparedness issues, 75, 80-82, 108, 112, 113, 116-117; on nuclear testing, 86; and Vietnam, 103-104
McNaughton, John, 89
Memorandum of Understanding between the United States and the Union of Soviet Socialist Republics Regarding the Establishment of a Direct Communications Link, 91
Middle East: Camp David Accords in, 170; superpower conflict over, 137-139. *See also individual countries*; Persian Gulf
Midgetman, 213
Military buildup: after coup in Czechoslovakia, 12; during Carter administration, 175; in Europe, 20-21. *See also* Europe; North Atlantic Treaty Organization (NATO); Warsaw Pact; during Kennedy administration, 75-76; as method of national security, 2; Soviet, 145-146, 175-177, 208-210
Military preparedness: during Bush administration, 238-242; during Carter administration, 171-179, 194, 211; conclusions regarding, 257-258; during Eisenhower administration, 40-44; during Johnson administration, 108-118; during Kennedy administration, 68, 72-87, 114; during Nixon administration, 142-152, 163; during Reagan administration, 208-218, 231, 232; during Truman administration, 15, 17-24, 26
Military spending: during Bush administration, 238-239, 255; during Carter administration, 173, 210; during Eisenhower administration, 28-32; during Ford administration, 210; during Kennedy administration, 68, 72-73; during Korean War, 16, 18; during Nixon administration, 126-127; during Reagan administration, 210-211; by Soviet Union, 175, 209; during Truman administration, 17-19
Minuteman missiles, 41, 44, 73, 81, 85. *See also* Strategic weapons
MIRV, 83; controversy surrounding, 112-113; development of, 110-112, 163; proposed freeze on Soviet, 159; rationale for development of, 110, 113; SALT negotiations and, 155, 156; Soviet view of U.S. acquisition of, 176-177; sufficiency and strategic stability and, 146-147
Missile Control Technology Regime (MCTR), 254
Missile Defense Act of 1991, 242
Missile gap: election of 1960 and, 63, 64, 73; as myth, 122
Missiles: development of U.S., 41; proposal to abolish U.S. and Soviet, 203. *See also individual types of missiles*
Mossadegh, Mohammed, 32, 33
Mozambique, 191
MRV (multiple re-entry vehicles), 111, 112
Multinational Nuclear Force (MLF), 78, 120
Mutual and Balanced Force Reduction talks (MBFR), 134, 137, 149, 161-162, 183, 230, 250
Mutual Defense Assistance Act, 13-14
MX ICBMs, 177, 194, 211-212, 213-214

Namibia, 203
Nasser, Gamal Abdel, 36, 37
National security, 1, 2
National Security Act of 1947, 17
National Security Council, 17, 19
NATO. *See* North Atlantic Treaty Organization (NATO)
Navy, Soviet, 210
Navy, U.S.: and attempt to demilitarize Indian Ocean, 190, 191; during Bush administration, 239; demobilization following World War II, 3; during Reagan administration, 215
Nehru, Jawaharlal, 33
Nervo, Padilla, 26
Neutron bomb, 180, 194, 215
New Deal, 98

Index 271

New Look, 28-32, 40
Newhouse, John, 154
Nicaragua: Carter administration and, 168; defeat of Sandinistas in, 207, 236; Reagan administration and, 206-207; Soviet transshipment of arms through, 200
Nitze, Paul, 145; investigation of CIA military estimates by, 135; on Soviet military buildup, 175; treaty ban on SLCMs favored by, 226-227; view of detente, 1321
Nixon, Richard: attempt to defuse anti-war movement by, 140-141; criticism of Bush by, 238; election in 1968 of, 99, 108; in election of 1960, 63; opinion on SALT agreements, 156; pardon of, 129; political astuteness of, 127; relations with China, 101, 135-136; resignation of, 129; social programs and, 98; as vice president, 51; view of arms control, 152; view of military preparedness, 126
Nixon administration: arms control during, 128, 129, 152-163, 257; assessment of, 163-164; impact of Watergate on, 134; Middle East conflicts during, 137-139; military preparedness during, 142-152; military spending during, 126-127; relations with China, 135-136; relations with Soviet Union, 130-135; Vietnam War and, 139-142
No first use doctrine, 229
Non-nuclear weapons states (NNWS), 120-121
Nonproliferation policy, 191-192
Nonproliferation Treaty of 1968: description of, 121; encouragement for participation in, 253; opposition to, 120-121; signing of, 123; Soviet fears regarding West Germany and, 122; Vietnam War and, 140
North, Oliver, 207
North Atlantic Treaty Organization (NATO), 11; during Carter administration, 179-182, 194; CFE Treaty and, 250; and demise of Soviet Union, 235, 236; deployment of INF in Europe by, 227; formation of, 13, 14; France's relations with, 102; nuclear weapons and, 76-78, 180-182, 192-193; for peacekeeping operations, 250-251; policy of, 16-17, 20-21; reduction of nuclear arsenal by, 249; U.S. commitment to, 75; use of ground-launched cruise missiles by, 214; Warsaw Pact as threat to, 180-182, 231, 250
North Korea: banning of nuclear cooperation with, 253; invasion of South Korea by, 14-15, 21; and MCTR, 254; seizure of U.S. vessel by, 103; and truce talks, 30, 33
North Vietnam: bombing of, 106, 107; negotiations with, 107-108, 142; Soviet role in, 103. *See also* Vietnam War
NSC-68: drafting of, 22, 175; provisions of, 16-19, 26
NSC-162/2, 28
Nuclear energy, 191-192
Nuclear Nonproliferation Act (1978), 192
Nuclear Nonproliferation Treaty. *See* Nonproliferation Treaty of 1968
Nuclear Suppliers Group (NSG), 253
Nuclear test bans: Bush administration and, 254-255; Carter administration and, 189; Eisenhower administration and, 50-58; Kennedy administration and, 93-96; and Limited Test Ban Treaty (LTBT), 69, 93-96, 119; Nixon administration and, 162; Soviet proposal for, 134
Nuclear tests: in China, 104, 120; conferences to discuss detection of, 55-57; in France, 120; Kennedy administration resumption of, 86-87, 92-93; by Soviet Union, 2, 50, 86, 87, 92-93
Nunn, Sam, 177

Office of Secretary of Defense, 17
Ogaden, 169
Olympic games of 1980, 173
1½-war doctrine, 152, 164
Open Skies proposal: explanation of, 47-50; fear of surprise attack and, 58, 59
Operation Northern Handshake, 242
Operation Provide Help, 237
Oppenheimer, J. Robert, 23
Organization of American States (OAS), 99-100
Outer Space Treaty (1967), 120

Pahlavi, Mohammed Riza (Shah of Iran), 33, 166-167, 171-172
Pakistan, 173
Panama Canal, 168-169
Pauling, Linus, 55

PD-18, 174, 177, 182
PD-59, 178, 194
Peaceful Nuclear Explosions Treaty (PNET), 162-163, 183
Pell, Claiborne, 193
People's Republic of China, 7; and 1-' war doctrine, 152; Carter administration and, 167, 170-171; challenge to Soviets by, 100-101; involvement in Indochina, 104; and Korean War, 18, 30-31; and MCTR, 254; Nixon administration and, 135-136; nuclear explosion in, 104, 120; protection against attack from, 116, 117; triumph of communism in, 14
Perestroika, 203, 234
Perle, Richard N., 198
Pershing II, 192-193, 214, 215, 221
Persian Gulf: buildup of U.S. forces in, 174; during Carter administration, 182. *See also* Middle East; *individual countries*
Persian Gulf War: bombers used in, 148, 211; enhancing fear regarding spread of nuclear weapons, 239; missiles used in, 213, 216, 254; Russia and, 236
Pescadores Islands, 38
Pipes, Richard E., 135
Point Four, 14
Poland: Democratic elections in, 205; democratic regime in, 235; Russian troops remaining in, 236; Soviet intervention in, 200, 204-205; Soviet occupation of, 6
Polaris missiles, 41, 43, 70, 73, 81, 85. *See also* Strategic weapons
Powers, Francis Gary, 44, 58
Presidential campaigns/elections: of 1948, 5; of 1952, 27; of 1956, 51; of 1960, 58, 62, 63; of 1964, 97-98; of 1968, 99, 107-108, 125, 140; of 1972, 128-129; of 1976, 132, 165, 168; of 1980, 172, 174, 195-196, 206, 208, 219; of 1984, 223; of 1992, 238
President's Science Advisory Council (PSAC), 54, 55
PRM-10, 174-175, 182
Progressive Citizens of America party, 5
Project Argus, 57
Propaganda, 26

Qaddafi, Muammar al-, 207
Quarles, Donald, 52
Quemoy, 34, 38

Rabi, I. I., 54
Radford, Arthur, 52, 94
Radiological weapons, 189-190
Rapid Deployment Force (RDF), 182, 194
Rarotonga Treaty, 231
Rathjens, George W., 112
Reagan, Ronald: accomplishments of, 199; arms control efforts by, 202-204, 258; and campaign of 1976, 130, 132; disinterest in arms control, 218-219, 222; election in 1980 of, 172, 195-196, 206, 219; position on Soviet Union, 195-196, 200, 218; "Star Wars" speech of, 201, 216-217
Reagan administration: arms control during, 202-204, 218-231, 257; assessment of, 199, 231-232; broadening of rapid deployment force during, 182; international situation during, 199-208; military preparedness during, 208-218; military spending during, 210-211; nuclear freeze movement during, 222; policymakers in, 196-199; relations with Soviet Union, 197-208; SALT II and, 186
Reagan Doctrine, 207
Republican party, 27
Roosevelt, Franklin D.: choice of Wallace by, 4; death of, 3; New Deal programs of, 98
Roosevelt, Kim, 33
Rostow, Walt, 104
Rumania, 235
Rumsfield, Donald, 175
Rusk, Dean, 89, 94, 97, 118
Russia: cooperation between U.S. and, 236-238; and decrease in U.S. military spending, 239; economic aid for, 237; joint naval exercises with U.S., 242; military in Europe, 236, 251; prevention of brain drain from, 254; relations with U.S., 236-238; threat of arsenal in, 241. *See also* Soviet Union

Saavedra, Daniel, 207
SAC aircraft, 43
Sadat, Anwar: and Camp David Accords, 170; conflict with Israel, 137-138
Safeguard, 149
Sakharov, Andrei, 166
SALT I: background of, 132; congressional review of, 128; criticism of, 155-157;

MIRV and, 147; negotiations regarding, 123, 140, 153-154; Nixon administration and, 129, 163; success of, 136; sufficiency and, 143, 153
SALT II: early guidelines for, 159; negotiations regarding, 133, 170, 171, 173, 183-186; provisions of, 219; Reagan's criticism of, 196, 219-220, 223; Soviet violations of, 225; support for, 220-221; weapons permitted by, 177; withdrawal from Senate of, 193
Samos, 64
Sandinistas, 207
Satellites, 188
Saud, King of Saudi Arabia, 37
Saudi Arabia: military aid to, 37; and Persian Gulf War, 239
Schilling, W. R., 23, 24
Schlesinger, Arthur M., Jr., 64, 93
Schlesinger, James, 130; as advocate of flexible options, 150, 178; view of detente, 132
Schmidt, Helmut, 180
Scoville, Herbert, Jr., 112
Scowcroft Commission, 213
Sea-launched intercontinental ballistic missiles (SLBMs): buildup during Carter administration of, 179; development of, 213; negotiations with Russians to limit, 246, 247; questions regarding, 79; SALT and, 155, 226; U.S. vs. Soviet, 82, 209, 246; Vladivostok Accord and, 159. *See also* Strategic weapons
Seabed Treaty, 120, 152-153
Seaborg, Glenn, 89
Seawolf hunter-killer submarines, 242
Sentinel, 117. *See also* ABM (anti-ballistic missiles)
Shah of Iran. *See* Pahlavi, Mohammed Riza (Shah of Iran)
Shultz, George P., 197, 202
Single Integrated Operations Plan (SIOP), 84
Skybolt missiles, 69, 70
SLBMs. *See* Sea-launched intercontinental ballistic missiles (SLBMs)
Slepak, Vladimir, 166
Smoke, Richard, 229
Solidarity, 204
Somalia, 169
Sorenson, Theodore, 238
South Korea: human rights violations in, 167; invasion by North Korea, 14-15, 21; security treaty signed with, 33, 34; Soviet downing of civilian airliner from, 200-201
South Vietnam: fall of, 139, 142; Kennedy and, 70, 105; Nixon administration and, 140-142. *See also* Vietnam
Southeast Asia: decline in U.S. power in, 169; superpower conflict over, 139-140. *See also individual countries*
Southeast Asia Treaty Organization (SEATO): formation of, 34; protection for nations who are members of, 105
Soviet Union: Afghani invasion by, 133, 167, 168, 171-174, 183, 186, 193; Afghanistan withdrawal by, 203, 236; Angola intervention by, 139; arms control proposals by, 9, 46-47, 49. *See also* Arms control; on arms transfer strategies, 187; arsenal in former, 241, 245, 254; assessment of nuclear capabilities of, 18-19; Atoms for Peace proposal and, 46; and attempt to demilitarize Indian Ocean, 190-191; biological weapons development in, 160; buildup of navy, 210; Bush administration and, 238; Carter administration and, 166-168, 171-173, 178, 183, 186, 199-200; challenge by China to, 100-101; Churchill's speech regarding, 4; on countervailing strategy, 178; and creation of West German state, 13; demise of, 233-235; Eisenhower administration and, 29-30, 35, 50-58, 60-62; during end of World War II, 5-7; fears regarding West Germany, 47, 121, 122, 136; grain embargo against, 173, 200; human rights issues and, 137, 166, 185; interest in Greece and Turkey, 11; interventions in Poland, 6, 200, 204-205; invasion of Hungary by, 37; Kennedy administration and, 66, 67, 72-74; Middle East conflict and, 138, 139; military buildup of, 145-146, 175-177, 208-209; military policy during Johnson administration, 113-116; military spending of, 175, 209; NATO-Warsaw Pact totals and, 181; Nixon administration and, 130-135; nuclear tests by, 2, 50, 86, 87, 92-93; objection to Baruch Plan by, 9; Reagan administration and, 196-208, 218, 223-225; SALT agreements and, 154-157; signature of Consular Convention

with, 99; Somalia intervention by, 169; under Stalin, 32; strategic forces of, 82, 115, 122, 175, 176; and Suez Canal seizure, 37; surprise attack conferences and, 58-59; suspension of ASAT tests by, 188-189; testing of long-range missiles by, 40-41; Truman administration and, 18-19, 21, 25-26; view of detente, 131-132; view of flexible options, 151; view of U.S. strategic forces by, 109; in Vladivostok meetings, 158-159; withdrawal of troops from Afghanistan, 203, 236. *See also* Russia

Sputnik, 30, 38, 41, 54, 80

SS-20 missile, 180-182, 192, 193

Stable deterrence, 85-86

Stalin, Joseph, 6; military buildup by, 32; post-World War II relations with U.S., 10

Star Wars. *See* Strategic Defense Initiative (SDI)

START talks, 222, 223

START Treaty, 243-245, 254

Stassen, Harold E.: as assistant for disarmament, 45, 47, 60; test ban negotiations and, 51-53

Stevenson, Adlai, 51, 65, 89

Stevenson Amendment, 128, 131

Stimson, Henry, 7

Strategic Air Command (SAC), 29

Strategic Defense Initiative (SDI), 157; Bush administration and, 242; controversy over, 216-218; Reagan's view of, 201, 203, 216-217; Soviet opposition to, 223

Strategic stability: MIRV and, 147; Nixon administration aim toward, 144-146, 163; SALT and, 163; Star Wars and, 218

Strategic weapons: assured destruction and, 80; Bush administration and, 243-248; Carter administration and, 179; and concept of stable deterrence, 85-86; controlled response and, 83-85; Eisenhower administration and, 29; explanation of, 79; force levels set for, 80-83; Reagan administration and, 211-214, 219-227; SALT agreements and definition of, 154; U.S. vs. Soviet, 82, 115, 122, 175, 176, 246. *See also* Atomic weapons

Strauss, Lewis, 51, 52, 55, 57, 94

Suez Canal, 36-37

Sufficiency: Eisenhower administration and, 42; MIRV and, 146-147; Nixon administration and, 142-144, 163; strategic stability vs., 145

Surprise attack conferences, 58-59

Syria, 138

Systems analysis, 108

Tachen Islands, 34

Tactical nuclear weapons: Bush administration and, 148-149; description of, 76-77; Nixon administration role for, 148-149

Taft, Robert, 4

Taiwan: Carter administration relations with, 171; Nixon administration relations with, 135-136; protection of, 34-35, 38

Talbot, Strobe, 154

Taylor, Maxwell, 72

Teller, Edward, 23, 52-53, 94

Terrorism, 239

Tet Offensive, 103, 107

Third World: Eisenhower and, 70; Kennedy and, 65, 70; Reagan and, 205-206; Republican vs. Democratic presidents' attitude toward, 70

Thor IRBM, 41, 44

Three Mile Island, 192

Threshold Test Ban Treaty (TTBT), 162, 183

Titan missile, 41, 81. *See also* Strategic weapons

Tito, Josip Broz, 13

Tonkin Gulf Resolution, 105, 106

Treaty Banning Nuclear Weapons Tests in the Atmosphere, in Outer Space, and Under Water, 95. *See also* Limited Test Ban Treaty

Treaty of Tlatelolco, 119, 120

Trident submarines, 147-148, 158, 163, 178, 194, 213, 214

Trujillo, Rafael, 99-100

Truman, Harry S.: background of, 3; firing of Wallace by, 4; on Korea, 14-15; Point Four program of, 14; speech at UN on arms control, 24-25

Truman administration: arms control during, 24-26, 257; assessment of, 26; domestic setting during, 3-5; European military buildup during, 20-21; hydrogen bomb and, 22-24; international situation during, 5-15; military doctrine during, 15-17; military spending during, 17-19

Truman Doctrine, 11, 16

Turkey, 10-11

2½-war doctrine, 76, 152

Index

Ukraine, 245
UNAEC. *See* United Nations Atomic Energy Commission (UNAEC)
United Nations, disarmament unit of, 25, 90, 159, 190
United Nations Atomic Energy Commission (UNAEC), 8, 25
United Nations Disarmament Commission (UNDC), 25
United States: relations with Russia, 236-238; strategic forces of, 82, 115, 122; vulnerability of, 1-2

Vance, Cyrus: appointment of, 166, 168; on Carter, 183; and SALT II negotiations, 184, 185; on Soviet intervention in Ethiopia, 169; view of Soviet Union, 167, 171
Vietnam: Chinese and Cambodian invasions of, 170, 172; division of, 33; French involvement in, 24, 33; impact of defeat in, 195; Kennedy and, 70; U.S. involvement in, 33-34
Vietnam War: as issue in 1964 election, 97-98; as issue in 1968 election, 125; during Johnson administration, 103-108; during Nixon administration, 140-142; opposition to, 106, 126-127, 140; winding down of, 141. *See also* South Vietnam; North Vietnam
Vietnamization, 140
Vladivostok Accord, 159, 184
Voting Rights Act of 1965, 99

Wadsworth, James, 56-57
Walensa, Lech, 204
Wallace, George, 125
Wallace, Henry A., 3, 5
War on Poverty, 98
War Power Act of 1973, 128
Warnke, Paul, 168
Warsaw Pact: buildup of forces of, 179, 180; conventional force reduction by, 230-231; and demise of Soviet Union, 235, 236; dissolution of, 236; formation of, 35; NATO troop count and, 161; as threat to NATO, 180-182, 231, 250. *See also individual countries*
Washington Agreement (1992), 245-247
Watergate: Ford administration and, 129-130; impact of, 127, 134, 165
Weapons of mass destruction (WMD), 253

Weinberger, Caspar W.: on Star Wars, 217-218; views on Soviet Union, 198-199, 214
Weisner, Jerome, 89
West Germany: formation of government in, 13; NATO and, 35, 120; neutron bomb and relations with, 180; nonaggression pacts signed by, 136; Soviet fears regarding, 47, 121, 122, 136; strengthening of armed forces in, 67; unification of, 235-236. *See also* Germany
Westmoreland, William, 107
Wheeler, Earle G., 118
White, Thomas D., 94
World War I, 159
World War II: home front during, 3; Soviet forces at end of, 5-6; Soviets aim in, 235; Truman and, 3; as watershed for military policy, 15
Worse-case planning, 109

Yeltsin, Boris: arms control efforts by, 245, 247, 255; as president of Russian Republic, 234; on test bans, 255
Yom Kippur War, 138
York, Herbert F., 54, 113
Yugoslavia, 235

Zorin, V. A., 89
Zumwalt, Elmo, 132